Texts and Monographs in Computer Science

Texts and Monographs in Computer Science

Selected Writings on Computing: A Personal Perspective

Edsger W. Dijkstra

Springer-Verlag
New York Heidelberg Berlin

Edsger W. Dijkstra
Burroughs Corporation
Plataanstraat 5
5671 AL Nuenen
The Netherlands

Editor

David Gries
Department of Computer Science
Cornell University
Upson Hall
Ithaca, NY 14853
U.S.A.

With 13 illustrations.

Library of Congress Cataloging in Publication Data
Dijkstra, Edsger Wybe.
  Selected writings on computing
  (Texts and monographs in computer science)
  Bibliography: p.
  Includes index
  1. Electronic data processing—Addresses, essays, lectures. 2. Computers—
Addresses, essays, lectures. 3. Programming (Electronic computers)—Addresses,
essays, lectures. I. Title. II. Series.
QA76.24.D54   1982   001.64   82-10260

Production: Michael Porch
Typeset by Science Typographers, Inc., Medford, NY.
Printed and bound by R. R. Donnelley & Sons, Harrisonburg, VA.
Printed in the United States of America.

9 8 7 6 5 4 3 2 1

ISBN 0-387-90652-5 Springer Verlag New York Heidelberg Berlin
ISBN 3-540-90652-5 Springer-Verlag Berlin Heidelberg New York

Preface

Since the summer of 1973, when I became a Burroughs Research Fellow, my life has been very different from what it had been before. The daily routine changed: instead of going to the University each day, where I used to spend most of my time in the company of others, I now went there only one day a week and was most of the time —that is, when not travelling!— alone in my study. In my solitude, mail and the written word in general became more and more important. The circumstance that my employer and I had the Atlantic Ocean between us was a further incentive to keep a fairly complete record of what I was doing. The public part of that output found its place in what became known as "the EWD series", which can be viewed as a form of scientific correspondence, possible since the advent of the copier. (That same copier makes it hard to estimate its actual distribution: I myself made about two dozen copies of my texts, but their recipients were welcome to act as further nodes of the distribution tree.)

The decision to publish a selection from the EWD series in book form was at first highly embarrassing, but as the months went by I got used to the idea. As soon as some guiding principles had been adopted —preferably not published elsewhere, as varied and as representative as possible, etc.— the actual selection process was much easier than I had feared.

Harder to decide was the question to how much editing the selected texts should be subjected. When the texts are viewed as historical documents, their editing should be minimal. When David Gries went through the texts with his fine-toothed comb he revealed so many opportunities for improvement that, eventually, the editing became quite extensive. As a result, the texts as published are not representative of my mastery of the English language.

A major obstacle to publication was my insistence that selected trip reports be included. Having decided that the selection should be representative, I had no choice, since the period in question covers years during which I was on the road a third of the time. Furthermore, few of my texts reflect my feelings and attitudes more clearly than the trip reports. (It has been remarked that my trip reports are more revealing about their author than about the people and places visited.) There was only one snag: there is no tradition of publishing such comments. While performing artists are quite used to being judged publicly by their peers, performing scientists are not. (Reviews of published books and articles are the closest approximation.)

In my appreciation, the feelings of the people involved are as much a part of the birth of a science as their "objective" scientific achievements, and when one publisher told me he would like to publish the selection after the removal of the trip reports, I looked for another one. I am very grateful to Marvin Israel for immediately insisting that the trip reports be included.

Even if you can convince the judge that it was never your intention to hurt or to offend, libel suits are awkward and eventually it was thought prudent to replace names in a few instances by "NN". I would like to stress that in no case should such a replacement be interpreted as our suspicion that the person in question would make trouble.

First and foremost I am indebted to Burroughs Corporation, which gracefully created the circumstances under which I could work. It is impossible to mention all those who have contributed, directly or indirectly. I make an exception for C.S. Scholten, with whom I have collaborated without interruption since 1952, and for W.H.J. Feijen, A.J. Martin, and M. Rem. Our regular discussions formed the root from which the "Tuesday Afternoon Club" grew. In its weekly gatherings, the Tuesday Afternoon Club evolved into a very critical and very inspiring environment; how much we have benefitted from each other is hard to fathom.

Finally, this book could not have been published in its present form without the very substantial assistance of David Gries, who spontaneously offered to correct my English. He ended up by screening all arguments and their presentation as well. He went far beyond the call of friendship and my feelings towards him are of deep gratitude on the verge of guilt, since I am afraid that he undertook the task without being aware of its size. I owe him many thousands of thanks for his many thousands of comments.

Nuenen, 19 July 1981   EDSGER W. DIJKSTRA

Table of Contents

This essay, though dating from February 1968, has been included because, in retrospect, it marks a turning point in my professional life: it represents my earliest conscious effort at orderly program development. The whole essay —and this explains to a certain extent its somewhat pathetic covering letter— was written while I felt mortally ill: it was written as my farewell to science. Fate has decided differently.

This technical note, though dating from 1972, has been included because we never published it. (Though typed, it was never decently edited until I did so for this collection.) When we discovered that we could not explain it to the data processing experts in our immediate environment, we somehow lost interest. In May 1977, Martin Rem —while temporarily at the California Institute of Technology, Pasadena— designed a special purpose "elephant" —a set of communicating sequential processes with a fixed connection pattern— for establishing whether a renumbering satisfying relation 7 (from this technical note) exists.

The algorithm developed here is not the best one possible: it is not linear in the number of arcs. It has been included for the sake of those interested in problem solving: it is one of my rare verbatim protocols of what I wrote down while developing this solution. (I started thinking about the problem while travelling by train from Eindhoven to Amsterdam; the text was written in my hotel room.) [See Hopcroft, J., and Tarjan, R. Efficient algorithms for graph manipulation. *Comm*. ACM 16, 6 (June 1973), 372–378.]

EWD385   Trip Report E.W. Dijkstra, Summer School Munich,
           July 25 to August 4, 1973   31

On August 1, 1973, during that NATO Summer School in Marktoberdorf, I became a Burroughs Research Fellow; I still remember how funny it felt to write my trip report in English instead of in Dutch, as I had been used to do. At that Summer School I learned —blessed are the English!— that Norman Vincent Peale is practically unknown in the United Kingdom.

EWD386   The Solution to a Cyclic Relaxation Problem   34

This is the solution referred to in the last paragraph of EWD385. Remarkably enough —see EWD391— the remark is missing in the end, that in the case that $m * p$ is *not* an integer multiple of N, the system will still converge to a completely stable situation, provided that the roundings don't all take place in the same direction. I was close to EWD391's "crucial observation", but not yet there....

EWD387   Trip Report IBM Seminar "Communication and
           Computers", Newcastle, Sept. 1973   36

The above title has been faithfully reproduced in this collection with due apologies to the University of Newcastle-upon-Tyne, U.K., which is always very careful to denote these yearly seminars differently (and rightly so). Had my then still recent association with industry made me so sensitive to what I observed? The reference to the documentary film made for the Monsanto Chemical Company is from *The Organization Man* by Willam H. Whyte, Jr. (Simon and Schuster, 1956), Chapter 16, titled "The Fight against Genius".

EWD391   Self-Stabilization in Spite of Distributed Control   41

As soon as I had found at last my first self-stabilizing system, I was so excited that immediately —on the 1st of October 1973— I wrote this paper with the intention of submitting it for publication. Just in time I remembered that such temptations should be resisted until the initial excitement has died out. On the 12th of October 1973 I found a solution with four-state machines, on the 1st of November 1973 one with three-state machines. Under the same title all three solutions were eventually published in *Comm*. ACM 17, 11 (Nov. 1974) 643–644.

EWD407   Acceptance Speech for the AFIPS Harry Goode
           Memorial Award 1974   47

This speech was delivered at the Conference Luncheon, Tuesday May 7, 1974, of the National Computer Conference and Exposition, May 6–10, 1974, Chicago, U.S.A.

Only at the 16th of June, 1974, it became public knowledge that since its inception, ten years earlier, I had been Chairman of the Board of "Mathematics Inc.", the company earmarked to become the world's leading manufacturer of mathematical products. One of my reasons for going public was my desire to broaden the range of my written English, which, as far as it had been developed, was becoming a mild prison. The communications of the Chairman of "Mathematics Inc." are as much linguistical exercises as genuine efforts to inform the reader about the world in which this wonderful company operates.

See EWD427. (Those former members of the IFIP Working Group 2.1 who, like I, have learned the English expression "utterly preposterous" from the German Prof.Dr.Dr.h.c.F.L. Bauer, will still remember the acronym "U.P."; for the benefit of the uninitiated reader, the acronym has not been used.)

Because the Proceedings of the 108th Annual Meeting of the International Federation of Mathematical Societies IFMS, 1976, Loempia, are out of print, their publishers could not withhold permission to reprint here at least excerpts from the Keynote Address. Their permission, so gracefully granted, is acknowledged in gratitude.

This essay —a credo, if you like— has been provoked by (I am afraid, rather depressing) discussions at the Eindhoven University of Technology about the computing science curriculum. Parts of it are as general as its title suggests, and deal with questions such as the role of scientific thought and the viability of scientific disciplines. The rest argues why computing requires a discipline worthy of the name "computing *science*". (Of all I wrote in those days, this essay is one I remember best. At the time of writing I liked it, and I still like it.)

This paper was submitted for publication and accepted, but never published. After the referee's conclusion:

"This paper formulates and illustrates some fundamental principles of software engineering which have been shamefully and disastrously neglected in the past; for this reason its publication is to be highly recommended.

However, the argument is in several places quite sketchy, and should be reinforced if the paper is to live up to its promise. The comments given below may indicate some further points that should be covered."

nine(!) pages of detailed comments followed. (The last sentence of the section "Temptations to be resisted." evoked from the referee the comment: "In every fibre of my body I agree. But I wish the author could bring more compelling arguments than merely italics.") But all my efforts at rewriting failed: I could not live up to my referee's expectations, and, eventually, I gave up. See also EWD465.

A problem from graph theory is solved by a circular arrangement of N synchronized machines that together manipulate an $N * N$ connection matrix, each machine starting at an element of the diagonal.

An elephant —more in the form of a snake!— built from a string of mosquitoes provides the "additional hardware" referred to in EWD462; a wise definition of "average page fault frequency" as a function of time presented an unexpected problem. Because this elephant was a patentable invention, this note was not distributed at the time of writing.

At which I was introduced to what later became known as "the Gries–Owicki Theory", and I decided not to become a logician.

A productive quickie (i.e. one of the attempted solutions to The Travelling Scientist's Problem). How mathematicians and physicists threaten to strangle computing science.

From a historical point of view, this letter, which I wrote in my capacity of Chairman of the Board of "Mathematics Inc.", is of great interest: it is the first record of our scientific progress being hampered by legal embroilments.

The teaching of programming as the teaching of thinking is the central theme of this Luncheon Speech. See also EWD494.

This report is typical for the texts that hardly see the light of day: the not too convincing deposit of a lot of hard work. I did send it around "hoping for helpful comments", but I got none: evidently, it was as hard to read as it had been to write. The suggestions made in its last paragraph still seem to place the effort in the right perspective.

With eight public performances at six different places and a week at Burroughs, Mission Viejo, this was a trip with a heavy schedule. The main events were the International Conference on Software Reliability, 1975, Los Angeles, U.S.A. and the IBM Conference on Software Engineering Education, Montebello, Canada.

Computing's misery captured in a dozen, easily remembered maxims.

This letter describes the start of an experiment with "shunting monitors" that was —and perhaps still is!— not without promise. Its aim was to combine what later became known as "the technique of the split binary semaphore" with the textual encapsulation of the monitor and —for the sake of more delicate control— the explicit manipulation of queues of blocked processes. Conceptually as well as notationally, the text is still quite raw —the introduction of the anthropomorphic "me" being only one of the minor sins!— . Discouraged by Hoare's lack of enthusiasm, and quickly thereafter thrilled by more exciting visions, I abandoned the experiment while it was still in its infancy. See also EWD503 and EWD504.

This was written the day after EWD501 had been mailed. Note that the procedure "release" at the end of the last example, in the "diskhead" monitor, contains a silly coding error that was corrected in EWD504.

As the text says: "Clearly, "shunting" is something I still have to learn!".

In retrospect this text is not without historical interest: it records the highlights of a discussion mentioned under Ref. 9 in C.A.R. Hoare's "Communicating Sequential Processes", *Comm.* ACM 21, 8 (Aug. 1978), 666–677. The text was evidently written in a state of some excitement; in retrospect we may conclude that this excitement was not entirely unjustified. Seeing Hoare keenly interested in the topic, I left that arena.

I wrote this text in Newcastle-upon-Tyne to serve as a starter for the discussion during the Symposium's closing session (see EWD513).

How I learned what I feared: "Computers and the educated individual" is an almost empty topic.

An analysis shows how the incorporation of error correction increases in general the probability that a wrong result will be delivered. (By and large, the warning was ignored during the years that followed; the pressure to use unreliable techniques proved often to be too strong.)

A very nice demonstration of a theorem that had been mentioned in EWD525 without proof.

A draft chapter of a book titled *On the Nature and Role of Mathematical Elegance*, which never got written (despite EWD538's closing sentence "To be continued in a later report."). The incentive to write the book is still there, namely the discovery that among all sorts of mathematicians the consensus about what is mathematically elegant is much stronger than they themselves suspect, and the conclusion that mathematical elegance cannot be such an elusive concept after all.

Being a private communication from its Chairman, this document is presumably the most revealing document we have about Mathematics Inc.; for the reader with a special interest in how to run a big business it could be illuminating to observe how the Chairman used what he had just learned in Newcastle (see EWD513) to the company's advantage.

This note was primarily written for my own clarification, and upon its completion I was very pleased with it. It is now a regular handout to my students, who seem to like it too. Its nonoperational approach to concurrency should be one of its distinctive features.

This was written to give the regular readers of the EWD series an idea of how I lived when I was not travelling. In retrospect it strikes me a bit as an idealization. It mentions, for instance, neither all the routine obligations of running an office nor the sleepless nights caused by university politics.

This invited speech, which describes one of my formal experiments in reasonable detail, was written for the Symposium on the Mathematical Foundations of Computing Science, Gdansk, 1976. It was, however, never delivered because, when I arrived in Gdansk and met my audience, I felt that a totally different talk would be more appropriate. So they got an impromptu instead (see EWD584).

I later learned that —in a very different connection— the function *fusc* had already been discovered (but not named that way) by de Rahm (see *Elemente der Mathematik*, Vol. 2 (1947), p. 95). The colleague who found and told me that discovery was very amazed to see no trace of disappointment from my side, but I couldn't care less: I had had my own fun in my own way. Burstall never picked up the gauntlet; later this was done at the Technische Universität München. (See EWD578.)

In my own publications I had given a very ugly formulation of the weakest precondition that the execution of a given statement is guaranteed to decrease a given integer function of the state by at least 1. During my absence from Eindhoven, colleagues of mine had found a much simpler expression, which is much simpler to work with.

This is an example of my activity as adviser, an activity of which I am not very fond; I also doubt that I am very good at it. Had I known E.T. Bell's book at the time of writing, I might have quoted him on "the twentieth-century mania for cooperation in everything". (*The Development of Mathematics* by E.T. Bell, McGraw-Hill Book Company, 1945.)

In its original version this technical note was unreadable, for what is called here $U(x)$ had been denoted there as $P(x)$ —my usual way of denoting the invariant relation of a repetition— ; as a result the poor reader had to guess whether $P(x)$ stood for the $P(x)$ of Manna and Waldinger or for mine! If I had written the text now, I would have used fewer implication signs; their lavish use —see, for instance, formula (7)— is definitely unattractive. Its conclusion, however, is most attractive: we can ignore subgoal induction because it is nothing but the Invariance Theorem in a complicated disguise.

This open letter to my co-members of the IFIP Working Group W.G.2.3 on "Programming Methodology" was very hard to write. It had been prompted by my observations at the Working Group's previous meeting (see EWD603). Its subject matter is intrinsically touchy, and not everyone appreciated the way in which I touched it in this letter. I didn't mind: I knew that I had done my best and that pleasing everyone is not my business.

I accepted the invitation for this visit to Australia shortly after I had decided that I should really reduce the amount of travelling to which I was subjecting my poor body. So much for good intentions! But I gave in because Dr. Robin B. Stanton's letter of invitation was so very nicely phrased, and I shall never regret having accepted his invitation, for the whole trip was in many ways a rare pleasure.

Occasionally I have found the "somewhat open letter" a very useful device. This was one of the first times that I applied it.

This is the type of comments on the computing community that you can't publish in a journal because they are not "scientific". It was written shortly after the introduction of the new Dutch postal codes, and I am still struggling to convince the world that my postal code is "5671 AL", ending on *two capital letters*!

This text is almost as painful to read as it was to write. And that is exactly the reason for its inclusion. It records a rough, groping experiment that is in strong contrast to what was harvested from it the next year, viz. "Finding the correctness proof of a concurrent program" (*Proceedings of the Koninklijke Nederlandse Akademie van Wetenschappen*, Amsterdam, series A, volume 81(2), June 9, 1978, pp. 207–215). It is almost the last text I wrote before I concluded that the implication sign is such an endless source of confusion that the less use we make of it, the better. In the years to come the problem tackled here would attract in one form or the other more attention, e.g. "Distributed Termination" by Nissim Francez (*ACM Transactions on Programming Languages and Systems*, Vol. 2, No. 1, January 1980, pp. 42–55) and EWD687a "Termination detection for diffusing computations" by Edsger W. Dijkstra and C.S. Scholten.

I tend to explain my discoveries in the way I made them, and, if I am not careful, all sorts of obsolete thinking habits surface during the explanation of my older discoveries. Explaining the Banker's Algorithm in a more modern way than I used to do —it dates from the mid-sixties— was an unexpected pleasure.

Well, on one actually. Somehow, I never included Martin Rem's second beautiful solution in the EWD series. After this had been written it was brought to my attention that two years earlier C. Bron had shown us essentially the same solution; his coding had been less "convincing" and the fact had completely escaped me.

Another trip report from Newcastle; it has been included because it describes one of my more intensive confrontations with the hardware community. The confrontation was disappointing.

Describing the insight I brought home from IFIP '77 (Toronto) or why to have dinner in a Chinese restaurant. I have had many requests for reprints of this report, mostly from France and from India.

This was written after I had explained the Three Golden Rules at the IFIP W.G.2.3 meeting at Niagara-on-the-Lake.

Mathematics Inc. is a remarkable company, as is demonstrated by the fact that all its Chairman's communications to date have been included in this anthology. At the same time this remarkable fact enhances the profound cultural significance of this selection of reports, which are now available for the first time to the public at large. Describing the full potential of Artificial Intelligence, this article is an absolute must for the well-educated, concerned layman.

This type of report is exciting at the moment it is being written: one has understood something! But in a way the discovery is so minor that after a while it is absorbed in that deposit called "experience".

The effect of an invitation that, eventually, I could not accept.

I still remember my modest excitement with which this little note was written. Firstly I realized that our strengthened mathematical grip on algorithms could open the way to new existence proofs. Secondly I was most pleased to see how well my heuristics had served me. Thirdly the little program that is the carrier of the argument is so beautifully simple.

Because the statement **do** $x > 0 \rightarrow x := x - 1$ **od** destroys an unbounded amount of information, its inverse would be a program of unbounded nondeterminacy; hence, within the realm of continuous programs, not each program has an inverse. But it is fun! Once, when I ended a one-week programming course by inverting programs, one of the participants called my last lecture "the longest joke he had ever heard". One of my colleagues called EWD671 "a rare intellectual delight". I think they meant the same thing.

This note was a pretty direct consequence of EWD671, which made me ponder what I really did when I inverted programs; quite naturally my attention was drawn to the different notions of termination.

A direct sequel to EWD671. So much for clearing up my own mind!

Fairy tales, I am told, are supposed to contain a core of truth. Well, this one certainly does, for the invention of QUICKSORT was C.A.R. Hoare's immediate reaction to his first exposure to ALGOL 60: its recursion was just what he needed! The moral of the story seems to be —but with fairy tales one is never quite sure— that the proof obligations to be fulfilled by the programmer provide the demarcation between his responsibility and the responsibility of the implementer of the programming language used. Hence, those proof obligations —and nothing more!— could be used to *define* the semantics of the programming language in question.

My dear Friend or Relation, Master, Colleague or Pupil,

Paraphrasing the ominous sentence: "This ... has been placed here for your convenience.", which is usually used to explain the presence of all sorts of American hotel room contraptions, I should like to say "The enclosed manuscript has been sent to you for your enjoyment.".

I would not dare to send it to you if you regarded it as the next item for the evergrowing pile of tasks still to be done. I know that the manuscript is long but I have let it grow that way in the hope that the intellectual effort needed for its digestion is inversely proportional to its length. And your enjoyment may be proportional to it. So I don't apologize for its length.*

There are no shattering discoveries in it: it is the kind of peaceful prose that I write (mainly for my own distraction?) when a somewhat poor condition forces me for some period of time to some sort of inactivity. It will certainly be less gloomy than this evening's front page news!

When you have read it and feel like dropping me a line, please don't hesitate to do so; I will receive it gladly.

Yours sincerely

EDSGER W. DIJKSTRA
Department of Mathematics
Technological University Eindhoven
P.O. Box 513
EINDHOVEN
The Netherlands

* There is no point in denying it: I do like Franz Schubert's music.

0

EWD227
Stepwise Program Construction

Over the past years I have been (heavily) engaged in a number of (at that time) advanced programming projects that could be considered as large in comparison to the available manpower. I am still in the active process of learning from the experience gained, one of the immediate goals of this learning process being the discovery of better ways to construct even "small programs" in a reliable fashion. Although large, advanced and sophisticated programming efforts are more spectacular, we must not forget that quite a lot of machine time and programmer's energy is really spent on small, down-to-earth projects and the present efforts to make computing facilities more directly accessible to the individual user will only reinforce this tendency.

For the interested reader I am going to make two programs and, besides that, I am going to show the individual steps in which they have been constructed. The examples serve to illustrate parts of my present understanding of the demands that the task of programming makes upon the human mind.

In my approach there are some central themes that I shall just mention for the proper understanding of the following. The first theme is that, although the program made by the programmer is his final product, the computations evoked by it are the true subject matter of his trade: he has to guarantee that the computations —the "making" of which he leaves to the machine— evoked by his program will have the desired effect. As a result, he has the duty to structure his program in a useful way, where usefulness (among other things) implies that the form of the program admits trustworthy statements about the corresponding computations. The second theme is that the mental aids available to the human programmer are, in fact, very few. They are enumeration, mathematical induction and abstraction, where the appeal to enumeration has to satisfy the severe boundary condition that the number of cases to be considered separately should be very, very small. The introduction of suitable abstractions is our only mental aid to reduce the appeal to enumeration, to organize and master complexity. Mathematical induction has been mentioned explicitly because it is the appropriate (and only!) established pattern of reasoning by which we can understand programs with either repetitive clauses or recursive procedures. As a corollary I mention the fact that for some time I knew that, as a programmer, I could live quite happily without any form of **go to** statement but that in the mean time my considered opinion is that I cannot live happily with the **go to** statement.

To avoid misunderstanding, I should like to state explicitly that I do not claim that the two programs produced are the best possible, measured (probably!) in terms of your private yard-stick. I do claim that they are fairly good and reasonable in terms of the average yard-stick, i.e. that they present utterly realistic solutions. I do claim to have achieved a degree of clarity and transparency of an order of magnitude better than the average programmer's solution, that my solutions have been reached with an intellectual effort considerably below average and that they admit exhaustive verification. And that is more than can be said about many a program.

The reason to treat two examples is because they have been drawn from vastly different fields. The one dealing with prime numbers is a so-called scientific application; the other, dealing with the idiosyncrasies of Flexowriters, is a so-called clerical application. These two fields are often regarded as completely foreign to each other: the successful application of the same discipline as illustrated below gives a strong support to the assumption that the difference between scientific and clerical machine usage is by no means an inherent difference, but more probably the result of a difference in intellectual level and professional training of the people engaged.

(Note. I do not feel myself called to justify the choice of my examples, which are a kind of random draws from what is happening around me: emotionally speaking, prime numbers leave me as unaffected as Flexowriters.)

The Construction of a Table of the First 1000 Prime Numbers

"Given an **integer array** $p[1:1000]$, make a program making the elements of p in order of increasing subscript value equal to the successive prime numbers, where 2 is considered as the first prime number."

Well-defined as this task may seem to the benevolent reader, as we go along we shall discover an undefined boundary between the amount of mathematical knowledge the programmer is willing to embody in his program and the amount of computation he leaves to the machine.

To start with, for the task to make sense it must be *known* that at least 1000 primes actually exist. We grant the programmer this knowledge and at a certain stage of program construction we allow him to appeal to this fact when he has to prove that his program does indeed halt.

We shall now give the coarsest version of the program, viz.

version 0:
begin "assign to the array *p* the prime table as described" **end**

When this action is in the well-understood and well-defined repertoire of actions from which the computation has to be composed, version 0 solves our problem. For the sake of argument we now assume that this action is *not* in the repertoire; in particular, we restrict ourselves to actions with which we can operate on arrays only elementwise. This implies that in our next version the order in which the elements of array *p* will get their desired value has to be expressed, and in it we shall try to express just that and preferably nothing more.

An obvious version of the program then starts with

begin $p[1] := 2; p[2] := 3; p[3] := 5; p[4] := 7; p[5] := 11; \ldots$

implying that the programmer's knowledge includes a table of the first 1000 primes. We shall not pursue this version, since it would imply that the programmer hardly needed the machine at all.

The first prime number being given ($= 2$), the thousandth being assumed unknown to the programmer, the most natural order of filling the elements of array *p* is in order of increasing subscript value, and if we express just that (with a simple repetitive **while do** clause) we come to

version 1a:
begin **integer** $k, j; k := 1; j := 1;$
      while $k \leq 1000$ **do**
      begin "increase *j* until the next prime number";
          $p[k] := j; k := k + 1$
      end
end

Identifying *k* as the subscript value of the element whose turn it is to be filled, the correctness of version 1a is easily proved by mathematical induction (under the assumption of the existence of a sufficient number of primes).

Version 1a is a perfect program when the operation described by "increase *j* until the next prime number" is in the repertoire, but let us suppose that it does not. In that case we have to express how *j* is increased, and in our next elaboration we shall try to express just that and preferably nothing more. With a simple repetitive **repeat until** clause (which may act upon a sequence of statements) we come for "increase j until the next prime number" to

version 2a:
begin boolean *jprime*;
     repeat $j := j + 1$; "give to *jprime* the meaning: j is a prime number"
     until *jprime*
end

If we substitute version 2a for the appropriate operation in version 1a our resulting program is undoubtedly correct. But if we assume that the programmer knows that, apart from 2, all prime numbers are odd, then we may expect that he will be dissatisfied with the obvious inefficiency of version 2a. The price to be paid for this, call it "lack of clairvoyance", is a revision of version 1a in which the prime number 2 is dealt with separately, after which the cycle can deal with the odd primes. So we come to

version 1b:
begin integer $k, j; p[1] := 2; k := 2; j := 1$;
     while $k \leqslant 1000$ **do**
     begin "increase odd j until the next odd prime number";
          $p[k] := j; k := k + 1$
     end
end

where the analogous elaboration of the operation between quotes leads to

version 2b:
begin boolean *jprime*;
     repeat $j := j + 2$;
          "give to *jprime* for odd j the meaning: j is a prime number"
     until *jprime*
end

The above oscillation between versions 1 and versions 2 is in fact nothing else but moving the interface between the overall structure and the primitive that has to fit in this structure. This is definitely not attractive, but with a sufficient lack of clairvoyance and being forced to take our decisions in sequence, I see no other way. We can regard our efforts as experiments to explore where the interface can be most conveniently chosen.

Encouraged by the success of treating the integer 2 separately, we investigate what can be gained by treating 3 separately as well. For this purpose we introduce the property "throdd", i.e. divisible by neither 3 nor 2. The throdd numbers are of the form $6N + 1$ or $6N + 5$. By definition, 2 and 3 are the only prime numbers not contained in the set of throdd numbers and so we come to

version 1c:
begin integer k, j; $p[1] := 2$; $p[2] := 3$; $k := 3$; $j := 1$;
    while $k \leqslant 1000$ **do**
    begin "increase throdd j until the next throdd prime number";
        $p[k] := j$; $k := k + 1$
    end
end

where the analogous elaboration of the operation between quotes leads to

version 2c:
begin boolean *jprime*;
    repeat "increase throdd j until the next throdd value";
        "give to *jprime* for throdd j the meaning: j is a prime number"
    until *jprime*
end

This is only an improvement when the operation "increase throdd j until the next throdd value" is easily implemented. The proper increase of j is a function of j; call it "INC(j)". Its value is $= 4$ when $j = 6N + 1$, its value is $= 2$ when $j = 6N + 5$. Instead of freshly evaluating the function INC(j) whenever we need it, we introduce a separate variable, *inc* say, to record the current value of INC(j), corresponding to the current value of j. Variable *inc* has to be set initially when j is set and it has to be adjusted whenever the value of j is changed. (The introduction of *inc* is an instance of a standard programmer's device to trade variable space for computation speed.) Using list-assignments to stress that *inc* is just a companion of j, the introduction of *inc* and the elaboration of "increase throdd j until the next throdd value" leads to

version 1d:
begin integer k, j, *inc*; $p[1] := 2$; $p[2] := 3$; $k := 3$;
    $(j, inc) := (1, 4)$;
    while $k \leqslant 1000$ **do**
    begin "increase throdd j, adjustment of *inc* included, until the next
        throdd prime number";
        $p[k] := j$; $k := k + 1$
    end
end

where the elaboration of the operation between quotes leads to

version 2d:
begin boolean *jprime*;
    repeat $(j, inc) := (j + inc, 6 - inc)$;
        "give to *jprime* for throdd j the meaning: j is a prime number"
    until *jprime*
end

There is no indication that any gain will result from taking the next prime (i.e. 5) out of the cycle as well, and we shall not try it.

Again, when "give to *jprime* for throdd *j* the meaning: *j* is a prime number" is an operation from the presupposed repertoire, then our program is finished. We now assume that it is not; in other words we have to evoke a computation deciding whether a given throdd *j* has a factor. It is only at this stage that the algebra really enters the picture. Here we make use of the knowledge that we only need to try prime numbers as factors; furthermore we shall use the fact that the prime numbers to be tried can already be found in the filled portion of array *p*.

We use the facts that:

(a) *j* being a throdd value, the smallest potential factor to be tried is $p[3]$, i.e. the first prime above 3;
(b) the largest prime factor we have to try is $p[ord - 1]$, where $p[ord]$ is the smallest prime number whose square exceeds *j*.

If this set is not empty, we have a chance of finding a factor and, as soon as a factor has been found, the investigation of this particular *j* value can be stopped. We have to decide in which order the prime numbers from the set will be tried, and we shall do so in order of increasing magnitude, because the smaller a prime number the larger the probability of its being a factor of *j*.

In our first elaboration of "give to *jprime* for throdd *j* the meaning: *j* is a prime number" we come to

version 3d:
```
begin integer n, ord; boolean nofactorfound;
      ord := 1; while p⌊ord⌋ ↑ 2 ≤ j do ord := ord + 1;
      n := 3; nofactorfound := true;
      while n < ord and nofactorfound do
      begin "give to nofactorfound the meaning: p[n] is not a factor of j";
            n := n + 1
      end;
      jprime := nofactorfound
end
```

Here we make two observations. Boolean variable "*nofactorfound*" is superfluous —we could have used *jprime* instead— so that the last assignment statement can be removed. Furthermore, *ord* is a function of *j* that we need not recompute freshly every time; we can and should treat it along the same line as *inc*. The latter remark causes the final revision of version 1, leading to

version 1e:
begin **integer** k, j, inc, ord; $p[1] := 2$; $p[2] := 3$; $k := 3$;
    $(j, inc, ord) := (1, 4, 1)$;
    while $k \leqslant 1000$ **do**
    begin "increase throdd j, adjustment of inc and ord included, until
          the next throdd prime number";
          $p[k] := j$; $k := k + 1$
    end
end

where the elaboration of the operation between quotes leads to

version 2e:
begin **boolean** $jprime$;
    repeat $(j, inc) := (j + inc, 6 - inc)$;
          while $p[ord] \uparrow 2 \leqslant j$ **do** $ord := ord + 1$;
          "give for throdd j, using p and ord, to $jprime$ the meaning:
          j is a prime number"
    until $jprime$
end

REMARK. Here "**while** $p[ord] \uparrow 2 \leqslant j$ **do**" can be replaced by "**if** $p[ord] \uparrow 2$ $\leqslant j$ **then**", but to my taste the marginal gain in efficiency is not worth the intellectual effort to prove its validity. A programmer should learn to be lazy at the right moment and to let the principle "Safety First" prevail!

Elaboration of the operation between quotes gives a variant of version 3d, viz.

version 3e:
begin **integer** n; $n := 3$; $jprime :=$ **true**;
    while $n < ord$ **and** $jprime$ **do**
    begin "give to $jprime$ the meaning: $p[n]$ is no factor of j";
          $n := n + 1$
    end
end

For "give to $jprime$ the meaning: $p[n]$ is no factor of j" we may write under the assumption of decent real arithmetic **begin** **real** q; $q := j/p[n]$; $jprime := (\text{entier}(q) \neq q)$ **end**. We shall assume the availability of the integer division and write

version 4e:
$jprime := (j \neq (j \div p[n]) * p[n])$

Finally we perform all substitutions to construct a single statement.

```
begin integer k, j, inc, ord; p[1] := 2; p[2] := 3; k := 3;
      (j, inc, ord) := (1, 4, 1);
      while k ≤ 1000 do
      begin begin boolean jprime;
                  repeat (j, inc) := (j + inc, 6 − inc);
                         while p[ord] ↑ 2 ≤ j do ord := ord + 1;
                         begin integer n;
                               n := 3; jprime := true;
                               while n < ord and jprime do
                               begin jprime := (j ≠ (j ÷ p[n]) * p[n]);
                                     n := n + 1
                               end
                         end
                  until jprime
            end;
            p[k] := j; k := k + 1
      end
end
```

We could have made the inner blocks into compound statements by moving the declarations for *jprime* and *n* to the outside. We have not done so: clarity does not gain by it and whether there is a point in doing it is rather dependent on the implementation.

Thus ends the treatment of the first example.

The Unique Reporting of the Printed Page as Produced on a Flexowriter

For our purpose we can regard a Flexowriter as a kind of electric typewriter which is operated only via the keys of its keyboard. Whenever a key is pressed, a configuration characteristic for this key is punched in a paper tape, which is then moved on over one position. Typing a page thus implies the production of a paper tape specifying what has been typed. (Actually, besides the punching station the Flexowriter has a reading station from which the printing mechanism can be controlled. By inserting the paper tape just produced into the reading station one can obtain another copy of the printed page.)

We want to write a program that reads such a paper tape and gives, when called repeatedly, a unique description of the corresponding page image, according to conventions to be described below. As we go along we shall see that this is no trivial matter, because (mainly due to the construction of the Flexowriter) many paper tapes, greatly varying among each other, may correspond to the very same page image. (In our example we shall simplify the real situation slightly: we shall exclude the unexpected occurrence of "end of tape" and exclude the situation that the paper tape reader of the computer discovers —due to some error in punching or reading— an illegal configuration. Even thus simplified, the problem is messy and intricate enough to serve our purpose!)

Two remarks are in order about the presentation of our solution:

(1) the routine will be coded as an operator, operating in a local universe of permanently existing variables; we shall use small letters for their identifiers.
(2) constants that refer to the integer values associated with characters will be denoted by identifiers composed from capital letters.

In its coarsest form the local universe contains one integer variable, called "*charf*" and the operator can be described by

version 0:
begin "assign to *charf* the next value" **end**

Our Flexowriter has equal spacing, i.e. each line has a fixed number of print positions. There is a finite number of so-called "position characters" (because of the absence of a backspace key on our Flexowriters, which would allow a practically unlimited number of superpositions) and each position character can occur at each print position of the page. A numerical code for the position characters has been chosen and the operator reports by assigning to *charf* the numerical value associated with the position character in the current print position, dealing with the print positions in each line in order from left to right and with the lines in order from top to bottom.

With respect to the left margin we assume that its position on the printed page is given; to indicate the right-hand end of a line we have extended the range of *charf* values with an additional one, denoted by "RET" (i.e. New Line, Carriage Return) and require for the sake of uniqueness that all "invisible" spaces at the right-hand end of a line be suppressed. It is as if RET is counted among the visible position characters but that its (symbolic) printing position has to be aligned to the left as far as possible.

The purpose of version 1 is to suppress any spaces at the right-hand end of each line; for its benefit the local universe has been extended with two integer variables:

charf 1: the range of this variable equals that of *charf*, but in the time sequence of its values, invisible spaces at the right-hand end of each line will still occur (if present, of course);

stock: this is a counter; its value equals the number of times that *charf* can be filled with a next value before *charf*1 has to be refilled. It requires the initial setting "*stock* := 0".

Version 1 implements the look ahead whenever one or more spaces are reported (using *charf*1); when followed by RET they have to be suppressed, otherwise they have to be transmitted.

version 1:
begin if *stock* = 0 **then**
      begin repeat "assign to *charf*1 the next value";
                    stock := *stock* + 1
          until *charf*1 ≠ SPACE;
          if *charf*1 = RET **then** *stock* := 1
      end;
      charf := (**if** *stock* > 1 **then** SPACE **else** *charf*1); *stock* := *stock* − 1
end

Our next complication is that the "position character" as reported in *charf*1 (with the exception of RET) may be composed of three parts: by means of the mechanism of a so-called non-escaping key (i.e. one that leaves the carriage position as it is) one can superpose various "key characters" in the same print position. We have in fact two such key characters, viz. underlining and a vertical stroke. The purpose of version 2 (an elaboration of "assign to *charf*1 the next value") is to combine the key characters referring to the same print position.

We have to take into account

(1) that non-escaping key characters have to be combined with the first following escaping key character;
(2) that repetition of the same non-escaping key character in the same print position must be considered as equivalent to its single occurrence.

For the benefit of version 2 we extend the local universe with one integer variable,

*charf*2:   the range of this variable is those *charf* values corresponding to position characters produced without non-escaping key characters, plus the values denoted by UNDER and STROKE.

As a matter of fact, $0 \leqslant charf2 \leqslant 127$ will be satisfied; the presence of underlining will be coded in *charf*1 by an increase of 128, that of a stroke by an increase of 256.

Our tentative elaboration of "assign to *charf*1 the next value" gives rise to version 2 (here CRAZY2 denotes a constant value that is outside the range of *charf*2).

version 2:
begin integer *under*, *stroke*;
   under := 0; *stroke* := 0; *charf*1 := CRAZY2;
   repeat "assign to *charf*2 the next value";
      if *charf*2 = UNDER **then** *under* := 128
             else
      if *charf*2 = STROKE **then** *stroke* := 256
             else
     *charf*1 := *charf*2
   until *charf*1 ≠ CRAZY2;
   *charf*1 := *charf*1 + *under* + *stroke*
end

We have said "tentative elaboration" because, as it stands, this version will not prevent, say, the transmission of an underlined RET: "*charf*2 = UNDER" followed by "*charf*2 = RET" requires the insertion of an additional space to be underlined. Since pure spaces (i.e. without underlining or stroke) preceding RET will be suppressed by version 1 anyhow, we can (and shall) remedy this situation by imposing upon "assign to *charf*2 the next value" the requirement that it will never transmit RET unless immediately preceded by a transmission of SPACE.

The next complication is that our Flexowriters are equipped with a tabulator key TAB, which, when pressed, gives rise to a punching in the paper tape, while the carriage moves on until the next tabulator stop that is more than one position to the right of the current position: the carriage moves over at least two positions. The positions of the tabulator stops are standardized (once every eight positions) but it implies that the algorithm deriving the number of spaces corresponding to TAB must be aware of the current position of the carriage (at least modulo 8). It is the purpose of version 3 —the elaboration of "assign to *charf*2 the next value"— to translate tabulations into the equivalent number of spaces and to insert a SPACE before RET.

For its benefit we introduce into the local universe three integer variables.

*charf*3: the range of this variable is that of *charf*2, extended with TAB.

pos: keeps track of the current carriage position; when "*charf*3 = RET" occurs *pos* will be set to zero, when "*charf*3 = TAB" occurs it will be increased to the proper multiple of 8. It requires an initial setting, say "*pos* := 0".

substock: this is a counter; its value equals the number of times that *charf*2 can be filled with its next value before *charf*3 has to be refilled. It requires the initial setting "*substock* := 0".

We arrive at the following elaboration of "assign to *charf*2 the next value".

NOTE. As it stands I am not very much satisfied with the coding of version 3. The way in which SPACE before RET is smuggled in, for instance, is too tricky. It is, however, the first version I wrote down for it.

version 3:
begin if *substock* = 0 **then**
    begin "assign to *charf*3 the next value";
        if *charf*3 ≠ UNDER **and** *charf*3 ≠ STROKE **then**
        pos := *pos* + 1;
        if *charf*3 ≠ RET **and** *charf*3 ≠ TAB **then** *charf*2 := *charf*3
                                  else
        begin *charf*2 := SPACE;
            if *charf*3 = RET **then**
            begin *substock* := 1; *pos* := 0 **end**
                          else
            begin *substock* := (*pos* ÷ 8 + 1) * 8 − *pos*;
                pos := *pos* + *substock* **end**
      end
    end   **else**
    begin *charf*2 := (**if** *charf*3 = TAB **then** SPACE **else** RET);
        substock := *substock* − 1
    end
end

The last complication presented by the structure of the Flexowriter is its built-in memory element, called "the case". It is in one of two states, called "upper case" and "lower case", respectively. When it is in state upper case it remains there until the key "LOWER CASE" is pressed, which furthermore results in punching the value "LC" in the paper tape. When it is in state lower case, it remains there until the key "UPPER CASE" is pressed, which results in punching the value "UC" in the paper tape. When pressing any other key, punching is only dependent on the key pressed, but printing is (except for the space bar, the tabulator and the carriage return) dependent on the current case as well.

In version 4 —an elaboration of "assign to *charf*3 the next value"— we have to implement the influence of the case punchings. For the benefit of it we extend the local universe with two integer variables
octade: used to record the next punching on the paper tape
case: this variable may have the values LC or UC (or possibly a third one, meaning "undefined", because space, tabulation and carriage return can be processed case independently). It must get an initial value, say "*case* := LC".

At this same level we implement that two legal punchings (BLANK and ERASE, corresponding to no holes and all holes respectively) are skipped without any possible effect on the page image. CRAZY3 denotes a constant outside the legal range of *charf*3.

version 4:
begin *charf3* := CRAZY3;
      repeat "give *octade* its next value";
               if *octade* ≠ BLANK **and** *octade* ≠ ERASE **then**
               begin if *octade* = LC **or** *octade* = UC
                         then *case* := *octade*
                         else *charf3* := fun(*case*, *octade*)
            end
      until *charf3* ≠ CRAZY3
end

With "give *octade* its next value" I indicate the paper tape read instruction and I shall not elaborate it any further. The function "fun(*case*, *octade*)" is also left undescribed: it is too much dependent on the special numerical codes; we only mention that upper and lower case space (tab or ret) must both be transmitted as SPACE (TAB or RET).

The successive insertions of version "*i* + 1" into version "*i*" are left to the industrious reader (or should I say "writer"?).

Concluding Remarks

Before stressing the similarity of the ways in which our two problems have been solved I should draw attention to a difference. In the first example I have paid considerable attention to the decision where to put the interface between the successive levels, in the second one I did no longer do so. I do not believe that the origin of this difference is in any way related to the supposed contrast between "scientific" and "clerical" machine applications, for it has a perfect historical and psychological explanation. The historical explanation is that I have used the prime number table generation problem in a number of oral examinations, the psychological explanation is that in treating the second example I am getting tired and perfectly willing to leave to my readers the intellectual satisfaction of improvement.

Personally I am much more impressed by the similarity of the ways in which the two rather different programs have been constructed. The successive versions appear as successive levels of elaboration. It is apparently essential for each level to make a clear separation between "what it does" and "how it works". The description of "what it does", the definition of its nett effect, requires introduction of the adequate concepts, and both examples seem to show a way in which we can use our power of abstraction to reduce the appeal to be made upon enumeration.

As stated in the introduction, we may expect that computers will become more directly accessible for the individual user and we may expect that the latter should like to use its capabilities for the text manipulations involved in program composition. At present I am rather unsure about the true nature of the text manipulations the user would then like to perform —it is certainly something more structured than just deletion and insertion of characters or lines! In the fervent hope of getting a better understanding of what these manipulations are I have reported two instances of program construction as detailed and as honestly as I possibly could.

Finally: if I did hit a worthwhile nail on its head, then this manuscript should end with a proper acknowledgement, giving honour where honour is due. Under the present circumstances I can only express my gratitude to... my Friends and Relations, my Masters, Colleagues and Pupils.

Eindhoven, February 1968

EWD338
Parallelism in Multi-Record Transactions

BY E.W. DIJKSTRA AND C.S. SCHOLTEN

We consider a data base, comprising a great number of individual records, and transactions to be carried out on this data base. Each transaction is a finite computation involving a number of these records. The computation to be carried out —and even the identity of the records involved— will in general be dependent on the state of the data base when the transaction is initiated. When the data base grows, the following conflict emerges: on the one hand one may expect the number of transactions to be carried out to grow as well; on the other hand the growing data base will make individual record selection a more and more painful process, slowing down the individual transaction executions. Comes the moment that the stream of transactions, carried out one after the other, no longer fits in real time. To solve this real-time problem we must be willing to carry out a number of transactions in parallel. This paper is devoted to the logical problems that then emerge.

The purpose of this paper is twofold: firstly, to isolate (and to solve to a certain extent) the logical problems involved and, secondly, to demonstrate the viability of our top-down approach in problem solving. This means that those readers that are unfamiliar with the top-down approach, but are familiar with a number of these logical problems, must be patient. If they find us ignoring a number of practical considerations in the beginning, they should read on quietly; there is a fair chance that they will be taken into account in due time.

The First Model

In the purely sequential execution of the transactions, we can execute the transactions in the (supposedly unique) order in which they are requested, and at any moment there is at most one transaction under execution. In our first model, we still assume that the requests for transactions reach the system in a unique order and with a speed regulated by the system in such a way that the system can cope with the requests. We admit, however, that at any moment the number of transactions currently under execution may be larger than one, although not exceeding some given finite upper bound. The execution of a transaction extends from the moment that the system has acknowledged the request for the transaction until the moment that the system has completed the transaction.

In the purely sequential execution, the system's nett reaction to a number of transaction requests may depend on the order in which the transactions are requested. In the case of parallelism we do *not* require that the system's nett reaction be identical to that of the sequential system when faced with the stream of requests in the order in which the parallel system has acknowledged these requests. We do require, however, that it is possible to order the requests in such a way that the nett reaction of the sequential system faced with the requests in that order will be identical to the reaction of the parallel system. (In many cases, viz. when we have two mutually non-interfering transactions, this order need not be unique.)

Our parallel system has three main obligations: it has to prevent 1) undesired interference, 2) deadlock and 3) individual starvation.

ad 1

Let each transaction be identified only for the period of its execution. Let $T[i]$ be a transaction currently under execution. Let $M[i]$ be the set of records manipulated until now by $T[i]$. This implies that during the execution of $T[i]$, the set $M[i]$ can not decrease, until $T[i]$ has been terminated and $M[i]$ ceases to exist. We can guarantee the absence of undesirable interference by requiring that at any moment

$$i \neq j \Rightarrow M[i] \cap M[j] = \varnothing \tag{1}$$

i.e. for two different transactions the intersection of the corresponding sets M is empty.

ad 2

If a and b are two different records and for $i \neq j$ we have at a given moment

$$a \in M[i] \quad \text{and} \quad b \in M[j]$$

then we will find ourselves in trouble when the progress of $T[i]$ requires record b to be added to $M[i]$ and also the progress of $T[j]$ requires record a to be added to $M[j]$, for then there is no way in which $T[i]$ or $T[j]$ can progress without violating relation 1. This is called "deadlock". If we insist on the absence of the danger of deadlock —and we do— the above observation tells us that, without any further knowledge about the future requirements of the transactions, parallelism is impossible. We therefore associate with each transaction $T[i]$ a set $F[i]$ of records, containing all the records that may possibly be added to $M[i]$. (Note that this definition implies $M[i] \cap F[i] = \varnothing$.)

When the current transactions can be renumbered so that

$$i < j \Rightarrow F[i] \cap M[j] = \varnothing \qquad (2)$$

the danger of deadlock is absent, for then $T[0]$ can be carried to completion, and after that the new $T[0]$, etc. We call the situation "safe" when, besides relation 1, transactions can be renumbered such that relation 2 holds. We shall keep the system in a safe state. From the above we can conclude that a decrease of the set $F[i]$ —as a result of progress of $T[i]$— will leave a safe situation safe; it furthermore follows that such a decrease is something to be encouraged, because as long as $F[0] =$ the universe, all $M[j]$ with $j > 0$ must be empty, i.e. parallelism is not possible.

When we start each transaction with its F equal to the universe, and insist that $T[i]$ can only add a record to $M[i]$ by transferring it from $F[i]$, then this is the only transition that might violate condition 1 or the safety, i.e. this is the only place where it might be necessary to hold up the further execution of the transaction, to "put the transaction to sleep". The "counter-occurrences", on account of which a sleeping transaction could be woken up again, are when another progressing transaction decreases its own F explicitly or terminates.

In the above we have assumed that, for each transaction, F would start equal to the universe and would only decrease. Because this set is so huge, one could think that it could be profitable to divide the execution of a transaction into two successive phases, a first phase in which F is still allowed to grow and a second phase in which this is no longer permissible. But as far as the avoidance of deadlock is concerned, such a transaction is equivalent to one with F equal to the universe during the first phase, decreasing F to the stated amount upon the transition from the first to the second phase.

ad 3

Our system has to allocate records to transitions. When the allocation strategy is such that each request of an $F \to M$ transition is honoured as soon as this is compatible with the simultaneity restriction 1 and the safety condition, it is well-known that the execution of an acknowledged transaction may be postponed indefinitely long. Suppose we have

$$M[1] = \{a\} \qquad F[1] = \{c\}$$
$$M[2] = \{b\} \qquad F[2] = \{c\}$$
$$M[3] = \varnothing \qquad F[3] = \{a, b, c\}$$

and suppose that $T[3]$ would like to transfer record c to $M[3]$. It cannot do so because doing so would introduce deadlock with respect to both $T[1]$ and $T[2]$. In the case of an infinite supply of transactions of type 1 and type 2, $T[3]$ could be kept asleep forever. This phenomenon is called individual starvation and, as a rule, it is considered to be undesirable.

A crude way to exorcize the danger of individual starvation is the following: as soon as a transaction is put to sleep, a fixed upper limit is imposed upon the number of transactions that may be initiated during that nap. We are not going to look for a more refined technique now, for there are other reasons why we consider our first model as too crude, and in our second model we shall depart from it.

The Second Model

Our main complaint about the first model is that a record once in set $M[i]$ remains in set $M[i]$ until the transaction has run to completion. We would like to be able to express that a transaction is such that a manipulated record is no longer essential for the correct progress of the transaction. We therefore split $M[i]$ into two disjoint sets $A[i]$ and $P[i]$, i.e. the records that are still active and the records that have been processed. A record in set $P[i]$ has arrived there from set $F[i]$ via set $A[i]$ and will remain there until termination of $T[i]$.

Obviously

$$i \neq j \Rightarrow A[i] \cap A[j] = \varnothing$$

is a necessary condition, but this is no longer sufficient to guarantee that the nett reaction of the parallel system is identical to the reaction of a sequential system after proper ordering of the requests, for it would not exclude

$$A[i] \cap P[j] \neq \varnothing \qquad \textbf{and} \qquad A[j] \cap P[i] \neq \varnothing \quad .$$

The first condition expresses that in the sequential ordering $T[i]$ should follow $T[j]$ and the second condition requires it to be the other way round. The situation is even worse, because if $P[i] \cap P[j] \neq \varnothing$, apparently, the order in which the shared record was processed was decided in the past, and this order is no longer expressed in the population of the various sets, even though in general it is still relevant.

In our second model, the virtual order for the pair $T[i]$, $T[j]$ is irrevocably decided as far as their interference with the data base is concerned, as soon as for the first time holds

$$A[i] \cap P[j] \neq \varnothing \quad \textbf{or} \quad A[j] \cap P[i] \neq \varnothing \quad .$$

Therefore we associate with each pair $(T[i], T[j])$ of transactions the function $V(i, j)\ (= -V(j, i))$, defined by

$$V(i, j) = 0 \qquad \text{no decision on the order of } T[i] \text{ and } T[j] \text{ has been made}$$

$$V(i, j) = +1 \qquad \text{in the virtual order } T[i] \text{ has to precede } T[j]$$

$$V(i, j) = -1 \qquad \text{in the virtual order } T[j] \text{ has to precede } T[i].$$

We now have the following invariant relations

$$i \neq j \Rightarrow A[i] \cap A[j] = \varnothing \tag{3}$$

$$A[j] \cap P[i] \neq \varnothing \Rightarrow V(i, j) = +1 \tag{4}$$

$$V(i, j) = +1 \Rightarrow A[i] \cap P[j] = \varnothing \tag{5}$$

$$P[i] \cap P[j] \neq \varnothing \Rightarrow V(i, j) \neq 0 \tag{6}$$

and deadlock is prevented, provided that we can renumber the transactions currently under execution in such a way that

$$i < j \Rightarrow \{F[i] \cap (A[j] \cup P[j]) = \varnothing \quad \textbf{and} \quad V(i, j) \geq 0\} \tag{7}$$

for then $T[0]$ can be carried to completion without violating the decided virtual order. (See, however, the note added while editing.)

The second model shows great similarity to the first one. Again, the only point where it might be necessary to put a transaction to sleep is where it would like to transfer a record from set F to set A. The points of progress in one transaction that could result in the situation that sleeping transactions could be woken up are (as before) explicit F-decrease and termination, but in addition to these two a transition from A to P.

The problem of individual starvation can be dealt with in the same crude fashion as in the first model, and for the time being we shall leave it at that.

The Third Model

The second model is appropriate when each transaction modifies all its active records. But that seems a rather exceptional situation, and in our third model we would like to exploit the fact that simultaneous inspection of a current record value by a number of parallel transactions is an absolutely innocent operation. For that reason we split all sets into two: F into FR and FW, A into AR and AW and P into PR and PW. Here AR are the "read only records", while records in set AW may also be modified. Initially, a transaction starts with FW equal to the universe and the other five sets empty. Permissible transfers of a record are: from FW to FR and AW, from FR to AR, from AW to PW and from AR to PR.

Now formulae 3) through 7) can be modified systematically by changing

$$X[i] \cap Y[j]$$

into

$$(XW[i] \cap YW[j]) \cup (XW[i] \cap YR[j]) \cup (XR[i] \cap YW[j])$$

i.e. from the four cross-products only the three in which writing is possibly involved, but not the fourth, the RR combination.

After this systematic change we have formulae 3') through 7'), describing a model in which records shared for inspection only impose no mutual exclusion or virtual ordering. The only difference between the third and the second model is that in one transaction the transfer of a record from FW to FR could have the side-effect of waking up a sleeping transaction.

NOTE. If a transaction, upon inspection of a record in set AW (because it might have to modify it), discovers that it can leave the record unchanged, we can, if we so desire, admit the transfer of this record from set AW to set AR. In that case also this transition could have the side-effect that another sleeping transaction can now be woken up.

Avoiding the Danger of Individual Starvation

In view of the formal relationship between the second and the third model it suffices to discuss the starvation problem in terms of the simpler formalism of the second model.

By the time, however, that we are going to tackle the starvation problem seriously, we should bear in mind that until now we have assumed that the only reason for preventing progress of a transaction would be that otherwise relations 3 or 7 would be violated. In a general system one must assume that there will be other reasons as well: by the time that we bring into the picture that most of the records will be in secondary store most of the time, reduction of the traffic density between primary and secondary store might become a worthy goal, and we can envisage a system trying to collect transactions involving the same records. The system can try to do so by postponing transactions, but such strategic postponement must be void of the starvation danger.

With each transaction $T[i]$ currently under execution we can associate a so-called "allowance counter" $ac[i]$, with value equal to the maximum number of other transactions allowed to run to completion before $T[i]$ will run to completion. This implies that upon termination of a transaction all ac's associated with the remaining transactions will be decreased by 1. We now superimpose upon our original safety condition the condition that the transactions can be renumbered in such a fashion that, besides relation 7, also

$$i \leqslant ac[i] \tag{8}$$

holds.

In that case $T[0]$ can run to completion, and its termination will decrease the remaining ac's by 1; simultaneously the remaining transactions will shift down one place (i.e. the old $T[1]$ will become the new $T[0]$) and as a result relation 8 will continue to hold.

Inside a transaction we have now three types of points where the system may decide to put a transaction to sleep:

> request for record transfer from F to A
> request for potential strategic postponement
> request to terminate.

Whenever a transaction makes such a request that can be honoured without violating conditions 3, 7 and 8, the system is in general free to refuse the request and to put the transaction to sleep. This would admit the possibility of a completely sleeping system, and no real-time guarantee could be given, even if a maximum execution time for a transaction is known. We therefore impose the requirement that

> when the set of current transactions is non-empty,
> at least one transaction must be non-sleeping.

When a transaction is initiated and its ac is introduced its initial value must be sufficiently high to guarantee 8; the number of transactions currently under execution will certainly be sufficient. The higher the initial value of the ac's, the greater the system's freedom in shuffling the transaction order, but the weaker any real-time guarantee about possible delays.

Finally, in the above parallel system, the order in which the transactions are terminated is a possible order for the transaction stream processed by the purely sequential system that should show the same nett reaction.

NOTE ADDED WHILE EDITING. In October 1979, Mr. Darryn Price from Burroughs Corporation, Austin, Texas, was the first to discover a flaw in the above.

With $V(i, j) = 1$ and $V(j, k) = 1$, the commitment that $T[i]$ should precede $T[k]$ in the virtual order may only remain recorded as long as $T[j]$ remains under execution. A solution is only to permit termination of a transaction provided it can be taken as $T[0]$ in the virtual order. (End of the note added while editing.)

EWD376
Finding the Maximum Strong Components in a Directed Graph

This essay records an exercise in orderly program composition. The record is not completely truthful in the sense that prior to its writing some thinking without pencil and paper was done. As a result, the following text contains a few "surprises" in the sense that suggestions are made without an elaborate heuristic justification. When I noticed myself doing so, some heuristic justification was added afterwards. The moral of all this is: in case of surprise, please go on reading!

Given a set of nodes and a set of directed arcs, each leading from a node to a node, it is requested to partition the set of nodes into maximal strong components. A strong component is a set of nodes such that the arcs between them provide a path from any node of the set to any node of the set. A single node is a special case of a strong component; then the path can be empty. A maximal strong components is a strong component to which no nodes can be added.

We shall use the acronym "*sa*" for a set of arcs, and the acronym "*sn*" for a set of nodes. Our final answer is a partitioning, that is a set of sets of nodes with empty intersections; for that latter object we shall use the acronym "*ssn*". Similarly, when the need arises, we shall use the acronym "*ssa*" for a set of sets of arcs with empty intersection. (Note added while typing out the manuscript: this need did not arise.)

Let "*sn*" be the given set of nodes, and "*sa*" be the given set of arcs. Let the final value of "*ssn*" be the desired answer. We then write the desired final relation as

$$ssn = \mathrm{MSC}(sa) \tag{1}$$

where MSC, the set of Maximal Strong Components, is regarded for constant *sn* as a function of the set of arcs *sa*.

We want to inspect the arcs one by one (in a suitable order still to be chosen), i.e. we introduce two disjoint subsets of sa, viz. $sa1$ and $sa2$, such that

$$sa = sa1 + sa2 \qquad (2)$$

where $sa1$ comprises the inspected arcs (initially empty, finally $= sa$) and $sa2$ the uninspected arcs (initially $= sa$, finally empty).

Similarly, we want to build up the final value of ssn. We shall do so by maintaining the invariant relation

$$ssn + ssn1 = \text{MSC}(sa1) \qquad (3)$$

Here each node of sn will occur either in an element of ssn or in an element of $ssn1$, but never in both. (Besides that we can, as will be shown later, restrict ourselves to $ssn1$-values that are sets of sets of single nodes.) The following idea underlies the introduction of $ssn1$: ssn is a set of maximal strong components, for which —we write an algorithm for a sequential machine!— we may expect to establish one after the other that they will occur as element of the final value of ssn. Our aim is that at any moment in time, ssn will only contain elements of its final value: they are the maximal strong components definitely found. Then we need $ssn1$ for the remaining nodes.

The initial condition corresponding to $sa1 = empty$ is $ssn = empty$ and each node of sn being a separate element of $ssn1$. When we succeed in establishing

$$ssn1 = empty \quad \textbf{and} \quad sa2 = empty \qquad (4)$$

under invariance of (3), the desired relation (1) has been established, since the second term of (4) implies on account of (2) that $sa = sa1$.

We have not established yet the relation between the way in which the nodes are divided over ssn and $ssn1$ on the one hand and the arcs over $sa1$ and $sa2$ on the other. We shall maintain the following relations (5) and (6):

each arc originating in a node of ssn is in $sa1$ \qquad (5)

each arc terminating in a node of $ssn1$ is in $sa2$ \quad . \qquad (6)

Relations (5) and (6) are compatible with the initial situation. Because $ssn = empty$, there are no arcs originating in a node of ssn and therefore $sa1$ can be empty (i.e. (5) is not violated) and because $ssn1$ comprises all nodes, all arcs should be in $sa2$, in accordance with the initial condition $sa2 = sa$ (i.e. (6) is satisfied).

Relations (5) and (6) are also compatible with the final situation, because then ssn will comprise all nodes, all arcs must be in $sa1$, in accordance with

$sa1 = sa$ (i.e. (5) is satisfied), while (6) is satisfied because then both $ssn1$ and $sa2$ will be empty (see (4)).

We observe that, because $sa1$ and $sa2$ have an empty intersection, there will be no arcs originating in a node of ssn and terminating in a node of $ssn1$. On the other hand, an arc originating in a node of $ssn1$ and terminating in a node of ssn may be in either $sa1$ or $sa2$.

The structure of our program becomes, if we want to apply the fundamental invariance theorem for loops:

$sa1 :=$ *empty*; $sa2 :=$ *sa*;
$ssn :=$ *empty*; $ssn1 :=$ "the set of all single node sets";
while $ssn1 \neq$ *empty* **or** $sa2 \neq$ *empty* **do**
    "transfer arc(s) from $sa2$ to $sa1$" and/or
    "transfer node(s) from $ssn1$ to ssn"
    under invariance of (3), (5) and (6)
                od

Relation (5) allows us to simplify the last boolean expression: $ssn1 =$ *empty* implies that all nodes are in ssn, which implies that all arcs are in $sa1$, which implies that $sa2 =$ *empty*. Therefore it can be simplified to

while $ssn1 \neq$ *empty* **do**

Relations (5) and (6), which may have come as a surprise, have been suggested by

Theorem 1. *When the set of nodes is subdivided into two sets nsA and nsB, such that there are no arcs originating in a node of nsA and terminating in a node of nsB, then the set of strong components is unchanged when the arcs (if any) originating in a node of nsB and terminating in a node of nsA are removed and, secondly, no strong component contains nodes from both sets.*

Here the nodes in ssn play the role of those in snA and Theorem 1 tells us that the maximal strong components they will give rise to cannot depend on the arcs still in $sa2$. Therefore they can only depend on the arcs in $sa1$, which have already been inspected. As a result each element (i.e. a maximal strong component) of an intermediate value of ssn will be an element of its final value.

In order to refine the repeatable statement we introduce a chain of strong components (a chain of sets of nodes), called "csn", empty at the beginning and at the end of the repeatable statement. The transfer of a node from $ssn1$ to ssn will take place in two steps: first the node will be transferred (individually) from $ssn1$ to csn; at a later stage the node will be transferred (together with all the nodes of the same maximal strong component) from *csn* to *ssn*.

The strong components in *csn* are so by virtue of arcs of *sa*1 and their chaining is performed by arcs of *sa*1. More precisely,

> two successive strong components in *csn* are connected by one arc from *sa*1 originating in a node of the predecessor and terminating in a node of the successor   (7)
> no arc in *sa*1 will originate at a node of an element of *csn* and terminate at a node of a preceding element in *csn*.   (8)

The chain *csn* has been introduced as a tool for searching for cycles, an activity that is suggested by

Theorem 2. *When a number of strong components can be connected via a cyclic path, they belong to the same maximal strong component.*

This theorem suggests that we try to extend the chain at one end: whenever we encounter an arc leading from its end element to a preceding element in the chain a cycle has been detected, and all elements of that cycle can be combined to form the new terminal element. We shall call this operation "combine end elements of *csn*"; its purpose is to restore the validity of (8).

When the chain *csn* is non-empty, we investigate whether *sa*2 contains an arc *f* having its origin in (one of the nodes of) the terminal element of *csn*.

If such an arc *f* points to one of the nodes in *ssn*, it can be ignored (on account of Theorem 1).

If such an arc *f* points to a node in the terminal element of *csn*, it can be ignored as well —we knew already that the nodes in this terminal element formed a strong component.

If such an arc points to (a node in) a preceding element of *csn*, the end elements of *csn* are combined.

If such an arc leads to a node in *ssn*1, that node is appended to the chain and will form, all by itself, the new terminal element of *csn*.

In all four cases the arc *f* is transferred from *sa*2 to *sa*1.

If no such arc exists, the terminal element of the chain must be a maximal strong component of the final graph; it will be removed from *csn* and added to *ssn*, which now grows by one element. This conclusion, again, is justified by Theorem 1. (Note. Here Theorem 1 is applied twice: the terminal node is a maximal strong component because it has no outgoing arcs in the reduced graph that we get by removing all arcs leading back to a node of *ssn* after it has been established that *ssn* already contains maximal strong components for the total graph.)

The structure of the repeatable statement —only starting when the chain $csn = empty$ and $ssn1 \neq empty$— can be the following:

transfer an arbitrary element of $ssn1$ and append it to an
initially empty chain csn;
while $csn \neq empty$ **do**
  if $sa2$ contains no arc f originating in a node of csn's terminal
    element
    then transfer csn's terminal element to ssn
    else transfer such an arc f from $sa2$ to $sa1$;
        if f terminates in (a node of) an element of $ssn1$
          then transfer that element from $ssn1$ to csn
          else **if** f leads to (a node of) a preceding element of csn
              then combine end elements of csn
            fi
        fi
  fi
od

We have now to choose a way to represent the information. It is assumed that the nodes are numbered from 1 through N. Because we intend to chain nodes, it is a wise precaution to add "a virtual node" with number 0.

In the representation of our sets of nodes we can exploit the fact that we know that the elements of $ssn1$ are single node sets. In ssn and csn our elements are strong components; in csn we can number them from $+1$ upwards, in ssn we can number them from -1 downwards and thus we come to the following representation with an integer array $sn[0:N]$:

$sn[i] > 0$ means: node i is a member of element $sn[i]$ of csn
$sn[i] < 0$ means: node i is a member of element $sn[i]$ of ssn
$sn[i] = 0$ means: node i is (a node of) an element of $ssn1$
$sn[0] = 0$.

In order to scan nodes we introduce for nodes in csn or ssn an integer array $pc[1:N]$, where for node i in one of the two sets of sets

$pc[i] = j$ means: with respect to node i, node j is the next oldest node in
           the same set of sets; when $j = 0$, node i is its oldest
           node.

In order to be able to trace these pc-chains we introduce two handles:

$yc =$ the number of the youngest node in csn; when $csn = empty$, $yc = 0$
$ys =$ the number of the youngest node in ssn; when $ssn = empty$, $ys = 0$.

In order to speed up the search for an arbitrary node in $ssn1$ for the initialization of csn, we introduce the integer variable k, such that $ssn1$ contains no nodes with a number $< k$.

Further we introduce, in order to be able to fix the ordinal number of a new element,

ec = the number of elements in csn
es = the number of elements in ssn

and, in order to decide whether $ssn1$ is empty,

$es1$ = the number of elements in $ssn1$.

In our program we have to establish whether $sa2$ contains an arc f originating from the terminal element of csn. We do so by investigating the nodes of the terminal element and on account of the pc-chaining we do so in order of increasing age in csn. Because quite a number of nodes may be a member of the terminal element it seems a bit wasteful in time to start this search always at the youngest node and therefore we introduce

yun = the number of "the youngest possibly unexhausted node" i.e. $sa2$
        contains no arcs originating in a node of csn younger than no. yun
        (if any). Again, in the extreme case, yun may be 0.

Our algorithm presupposes that for each node we can find "its outgoing arcs". We therefore assume that the arcs are sorted in order of increasing starting node and that in that order their terminal nodes are listed in global integer array $t[1:\text{number of arcs}]$, while the boundaries are given by integer array $b[0:N]$, such that $b[0] = 0$, $b[N] = $ number of arcs, and the nodes at which the arcs originating at node i terminate will be $t[j]$, with j ranging

$$b[i-1] < j \leqslant b[i].$$

For the representation of the partitioning $sa = sa1 + sa2$ we introduce

integer array $c[0:N]$

such that all arcs originating in node i and belonging to $sa1$ will have an ordinal number j satisfying

$$b[i-1] < j \leqslant c[i]$$

and those in $sa2$ a j satisfying

$$c[i] < j \leqslant b[i].$$

We assume $c[0] = 0$ for the sake of safety (i.e. $sa2$ contains no arcs originating from the virtual node).

In the following program variable ft is used to identify the terminal node of arc f, while variable h is used for a wild collection of short range purposes. I know that this is a poor style; I too have my weak moments!

```
begin integer array sn, c[0:N], pc[1:N];
      integer yc, ys, ec, es, es1, yun, h, ft, k;
{initialize sa1 and sa2}
      c[0] := 0; h := 0; while h < N do h := h + 1; c[h] := b[h − 1]
                                                    od;
{initialize ssn and ssn1}
      h := 0; while h ≤ N do sn[h] := 0; h := h + 1 od;
      ys := 0; es := 0; es1 := N; k := 1;
      while es1 > 0
      do
      {search for a node k in ssn1}
        while sn[k] ≠ 0 do k := k + 1 od;
      {remove it from ssn1 and initialize csn with node k}
        es1 := es1 − 1; sn[k] := 1;
        pc[k] := 0; yc := k; ec := 1; yun := k;
      {note that at this moment node k is oldest, youngest, and youngest
       possibly unexhausted node of csn}
        while ec > 0
        do
        {search for the youngest unexhausted node of the terminal
         element of csn}
          while sn[yun] = ec and c[yun] ≥ b[yun] do yun := pc[yun] od
        {this loop will certainly terminate, possibly with yun = 0};
          if sn[yun] ≠ ec
            then {there is no arc f in sa2 originating in the terminal
                  element no. ec of csn and therefore this terminal element
                  will be transported to ssn}
                  es := es + 1;
                  while sn[yc] = ec
                  do sn[yc] := −es; h := pc[yc]; pc[yc] := ys;
                     ys := yc; yc := h
                  od;
                  ec := ec − 1; yun := yc
            else {c[yun] < b[yun], therefore the next arc originating at
                  node no. yun will be transferred from sa2 to sa1; this is
                  arc f}
                  c[yun] := c[yun] + 1; ft := t[c[yun]]; h := sn[ft];
                  {now ft is the terminal node of arc f and h = sn[ft] to
                  save dynamically a few subscriptions!}
                  if h = 0
                    then {node ft has to be removed from ssn1 and to be
                          attached to csn}
                          es1 := es1 − 1; ec := ec + 1; sn[ft] := ec;
                          pc[ft] := yc; yc := ft; yun := yc
                    else if 0 < h and h < ec
```

then { *ft* is a node of the non-terminal element
no. *h* of *csn*, with which the younger elements
have to be combined}

    ec := *h*

{this ends the use of *h* as $h = sn[ft]$};

    h := *yc*; **while** $sn[h] > ec$

          do $sn[h] := ec$; $h := pc[h]$

          od

{note that in combining, *pc*, *yc* and *yun* can
remain unchanged}

else {arc *f* points either to *csn*'s terminal
element or to an element of *ssn*; in either
case it can be ignored}

    fi

  fi {the case that arc *f* existed has been dealt with}

 fi {*csn*'s terminal element has been inspected}

od {*csn* is again empty}

od {*ssn*1 is empty, the computation is done};

{print the results; the maximal strong components appear numbered in decreasing order}

  while $es > 0$

  do newline; printtext("maximal strong component *nr.*");

    printvalue(*es*); printtext("consists of the nodes:");

    while $sn[ys] = -es$ **do** printvalue(*ys*); *ys* := *pc*[*ys*] **od**;

    es := *es* − 1

  od

end

Concluding Remarks

In order to avoid the usual misunderstandings it might be a good thing to
point out, once again, that the approach illustrated in this exercise does not
pretend to be an infallible cure against fallibility. We have tried two things:
we have tried to develop a program in a way that leads to a higher
confidence level than the one that can be reached when the designer "rushes
into coding" and we have tried to make the reader share our conviction
—strengthened by the above experience!— that the simultaneous development of the correctness proof gives indeed a strong heuristic guidance in the
process of shaping the program.

    As the reader will have noticed we have not spent a single word of
explanation on the repeatable statements of the small innermost loops. I
think that this is in accordance with normal mathematical practice: the
reasoning has to be broken down in steps so small that they can be made

"in confidence" and that a more detailed proof, a more detailed justification could be given when they are challenged, but that that should not be done without compelling reason. We should not waste our time on trivia!

The situation at the innermost loops, where we deal with quite standard coding techniques, is quite different from the situation at the outermost levels, where we have to manipulate with concepts and relations cooked up and discovered for the specific purpose of solving this specific problem: it is at the latter level that the greater explicitness seems most urgently needed. Also, it is in that part of the analysis and synthesis that the most heavy demands are made upon the programmer's ability to express himself effectively.

Finally we draw attention to the fact that we did not need a single example to explain what we were talking about or (even worse!) to discover what the program should do. And this, of course, is as it should have been.

Acknowledgments

We express our gratitude towards J.A.G.M. Kerbosch and J.C. Wortmann for bringing this problem to our attention and thereby presenting the challenge.

Nuenen, 30th May 1973   EDSGER W. DIJKSTRA

EWD385
Trip Report E.W. Dijkstra, Summer School Munich, July 25 to August 4, 1973

Well, actually it was not Munich, but the little town of Marktoberdorf, which meant that upon arrival in Munich we had another two hours of travel to survive and that upon departure we had to leave so early that I bought a travel alarm clock just to be on the safe (i.e. "early") side, since I had found the waking service of Hotel Sepp on previous tests unreliable! At both occasions, the international trains were perfect and dead on time, it is, for distances of that order of magnitude, the most civilized way of travelling through Europe.

This NATO-sponsored Summer School is establishing quite a position in the field. Last time there were about 80 participants, this year they could accommodate 105, but the number of applications had been three times as much! It was a difficult audience: it was large and highly inhomogeneous. I always try to adapt my presentations to my audience as much as possible, and for such a mixed audience this is always difficult. But during the first three days I could not even try it, because they were very passive and did not give any feedback. Part of that can be explained by the language barrier —there were participants from 22 different countries, including France— but not all of it. I had to give ten lectures (of 45 minutes each), the last six —i.e. after the weekend— were less of a monologue. I got the impression that eventually I reached practically all the participants. Wladislav Turski and Alan Perlis had an equal share of the burden.

Turski (Warszawa, Poland) lectured under the title "Morphology of Data." What he tried to do seemed quite reasonable: he tried to separate "naming conventions" on the one hand from storing on a (addressable) medium on the other hand. But he suffered quite clearly from the pressure of his Polish environment, where pure mathematicians are very much in power and enforce their notational prejudices (probably justified for their own requirements) ruthlessly upon everyone else; I know that Turski has suffered from this pressure, and that he has made a conscious effort to undo its harmful effects as much as possible. Having heard his presentation I must come to the conclusion that he has not fully escaped (yet).

Perlis (Yale University, USA) is quite a different person! He is fun to listen to as long as you do not listen too carefully, for as soon as you start doing that his words dissolve into loose talk, so superficial that after a while it becomes annoying, his jokes excepted. His presence was valuable insofar he provided the contrast, trying to make his case for "unstructured programming" and his presence was responsible for a number of discussions and even arguments. But I have the feeling that the level of these discussions could have been higher if someone else had provided that contrast. Brian Randell (who is very good at such things) saved a few discussions.

Niklaus Wirth —who spoke also a little bit on behalf of Tony Hoare— spoke on "An Axiomatic Definition of the Programming Language PASCAL". His presentations were very well prepared and it was a pleasure to listen to him. He gave a striking demonstration of our increased powers of annotating and explaining non-trivial programs! It was really impressive. (The demonstration suffered slightly from the fact that the program he showed was not very nice, and some in the audience found their thoughts drifting away in the mood of "How should I solve that problem by means of a program?") In other respects he was not convincing: in the design of PASCAL the axiomatic definition did not play a significant role, and to give an axiomatic definition was an afterthought. The result shows that and you cannot conceal that.

Personal reasons prevented M. Griffiths of Grenoble from speaking as scheduled, but we were lucky in having Per Brinch Hansen (California Institute of Technology) as a substitute. He went through the highlights of his recently published book "Operating System Principles" and he did that much, much better than two years ago, when he covered the same material in a very biased and even aggressive manner. Now he gave a neat, balanced survey. It is a pity that he has a very monotonous voice; it is really soporific and now I cannot even read one of his publications without hearing it!

Brian Randell gave a two-lecture talk on the PEARL system, and did so very nicely. (He had to, for its author, Bob Snowdon, was sitting in the audience!). The remaining three speakers, I am afraid, failed to get their message across the limelight; in one or two cases there was some doubt whether there was a message...

Having talked about factorization of a solution and having illustrated this by comparing two different types of circuits found in clocked machines, I wanted to expose the audience to the design of a mouse that follows a contour, because you can then meet that same factoring principle in a completely different environment (and in its full glory, even!). I did not quite know how to stage it: the whole crowd of 105 people seemed too large for active participation. I announced "an interactive programming session", announced that I had found two "intelligent terminals" —in the form of David Redell and Paul McJones, both from Berkeley— and predicted a successful session because our communication language (viz. English) was "an interpretive language". (I was so cross with Al for all his platitudes; I think that this ridicule was the only time I showed my temper in public!) It was a very nice session, I was lucky in the choice of my "intelligent terminals"!

Compared with earlier Summer Schools, there was a change. A greater percentage of the participants seemed to have come with the rather stupid hope, essentially, for a recipe for thinking, or under the false assumption that "the good programming language" is the end to all your problems! Who has taught them that nonsense? I observed this attitude most markedly among the American and the Israeli participants (but as the French kept their mouths hermetically sealed ... who knows?). This false and primitive idea surfaced over and over again; in utter exasperation I recommended at the beginning of my last lecture "A Guide to Positive Programming" by Norman Vincent Peale...

Another difference was caused by a drastic change (or shift) on the German Academic scene. For years computing science has been neglected. Since the term "Informatik" has been invented for it, the German government is backing the subject with all its force and marks: departments of "Informatik" are mushrooming all over the country. And how did they staff them? With what they had, pure mathematicians and automata theorists in particular. I am afraid that the result is a disaster, at least for German Computing Science. German Computing Science is in danger of being taken over either by the mathematicians or by APL; in both cases the result will be very much the same, viz. the end of German Computing Science!

I solved the convergence properties of a tricky cyclic relaxation problem while the others visited mad Ludwig's castle Neuschwanstein. It came out of my search for self-stabilizing systems.

Nuenen, 7th August 1973   DR. EDSGER W. DIJKSTRA

EWD386
The Solution to a Cyclic Relaxation Problem

The problem solved in this note arose in connection with the (just initiated) study of self-stabilizing systems.

Consider a circle and N points numbered from 0 through $N - 1$, placed in an *arbitrary* order around the circumference. For "the adjustment of point $nr.i$" we consider the shortest clockwise path along the circumference from its predecessor —i.e. point $nr.(i - 1)$**mod** N— to its successor —i.e. point $nr.(i + 1)$**mod** N—; the new position of point $nr.i$ will be halfway (i.e. the middle) of that path. In formula (taking the circumference of the circle as unit) with $pred = x[(i - 1)$**mod** $N]$ and $succ = x[(i + 1)$**mod** $N]$

$$x[i] := \textbf{if } pred \leqslant succ \textbf{ then } (pred + succ)/2$$
$$\textbf{else } ((pred + succ + 1)/2)\textbf{mod } 1 \textbf{ fi}$$

If we start doing adjustments, will the system converge to a stable state?

This is not necessarily the case if we do the adjustments simultaneously, i.e. determine all the new positions in terms of all the old ones, as is shown by the following examples.

	$N = 3$				$N = 4$		
t	0	1	2	t	0	1	2
$x[0]$	0	1/2	0	$x[0]$	0	3/4	0
$x[1]$	2/3	1/6	2/3	$x[1]$	0	1/4	0
$x[2]$	1/3	5/6	1/3	$x[2]$	1/2	1/4	1/2
				$x[3]$	1/2	3/4	1/2

For both odd and even N we have an example that will oscillate with a period 2. If, however, we do the adjustments one at a time in a fair random order (i.e. without permanent neglect of certain points), then the system is bound to converge.

Consider, instead of the N points, the N clockwise paths leading from each point to its successor. After a point adjustment the two paths meeting at that point will both be less than $1/2$ and no future adjustment can ever undo that! After adjustments all around the circle each path will be less than $1/2$, and from that moment onwards each triangle "$i - 1, i, i + 1$" is a clockwise one. The total clockwise path from 0 to 1, from 1 to 2,..., from $N - 1$ to 0 will go around the circle a fixed number of times, m say ($0 \leqslant m \leqslant N/2$). No adjustment can anymore change the value of m, from now onwards we could even do simultaneous adjustments. The final state will satisfy for all i

$$(x[(i + 1)\mathbf{mod}\ N] - x[i])\mathbf{mod}\ 1 = m/N$$

The system converges linearly (imagine successive points connected by spiral springs or rubber bands of equal length).

The above was written under the assumption that along the circumference we had the continuum at our disposal, i.e. that the fractions x, satisfying $0 \leqslant x < 1$, could be represented in arbitrary precision. Suppose now that we have to represent the fractions x as integer multiples of $1/p$ (where we may assume the integer p to satisfy $p \gg N$).

The extent to which the system converges seems to depend on how we round off when necessary, i.e. when the clockwise path from predecessor to successor turns out to be an odd multiple of $1/p$. If we impose the rule, that rounding will always take place in the same cyclic direction (say "anticlockwise"), then the following will happen.

With m defined as in the continuous case, define q and r by

$$m * p = q * N + r \qquad \text{with } 0 \leqslant r < N$$

Of the paths $p[i]$ leading from $x[i]$ to its successor, $(N - r)$ —the "short" paths— will be of length q/p and r paths —the "long" paths— will be of length $(q + 1)/p$. If $p[i - 1]$ is "long" and $p[i]$ is "short", adjustment of point $nr.i$ —with anti-clockwise rounding— will have the effect that the predicates "short" and "long" have interchanged position. The short ones will be travelling anti-clockwise through the cycle, simultaneously the long ones will travel clockwise through the cycle.

The two types of paths travelling in opposite direction through the same cycle makes it quite clear that if $m * p$ is an integer multiple of N, the system will converge to a completely stable situation.

Nuenen, 8th August 1973   DR. EDSGER W. DIJKSTRA

EWD387
Trip Report IBM Seminar "Communication and Computers", Newcastle, Sept. 1973

It was a very mixed affair and I have not yet succeeded in sorting out my feelings completely. Let me try.

There are two completely different views of programming. On the one hand we have the (academic) study about the nature of the intellectual challenge, on the other hand we have programming as it is done and can be done by the hundreds of thousands that are called "programmers" today. These are two completely different subjects, and when two groups are talking about them as if it were one subject, unaware of the "twoness", endless confusions arise. I have now witnessed this confusion so many times that it does no more catch me unaware. During this seminar on "Communication and Computers" there was a similar confusion; being less familiar with that one, I only discovered it well after the Seminar had finished.

On the one hand there are the technical and logical problems connected with the organization of the cooperation between two or more computers, so far apart that by definition they are asynchronous. In this field there are enough intriguing and logically very difficult problems to justify a seminar to them. On the other hand the American scene presents us with a few large, powerful bodies: the giant IBM forcing a de facto standard upon the world of computing, "ma Bell" forcing in a very similar fashion a de facto standard upon the world of communication and finally as a third (politically very powerful) party the ARPA network, an achievement that, in spite of all its patent shortcomings, will be a model for many future efforts, if only because it has been such an expensive experiment.

Much of the discussion and the talks was really about the problem of organizing fruitful cooperation —how to organize some sort of merge— between the now separate communication and computer industries, each with their different pasts and tremendous vested interests. But this was done in veiled terms, addressed to an audience of European academic computer scientists! Some misunderstanding —to put it mildly— was only to be expected.

The academic computer scientists were not quite sure whether the problem really concerned them and their educational responsibilities, and I cannot blame them either. From the rostrum the problem was approached from an academic point of view as well, but...! L. Kleinrock of UCLA gave three excellent and inspiring tutorials on "Analytical Techniques for Computer Communication Networks". A highly gifted teacher, so gifted that he made you forget that his dealing with the whole subject was very one-sided! He showed queueing theory at work, unavoidably suggesting that the contribution of mathematics should always have the form of "applying an existing mathematical technique for solving a specific class of problems". The result is not inspiring for mathematicians: on the one hand most of the results can be obtained with the aid of what Kleinrock characteristically described as "baby queueing theory" and that was not too much: quickly one had to turn to simulation! In another respect it was also misleading: his stress on the quantitative aspects of the game —what else can you expect from a queueing theorist?— tended to make the audience believe that the logical problems were either solved or unimportant or nonexistent. (The stress on the quantitative aspects is, of course, a very American attitude: this time it was vigorously enforced by the really gigantic size of the investments made by all sides. We don't really know what to do, but let us minimize our cost/performance ratio nevertheless!) But he was a great lecturer and it was a pleasure to see him at work.

Sandy Fraser, now at Bell Labs, did an excellent job. He was very concerned about bringing communication and computing industries together. (Let the universities, too, think about sound protocols: now all nets are still "experimental" but what will happen in the next ten years will bind us for the next 200 years.) He was in many ways bound; the fact that Bell and IBM are engaged in a lawsuit of gigantic proportion required all sorts of statements (from Ewan Page, when he was introduced, and from himself, when he started). As far as his technical message was concerned, he was also very careful —alarmingly careful, one might say— : he made the impression of arguing that all technical considerations pointed in a direction opposite to the store-and-forward techniques chosen for the ARPA network, but clearly he wished to avoid making all ARPA fans his declared enemies. It is somewhat sickening that an undoubtedly gifted, honest and sensitive scientist like Sandy must so constantly be on his guard. He, too, is a gifted speaker, very different from Kleinrock, but also and always a pleasure to listen to. Kleinrock and Fraser were the only two speakers that received an applause at the end of their last lecture; and they fully deserved it.

The other two speakers that gave three one-hour lectures were NN_0 from IBM, Yorktown Heights, and NN_1, SRI, Menlo Park. NN_0 spoke undiluted IBMerese for three full hours and I am not going to give any further comments; I only heard the first hour —like many participants— and that was enough (too much). Because I had an urgent letter to write, I missed NN_1's first lecture —it was not really a lecture, he showed a movie— but I attended his next two performances. He was not only terribly bad, he was dangerous as well, not so much on account of the product he was selling —a sophisticated on-line text-editor that could be quite useful— as on account of the way in which he appealed to mankind's lower instincts while selling it. The undisguised appeal to anti-intellectualism and anti-individualism was frightening. He was talking about his "augmented knowledge workshop" and I was constantly reminded of Manny Lehman's vigorous complaint about the extremely "knowledge-oriented" American educational system, which fails to do justice to the fact that one of the main objects of education is the insight that makes quite a lot of knowledge superfluous. (Sentences like "the half-life of a fresh university graduate is five years" are only correct if you have crammed the curriculum with volatile knowledge, erroneously presented as stuff worth knowing.) His anti-individualism surfaced when he recommended his gadget as a tool for easing the cooperation between persons and groups possibly miles apart, more or less suggesting that only then are you really "participating": no place for the solitary thinker. (Vide the sound track of the Monsanto movie, showing some employees, "No geniuses here: just a bunch of average Americans, working together."!) The two talks I heard were absolutely insipid, he had handed out a paper "An augmented knowledge workshop."; the syntactical ambiguity in the title is characteristic for the level of the rest of the article. As a result of his presentation, I told a few participants that I had found, thanks to this seminar, a new software project. "Because in the years to come there will be a crippling shortage of competent programmers, I shall develop a software package, called "The Instruction Interpreter". From the moment of its completion, users no longer need to program, they just give their instructions to the system." (This is only an edited version of one of the paragraphs of the NN_1 article!) I would have liked to start a discussion with him, but I knew that my lack of mastery of the understatement would have made me too rude for English ears if I had spoken. Finally —after a more than two-hour effort in the middle of the night in sorting out his muddle— I decided that it was not worth the trouble.

Besides the four main speakers there were six others who gave one-hour presentations.

On the schedule was mentioned Mr. T.R.M. Longam from IBM International Information Services. He was prevented from coming and his place was taken by one of his staff members, whose name I failed to catch. He did not speak IBMerese and gave a clear survey of intent and scope of his organization. In my memory will stick the tremendous amount of equipment he had in his place: 4 IBM360 model 65, a similar number model 50 plus peripheral gear. From the type of work he described, one could not fail to conclude that the arithmetic capabilities of these machines could hardly be expected to get very tired, and presumably they spend an awful lot of time idling or doing internal red tape. But he was a good speaker.

J. McNeil of Logica Limited gave a talk on "Graduates in the Computer Industry: A Consultant's View." It was a talk on a similar topic as covered by Alex d'Agapeyef a few years earlier but McNeil's presentation was more convincing. On the whole he was happy with graduates. He made it quite clear that their ability to write another compiler for a baby language was in his eyes not their most important asset, because the range of their activities was much broader. He complained —and I can well believe that he was fully justified in doing so!— about their crippling inability to use English effectively. In the discussion afterwards no one took up that point; at some stage I felt inclined to do so, but the moment passed. Nice talk.

There were two talks from PTT officials, a management talk by Mr. G. Dale from the English PTT and a technical one by ir.A. Boesveld of the Dutch PTT. The first speaker dealt with international politics, the second one described Stored Program Controlled Telephone Exchanges. As far as the clarity and truthfulness of the picture as given by Boesveld is concerned he did an excellent job; the programming techniques applied seemed to be rather old-fashioned, but my guess is that that is typical for the field. (As a Dutchman it was nice to hear that the Dutch telephone system ranks high in quality and low in tariff among its European fellow systems.) After both talks the audience misbehaved, at least to my standards; the audience started to attack the (his) PTT for monopolistic attitudes, misuse of power, failing public relations etc. I understand that it can be quite frustrating to get PTT's permission to hook an unusual gadget to their lines, but this seminar was *not* the proper place or moment to air(?) those frustrations.

Mr. R. Scantlebury from the NPL, Teddington, described the —again experimental!— NPL Data Communication Network. The subject, I gather, was appropriate. It was, however, a little bit too obvious that the speaker had done so before; it was a nice, polished presentation, but the speaker could not get excited about his subject, nor could his audience. I always like to listen to him lecturing, but that is because I like his English.

I used my hour to talk not on my announced subject, but on the many-mosquito elephants in general and the hyperfast fourier transformer in particular. (Patent restrictions prevented me from announcing this subject when I was invited to talk.) My subject fell a little bit outside the scope of the seminar (so did McNeil's) but I felt that this was not too bad in view of the background of the audience. Although I thought that I did a reasonably competent job in explaining it, they found it very difficult to follow and did not seem to be excited. This amazed me because, in my introduction, I had told them the various reasons why I had chosen to talk on this subject, among them the fact that elephant design had turned out to present problems that had stretched my mathematical gear, my notational techniques and my conceptual abilities to the limit. But perhaps it was a mistake to present a new intellectual challenge, even to an audience consisting almost exclusively of university professors. (When I showed it —in strict confidence of course!— earlier this year to Peter Naur, at the end of my presentation he looked silently to the blackboard for more than a minute and then exclaimed "Jezus!". My sad guess is that there were too few Peter Naurs in this audience ...)

That was the conference. Before it started we had "an evening" at the home of Ewan Page, the next afternoon, just before dinner, a sherry party, the next afternoon an excursion to Hadrian's wall —with a *true* archeologist explaining all about one of the excavations; he was an absolute delight!— and the next evening the closing banquet. So we were kept quite busy!

I wonder whether the seminar as a whole was a success. If you set "instruction" as your goal, then I gather that it was successful. The academic computer scientists saw stuff from a closely related field that was largely new for them. The question of course is what are they going to do with it. Mostly nothing, I am afraid. Besides that, I observed a general "malaise". On the whole, technical or scientific excitement was lacking —in spite of Kleinrock's superb lecturing technique!— and the little bit there was damped by the feeling that eventually political considerations would force the "wrong" decision anyhow. In that sense it was not only not exciting, it was even depressing. Is computing science nearing its completion? Is computing practice settling down in a way beyond recovery? Or are, as a result of current circumstances, university professors tired and discouraged?

Nuenen, 12th September 1973   DR. EDSGER W. DIJKSTRA

EWD391
Self-Stabilization in Spite of Distributed Control

A systematic way for finding the algorithm ensuring some desired form of co-operation between a set of loosely coupled sequential processes can in general terms be described as follows: the relation "the system is in a legitimate state" is kept invariant. As a consequence, each intended individual process step that could possibly cause violation of that invariant relation has to be preceded by a test that it won't do so, and depending on the outcome of that test the critical process step is either caused to take place or it —and with it the process of which it is a part— is delayed until a more favourable system state has been reached. With a suitable choice of the set of legitimate states one can indeed introduce the rule that a critical process step will be delayed only as long as its execution would lead to violation of the corresponding invariant relation.

The resulting design is readily implemented if the different sequential processes can be granted mutually exclusive access to a common store in which the current system state is recorded. Then a relation between (the values of) the variables in that commonly accessible store is the core of what we could call "the centralized control".

A complication arises when there is no such commonly accessible store and "the system state" must be recorded in variables distributed over the various processes, and furthermore the communication facilities are limited in the sense that each process can only exchange information with "its neighbours", a (possibly small) subset of the total set of processes. (We can view the processes as nodes of a connected graph in which each of the (sparse) set of edges denotes the neighbour relation.) The complication is that a node's behaviour can only be influenced by the part of the total system state description that is available in that node: local actions taken on account of local information must accomplish a global objective. Such systems (with what is quite aptly called "distributed control") have been designed, but all such designs I am familiar with are unstable in the sense that, when once in an illegitimate state, they could remain so forever. I call a system "self-stabilizing" when, regardless of its initial state, it is guaranteed to arrive at a legitimate state in a finite number of steps. (Whether the property of self-stabilization is interesting as a start procedure, for the sake of system robustness, or merely as an intriguing problem, is a question that falls outside the scope of this article.)

Unable to decide on theoretical grounds whether non-trivial self-stabilizing systems with distributed control could exist at all, I decided to try to design one under the following constraints and objectives.

We consider a system built from $N + 1$ finite state machines numbered from 0 through N. (The state space for the total system is then the Cartesian product of the $N + 1$ individual state spaces of the respective machines.) The machines are arranged in a ring, i.e. for $0 \leqslant i < N$, machine $nr.i$ has machine $i + 1$ as its right-hand neighbour, and machine N has machine 0 as its right-hand neighbour.

In the middle of the ring stands a demon, each time giving, in "fair random order", one of the machines the command "to adjust itself". (In "fair random order" means that in each infinite sequence of successive commands issued by the demon, each machine receives the command to adjust itself infinitely often.) Upon "adjustment" a machine goes into a (new) state, which must be a function of its own (old) state and the current states of its (two) neighbours.

Furthermore, as a function of its own state (and possibly of the states of its neighbours) a machine may be "privileged". The legitimate states are defined as those states in which exactly one machine is privileged and for which all possible successor states are legitimate as well; furthermore it is required that then the privilege will rotate around the ring.

SIDE REMARK. I was hoping for an existence proof of self-stabilizing systems with distributed control: a ring is then one of the most natural, simple connection graphs. My choice of legitimate states, viz. requiring convergence towards a solution of the mutual exclusion problem, is understandable for historical reasons [1], [2], [3], [4], it is also justified by its central position in the whole field of controlling co-operation between loosely coupled processes. Finally, the choice of the demon was suggested by a recent experience with a cyclic relaxation problem in which "fair random relaxation" would converge to a limit, while simultaneous relaxation could lead to oscillation (EWD386, unpublished). So much for the justification of the problem choice.

Again I beg my intrigued readers to stop reading here and to try to solve the stated problem themselves, for only then will they (slowly!) build up some sympathy with my difficulties: the problem has been with me for many months, while I was oscillating between trying to find a solution

—and many an at first sight plausible construction turned out to be wrong! — and trying to prove the non-existence of a solution. And all the time I had no indication in which of the two directions to aim, nor of the simplicity or complexity of the argument —if any!— that would settle the question.

*   *
*

The crucial observation is that, in general, the problem cannot be solved if, in addition, we require our machines to be identical. For if the number of machines is non-prime, our starting situation can have a cyclic symmetry of degree n ($2 \leqslant n \leqslant N/2$) and if then the demon —and he is free to do so!— gives his first n commands equally spaced around the ring, the cyclic symmetry will not have been destroyed. If the demon continues with such fair (but nasty) behaviour, we shall never reach the state after which, forever, a single machine will be privileged. Making not all machines identical can be accomplished in two extreme ways: either by making them all different or by making one exceptional. In view of our obligation to enforce asymmetry, one exceptional machine and all others mutually equal seems the most promising choice.

Secondly, it is not a priori excluded that the nett effect of the command "adjust yourself" is nil, viz. that the new state of the machine to which the command was given equals its old state. In a legitimate state we have no particular desire to let the adjustment command have any effect when given to a machine far away from the privileged one. To simplify matters we can look for a solution in which the adjustment command has only effect when directed towards a machine that at that moment is privileged, and the result of whose adjustment will be that it loses its privilege. When now the function "privileged" is chosen such that at least one machine must be privileged, then "dead ends" are excluded a priori: the ring will remain alive, and we can concentrate on the requirement that the system converge to the state from which a single privilege will rotate past all machines.

Thirdly, we may feel tempted to introduce some sort of counter, but because we are confined to finite machines, true counters are excluded and the best we can hope for are counters counting modulo K, where K is some sufficiently large constant (certainly > 1). For two counter values modulo K, the maximum or minimum is not defined and we cannot hope to establish progress towards the legitimate state because some "maximum counter value" decreases. But equality and a successor function that can be applied a limited number of times without leading to ambiguity are well-defined. This suggests defining the function "being privileged" in terms of equality of states.

In terms of equality we can define a function "being privileged" such that at least one machine is privileged quite easily when bearing in mind that one machine —let it be machine 0— should be exceptional. Let for $1 \leqslant i \leqslant N$ machine i be privileged when its state differs from that of machine $i - 1$, i.e. when $x[i] \neq x[i - 1]$. We choose this —rather than the other way round— because now non-privileged implies $x[i] = x[i - 1]$ and equality is transitive: in other words, when all machines except machine 0 are non-privileged, $x[0] = x[N]$ and when we define this as the condition for machine 0 being privileged, our requirement of at least one machine being privileged is therefore met.

Furthermore we had suggested that adjustment would cause the machine in question to loose its privilege. For the normal machines ($1 \leq i \leq N$) we have no freedom anymore: adjustment of machine i means

"**if** $x[i] \neq x[i - 1]$ **then** $x[i] := x[i - 1]$ **fi**"   .

For the exceptional machine, 0, I now suggest

"**if** $x[0] = x[N]$ **then** $x[0] := (x[0] + 1)$**mod** K **fi**"

and it is only here, where a new state has to be generated, that it becomes significant that we consider the machine states x as a counter modulo K.

To start with, we remark that when a machine "fires" —if we may use that term for the non-nil adjustment that takes place when the demon gives the command to a privileged machine— it loses its privilege, it may give the privilege to its righthand neighbour and to no one else. Because at least one machine must be privileged, firing of the only privileged machine will always give the only privilege to its righthand neighbour: once in a legitimate state the system will remain in a legitimate state and the privilege will rotate around the ring.

Furthermore: suppose that the exceptional machine is not privileged, i.e. $x[0] \neq x[N]$, then in a finite number of commands it will become privileged. For let j be the minimum value such that $x[j] \neq x[0]$; because j is the minimum value, $x[j - 1] = x[0]$ and therefore $x[j] \neq x[j - 1]$, i.e. machine j is privileged. In a finite number of commands the demon will point to it, thus increasing j if $j < N$ or making $x[N] = x[0]$ if $j = N$, i.e. making the exceptional machine privileged. So the exceptional machine will continue forever to get the opportunity to fire.

Let us now investigate what happens when we start the system in an arbitrary state. When the exceptional machine fires for the first time, we colour its new state blue and all other states white; from then onwards each state created by the exceptional machine or copied from a blue state by a normal machine will be blue as well. If h is the number of times the exceptional machine fires while $x[N]$ is still white, then —because $K > 1$— h will satisfy $h \leq N$: after the first firing, the copying process along the chain of normal machines can supply machine N at most with another $N - 1$ further white states, differing in succession.

Without loss of generality we could have chosen initially $x[0] = K - 1$. If $K > N$, then the first N firings of the exceptional machine have created the blue states from 0 through $N - 1$, and scanning the blue states, starting at the exceptional machine and going to the right, we find a sequence of non-increasing blue x-values. At the next firing of the exceptional machine with $x[0] = N - 1$, also $x[N] = N - 1$ must hold. At that moment, however, $x[N]$ must be blue as well and therefore *all* states must be $= N - 1$, i.e. the system has arrived in one of its legitimate states. And this completes the proof for self-stabilization provided $K > N$ (and, for smaller values of K, counter examples kill the assumption of self-stabilization).

*   *
*

So far, so good, but one may object to using a rather powerful demon that may be very awkward to implement. Can we eliminate that centralized agency, can we replace it by "a distributed demon"?

Each variable $x[i]$ is only inspected and assigned to by machine i and only inspected by its right-hand neighbour. We assume each variable $x[i]$ equipped with its own, private, two-way switch, which excludes simultaneous access by the two neighbours it connects. And we assume that the machines will adjust themselves with a finite speed and a finite frequency, instead of waiting for the demon's command. Does it work? Amazingly it does without any further refinements.

Two simultaneous adjustments of non-neighbouring machines have no mutual interference at all. An adjustment by the exceptional machine cannot suffer from simultaneous activity of its lefthand neighbour N, because $x[N]$ is inspected only once per adjustment. But adjustment of a normal machine i, although possibly inspecting $x[i - 1]$ twice during a single adjustment, cannot suffer from its lefthand neighbour activity either: if $x[i - 1]$ changes its value between the two inspections, the first value differed from $x[i]$; if the second value differs from $x[i]$ as well, the program behaves as if this value was also offered the first time, while if the second value equals $x[i]$, the assignment has no effect and it is as if the adjustment had not taken place at all!

Conclusion

Self-stabilizing systems with distributed control do exist in the sense that local decisions force the system towards satisfying and then maintaining a global requirement. In particular, local mutual exclusion is a sufficient building block for eventually achieving mutual exclusion globally.

References

[1] Dijkstra, E.W. Solution of a problem in concurrent programming control. *Comm.* ACM 8, 9 (Sept. 1965), 569
[2] Knuth, D.E. Additional comments on a problem in concurrent programming control. *Comm.* ACM 9, 5 (May 1966), 321–322

[3] de Bruijn, N.G. Additional comments on a problem in concurrent programming control. *Comm*. ACM 10, 3 (March, 1967)
[4] Eisenberg, M.A. and McGuire, M.R. Further comments on Dijkstra's concurrent control problem. *Comm*. ACM 15, 11 (Nov. 1972), 999

EWD407
Acceptance Speech for the AFIPS Harry Goode Memorial Award 1974

Before focussing on today's occasion, viz. my receiving the AFIPS Harry Goode Memorial Award, I would like to say a few things about awards and getting them in general. You see, it has been argued that the whole system of giving awards and bestowing distinctions is obsolete, and that therefore we should stop doing so.

One argument in favour of abolition is that it is so difficult to select the recipient in all fairness, both fairness to those candidates that don't get the award and fairness to its past recipients. The argument is that nearly always one is faced with either too many or too few eligible candidates. I cannot regard this as a valid objection: something cannot be wrong just because it is difficult to do it well! Besides that, the past history of the Harry Goode Memorial Award has shown the way out of this dilemma: the abundance or lack of suitable candidates has resulted in a shared award in some years and no award at all in other years. That such a wise policy maintains and even enhances the value of the distinction is something of which —as you can guess— I am painfully aware.

A next argument in favour of abolition is that they are superfluous, because one only wants to give them to first-rate scientists, and they are sufficiently known from their work anyhow. But are they? Well, certainly in some circles, including the selection committee. But a wise committee realizes that such distinctions also act as signposts, as a kind of reading guide for the general public, and I would not like to deprive responsible bodies of such means of exerting a hopefully beneficial influence. For the recipient that is aware of this aspect, the whole happening becomes some- what embarrassing and perhaps even frightening, but that is his problem.

A third objection against the whole award system is that the distribution of fame suffers, by its very nature, from a built-in instability, so why aggravate it? The only thing you do is to make the already famous still more famous! But in all honesty: "What else can you do with a famous man?". To be serious, underlying this last objection is the doubt as to whether "fame" as an institution in our civilization is a good thing or not. I think it can be a good thing. There are all sorts of things that should be said but will only be noticed when said by someone supported by fame. We may not like this state of affairs, but for the time being it seems a fact of life. Fame creates responsibility at both sides; the famous have the obligation to decide wisely when, where and how to open their mouths, their audience has the complementary responsibility *not* to accept everything they say unchallenged, just because a famous man has spoken. Trying to abolish fame is trying to shrink from those responsibilities, and I do not think that our civilization should do that.

In short, I am greatly in favour of honours, titles, awards, distinctions, golden medals etc. and you find in me not only an experienced, but also enthusiastic recipient!

So much about awards in general; now about getting them. When such a distinction hits you, and particularly when this happens during one of those agonizing periods of doubt and despair, it can be an encouragement stronger than I can describe it in words; it can revive one to the extent that suddenly one can hear again the angels singing in one's heart. It can evoke a frightening joy .... . And when it happens to you, I must warn you not to be disappointed when you discover that you can share this joy with only very few people: again you will find yourself very lonely .... .

Let us now switch from the general considerations to this specific occasion. I interpret this granting of the Harry Goode Memorial Award as a symptom of a broadening recognition of the relevance of a cause to which I have devoted more than the last decade of my life, and as such it is very gratifying. I have not been the only one to promote it, but I am willing to accept the point of view that I have been its principal advocate and in that capacity I accept the Award in name of all those colleagues, known or unknown, who have contributed. The cause in case is the conviction that the potentialities of automatic computing equipment will only bear the fruits we look for, provided that we take the challenge of the programming task seriously and provided that we realize that what we are called to design will get so sophisticated, that Elegance is no longer a luxury, but a matter of life and death. It is in this light that we must appreciate the view of programming as a practical exercise in the effective exploitation of one's powers of abstraction. It is in this light that we must appreciate all current efforts towards raising the level of confidence in the correctness of our programs, the reliability and robustness of our machines, all efforts to discover the intellectual disciplines needed for controlled design.

We are in the midst of an exciting process of clarification, of improvement of our understanding of the true nature of the programming task and its intrinsic difficulties. A few notes of warning, however, are not out of place, because, to my great regret, already now progress is being oversold. Simple souls have been made to believe that we have a retail shop in Philisopher's Stones that, by magic, will cure all diseases; in a few years time it will, of course, become apparent that there are still a few diseases uncured and then the same simple souls will denounce us as quacks. Secondly, as one may expect, programming discipline reflects itself in a coding discipline, but this does *not* justify the expectation that the problems of programming can be solved by a few measures such as a new, clean programming language or a new management structure or a new mechanical aid! Such measures may assist, certainly, but only provided that we do not overestimate their significance.

I would like to end my brief acceptance speech with a quotation from the English artist William Blake, who lived from 1757 until 1827:

"He who would do good to another must do it in minute particulars
General Good is the plea of the scoundrel, hypocrite and flatterer
For Art and Science cannot exist but in minutely organized particulars."

I thank you for your attention.

PROF. DR. EDSGER W. DIJKSTRA

EWD427
Speech at the Occasion of an Anniversary

BY EDSGER W. DIJKSTRA

Ladies and Gentlemen!

It is my pleasure and privilege, as Chairman of the Board of "Mathematics Inc.", to address you, its shareholders, at the 10th Anniversary of our Company. At this occasion it seems befitting to give you a short survey of its illustrious history.

All of you, of course, know how the company was founded, when three young, eager and enterprising mathematicians left their common employer, dissatisfied as they were with its purely commercial objectives and also convinced that, on their own, they could make much more money. And right they were!

We are all here as witnesses of the fact that it was *not* the inside information they took with them, but the vigor of the fresh young organization they founded, based on professional competence only, that made the enterprise the financial and scientific success their initiative deserved. Their native abilities were, of course, supported by keen insight into the problems and possibilities of their former employer's market, but it clearly needed people of their keen intellectual perception to see that the old four-colour problem —almost forgotten to be a problem!— could serve as the basis and starting point of a business as successful as ours.

Up till that moment all cartographers had always thought that they would never need more than four different colours on their maps. Similarly, eye tests for colour sensitivity of pilots and ship captains had never required the ability to distinguish between more than four different colours. It was in this sensitive area of map making and traffic by air and sea that these three gentlemen pointed out that up to that moment the sufficiency of the number "four" was no more than a mere assumption that could be killed by the first counter-example.

50

In view of the reorganizations that would be needed when a fifth colour would be discovered to be necessary, a great nervousness was aroused and at that moment the young company saw the possibility of one, or possibly two contracts in connection with the four-colour problem. A quick but thorough piece of market research was launched in order to discover where the greatest opportunities would lie: would it be in the proof that four colours would always suffice or would it be in the proof that occasionally five (or perhaps even six!) would be needed? For the first product they had the support of the Map Makers Association and of the International Union of Airline Pilots, for the second product the support of printing ink manufacturers and some small shipping companies that would like to use the result as a means of getting rid of a few of their older captains. The critical question, of course, was which of the two products would be preferred by the Navy and the Air Force. As luck would have it, the needs of the latter two pointed into the same direction and within two months, based on solid contracts with both the military and the civilian, our Company was founded.

In its earliest time it was beset by all problems of a young and growing company: moving from modest dwellings to more sumptuous quarters, readjusting the planning, the budget etc. and, as was to be expected, after the almost canonical period of nine months, serious disagreement between the three founders caused one of them to leave the Company and to start all by himself. His parting —I am happy to say— did not create any ill-feelings: he still owns a part of the company's stock and occasionally he acts as independent consultant. The disagreement was on planning.

The remaining two directors felt that a first working version of the Proof could be delivered 27 months after the contract had been signed and this planning was not reconsidered until the 12th month. At that critical stage it became apparent that the project had suffered from two misfortunes. Upon closer scrutiny one of the smaller Proof Modules had presented difficulties that, with the then present state of the art, proved to be unsurmountable. For a few weeks the company hesitated between two different courses of action, either to redesign the interfaces between the Proof Modules such as to make each of them more manageable, or to launch a research effort that would yield the technology enabling us to deal with the obstinate, unruly Module. As some of you will remember, this was the Company's most critical moment, not in the least because each course of action was preferred by one of the two remaining directors.

Within a few weeks, however, one of them managed to get the Navy's support for his approach, as a result of which the other director got the Air Force's support the next day. Of course this meant doubling the Company's size, a move to new quarters and all that: the Company's two Divisions, I am happy to say, work together in full harmony and the Board was very happy to see the broadening in scope: a one-product company is always somewhat vulnerable.

A second misfortune —that really could not have been forseen and for which we cannot blame our Company— was that two Universities failed to fulfil their obligations: in January they had accepted the obligation to produce at the end of the academic year a given number of brilliant mathematicians. At the end of term time the two Universities, however, de-committed themselves in the most shameful manner; since there was no written contract we could not sue them. But this is typically what happens to young companies only: we have learned our lesson and since the second year of our existence our contracts with Universities as regards the delivery of brilliant mathematicians protect our interests so well that, as a matter of fact, we often prefer to recover the damages.

We had to redo our PERT-planning and we had a hard time explaining to our clients that the first delivery of a Proof had been re-scheduled at month 35 instead of 27, but we succeeded. A next critical moment occurred when that second deadline was approaching. In the meantime, however, we were more firmly established. Firstly we could point to the fact that we had over 200 mathematicians working on the project, secondly we had been able to reshape the decommitment of the two Universities into an advantage: as they felt somewhat guilty, pressure could be exerted to make them our first two so-called "Institutional Members" of our organization. As the two Universities in question were both very influential and also anxious to share the responsibility, we had 12 Institutional Members —7 of which were well-known— by the time that the 35-month deadline approached.

As a result it was not too difficult to appoint a fully independent Supervisory Board that was willing to assert that the 35-month deadline —the result of youthful optimism and all that— had to be postponed: at the modest price of a few megabucks we bought the officially approved postponement until month 48.

When that deadline approached we indeed delivered the first release of the Proof. Admittedly it contained still a number of bugs, but the Company, in the meantime, had grown up to 350 mathematicians and was fully confident that, with the aid of the trouble reports coming from the field, it would get the Proof basically straightened out within the next four releases, a confidence that, as you all know, turned out to be fully justified.

The Proof of the four-colour conjecture turned out to be a most success-ful product of the Company. After our first customers had reported that, on the whole, they could live with it, general confidence grew and at month 75, shortly after our third release, the number of customers had grown by a factor of three. The more extensive field testing, leading to more experience and trouble reports, was met by a healthy growth of the Company which at the age of six years had grown to 720 brilliant mathematicians.

Although the Proof was not yet fully completed, it became obvious that with new products we had to open new markets. It was not quite obvious which. The progress with the four-colour problem eventually had been so rapid that the accompanying decrease of its personnel budget came some-what as a surprise to our young management that had had no earlier experience with projects in the stage of successful completion. Again we had a hectic period: should we fire the surplus mathematicians with the risk of not having them at our disposal when we would need them for our next project?

In the meantime, the government was so heavily committed that a few of its organizations and persons, who first had been our foes, could be turned into our friends at a price modest compared to what our Company gained in terms of continuity and stability. It was observed that for Pythagoras' Theorem at least 100 different proofs were hanging around, and practically all incompatible with each other! We managed to lend 150 mathematicians on a temporary basis to the appropriate Standardizing Body to sort out that mess and decide upon a Standard Proof for Pythagoras' Theorem. And as you all know, a few of our Institutional Members have been most successful in rejecting with their Academic Authority all constructive proposals for a Standard, thereby prolonging the proceedings until, within the Company, a new project would be well on its way. What did I say, a new project? No! Two projects even!

The Company hesitated between Fermat's Last Theorem, Goldbach's Conjecture and Riemann's Hypothesis. After careful market research Fermat and Goldbach —having more appeal to the man in the street— proved to be more promising than Riemann at this stage. As they seemed equally profitable, both were selected.

Now we have our 10th Anniversary: the four-colour problem has been nearly solved, for Goldbach's Conjecture and Fermat's Last Theorem we have solid contracts and the size of our Company has grown to nearly a thousand! You, shareholders, are of course mostly interested in the Com-pany's growth potential. To you I can only describe it as "magnificent"! Know your shares supported by the loyal devotion of one thousand brilliant mathematicians, by a Company that, by its earlier successes, has established itself firmly in the market place. We have often been copied, but never been equalled! "Semper floreat et crescat Mathematics Inc!"

(Applause.)

Nuenen, 16th June 1974

EWD442
Inside "Mathematics Inc."

From the private correspondence of the Chairman of the Board:

"In passing it is a pleasure to inform you that Mathematics Inc. fully lives up to its device "Semper floreat et crescat." Recently, the chairman of its board has been invited to deliver the keynote address at the 108th Annual Meeting of the International Federation of Mathematical Societies IFMS, to be held in the fall of 1976 in Loempia, the capital of Angora. In order to reflect this international recognition we are considering moving to more sumptuous apartments, viz. the top twelve floors of the Hosanna Building. But the negotiations are very difficult, as the even floors are owned by Mr. J. Simpson —not the well-known J.F. Simpson, just J. Simpson— while the odd floors are the property of a certain Mr. Hayes, Mr. Simpson's father-in-law's brother, a very old gentleman who considers himself a keen businessman. His price is exorbitant and his conditions are utterly preposterous: currently he wishes to impose upon our personnel that they will only use the toilets on Simpson's floors! To appease the old gentleman we may have to install —at our expense, of course— a Toilet Flushing Water Recycling System; I have already contacted an architect. Mr. Hayes, however, is already 87 and his health, I am told, is not too good.

But as you will understand, all these negotiations, time-consuming as they are, make me a very occupied man, and whether I can accept the IFMS invitation depends on whether I can find a free weekend to write my address; the deadline is 1st October 1974 (in duplicate, double-spaced)."

From an address to the senior staff members:

"As a token of our deeply felt gratitude for what he has done for the Company we shall send a large bunch of orchids to Mr. Hayes, the weary traveller who has, at last, reached his final destination .... "

From the minutes of the Board of Directors:

"Our Manager International Promotion has reported political troubles in some countries, caused by the fact that in our Brochure MX-783-5456-a: "What Counts what Counts", a reference is made to "Arabic Numerals"; a quick investigation has shown that a switch to "Arabian Numerals" would solve the problems there, but would create similar difficulties in the rest of the world. If switching to "Arabesque Numerals" is not an internationally acceptable solution, we shall try to escape nationalization by delegating, where necessary, our activities to a full daughter "Algebraics Inc." After a long and nostalgic monologue by our Chairman about the good old days when we were not operating on a multinational basis, the Meeting returns to the order of the day. The decision is postponed until the next meeting."

EWD443
A Multidisciplinary Approach to Mathematics

BY EDSGER W. DIJKSTRA*

(Extracts from the keynote address to be delivered at the 108th Annual Meeting of the International Federation of Mathematical Societies (IFMS) at Loempia, Angora, Monday 11–Friday 15 October 1976.)

Ladies and Gentlemen,

Now and again the great public is taken by surprise by the announcement of some startling discovery, some exciting invention or scientific breakthrough, and they cannot but get the impression that such things happen suddenly, even the scientists themselves being utterly unprepared for it. But the student of the history of science knows differently: even if he cannot smooth the discontinuity completely, he knows that in all cases such a breakthrough is the natural consequence of a usually long preparation —be it hidden for the casual observer— like the development of a carbuncle, deep under the skin.

The same holds for the current breakthrough in the practice of Mathematics, for which, as I hope to show, the seeds have been sown during the last three decades. For, this time the breakthrough did not only surprise the outsiders, it surprised many mathematical insiders as well, the reason being that the first seeds were sown and took root outside the Mathematical world itself.

We all still carry with us the cherished and endearing image of the Mathematician as it has come to us through the ages: half genius, half nitwit, partly deep thinker and partly just juggler with symbols, a man so absorbed by his own artificial world that he hardly belongs to the real one.

*Author's address: Mathematics Inc., Hosanna Building.

Are not Archimedes' words to the Roman soldier: "Don't disturb my circles!" the archetypical ones? And when the Roman soldier did as is usually done with someone who is not understood, and killed Archimedes with a single thrust of his glorious sword, we all feel that sword piercing our own romantic hearts . . . .

The image may have been a true one, but World War II has changed the world: it caused a collision not only between nations, but between sciences and between different walks of life as well. The intercommunication has broken the isolation, the lonely scientist burning the midnight oil has been replaced by the scientific worker keeping normal office hours, the romantic thinker believing in truth for truth's sake has been replaced by the businesslike and efficient solver of problems of social, economic and technical relevance.

As Chairman of the Board of "Mathematics Inc." —now the world's leading mathematical industry with a firm grip on more than 75 percent of the world market— I am in a better position than anyone else to give you all the inside information about the refreshing breeze that has blown new life into the mathematical science, at a moment that it was getting stale and in danger of dying of old age.

*   *
*

The decision to give the mathematical industry, for the first time in history, a solid foundation based on market research has, of all the changes, probably had the most profound effect. For instance, one of the most successful discoveries of our sales department was directly related to a significant trend in today's civilization, viz. the use of square tiles instead of wall-to-wall carpeting. The result was a revolutionary re-edition of the old-fashioned multiplication tables, but now, in order to ease the estimation of the number of tiles needed, in the form of a two-colour halftone division table. Its title alone: "Tiles for Everyone." is, all by itself, a masterpiece of mathematical popularization. (Our original title "Tile estimations made understandable for the layman." was completely demolished by our sales department as being too condescending; so was our next effort "Tile estimations made easy.".) In a sense, it was only a minor product, but in another sense it was the beginning of a mathematical revolution: as for years this table has been responsible for over 20 percent of our revenue, it has taught us all that, in the past, mathematicians, guided by their intuition instead of by scientific market research, have tackled the wrong problems.

*   *
*

Another discovery, perhaps surprising for the older ones among you, is that there is absolutely no market for the so-called "eternal truths" previous generations of mathematicians have been after. But we have understood that in the world of fast progress we are living in now, the only important results are those with a halflife of at most five years. As in the traditional mathematical papers the delay between submission of a paper and its eventual publication is of the same order of magnitude, we had to bypass the established channels, but as the lack of referees with social responsibility forced us to do so anyhow, this posed no additional problem.

*   *   *

We have also found out that, as important as what you publish is how you publish it. A small example: when it was made a company regulation to replace "etc." —as most readers are not quite sure of which obsolete Latin expression this is an abbreviation— by the more homely "and so on", sales immediately jumped by more than 15 percent! That shows what public relations can do for mathematics!

*   *   *

The mathematical establishment works on paper that is higher than wide. Our ergonomics department did a work analysis and discovered that the hand's horizontal mobility exceeds its vertical mobility by a factor of 1.4 and, as a result, it became a company rule to turn the normal office paper over 90 degrees. The results were startling. At first, Productivity Control was very disappointed, because, after the change, productivity measured —as they were used to— in lines of mathematics produced per manday seemed to have decreased slightly. Measured in number of symbols written down per manday, however, the increase was significant! Measured in number of pages of mathematics produced per manday the improvement was still more striking! Needless to say, the discovery of that last productivity unit must be considered as one of the greatest recent contributions to the gross national product in all countries where we are represented. (White, oval office paper has been tried, but the experiment has been abandoned: it led to too many circular arguments.)

*   *   *

As a company with the avowed aims of not enriching itself at the expense of others, but to work for the benefit of our total civilization, a thorough study has been made of the thresholds that, traditionally, restrict the benefits of bourgeois mathematics to an elite minority. As a socially responsible organization, and also from market considerations, we felt it, already early in the company's history, as one of our primary duties to try to bring Mathematics to the Millions. The major stumbling block turned out to be the abundant use of Greek and Hebrew characters and other fancy symbolisms, which, since then, have been rigorously abolished. (The re-education of our mathematical staff, implied by this abolishment, I am sorry to say, has not been without problems, because, although apparently converted, many staff members tended to persist in their bad habits in secret. A number of strong measures, based on undeniable evidence of guilt from the staff members' wastepaper baskets, has implemented the ultimate solution to the Greek-and-Hebrew-letter problem.) As new educational experts —so-called "enlightening specialists"— have been attracted, we are confident that future re-orientations of our technical staff will be implemented so smoothly as to remain totally unnoticed by them.

We have taken this measure, as new re-orientations are only to be expected: a current experiment to restrict, for instance, the use of the alphabet to that of capital letters only, is underway and looks very promising. In retrospect, it is no surprise that, in spite of a tradition of 2500 years, Mathematics has no more achieved than the little it has: all through those 25 ages, a thorough scientific study of the Man-Paper Interface has never been made!

*   *
 *

Compressed into a single sentence my message is that the Interdisciplinary Approach to Mathematics will lead to a better world. The chains of inhuman formalism being broken, intellectual slavery will become intellectual freedom, "the happy few" will become "the happy many"!*

And finally, for Mathematics in general, and for Mathematics Inc. in particular —what, after all, is the difference?— I can only end with the deeply felt prayer: "Semper floreat et crescat."!

11th August 1974

---

*For those interested in further details, we refer to "A Guide to Positive Problem Solving" to be published shortly by the Hosanna Press.

EWD447

On the Role of Scientific Thought

Essentially, this essay contains nothing new; on the contrary, its subject matter is so old that sometimes it seems forgotten. It is written in an effort to undo some of the more common misunderstandings that I encounter (nearly daily) in my professional world of computing scientists, programmers, computer users and computer designers, and even colleagues engaged in educational politics. The decision to write this essay now was taken because I suddenly realized that my confrontation with this same pattern of misunderstanding was becoming a regular occurrence.

Whether the misappreciation of the proper role of scientific thought that I observe within the "computing community" is a phenomenon that is specific for the computing community, or whether it is also a current phenomenon in other disciplines, is not for me to judge. One thing seems certain. In the computing community itself we can find enough historical explanation, and we don't need to look for outside influences when we try to understand how the phenomenon came about. (This is not meant to say, that outside influences have been absent!)

As we shall see in a moment, the adjective "scientific" when used in the expression "scientific thought" refers more to a *way* of thinking than to *what* the thoughts are about. To use the Latin expressions: it refers to the "quo modo" rather than to the "quod". This explains partly why the tradition of scientific thought has been imported into the computing world only to a limited extent by the many pioneers who immigrated in the early days from other scientific disciplines. The early academics who became involved with computers all had had their training in other scientific disciplines, and many of them were quite able to practise "scientific thought" in their original field of intellectual activity. But for a great number of them, that had been the only confrontation with scientific

60

thought. As a result, it is understandable that they associated their notion of scientific thought as much with the specific field in which they had practised it as with a *general* way of thinking that could (and should!) be transferred to their new field of activity. In addition, many of them must have felt that scientific thought was a luxury that one could afford in the more established disciplines, but not in the intellectual wilderness they now found themselves in. But, as we shall also see in a short while, scientific thought is not a luxury made possible in established scientific disciplines, on the contrary: it was the tool that made the establishment of those disciplines possible!

Besides emigrants from other academic fields, the computing world has attracted people from all over the world: businessmen, administrators, operators, musicians, painters, unshaped youngsters, you name it, a vast majority of people with no scientific background at all. By their sheer number they form all by themselves already an explanation for the phenomenon.

To introduce the subject, I would like to quote two paragraphs from a letter I recently wrote to a professional friend.

"Let me try to explain to you what to my taste is characteristic for all intelligent thinking. It is that one is willing to study in depth an aspect of one's subject matter in isolation for the sake of its own consistency, all the time knowing that one is occupying oneself only with one of the aspects. We know that a program must be correct and we can study it from that viewpoint only; we also know that it should be efficient and we can study its efficiency on another day, so to speak. In another mood we may ask ourselves whether, and if so, why, the program is desirable. But nothing is gained —on the contrary!— by tackling these various aspects simultaneously. It is what I sometimes have called "the separation of concerns", which, even if not perfectly possible, is yet the only available technique for effectively ordering one's thoughts that I know of. This is what I mean by "focussing one's attention upon some aspect": it does not mean ignoring the other aspects, it is just doing justice to the fact that from this aspect's point of view, the other is irrelevant. It is being one- and multiple-track minded simultaneously.

I remember walking with Ria when we were engaged —it was near Amsterdam's Central Station— when I explained to her that I wanted to be glad and happy with my eyes fully open, without fooling myself in the belief that we lived in a pink world: to be happy to be alive in the full knowledge of all misery, our own included...." (End of quotation.)

Scientific thought includes "intelligent thinking" as described above. A scientific discipline emerges with the —usually rather slow!— discovery of which aspects can be meaningfully "studied in isolation for the sake of their own consistency" —in other words, with the discovery of useful and helpful concepts. Scientific thought includes in addition the conscious search for useful and helpful concepts.

The above should make it clear that I want to discuss the role of scientific thought for the sake of its practical value, that I want to explain my pragmatic appreciation of a tool. It is no slip of the pen that the above quotation refers to the "effective ordering of one's thoughts": the efficiency of our thinking processes is what I am talking about. I stress this pragmatic appreciation, because I live in a culture in which much confusion has been created by talking about the so-called "academic virtues" (sic!) with moral, ethical, religious and sometimes even political overtones. Such overtones, however, only confuse the issue. (If you so desire, you may observe here scientific thought in action. I do not, for instance, deny political aspects —I would be a fool if I did so! The anti-intellectualistic backlash against "the technocrats", which is so en vogue today, is inspired by a —largely unjustified— fear for the power of him who really knows how to think and by a —more justified— fear for the actions of him who erroneously believes to know how to think. These political considerations, however, have *nothing* to contribute to the technical problem of ordering one's thoughts effectively, and that is the problem that I want to discuss "in isolation, for the sake of its own consistency".)

I intend to describe for your illumination the most common cases in which the "average" computing scientist fails to separate the various concerns; in doing so I hope and trust that my colleagues in the profession do interpret this as an effort to help them, rather than to insult them. For the sake of the non-professional, I shall present the least technical cases first.

One of the concerns, the isolation of which seems most often neglected, is the concern for "general acceptance". (In the world of pure mathematics —with which I have some contacts— this problem seems to be fairly absent.) The concern itself is quite legitimate. If nobody reads the poems of a poet that wanted to communicate, this poet has failed, at least as a communicating poet. Similarly, many computing scientists don't just solve problems, but develop tools —theories, techniques, algorithms, software systems and programming languages. And if those that, they feel, could profit from their designs prefer to ignore these inventions and to stick to their own, old, rotten routines, the authors get the miserable feeling of failure. Have they? Yes and no. They can adopt the Galileian attitude: "Nothing becomes true because ten thousand people believe it, nor false because ten thousand people refuse to do so", and can decide to feel themselves, in splendid isolation, superior to their fellow computer scientists for the rest of their lives. I can deny no inventor that feels underappreciated such a course of action. I don't recommend it either; the sterile pleasure of being right tends to get stale in the course of a lifetime. If one's aim is to design something useful, one should avoid designing something useless because unused. In other words, I fully accept "general acceptance" as a legitimate concern. We must, however, be willing to ignore this concern temporarily —for a few days or a few years, depending on what we are undertaking— for unwillingness to do so will paralyze us.

Some time ago I visited the computing center of a large research laboratory where they were expecting new computing equipment of such a radically different architecture that my colleagues had concluded that a new programming language was needed for it if the potential concurrency was to be exploited to any appreciable degree. But they never got their language design started because they felt that their product should be so much like FORTRAN that the casual user would hardly notice the difference, "for otherwise our users won't accept it". They circumvented the problem of explaining to their user community how the new equipment could be used to best advantage by failing to discover what they should explain. It was a rather depressing visit....

Clearly the proper technique is to postpone concerns for general acceptance until you have reached a result of such a quality that it deserves acceptance. The significance of your message should justify the care you give to its presentation; its "unusualness" may make extra care necessary. And, furthermore, what is "general"? Did Albert Einstein fail because the Theory of Relativity is too difficult for the average high-school student?

Another separation of concerns that is very commonly neglected is the one between correctness and desirability of a software system. Over the last years I have lectured to all sorts of audiences about techniques that may assist us in designing programs so that one can prove a priori that they meet their specifications. One of the standard objections raised from the floor is along the following lines: "What you have shown is very nice for the little mathematical examples with which you illustrated the techniques, but we are afraid that they are not applicable in the world of business data processing, where the problems are much harder, because there one always has to work with imperfect and ambiguous specifications." From a logical point of view, this objection is nonsense: if your specifications are contradictory, life is very easy, for then you know that no program will satisfy them, so, make "no program". The greater the ambiguity, the easier the specifications are to satisfy (if the specifications are absolutely ambiguous, every program will satisfy them!).

Pointing that out, however, seldom satisfies the man who raised the objection. What he meant, of course, was something different. He meant something along the following lines. "We make something with the best of intentions in the hope of satisfying a need as we understand it, but when our product has been put into action, it does not perform satisfactorily. How are we to discover whether we have correctly made the wrong thing or whether there is just a silly bug somewhere?". The point is that this question is empty as long as the specifications do not define —are not accepted to define by definition— what the system is supposed to do. It is like asking the judge to settle a business dispute caused by the absence of a contract stating the mutual rights and obligations. It is the sole purpose of the specifications to act as the interface between the system's users and the system's builders. The task of "making a thing satisfying our needs" as a single responsibility is split into two parts: "stating the properties of a thing, by virtue of which it would satisfy our needs" and "making a thing guaranteed to have the stated properties". Business data processing systems are sufficiently complicated to require such a separation of concerns, and the suggestion that in that part of the computing world "scientific thought is a non-applicable luxury" puts the cart before the horse. The mess they are in has been caused by too much unscientific thought.

But from the above, please don't conclude that unscientific thought is restricted to the business world! In Departments of Computing Science, one of the most common confusions is the one between a program and its execution, between a programming language and its implementation. I always find this very amazing: the whole vocabulary to make the distinction is generally available. Moreover, the very similar confusion between a computer and its order code, remarkably enough, is quite rare. But it is a deep confusion of long standing. One of the oldest examples is presented in the LISP 1.5 Manual. Halfway through their description of the programming language LISP, its authors give up and from then onwards try to complement their incomplete language definition by an equally incomplete sketch of a specific implementation. Needless to say, I have not been able to learn LISP from that booklet! I would not worry if the confusion were restricted to old documents, but, regretfully enough, the confusion is still very popular. At an international summer school in 1973, a very well-known professor of Computing Science made the statement that "ALGOL 60 was a very inefficient language", while what he really meant was that, with the equipment available to him, he and his people had not been able to implement ALGOL 60 efficiently. (That is what he meant, he did not mean to say it!) Another fairly well-known professor of computing science has repeatedly argued in public that there is no point in proving the correctness of one's programs written in a higher-level language "because, how do you know that its compiler is correct?". In the motivation of a recent research proposal, doubt is cast upon the adequacy of "the axiomatic semantics approach" since it may lead to deductive systems that are "undesirable in that they may not accurately reflect the actual executions of programs". It is like casting doubt on Peano's Axiomatization of the Natural Numbers on the ground that some people make mistakes when they try to do addition!

On the one hand we have the physical equipment (the implementation); on the other hand we have the formal system (programming language). It is perhaps a question of taste —I don't believe so— to whom of the two we give the primacy, that is, whether it is the task of the formal system to give an accurate description of (certain aspects of) the physical equipment, or whether it is the task of the physical equipment to provide an accurate model for the formal system. I prefer the latter. But under no circumstance we should confuse the two!

I have, I think, very good reasons for my preference, because if I cannot appreciate a formal system for the sake of its own consistency but must view it as description of physical equipment, I could not deal with a pro-gramming language that has not been implemented! (And that is, for instance, exactly what a language designer has to do.)

The confusion is perhaps most clearly demonstrated by the often ex-pressed opinion that "one cannot use a programming language that has not been implemented". But this is nonsense, of course one can! One can use any well-defined programming language, whether implemented or not, for writing programs; it is only when you want to use those programs to evoke computations that you need an implementation as well. Being well-defined, rather than being implemented, is a programming language's vital character-istic.

The above remarks are neither jokes nor puns; on the contrary, they are pertinent to multi-million-dollar mistakes. They imply, for instance, that the development projects —erroneously called "research projects"— aimed at the production of "natural language programming systems" —currently en vogue again— are chasing their own tails.

NOTE (which I hate to add, because it is nearly an insult to my readers, whom its inclusion accuses of possible superficiality). I have *not* said that when considering a programming language, one should not care about its implementability: one had better! But this concern, no matter how serious, is one we should try to isolate. (End of note.)

In my opening paragraph I also mentioned colleagues engaged in educa-tional politics. The writing of this essay was, as a matter of fact, also prompted by a recent study of two Computing Science Curricula at the university level. They were from different sides of the Atlantic Ocean, but shockingly similar in two respects: unbelievably elaborate budgets and a total lack of understanding of what constitutes a scientific discipline.

A scientific discipline separates a fraction of human knowledge from the rest: we have to do so, because, compared with what could be known, we have very, very small heads. It also separates a fraction of the human abilities from the rest; again, we have to do so, because the maintenance of our non-trivial abilities requires that they be exercised daily and a day, regretfully enough, has only 24 hours. (This explains, why the capable are always busy.)

But of course, any odd collection of scraps of knowledge and an arbitrary bunch of abilities, both of the proper amount, do not constitute a scientific discipline: for the separation to be meaningful, we also have an internal and an external requirement. The internal requirement is one of coherence: the knowledge must support the abilities and the abilities must enable us to improve the knowledge. The external requirement is one of what I usually call "a narrow interface": the more self-supporting such an intellectual subuniverse, the less detailed the knowledge that its practitioners need about other areas of human endeavour, the greater its viability. In the terminology of the computing scientist, I should perhaps call our scientific disciplines "the natural intellectual modules of our culture". (When the layman asks the computing scientist what is meant by "Modularization", a reference to the way in which the knowledge in the world has been arranged is probably the best concise answer.)

In view of the preceding, it becomes quite obvious why many earlier efforts to concoct Computing Science Curricula at our universities have been such dismal failures. They were just cocktails! For lack of other ingredients, they tried to combine scraps of knowledge from the most diverse fields that seemed to have some relation to the phenomenon Computer. That the ingredients of the cocktail did not mix into a coherent whole is not surprising; that the cocktail did not taste too well is not surprising either.

In those early days, the only alternative was waiting, as for instance Strachey urged in 1969: "I am quite convinced that in fact computing will become a very important science. But at the moment we are in a very primitive state of development; we don't know the basic principles yet and we must learn them first. If universities spend their time teaching the state of the art, they will not discover these principles and that, surely, is what academics should be doing." I could not agree more.

Now, of course, one can argue whether five years later we computing scientists have enough of sufficiently lasting value that can be "studied in isolation, for the sake of its consistency". I think that we now have enough to start, but if you think Strachey's advice still appropriate, you have my full sympathy.

The two recent(!) curriculum proposals I just referred to, however, presented the old cocktail as if absolutely nothing had happened, and, not as a timid first step, but as the final goal.... And when scientists no longer know what science is supposed to be about, we are in bad shape. Hence this essay.

Nuenen, 30th August 1974   PROF. DR. EDSGER W. DIJKSTRA
                                                                 Burroughs Research Fellow

EWD462
A Time-Wise Hierarchy Imposed upon the Use of a Two-Level Store

Abstract: *Following general design principles a paging system has been developed in which the aim has been high efficiency, a strong separation between store management and processor scheduling, and a minimal influence of the program mix upon the system's performance. It is, furthermore, described how some dedicated hardware can be expected to contribute effectively to memory management and the prevention of thrashing. Finally, the properties of the system should be such that a mismatch between configuration and workload gives a clear indication on a change of configuration.*

Key Words and Phrases: *demand paging, window size, thrashing control, smoothness, virtual store, two-level store, operating systems, design, reconfiguration, separation of concerns.*

C.R. Categories: 4.32, 4.34, 6.21, 6.34, 6.39.

This paper is really two articles merged into one. On the one hand it deals with a general design principle, on the other hand it deals with the design of a virtual storage system, to which the principle has been applied. Although the first aspect is the more general one, the title refers only to the second aspect, firstly because its elaboration occupies most of the space, and, secondly, because the virtual storage system to be developed below seems to be new and not without attractive properties.

The design principle in its most general form is that, whenever we have to design a mechanism meeting certain requirements, it does not suffice to design something that we *hope* meets the requirements: on the contrary, we must design it in such a way that we can *establish* that it meets the

67

requirements. As far as program correctness is concerned, this design principle has led to a programming methodology that is becoming more and more widely accepted: instead of making the program first and trying to establish its correctness afterwards —which may be nearly impossible— correctness proof and program are now developed hand in hand. (As a matter of fact, the development of the correctness proof is often slightly leading: as soon as the next argument in the proof has been chosen, a program part is designed to meet the proof's requirements.) Besides the mathematical requirement of correctness, we have the engineering requirement of "reasonable performance". This time the principle tells us that it does not suffice to design a mechanism that we hope will perform "reasonably well": on the contrary, we should (at least try to) design it in such a way that we can predict *a priori* how well it will perform. If we ask very precise questions about the performance, these questions may become very hard to answer. To predict that the computation time for the Horner scheme grows linearly with the degree of the polynomials is not hard. Estimation of the computation time needed for iterative computation of eigenvalues and eigenvectors of a symmetric matrix, however, is harder and probably most easily expressed in terms of the separation of the eigenvalues, i.e. in terms of part of the answer; this dependence is something that we should try to derive and prove! Often we have to be content with "worst case" bounds (which in contrast to averages have at least the advantage of not depending on the usually unknown input population). Sometimes we even have to be content with still vaguer definitions of what "reasonable performance" means. Yet this is no licence to design, for instance, a mechanism whose performance is occasionally surprisingly bad.

The actual performance of a machine with a virtual storage system is dependent on what is usually denoted as "the workload characteristics". In the name of the predictability of that performance we shall try to design the system to make that dependence as simple as possible: in particular we require that a mismatch between configuration and workload does not only make itself manifest in the form of poor performance, but will in addition give a clear indication what type of change —if any— of the configuration would improve the performance.

In order not to complicate the discussion unduly at the start, we shall make a few simplifying assumptions about the hardware. Later we can reconsider these assumptions. Some may be weakened easily, of others, however, we may come to the conclusion that if our hardware does not allow such idealizations, the scheduling problem will be "complified" seriously, perhaps even beyond our comprehension and control. In the latter case we don't need to feel having failed "to cope with the problem": on the contrary, the identification of seriously "complifying" hardware characteristics seems in the light of the present state of the art a valuable discovery.

As primary store we assume a random access store as randomly accessible as, say, a core store. As secondary store we assume a device with the characteristics of, say, a drum or a head-per-track disc, such that

(1) the place of information in secondary store need not influence decisions to change the contents of primary store, i.e. page-wise it can be regarded as a random access store;
(2) the processor speed is sufficiently slow and/or the cycle time of the primary store is sufficiently small and/or the transfer rate between primary and secondary store is sufficiently low that any slowing down of the processor as a result of cycle stealing by the channel can, to all intents and purposes, be ignored;
(3) transport between the two storage levels is taken care of by a single, dedicated channel.

　　Furthermore I assume

(4) a single processor;
(5) demand paging with fixed-size pages;
(6) such a modest amount of processor-status information (registers included!) that the time needed to switch the processor from one process to another can, to all intents and purposes, be ignored in view of an upper bound on the frequency with which these switchings may have to take place;
(7) no page-sharing between user programs (for instance on account of a common procedure library).

REMARK 1. The above assumptions are —or at least: were— not unrealistic. We shall later discuss some of the temptations that should be resisted when they are only partly fulfilled. (End of remark 1.)

REMARK 2. Assumption 6 means that as far as scheduling processor time is concerned, we can regard the total processor time as the sum of the periods of time devoted to actual program progress, and we are at any time free to grant the processor to what is considered the most urgent task. If the price of switching the processor from one task to another has to be regarded as high, one is faced with the often conflicting aim to grant the processor to the task with the maximum expectation value for the period of time for which full-speed progress is possible. (End of remark 2.)

The Role of the Replacement Algorithm in a Multiprogramming Environment

The idea of demand paging is that processing proceeds at full speed as long as the information is present in primary store. Upon a so-called "page fault" —i.e. the detected desire to access a page that is currently not in main store— the missing page must be brought in from secondary store. (The program causing the page fault has to wait until the channel has completed that transport; in a multiprogramming environment the processor is in the mean time available for other programs.) Besides bringing in the missing page, another page has to be dumped. The task of the so-called "replacement algorithm" is to choose that victim; its goal is to keep the interesting pages in primary store. Obviously, with each reasonable replacement algorithm, permanently unreferenced pages have a tendency to disappear sooner or later from primary store.

The ideal replacement algorithm embodies clairvoyance: it kicks out the page that in view of future needs can be missed best. Clairvoyance, however, is hard to implement, and actual replacement algorithms are based upon, essentially, three different ideas. (We shall see later that for our purposes the first two have to be rejected.)

(1) With a (quasi-)random number generator an "arbitrary" page residing in primary memory is chosen as the victim. It is reasonable in the sense that permanently unreferenced pages have indeed a tendency to disappear from primary store, it is simple and its performance is not half as bad as might be expected.

(2) In an effort to speed up the disappearance of permanently unreferenced pages the machine keeps track of the order in which the pages currently residing in primary store came in, and the older ones are given a greater probability of being chosen as the victim. In the extreme case, always the oldest is chosen and the algorithm becomes a FIFO ("First-In-First-Out") rule.

(3) Predicting tomorrow's weather according to the principle "the same as today", the machine keeps track, to a certain extent, of the order in which pages currently in primary store have been accessed, and pages which for a relatively long time have not been accessed are given a greater probability of being chosen as the victim. In the extreme case we get the so-called LRU-algorithm ("Least Recently Used").

NOTE 1. In the case of cyclic access to $n + 1$ pages with room for only n, both FIFO and LRU give the worst possible choice. Since purely periodic access patterns are not unrealistic, it has been suggested to incorporate always a randomizing element in the page replacement algorithm, so as to reduce the probability of such a "disastrous resonance" to nearly nil. (End of note 1.)

We shall resume the discussion of the replacement algorithm later, because in a multiprogramming environment a more crucial decision has to be taken first. When a new victim has to be chosen, there are two alternatives:

(1) either we regard primary store as a homogeneous pool of page frames and the victim is chosen on account of the total history in core, independent of the identity of the program that caused the page fault;
(2) or we regard the page fault as a private occurrence of the program in which it happened, only the history of the pages of this program is taken into account and one of its own pages will be selected as the victim.

In the design of the THE-multiprogramming system in the early sixties I chose the first alternative, and I remember the (opportunistic) arguments in favour of that decision. Firstly, it removed the obligation to keep track of which page frames were occupied by which programs —an administration that would have been complicated by the presence of shared library pages. Secondly, it would automatically see to it that a program idling for other reasons would not continue to occupy page frames, since its then permanently non-accessed pages would disappear through the normal mechanism (which was LRU, related to the total history). This paper is a peccavi in the sense that —as I hope to demonstrate convincingly in the sequel— this decision was more than a mistake: it was a sin against proper design. (One of its unattractive features was that a large high-vagrancy program always lost its pages, and, as a result, suffered from very slow progress.) In the mean time we know that "separation of concerns" should be one of our dearest goals, and in the case of choice 1 the page faults caused by a single program are dependent both on its fellow programs and on the relative speeds with which they are allowed to proceed. In the case of choice 2, however, where each program has its own, fixed number of page frames at its disposal, the generation of page faults is each program's private business, only dependent on that number of page frames, its access pattern and its(!) replacement algorithm. The mistake we made ten years ago was to allow a hardly controllable fine-grained interference between fellow programs that had been independently conceived but found themselves by accident mixed, instead of keeping the interference between the computational histories of these mutually independent programs more coarse-grained in time.

In the following we make a weak assumption about the replacement algorithm(s) used: the average frequency of a program's page fault generation is a non-increasing (and usually even: a decreasing) function of its so-called "window size", i.e. the number of page frames allocated to it.

About the Ideal Window Size

In this section we shall describe how we propose to exploit our first three assumptions. After having observed that it is the function of the replacement algorithm to try to reduce —with a given window size— the number of page faults caused by that program and, therefore, the total amount of time the channel is busy for the benefit of that program, our next purpose is to keep the channel nicely busy.

For each program we can introduce the total time C the processor has performed "computation" for that program and the total time T the channel has been occupied with "transports" between storage levels as a result of page faults caused by that program, both times C and T being recorded for that program from the same moment. When deciding how to allocate page frames to programs, i.e. when deciding the window size for each program, we seem to be managing three resources, viz. processor, channel and primary store. In this management problem, general dimension considerations tell us that the dimensionless quantity C/T must be significant. The point is, that processor and channel are resources *doing* something at a certain *speed*, but we cannot change the "speed" with which something is kept in store (no more than we are able to wait twice as fast for something).

Under the (temporary) assumption that for each program such a window size exists, we define for each program the "ideal" window size as the one that would give rise to a ratio $C/T = 1$, i.e. the window size that would cause on the average equal demands on processor time and channel time, the reason being that then processor and channel can be scheduled as a single resource. The result of demand paging is that a program has no use for the processor during the period of time that the channel is busy for it; as a result no program can occupy more than 50 percent of this combined resource, and if we want to keep the latter busy, we conclude that our degree of multiprogramming should at least be equal to two. This degree will usually not suffice (see below).

About the Degree of Multiprogramming

In this section we assume that for each program the vagrancy characteristics are such that for each program a constant —and known— window size can be considered as ideal.

In order to keep the combined resource constantly busy, individual C/T-ratios close to 1 is in general not enough. Suppose that the one program generates its page faults —when executed all by itself— quite regularly, one at a time, while the other program generates under the same circumstances bursts of two page faults at a time with half the frequency. The combination would not fit, and both processor and channel could be busy for at most 80 percent of the time. With a third program (of either type) full occupation is possible and an arbitrary program can use the maximum 50 percent. The typical purpose of multiprogramming is clear as far as utilization of the active resources is concerned: to absorb the bursts in which programs may generate page faults. After some consideration —and in analogy to other statistical phenomena— it becomes hard to believe that the desire to absorb the bursts would ever give rise to a degree of multiprogramming exceeding 4 or 5.

About the Adjustment of Window Sizes

We have introduced the notion of the "ideal" window size as the one by which program progress implies *on the average* equal loads C and T for processor and channel respectively. As a result the question whether for a given program the actual window has the ideal size is meaningless unless it is related to a sufficiently large section of computation history, in which the increase of $C + T$ is an order of magnitude larger than the T-increase caused by a single page fault (say: 20 times). Until now, we have acted as if during each computation the access pattern was sufficiently constant so that from beginning to end a single window size could be regarded as "ideal" for it, and also that for each program this size was known. In practice, neither of these two conditions is fulfilled and, therefore, the system is required to discover for each computation what the ideal window size is, and to adjust the window size when needed. For each program, reconsideration (and possibly adjustment) of the window size should only take place with a frequency that is an order of magnitude smaller than that of the target frequency of page fault generation: it is pointless to be willing to vary a program's window size so rapidly that the periods during which it is by definition constant are so short that the question of "idealness" becomes meaningless!

Let us assume therefore that for each program the system reconsiders its window size each time that program has increased its $C + T$ by a certain amount (equal to, say, 20 times the T-increase corresponding to a single page fault). When C has increased much more than T, a smaller window might be more adequate; when T has increased much more than C, a larger window might be more adequate. We could think of a simple negative feedback, based upon the quotient of the observed increases of C and T, say decreasing the window size by one page frame when that quotient exceeds 1.1 and increasing the window size by one page frame when that quotient is less than 0.9. Such a simple negative feedback, however, will not do the job, because even if our replacement algorithm is such that we can prove that a larger window would never lead to more page faults, the program might be such that a larger window would not lead to fewer page faults either!

A computation with high-frequency access to two fixed (program) pages and random access to 10,000 other (data) pages will not perform any better with a window of 100 frames (our maximum say) than with a window of 3. If it has a window of 3 and its C/T-ratio is too small, there is no point in increasing the window size. The simple negative feedback would continue to increase it and (like a young cuckoo) this program would eventually push the other programs out of primary store. This cuckoo effect cannot be remedied without penalty by suppressing growth of the window —although desirable on account of C/T— as soon as no improvement is observed, and the reason is the following. A program with high-frequency access to 12 pages may perform equally poorly with windows up to 11 frames and beautifully with a window of 12 frames, and this is something we would like to be discovered when its current window happens to be 4. In other words: it is not enough to know the C/T-ratio caused by the current window size, we should also know it for other ones!

Monotonic Replacement Algorithms

There is an important class of replacement algorithms —LRU is one of them, RANDOM and FIFO are not— which we might call "monotonic". They are characterized by the following property. Considering two synchronized executions of the same program but with different window sizes, we call the replacement algorithm "monotonic" if at all times all pages contained in the smaller window will be contained in the larger window as well, provided that this was true at the beginning. As a result, in the computation with the larger window no page fault occurs that does not occur in the other computation as well.

Therefore, if a program is executed with a monotonic replacement algorithm and an actual window size w, it cannot cost much to record how many page faults would have occurred if the window size had been $w + 1, w + 2 \ldots$ up to the maximum: it would only be a minor overhead on the *actual* page faults and would, therefore, be negligible. This information can be used to prevent the growth of a cuckoo, but it does not cater for the detection of an existing cuckoo, i.e. a program whose window size can be decreased without any ill effects.

To record the page faults that would have occurred with window sizes smaller than the actual ones, additional hardware seems indicated. The knowledge of the number of page faults that would have occurred with smaller-sized windows (particularly for the size $w - 1$) is so attractive to have, that the additional hardware seems justified. (In the latter case it can probably also take care of the recording of the number of page faults corresponding to window sizes larger than w.) Quite often, a page fault frequency—window size curve has a very sharp bend: we may expect programs that for size w will give a ratio $C/T > 1$ and for size $w - 1$ a ratio unacceptably close to zero. With the simple feedback mechanism the effort at window size adjustment would lead to thrashing half the time — a nasty property that has been used as an argument against virtual storage systems as such. If additional hardware counts the virtual page faults that would have occurred with window sizes smaller than the actual one, this thrashing is easily avoided.

In view of the above it is doubtful whether the introduction of a randomizing element in the page replacement algorithm in order to avoid "disastrous resonance" —see Note 1— is still desirable: most disastrous resonances occur when the window size is a few frames too small. But now that we can detect this and know how to remedy it, it seems better not to obscure the detection by the noise of a randomizer.

The Time-Wise Hierarchy

At our lowest level we have the individual access: its recording (for the sake of the replacement algorithm) and the test whether it causes a (virtual or actual) page fault are obvious candidates for dedicated hardware.

At the next level we have the actual page faults, which occur several orders of magnitude less frequently. Taken in isolation they only influence the program in which they occur.

At the next level, but again an order of magnitude less frequently, the window size is reconsidered. In the decision to increase or decrease the window size a threshold should be introduced so as to increase the probability that the result of reconsidering the window size will be the decision to leave it as it stands. Furthermore, if available information suggests a drastic change in window size, follow this suggestion only partly (half-way, say): either the suggestion is "serious" and the total change will be effectuated within two or three adjustments anyhow, or the suggestion is not "serious", because the access pattern is so wild that the notion of an "ideal" window size is (temporarily or permanently) not applicable to that program. In the latter case, it is better to allow this program to contribute unequal loads to the processor and the channel; if it only occupies one tenth of that combined resource, it can only bring the two total loads mildly out of balance.

At the last level, but again at a lower frequency, change of window sizes may have to influence the degree of multiprogramming: growing window sizes may force load shedding, shrinking window sizes may allow an increase of the degree of multiprogramming.

As a result of past experience, the fact that these different levels (each with their own appropriate "grain of time") can be meaningfully distinguished in the above design gives me a considerable confidence in its smoothness, in its relative insensibility to workload characteristics.

Efficiency and Flexibility

The purpose of aiming at C/T-ratios close to 1 was to achieve for the active resource (i.e. processor and channel combined) a duty cycle close to a 100 percent, to a large extent independent of the program mix. This freedom can still be exploited in various ways. A program needing a large window on account of its vagrancy can be given the maximum 50 percent of the active resource in order to reduce the time integral of its primary storage occupation. Alternatively, we can grant different percentages of the active resource in view of (relatively long-range) real-time obligations: to allocate a certain percentage of the active resource to a program means to guarantee a certain average progress speed. (This seems to me more meaningful than "priorities", which, besides being a relative concept, can only be understood in terms of a specific queueing discipline that users should not need to be aware of at all!)

REMARK 3. When a producer and a consumer are coupled by a bounded buffer, operating system designers prefer to have the buffer half-filled: in that state they have maximized the freedom to let one partner idle before it affects the other, thus contributing to the system's smoothness. Granting no program more than 50 percent of the active resource is another instance of consciously avoiding the extreme of "skew" system states! (End of remark 3.)

Temptations to be Resisted

If we enjoy the luxury of a full duplex channel, the page being dumped and the page being brought in can be transported simultaneously (possibly at the price of one spare page frame). Usually, however, such a page swap between the two storage levels takes twice as much time as only bringing in a page. If the channel capacity is relatively low, it is therefore not unusual to keep track of the fact whether a page has been (or: could have been) written into since it was lastly brought in: if not, the identical information still resides in secondary store and the dumping transport can be omitted. This gain should be regarded as "statistical luck" which no strategy should try to increase and which should *never* be allowed to influence one's choice of the victim (quite apart from the fact that it is hard to reconcile with the monotonicity of the replacement algorithm, since the monotonic replacement algorithm is defined for all window sizes simultaneously, independent of the size of the actual window).

We have also assumed the absence of page sharing. But this was not essential: if program A wants to access a page from the common library that at that moment happens to reside in program B's window, a transport can be suppressed by allowing the windows to overlap on that page frame. Both programs keep, independently of each other, track of their own usage of that page for the sake of their own replacement algorithm and the page only disappears from main store when it is no longer in any window at all. Again, this gain should be regarded as "statistical luck" which should *never* be allowed to influence our strategies. *Such pressure should be resisted; yielding to it would be terrible!*

Analyzing the Mismatch Between Configuration and Workload

If the channel achieves a duty cycle close to 100 percent, but the processor does not, a faster channel, more channels, or a slower processor may be considered. If the processor achieves a duty cycle close to 100 percent, but the channel does not, a faster processor, more processors, or a slower channel may be considered. (With two processors and one channel each program has the target C/T-ratio $= 2$.)

NOTE 2. A change in the quotient of processing capacity and transport capacity will give rise to other window sizes. With the built-in detection of virtual page faults as well, a user can determine himself what effect on the window sizes the change in that capacity ratio would have for his workload, without changing the actual window sizes. He should do so before deciding to change the configuration. (End of note 2.)

If neither processor nor channel achieves an acceptable duty cycle, we either have not enough work or are unable to buffer the bursts. If we have enough independent programs, a larger primary store could be considered in order to increase the degree of multiprogramming. Otherwise we should consider the attraction of more work, reprogramming (in order to change vagrancy characteristics), or a completely different installation (e.g. with very different secondary store characteristics). Or we may decide to do nothing about it at all and live with it.

Acknowledgments

Collective acknowledgments are due to the members of the IFIP Working Group W.G.2.3 on "Programming Methodology" and to those of the

Syracuse Chapter of the ACM. Personal acknowledgments are due to the latter's Chairman, Jack B. Cover, to Steve Schmidt of Burroughs Corporation, to John E. Savage of Brown University, and Per Brinch Hansen of the California Institute of Technology.

Nuenen, 6th December 1974   PROF. DR. EDSGER W. DIJKSTRA
                                              Burroughs Research Fellow

EWD464

A New Elephant Built from Mosquitoes Humming in Harmony

In an earlier document —EWD456— I mentioned a problem, suggesting that it boiled down to forming a transitive closure. M. Rem pointed out to me that the suggestion was wrong; this report deals with the problem in question.

We consider a non-deterministic finite state automaton with N states, each state being either a terminal or a non-terminal state. We can associate each state with a different node of a directed graph —and vice versa— in which each node has at least one outgoing arc. Terminal nodes —i.e. nodes corresponding to a terminal state— are the nodes whose *only* outgoing arc leads back into themselves: the only outgoing arc of a terminal node is also one of its incoming arcs. For each node the outgoing arcs point to the set of permissible "successor nodes". A node with only one outgoing arc is a deterministic node and all directed paths along the graph correspond to a possible computation of the machine.

Let R be a set of terminal nodes. We can then ask for the set V of nodes v such that any directed path starting at a node v will arrive after a finite number of arcs in a node from R. (This is asking for the weakest pre-condition for the finite state automaton.) After reducing the given graph by removing from each node from R its only outgoing arc, with respect to that reduced graph we can also define the set V as all the points v such that each directed path starting at v is finite.

The following sequential program would do the job. Assuming the nodes to be consecutively numbered, we introduce an array *nia* —i.e. "number of ill-directed arcs"— that (after the removal of the outgoing arcs from nodes r in R) count for each node the number of its outgoing arcs that lead to a node outside V.

"initialize *nia* such that $nia(r) = 0$ for r in R and $nia(n) =$
number of node n's outgoing arcs for any node n not in R;
$C := R$; $V := empty$;
do $C \neq empty \rightarrow$ transfer an arbitrary node c from C to V;
                $PC :=$ predecessor set of c;
                do $PC \neq empty \rightarrow$
                      remove an arbitrary node pc from PC;
                      if $nia(pc) > 1 \rightarrow nia{:}(pc) = nia(pc) - 1$
                      [] $nia(pc) = 1 \rightarrow nia{:}(pc) = 0$; $C := C + pc$
                      fi
                od
od"   .

And this sequential program demonstrates the ugliness of the problem
quite nicely: for the initialization of *nia* we need for each node outside R
(the size of its) successor set; thereafter we need for each node c its
predecessor set.

The following "program" is a little bit less sequential: it manipulates the
connection matrix. Let $con(i, j) = 1$ if there is an arc from i to j, otherwise
$con(i, j) = 0$. (To each terminal node corresponds a 1 on the diagonal,
which is the only 1 in its row.) Array *con* will be broken down as the
computation proceeds:

$C := R$; $V := empty$;
do $C \neq empty \rightarrow V := V + C$;
                make all columns corresponding to the elements of
                    C equal to all zeros;
                $C :=$ all elements outside V to which correspond
                    all-zero rows
od   .

Here the "ugliness" observed above is reflected by the repeatable statement
itself, in which the connectivity matrix is accessed either by rows or by
columns. In its second form the algorithm reflects, however, the potential
parallelism, because each time all columns or all rows, respectively, can be
treated concurrently.

One and a half years ago I designed a number of so-called "elephants
built from mosquitoes". The idea was to have a large set of micro-computers
—mosquitoes— with only very few input legs and output legs (and possibly
some antennae for synchronization). According to a *fixed* pattern, input and
output legs would be paired, each pair thus providing a directed communication link between two mosquitoes. The question was whether we could
design powerful special-purpose elephants built from such mosquitoes,
harmoniously humming together. (The hyper-fast Fourier elephant was the
most spectacular output of that effort, but it turned out to be known.) The
remainder of this report deals with the design of an elephant solving the
problem posed above. It is reasonable to wish to design an elephant for this

task. The modifications to which the matrix *con* is subjected are strictly monotonic and that should simplify the problems otherwise present in elephant design considerably. We are *not* interested in a one-mosquito elephant, not in an N^2-mosquito elephant either; we are heading for an N-mosquito elephant, and we shall try to get away with the simplest strongly connected arrangement I can think of: a cyclic arrangement with traffic in one direction only, with a mosquito associated with each node.

We consider the nodes and the associated mosquitoes numbered from 0 through $N - 1$. In order to do away with superfluous subscripts, each machine j refers to machine $(j + 1)$**mod** N as "its right-hand neighbour". All machines have a variable called "x", and transmission of information to one's right-hand neighbour will be coded as "$xR := \ldots$". (We are heading for fully synchronized mosquitoes.)

We shall now describe mosquito j. It is primarily the manager of the j-th column of the matrix *con*. We shall represent it as a boolean vector *arc* (with "*true*" for "1", i.e. the presence of an incoming arc for node j):

$arc(i)$ means: from node i leads (still) an arc to node j.

Furthermore, we observed that in an arrangement like this, it does not seem to do any harm if a mosquito, once in set V, continues to set its vector "*arc*" to all elements *false* (for the time not bothering about termination). We introduce for each mosquito j a boolean:

out means: node j is (still) outside set V.

We initialize $V := R$, i.e. *out* = *false* for all terminal nodes and *true* for all the others.

Consider what will happen if all machines j are now, after this initialization, simultaneously started on a synchronous execution of the following program:

mosquito j: $arc{:}(j) = arc(j)$ **and** *out*; $xR := arc(j)$;
        $i := (j - 1)$**mod** N;
        do $i \neq j \rightarrow arc{:}(i) = arc(i)$ **and** *out*;
                $xR := x$ **or** $arc(i)$;
                $i := (i - 1)$**mod** N
    od;
    out := *out* **and** x .

Each row is inspected starting at the diagonal and then towards the right. Each mosquito starts updating its column at the diagonal and then upwards. Each time a mosquito has updated element $arc(i)$, x means "in row i a 1 (or *true*) occurs to the left of column j up to and including the diagonal element of row i", and updating and confrontation take place in complete synchronism. The above program should be repeated as many times as necessary. The following program will see to that with the same initialization.

mosquito j: $new :=$ **non** out; $act := true$;
               do $act \rightarrow$
                   $goonR := new$;
                   $arc{:}(j) = arc(j)$ **and** out; $xR := arc(j)$;
                   $i := (j - 1)$**mod** N;
                   do $i \neq j \rightarrow$
                       $goonR := goon$ **or** new;
                       $arc{:}(i) = arc(i)$ **and** out;
                       $xR := x$ **or** $arc(i)$;
                       $i := (i - 1)$**mod** N
                   od;
                   $new := out$ **and** **non** x;
                   $out := out$ **and** x;
                   $act := goon$
          od   .

All mosquitoes will terminate simultaneously. (The local boolean act is not strictly necessary: we could have done it with "$goon$" itself.)

*   *   *

Time-wise, the above elephant is not very spectacular. Perhaps this is not too surprising: it has been remarked before —for instance by Hopcroft and Tarjan in print— that algorithms manipulating graphs in terms of the connection matrix tend to be relatively poor. This elephant has been recorded for a few other reasons.

Firstly —with the exception of the hyper-fast Fourier elephant— very little has been documented about our earlier efforts at elephant design.

Secondly, this is the first time that I have been able to solve a problem from graph theory with an elephant whose internal connection pattern between the mosquitoes does not depend on the structure of the graph. (If it does, the elephant is such a very special-purpose one to be hardly interesting.) In view of the remark by Hopcroft and Tarjan it remains questionable whether much may be expected from such elephants, but that is still an open question.

Thirdly, it has been recorded as "a reminder", viz. a reminder of the fact that we do not have any systematic methodology for elephant design as we now seem to have for the design of sequential programs. The latter we can now usually present as the "natural" outcome of a number of stepwise refinements. The reader who has seen a number of such program developments will have noticed the completely different presentation of the above elephant. I can only say: "Well, here it is." and the reader, at the moment of understanding it, is expected to react with: "Ain't that cute!". But this is, of course, very unsatisfactory, for it just means that we have not yet understood the problems involved in elephant design. (The interlocking of updating the columns and scanning the rows is, of course, "cute" and there is no point in denying that I show it with some pride!)

Fourthly, the way in which simultaneous termination of mosquito activity is controlled —although not "deep" in any sense— seems to have the virtue of generality and, therefore, deserves recording.

Fifthly, the solution seems remarkable for its very low demands on the facilities for inter-mosquito communication.

Nuenen, 28th November 1974   Prof. dr. Edsger W. Dijkstra
                                    Burroughs Research Fellow

EWD465

Monotonic Replacement Algorithms and Their Implementation

(The following is written with demand paging for fixed-size pages in mind; the size of the pages being fixed is probably not essential.)

The idea of a virtual storage implementation is that not all the stored information (both program and variables) needed for the progress of a computation need to be in primary store simultaneously, but that for large periods of time parts of it may reside in secondary store. For this purpose the information is partitioned over a number of chunks such that during progress the information of a chunk will be either totally present in, or totally absent from, primary store. In this sense the chunks are our "units of presence". If all the chunks have the same size, they are called "pages"; primary store is then subdivided into so-called "page frames", i.e. units of store able to contain exactly one page.

The idea of demand paging is that the computation can proceed at full speed until access to an absent page is required. Such a requirement is called " a page fault": the computation causing it comes to a grinding halt until the page needed has been brought in. If only pages were brought in, the capacity of primary memory would be exceeded very quickly; therefore, upon a page fault a page *swap* takes place: one of the pages present in primary memory while the page fault occurs is sent back to secondary store, is "dumped". The page subjected to this fate is called "the victim" and it is the purpose of the so-called "replacement algorithm" to choose the victim.

Elsewhere —in EWD462 (and in its preliminary version EWD408)— I have argued that in a multiprogramming environment the victim should be chosen from the present pages of the program causing the fault. The number of pages that a program has present in primary store, its so-called "window size", is, as a result, not changed by the occurrence of a page fault. The purpose of this note is to describe how the information is to be collected on account of which a reconsideration of the window size can be justified.

We call a replacement algorithm "monotonic" iff (i.e. if and only if) it has the following property. If the program is executed twice (but in strict synchronism) with two different window sizes, the pages present in the smaller window will at any moment all be present in the larger window, if this is the case at program start. Monotonic replacement algorithms have the pleasant property that the page faults occurring with the larger window size are a subset of those occurring with the smaller window size, and an increase of the window size can *never* lead to a higher page fault frequency. It is easily seen, however, that a larger window size need not lead to a lower page fault frequency either.

NOTE 1. Here "frequency" is not meant as "number of times per unit of real time", but as "number of times per unit of computation time", i.e. with respect to a clock that runs while the program is being executed at full speed and is stopped while the computation is not in progress. (End of note 1.)

NOTE 2. In the sequel we shall take the freedom to consider for fixed window size the page fault frequency as a function of (computation, see previous note) time, although a frequency cannot be the function of a moment, since it is only defined as an average over a period. For the time being we can think of something like

8/(now —the moment of the last page fault but 7).

Physicists —vide Lorentz— do things like this all the time; we shall return to this later. (End of note 2.)

Although we know that at any moment the page fault frequency is a non-increasing function of the window size, we have without further information no knowledge about the *slope* of that curve (nor needs, for a given computation, that slope be constant in time). As a result, with a certain target page fault frequency in mind, we cannot trust the effectiveness of the simple feedback mechanism that increases or decreases the window size if the page fault frequency observed with the current window size is too high or too low respectively. (This would be like trying to keep a car on the road for which the actual steering mechanism reacts with unknown and varying sensitivity to a rotation of the wheel!)

In particular:

(1) If the current window size gives a page fault frequency that is higher than the target value, we would like to know the larger window size (if any!) for which the page fault frequency would be small enough. (We just cannot expect to find this larger value by trial and error: if within the bounds of primary store no such window exists, all trials become errors, and quickly even expensive ones!)

(2) If the current window size gives a page fault frequency that is higher than the target value —and, therefore, decreasing the actual window size is not something one feels tempted to suggest— we would like to know how much the window size can be decreased without increasing the page fault frequency.

(3) If the current window size w gives a page fault frequency that is lower than the target value, we would like to know the page fault frequency for a window of size $w - 1$: if that is much higher than the target value, we must abstain from decreasing the window size.

NOTE 3. The page fault frequency curve as a (non-increasing) function of the window size has very often rather sharp knees. In such a situation the simple feedback system can easily lead to thrashing half the time. (End of note 3.)

The moral of the above is that in order to justify an adjustment of the window size, we would like to know the (current) page fault frequency for *all* possible window sizes, and not just for the actual window size w. In the sequel we shall show how this information can be obtained for monotonic replacement algorithms.

Monotonic replacement algorithms define (independent of actual window sizes!) after each access a unique order for the pages of the computation that have been accessed at least once during program start. (In the following that ordering only interests us for the first *maxw* elements, if *maxw* is the maximum window size.) At any moment the k-th page in that order is the unique (!) page that would be contained in the window of size k, but not in that of size $k - 1$.

Consider now the effect of an access to a page that, prior to the access to it, is at position K in that order; upon completion of that access it must be at position 1. (If we had executed the program with a window size $= 1$, the page concerned would have been in that single page frame window.) If $K > 1$, then the page originally in position 1 has to move to a position higher up in the order, k_1 say; then the page originally in position k_1 has to move to a higher position, k_2 say, etc. until a page is brought into position K. More precisely:

$$\text{with } k_{i_0} = 1, \qquad k_{i_n} = K \qquad \text{and for } 0 \leqslant j < n: \qquad k_{i_j} < k_{i_{j+1}}$$

a cyclic permutation of pages has to take place with the page originally at position K moving to a lower position (viz. 1), all other ones moving to a higher position. For position k with $k > K$, the ordering remains unaffected.

NOTE 4. If, for $0 \leqslant i < K$ we take $k_{i+1} = k_i + 1$, i.e. each page originally at a position $k < K$ moves one position higher up in the order, we have the LRU-algorithm (Least Recently Used). For each window size w we have that $K > w$ indicates a page fault, the page originally at position w is indeed both the least recently used one and also the one that will be pushed outside the window. (End of note 4.)

NOTE 5. All reorderings other than the cyclic permutations described above would lead to more than one page moving to a lower position in the order, i.e. for some window sizes an unasked-for page would be brought inside the window, but that is not what we call "demand paging": the combination of demand paging and monotonicity makes the above cyclic permutations the only permissible ones. (End of note 5.)

*   *   *

The mechanism consists of a string of mosquitoes numbered from 1 through *wmax*. Mosquito nr. *i* has a variable *cp* (current page) whose value equals —for the moment we assume that the mosquitoes are fast enough— the name of the page currently in the *i*-th position of the order. Furthermore each mosquito is activated by placing a page name on its "*A* input" and one on its "*B* input". The *A* input will equal the name of the page that arrives in its position, the *B* input is the name of the page being accessed. Upon access of a page, its name is placed on both *A* input and *B* input of mosquito nr. 1. The code for mosquito nr. *i* is: (for LRU)

```
if cp ≠ B input →A output := cp;
                 B output := B input;
                 cp := A input
 ▯ cp = B input → cp := A input
fi
```

where the output of mosquito *i* is the input for mosquito *i* + 1.

Left alone, the mosquitoes will update their *cp*-value in the order of increasing ordinal number. If the accessed page was originally in position *K*, the first *K* − 1 mosquitoes will select the first alternative, the *K*-th mosquito will select the second alternative and there the "ripple" ends. If *K* > *w*, a genuine page fault occurs.

If this string of mosquitoes were used to detect the presence or absence of a page, the transmission speed of the ripple would have to be very high viz. *wmax* mosquitoes per memory access at least. Under the assumption of independent presence/absence detection with respect to the current window, higher mosquitoes may lag behind! It suffices if they can go through the above motions with a speed of once per memory access: they are like the elements of a fancy shift register.

For the *i*th mosquito each selection of the first alternative corresponds to a page fault that would have occurred if *i* had been the actual window size. Each mosquito has to extract from this series a corresponding "page fault frequency". They can do so by taking the past into account by an exponentially decreasing weight, for instance by keeping each a variable *amppf* ("average moment previous page faults") and transmitting "*now*", and adjusting each time the first alternative is selected *amppf* for instance by

$$amppf := amppf + (now - amppf)/8,$$

(where "*now*" refers to the moment that the ripple entered the string of mosquitoes). If for a certain window size the page faults occur at regular time intervals "*delta*", then in the limit:

before each adjustment: $now - amppf = 8 * delta$ and
after each adjustment: $now - amppf = 7 * delta$.

If we don't like this discontinuity, we can also store, per mosquito, the value *amppf'*, each time updated by

$$amppf' := amppf' + (now - amppf')/2 \qquad .$$

With page faults occurring at regular time intervals "*delta*", we then have in the limit:

before each adjustment: $now - amppf' = 2 * delta$
after each adjustment: $now - amppf' = 1 * delta$.

As a result we constantly have $amppf' - amppf = 6 * delta$, and with the above we have achieved a Lorentz-like smoothing (see Note 2).

*   *   *

Two questions have been left unanswered, but it seems premature to try to settle them now.

The first question is what to do when a processor switches from one program to another. As an elephant contains the information of *wmax* mosquitoes, *wmax* may be high and processor switching may occur at great frequency, switching one elephant with equal frequency from one program to another might lead to unacceptable switching delays. I can only think of the crude solution: have at least as many elephants as high-priority programs. With LSI-techniques   the more of the same hardware, the better— this is perhaps not so unacceptable as it sounds in my puritan ears.

The second question is how the collected information for a program is to be delivered. This has to occur at a page fault —when the victim has to be chosen— and upon reconsideration of the window size. Particularly in the first case the "lagging behind" of the mosquitoes higher up in the order presents some difficulties: it makes instantaneous selection of the victim impossible.

Nuenen, 19th December 1974   PROF. DR. EDSGER W. DIJKSTRA
                                    Burroughs Research Fellow

EWD466
Trip Report E.W. Dijkstra, Meeting IFIP W.G.2.3., Munich, 8–14 December 1974

"Schlaf aus deine Freude, schlaf aus dein Leid...." (My translation: "Sleep off your joy and sleep off your sorrow....")

Wilhelm Müller (1794–1827)

The first record I placed upon the turntable after arrival back home was the (2nd) Fischer-Dieskau/Moore recording of "Die schöne Müllerin" by Schubert/Müller. In view of the poet's avowed longing for death —"Das Wild, das ich jage, das ist der Tod" (again my translation: "The game that I hunt is death itself.")— and the fact that 1827 − 1794 equals only 33, Wilhelm Müller has done fairly well....

I made the trip from Eindhoven to Munich —on Sunday— and vice versa —on Saturday— by train: it is a through connection and the fact that it takes slightly more than nine hours does not worry me. Trips like these remind me of the story, told to me by Brian Randell, of the man who commented on his ability to do two things concurrently "I can sit and think." and then added "and often I only sit...". On the trip to Munich —German international railway carriages really run smoothly!— I wrote the major part of a paper on the implementation of monotonic replacement algorithms —in the literature erroneously known as "stack algorithms"—; on the way back I thought —rather unsuccessfully, I must admit— on grammars for defining the structure of classes of strongly connected graphs, and, when that alley seemed dead for the moment, on redundant object code representation. (To think again thoughts with a possibly direct bearing on machine design is great fun!) By the time I crossed the German/Dutch border I had arrived at a few firm conclusions (according to which all machines in the design of which I have ever been involved —and many others, for that matter— contained the same flaw).

I am not sure when I shall find the time to work this out and write a readable report about it. Arriving home after a week's absence I received from my dear wife the carefully collected mail. (For the purpose of this report I weighed it: 2300 grams, all from people I had never written to before. In about one hour I read a —French— thesis of 500 grams, which I shall direct along the appropriate channels, but the remaining 1800 grams I have to process myself more seriously.) My youngest son saw me browsing through all that mail and announced that he did not want to become a professor! Blessed are the innocent children, even one's own.... (At the party on Thursday evening, quite a few people asked me what it meant and how it felt to be a Burroughs Research Fellow. After my explanation that it is my main commitment "to do my own thing", the usual reaction is something like "That must be an exciting, but also frightening challenge.". It was quite remarkable that all German-speaking colleagues only saw the exciting part and that none of them saw the frightening side of it: they all reacted with undiluted envy. Thus they confirmed my earlier impression that at the German-speaking Universities the level of life is not just as bad as everywhere else, but distinctly below average.)

The Working Group "On Programming Methodology" met from Monday morning to Friday afternoon. I spoke to them on Monday afternoon on highlights from my book and I was only moderately successful. I should have given them a list of highlights and the chance of selecting from them; I made the choice instead. Secondly I should have taken the time to prepare a number of transparencies, for now I struggled continuously with a lack of blackboard space. Friday afternoon I tried to get a discussion going on the purpose of "types" and the "pros and cons of polymorphic functions". That seemed a disaster, but I think that we miss the point when we blame that on our being tired and my having half a flu. Later I remembered that my effort to bring that topic to discussion in Bristol had been equally unsuccessful. In all probability, the moral of the story is that types do not play such a predominant role as we may have thought and are certainly no good for abolishing the notion of partial functions. And secondly —but that conclusion was not drawn that afternoon— that "scope rules" (both positive and negative ones) provide probably a much more useful form of redundancy.

Doug McIlroy from Bell Labs described a program structure built from modules connected by "pipes", which was nice for the way in which he used the —not unknown— ideas for program composition and modification. It was his talk that made me think about grammars for strongly connected graphs; because the latter is not a trivial problem, it remains to be seen whether we shall see modules in a much more complicated arrangement than, say, a pipe line. (Note that with one noteworthy exception, all my elephants up to now are built as a cyclic arrangement of mosquitoes: I sometimes have the feeling that this is not just lack of originality on my side!)

The next morning I missed Doug Ross (SofTech), since I had to act as the opening speaker at a meeting of the German Chapter of the ACM. This, again, was only moderately successful: I was amazed to find in the Max Planck Institut no throat microphone; besides that I had to work on a grey blackboard. Shortly after my performance I went back to the Leibniz Rechenzentrum, where first Peter Naur (Copenhagen) and then Jim Horning (Toronto) described experiments with large numbers of students. Peter's statistical material came from inquiries filled in by the students, Jim's statistical material came from mechanically observed errors. It was instructive in the sense that they described experiments I would never do myself; on the other hand the results seemed very inconclusive. I do not expect that with respect to such an individual activity as "thinking" any deep insights can be obtained by observing group behaviour. I have similar doubts regarding Lehman's (London) "Evolution dynamics of large pro-grams".

In the course of the week it was suggested that my sequencing discipline would lead to an unusually great fraction of complicated boolean expres-sions. To stay in tune with the statistical approach I counted the "guards" in the program texts in my manuscript: 155 simple ones (either a relation or a boolean variable or a negated boolean variable) and 27 complicated ones (in which I had counted all *cand*'s and *cor*'s double): 15 percent. I then conducted an inquiry among the people present, asking for their personal estimation of the percentage of complicated boolean expressions in their programs: the average of the answers was 17.5 percent. " ... but, please, always be sure to call it: Research" (Tom Lehrer).

Niklaus Wirth (Zurich) gave a very illuminating (critical) review of PASCAL: illuminating because he was more explicit than ever about the motivations that had gone into the design and, besides that, was not defensive. He was the first to evoke a real discussion among the members; in some other cases I think members were afraid to give their minds. David Gries showed how he tried to extend the axiomatic approach of Tony Hoare. It was not complete yet, but looked promising and eminently manageable. In any case he has already made clear to me that the technique of "ghost variables" is more powerful than introducing "progress functions", which are just a special case. Brian Randell (Newcastle-upon-Tyne) de-scribed the current state of their recovery project. It was only after the meeting, when Brian had already left, that I remembered having a precious document in my pocket. It was titled "THINGS TO BE PUT INTO A SYSTEMS DESIGN LANGUAGE" and compiled by him and me at the first ACM Symposium on Operating Systems Principles, Gatlinburg, 1967, when a number of the participants blamed the difficulties of operating system design on the absence of a suitable "language" and founded an ad-hoc subcommittee for the design of such a tool. We did not join that subcommittee but, during dinner time, compiled a list of recommendations instead. (When it was completed, we did not want to keep our fun for ourselves; at the other end of the dining room a larger group of participants was having dinner and for their amusement we let our list circulate around their table. It was only the next day that we discovered that at that other table... the subcommittee had its meeting!) Our list contained:

automatic backup feature
dynamic maintenance feature
condition reallocation facility
built-in heuristic procedures
levelling and delevelling concepts
file system generators
interrupt dispatcher control
automatic flaw recovery
system retry
parametric fork and spoon generators
system into madness putter
peripheral abstraction detector
general purpose modularity device
page fragmentation absorber
recursive scheduler
symbolic resource optimizer
graceful degradation (of female operators) (Brian's handwriting)
garbage assembly
maximized cost performance
self-documentation
underware (= system support)
cognitive self-reproducibility
interruptable virtuality
delay module insertion coordinator.

I have the feeling that many of the subjects listed above were discussed last week in one way or another. A sobering thought.. . .

Tony Hoare (Belfast) spoke on "Levels in Operating Systems" and this looked very promising. He had bent SIMULA to his purpose. Although I was very keen on getting a good grasp on what he was proposing and why, I intentionally made no notes, because I know that the only way in which I can hope to come to grips with that problem —a rather continuous evolution from rather bare machine to user programs added as "the last layer"— is by writing it down myself. I had tried to design something like that many years ago and remember where I got hopelessly stuck and I think that Tony showed how to get out of it. But his presentation —usually he is crystal clear— was influenced by its historical origin, and carried a lot of the SIMULA confusions with it. So I guess that I must reinvent the wheel in such a way that also simple-minded persons like myself can see that it is round.

George Rabin (Poughkeepsie) gave a talk in which he failed to communicate to me. My guess is that his problems have meaning only when one takes a number (how many?) of OS/360 positions for granted. I was wondering what he was talking about, and so did a few others.

The encounters outside the official sessions were more rewarding and covered all sorts of things. Tony made a promising suggestion as how to deal with "dual elephants", although it will require at least a very good taste if the notation is not to become too hairy. Two subscripts, which in turn may be associated with time and space, seems a minimum. Niklaus told a terrible story about CDC-software. With 10 six-bit characters (from an alphabet of 63) packed into one word, CDC used the 64th configuration to indicate "end of line"; when for compatibility reasons a 64th character had to be added, they invented the following convention for indicating the end of a line: two successive colons on positions $10k + 8$ and $10k + 9$ —a fixed position in the word!— is interpreted as "end of line". The argument was clearly that colons hardly ever occur, let alone two successive ones! Tony was severely shocked "How can one build reliable programs on top of a system with consciously built-in unreliability?". I shared his horror; he suggested that at the next International Conference on Software Reliability a speaker should just mention the above dirty trick and then let the audience think about its consequences for the rest of his time slice! At another occasion Mike Woodger (Teddington) gave a verbal clarification for his enthusiasm for the work of the Polish logician Lesniewski, an enthusiasm he had earlier communicated to me by mail. If Mike says that this work is far superior to the work of better known logicians like Quine, Fraenkel, Bernays and Rosser, who have "abandoned hope of relying on intuitive logical common sense in the face of the antinomies", because Lesniewski has successfully avoided the paradoxes by introducing "sets" as coins with two faces, I believe him. But it will take a long time before it will soak in. Firstly Lesniewski's notation is somewhat hair-raising, secondly, practically all people that could read it would have to unlearn the Principia Mathematica first. I came to the conclusion that I am not a logician, nor that I feel a strong desire to become one.

On Friday evening Tony —who had also addressed the German Chapter of the ACM— and I were invited for dinner by Christiane Floyd and Peter Schnupp, who had organized the meeting of that Chapter earlier that week. We were joined by four other Germans and had a quite pleasant dinner, which did not start or end very early. (As my train left the next morning at 11:42, I did not mind too much.) The spirit at the dinner table was quite well characterized by one of the Germans quoting "You may be consistent or inconsistent, but you should not switch all the time between the two.".

Gerhard Seegmüller had organized the meeting in the Leibniz Rechenzentrum and the party in his home on Thursday evening as smoothly as at the previous occasion. At that party I also met Manfred Paul and Fritz Bauer. The latter was very busy, because that very week there was in Munich a meeting of numerical analysts in honour of Householder. Olga Tauski and Dick Varga —with whom I had one or two breakfasts— shared our hotel.

I left Munich on Saturday morning gladly; when I came home in the evening I was a little sad.

Nuenen, 16th December 1974   PROF. DR. EDSGER W. DIJKSTRA
Burroughs Research Fellow

EWD474
Trip Report Visit ETH Zurich, 3–4 February 1975 by E.W. Dijkstra

Invited by Niklaus Wirth I gave three lectures at the Eidgenössische Technische Hochschule Zurich. The first one (Monday 16.00–18.00) was reasonably successful, the second one (Tuesday 11.00–12.00) was bad —at the end I lost my way in a trivial proof and had to give up— , the last one (Tuesday 14.15–16.00) went perfectly. For some reason I was very tense. For instance, I completely forgot to open each lecture (as usual) with a quotation! I also forgot the first day to invite "interrupting questions". Niklaus suggested that at my second talk I should give the audience some "homework" for the break at lunch. I did so, but at the beginning of the second talk instead of at its end: one question was so intriguing that more than one member of the audience tried to solve the problem during the lecture.

My trip from Eindhoven (dep. 9.08) to Zurich (arr. 18.14) was most comfortable. I had to change twice (Köln and Basel), but as all trains kept perfect time and I travelled light, this was no problem at all. It was my intention to prepare the lectures during the journey, but that was not entirely successful: my thoughts wandered away and I ended up reading in "Mathematics in Western Culture", a book that I can highly recommend (in spite of the sad foreword by R. Courant, which refers to today's "anti-mathematical fashion in education"). It was written by Morris Kline. I find such accounts of the birth of new sciences very instructive and inspiring: the analogy with what happens in computing science is sometimes quite close.

Niklaus picked me up at the Zurich railway station and took me to his house where I slept the next two nights. Sunday evening he had some family over from various parts of the world and, not counting Dutch, four languages were spoken at the dinner table. (At the end of the dinner I addressed their oldest daughter upon her request in Dutch: it was truly a multi-lingual dinner!) The next evening, after dinner we —i.e. Niklaus's wife and children and I— gave a small "house concert" (piano, recorder, ukulele, clarina and vox humana) and I found it touching to observe the earnest devotion of the young performers. Later that evening Niklaus and I were joined by Gene Golub —the numerical mathematician who is now at Stanford— and an American statistician called "Grace" —I am sorry that I do not remember her full name, for she contributed a fair share to an enjoyable evening— who came from Oxford and was on her way to Rehovot, Israel. The last evening —knowing that I wanted to sleep on the night train— I drank more freely. As a result I slept very well, but I am afraid that, when I was woken up at 5:15 so that I could leave the sleeper at Köln at six o'clock in the morning, I did not feel too happy. (Whether I would have felt any better without the alcohol of the previous night is, of course, an open question!) At 9:04 I arrived in Eindhoven, where my wife was with the car to pick me up.

I had two unexpected, but pleasant, encounters. The one was with Dana Scott, who happened to pass his sabatical leave at the ETH Zurich. On Sunday evening Niklaus gave me a 15-page letter from Scott, which I studied before I went to bed and discussed with Scott the next afternoon, during the hours before my first performance. The other was that, after I had spoken a few minutes, I suddenly discovered Robert Fano in my audience (he was the director of Project MAC at the time that I was guest-professor at MIT); he happened to pass his sabatical year at the IBM Laboratory in Zurich. It was a pleasure to meet him again.

The remaining time I talked with Niklaus, his colleagues and assistants, mainly about their work and their ideas. I observed a consensus that skepticism about automatic program composition is as justified as skepticism about automatic theorem provers. (As I have always stayed far away from these subjects, I have to rely upon opinions and expectations of those with more experience or better insight in the field.) I was shown a very nicely decomposed "message switching system" designed for a "terminal": in particular the high degree of isolation of hardware-dependent parts was impressive. It had been implemented for a Hewlett-Packard machine, and a few PDP-machines were the next candidates. To write the system —i.e. nearly all of it— in an extended version of PASCAL and then perform a "hand translation" is, indeed, the most sensible approach.

We also talked about the teaching of programming and the position and role of computer science. My strong impression is that the way in which the mathematical department in Chicago first absorbed and then strangled computing science —Golub told the story— is not an isolated case: such things are in danger of occurring at more places, universities and journals. Apparently it has happened already with ACTA INFORMATICA; Niklaus expressed himself very strongly (like Turski did in November), viz. that

ACTA INFORMATICA is now doomed beyond salvation. The mathematicians immediately restrict and extend the subject to what they see in it. I may write a letter to the Editor, Niegel, but it won't help much, for we know his answer: he will explain the situation by saying that such are the papers he receives (and we all believe it, for they are so much easier to write!).

The other threat comes from organized user groups that prefer complete stagnation ("the physicist's FORTRAN"). Upon closer scrutiny, their arguments are alarming. The argument for standardization is the exchange of their expensive programs, but that means that they exchange the bugs as well. (And it is somebody's law that, the more expensive a program, the greater the number of bugs.) In the old days, physicists used to repeat each other's experiments, just to be sure. Now they repeat each other's mistakes, fully automated repetition! The only justification for exchange, for sharing, is the *ultra-high quality* of the shared object, but now they insist upon sharing because it was expensive to make, although it is almost certainly expensive junk. On account of their desire to share, they should welcome all improvements that could raise the quality of the shared object, but they resist all change with the fallacious argument that they cannot afford to do so. I sometimes smell also the unwillingness to admit that their professional responsibility extends itself to the quality of their "vital" programs. It is frightening: here we have a mechanism that could easily kill a science on a world-wide scale! The only respectable answer of computing science is *never* to yield to the pressure.

In one respect I found the intellectual climate a little bit "sticky"; I do not know whether this is characteristic for the ETH Zurich or whether it is a Swiss national trait to be "solid" first and only "adventurous" as far as then allowed (and that is not very far). Part of my talk dealt with guarded commands. Now, for anyone with some understanding, it is clear that as sequencing tools they are much more attractive to use than the traditional while-do and if-then-else, and if, fifteen years ago, someone had thought of them, while-do and if-then-else would perhaps never have become established the way they are now. While at other places —Albuquerque and Toronto, for instance— it sufficed to show the difference, I felt this time more or less pressed to quantify the improvement, to demonstrate that "the improvement justified the change". I am not preaching irresponsibility, but the danger of such a climate is, of course, that you lose the ability of having day-dreams, just for fear that you can never turn them into reality. In view of this "stick-to-what-you-have" attitude it is a marvel that Niklaus managed to get PASCAL implemented at all! (The design of PASCAL itself has, of course, been heavily influenced by the local facilities and political situation. But, how else could it be?) It is, in view of the prevailing attitude of "clinging to the soil", remarkable how the computing science there has managed to remain relatively unaffected by the awful properties of the CDC-machine they have to use. They have probably been saved by knowing

its flaws very well; usually the obligation to use a poor machine ruins a
computing science department. They have survived!

Nuenen, 10th February 1975   PROF. DR. EDSGER W. DIJKSTRA
                                                    Burroughs Research Fellow

P.S.   The problem that intrigued parts of my audience was the following.
Consider for $X > 0$ **and** $Y > 0$ the following program part:

$x := X; y := Y; u := Y; v := X;$
do $x > y \rightarrow x := x - y; v := v + u$
☐ $y > x \rightarrow y := y - x; u := u + v$
od;
print$((x + y)/2)$; print$((u + v)/2)$

The knowledge of Euclid's algorithm suffices to see that the first number
printed is $gcd(X, Y)$; the question was to discover the functional dependence of the second number printed on X and Y and to prove it. (It is, of
course, the type of "inverted question" that I detest, but letting people
struggle with it makes them more receptive for the beauty and the power of
the invariance theorem.)

EWD475

A Letter to My Old Friend Jonathan

My dear Jonathan,

After so many years of silence, you will be surprised to receive such a long letter from me. But, read on, and you will understand that this time I must address myself to a lawyer I can *trust* and of whom I know that he *understands*.

Remember our schooldays, when we argued about the relative merits of the Greek and the Roman culture? How I defended the Greeks by quoting Plato and you the Romans by quoting Cicero, and how the unsettled question did not impair the friendship and companionship between the two of us? (Happy youths, who could argue hotly about the relative superiority of classical cultures, whereas, today, the inferiority of contemporary civilization seems to be the only common meeting ground!) Our fates were decided that evening by the choice of our heros: you chose law and I chose mathematics and our ways parted. (It is a strange thought that, if in that same discussion, I had chosen Homer and you Horatius, we might both have become professional poets and our paths might have continued to cross each other....)

Dear Jonathan, I am in a fix. I leave it to your great wisdom or to your worldly experience to decide for yourself whether my problem is that I don't understand them, or whether they are so short-sighted that they are unable to understand me. But the long and the short of it is that I am in a fix, I have painted myself into a corner to the extent that I need legal advice, imagine! As you know —Hugo has certainly told you something about it— I am presently responsible for Mathematics Inc., the most exciting and most miserable business ever conceived. It is really most exciting, because —besides being a most flourishing business (and that is saying a good deal, these days)— by blending the strength of Greek contemplation with that of Roman enterprise, we *are* changing the face of the world! Our problem is, however, that apparently the world is not quite ready for this (truly!) "Cultural Revolution" and is beginning to fight back in a most unartistic manner, just because it —and in particular: its legal procedures!— cannot cope with it. There are legal procedures for the protection of property of "things", but there is no true protection of property of "ideas", and of such nature are the products of Mathematics Inc. (There are, of course, patent law and copy-right, but as you read on, you, as a lawyer, will immediately see that in our case they are insufficient.)

One of our most successful product lines is connected with what used to be known as the Riemann Hypothesis, but now should be named our Theorem. To bring you into the picture, Riemann —originally trained to become a Lutheran minister!— was one of those romantic mathematicians of the nineteenth century, who maintained his fame by dying young enough to ensure that nobody saw that he himself was also unable to prove his conjecture. Riemann completely missed the vision and imagination needed to escape from the prejudices of the preindustrial society and, according to the tradition of the period, he fought his problem single-handed: the amateur, needless to say, failed miserably.

To supply the missing proof was for Mathematics Inc. an obvious target, not only because we have built up the first (and only) corporation in the world that is technically capable of constructing such a proof, but also, because commercially it is a most attractive proposition. The point is that whole flocks of mathematicians have made themselves dependent on it and have (somewhat irresponsibly) based whole branches of mathematics on Riemann's assumption. Think what a market! All those dangling results, ready to be harvested by the first company that provides the missing link! We have provided that link and, having the Proof, besides claiming *all* previous results based on Riemann's Hypothesis, we insist on substantial royalties for all future use of it. That is fair, isn't it? You cannot expect a huge company like Mathematics Inc. to distribute its goodies like Father Xmas, can you? But, reasonable as our claims are, we experience the greatest difficulties in getting our rights recognized.

As most royalties would come from abroad, our own government —with an eye on the balance of payments— is in principle eager to assist us and to support our foreign claims, but, Good Heavens!, it is incredible how it paralyzes itself (to the point of complete ineffectiveness) by insisting upon all sorts of clearly inadequate, inappropriate and impossible legal procedures. I have now received three letters from three different departments (Science and Education, Commerce and Foreign Affairs), all of them stating that according to (different!) articles so-and-so they can do nothing for us before we have *shown* our Proof! What do they think? For, as they also explain, this disclosure does not guarantee that they can do anything *real* for us, oh no, only after the disclosure can they start the investigations whether our claims can be supported! Knowing how our departments work, my heart sinks, for it would take at least another five years!

But, besides that, disclosure of the Proof is *absolutely out of the question*! Has no one heard of industrial property? You see, we want to sell the *result* of the Proof —viz. that Riemann's Hypothesis is no longer a hypothesis but a truth— , but certainly not disclose the Proof itself, for that embodies a radically new technique of mathematical reasoning that, as long as it is ours and exclusively ours, we would like to apply to a few similar outstanding problems. Disclosure of the Proof would be similar to the disclosure of "manufacturing secrets" of classical industries. How can we make them understand this situation?

(There is another reason —but this is strictly between you and me— why I do not care too much about disclosure of the Proof right now, because the Proof, although essentially correct, is still in the prototype stage: minor deficiencies —of which *we* know that they are easily mended: it has already all been planned— could be misused to weaken our claims. My marketing division has made quite clear that, as far as they are concerned, disclosure has to be postponed until the Proof has reached such a state of stability that it won't require significant maintenance for the first five years after delivery.)

Another serious problem —in view of the huge amounts of money involved— is connected with exportation within the European Community, viz. how to compute the Value Added Tax to be paid, when we sell the Proof. As you no doubt are aware of, the rules don't provide for it, since we cannot define our "raw materials": are they the symbols we use, or the Laws of Aristotelean Logic? (Here, I am sorry to say, I expect from my government an even less cooperative attitude!)

*   *
*

Thank goodness we don't have only serious problems, but ridiculous ones as well. Before we could get the top twelve floors of the Hosanna Building, I had (to humour the old gentleman who owned half of them) to order from an architect a Toilet Flushing Water Recycling System —I have included a copy of his design— . As the old gentleman died, he did not need any humouring anymore and we decided not to implement the TFWR System, although brilliantly designed, in view of the risks involved. But now the architect complains, even after having received his fee. His argument is that he is entitled to have his ideas realized. He points out that if all his customers would act as we have done, he would end his days with lots of money, received but not earned, and none of his brain-children to survive him. He is now threatening to sue us for wasting his creative powers. I am afraid he is an uncurable artist. (Don't worry, our regular lawyer will deal with him in the usual way.)

*   *
*

Dear Jonathan, one of these days I shall ask my secretary to make an appointment for an afternoon. Can we have dinner afterwards? (I suggest

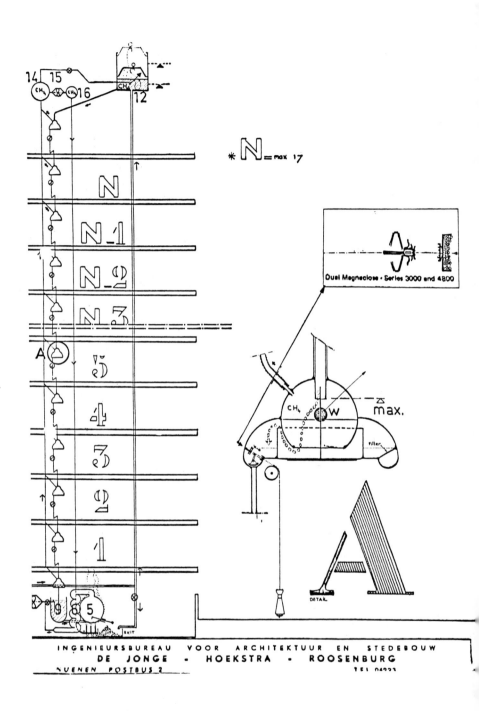

the Restaurant "Bali": it adds to an excellent kitchen the advantage of the proximity of a cafeteria where my chauffeur can have some food while we are having dinner.) I would like to discuss with someone like you the current mis-education provided by our Universities. Today's graduates leave the campus made to believe that it is Knowledge that matters, while all of us know that only Secrets matter. If all goes well, I could endow the major Universities with an appropriate chair. How should I call it? "The Edsger W. Dijkstra Chair of Industrial Espionage" or "The Mathematics Inc. Chair for Security and Privacy"? I shall ask my P.R.-man anyhow, but would appreciate your unbiased opinion.

I am very much looking forward to meeting you again. Till then!

Yours ever

9th February 1975

EDSGER W. DIJKSTRA
Mathematics Inc.
Hosanna Building

EWD480
"Craftsman or Scientist?"

(Luncheon Speech to be held at "ACM Pacific 75" at San Francisco, Friday 18th April 1975, by Edsger W. Dijkstra, Burroughs Research Fellow.)

My somewhat elliptic title refers, of course, to the programmer; so much you may have guessed. What, in all probability, you could not have guessed is that I have chosen to use the words "craftsman" and "scientist" in a very specific meaning: they have been chosen to characterize the results of two extreme techniques of education, and this luncheon speech will be devoted to a (be it short) discussion of their role in the education of programmers, in the teaching of programming. For the transmission of knowledge and skills both techniques have been used side by side since many centuries.

The future craftsman joins a master for seven meagre years, he works as an apprentice under his guidance and supervision, absorbing gradually, by osmosis so to speak, the skills of the craft, until he may be called a master himself. Craftsmen typically form Guilds and the guild members tend to keep their common craft as a well-guarded secret among themselves: not blowing the gaff is one of their rules of professional conduct. Note, finally, that old crafts have been lost, dependent as their survival was on the continuing transmission from one generation to the next.

The future scientist learns his trade as a student from a teacher, who, in contrast to the master who transfers his knowledge implicitly to his apprentice, tries to formulate the knowledge and to describe the skills as explicitly as possible, thereby bringing both into the public domain. The latter technique is the prevailing one at the Universities. It is no coincidence that the rise of the Universities occurred when the printing press became widely established, and it is no accident that each University regarded its

Library as its greatest treasure: the library was the embodiment of its specific calling. Scientists regard the free interchange of knowledge and insights as essential, and, in consequence, being non-secretive is one of their rules of professional conduct.

To this very day, both techniques are applied side by side: physicists, for instance, are mostly scientific, physicians, however, are mostly much more like guild members. Mathematicians are somewhere in between: mathematical results are published and taught quite openly, but there is very little explicit teaching on how to *do* mathematics, and publishing besides the results also the heuristics that led to them is regarded by many as "unscientific" and, therefore, bad style. Quite often the editor's censorship will try to prohibit their publication.

I have sketched for you two extreme educational techniques, but this was only preparation: my real topic is "Where along this scale should we place the teaching of programming?". This, as I have learned by sad experience, is a risky subject to discuss, because one always discusses it with people who themselves are involved in one way or another in the programming profession, and their personal involvement tends to evoke strong emotional reactions. Let us try to understand them, for only then we may be able to cope with them.

To make implicit knowledge explicit and to discuss how to describe skills, so that they can be transferred, implies, if not the birth at least the conception of a new science. But we should realize that changing a craft into a science, and making public property of the secret knowledge of the guild will always cause the guild members to feel threatened. For many a "puzzle-minded" virtuoso coder of the early sixties, the scientific development of the last decade has been most unwelcome. He feels like the medieval painter that could create a masterpiece whenever his experience enabled him to render proportions well, who suddenly found himself overtaken by all sorts of youngsters, pupils of Albrecht Dürer and the like, who had been taught the mathematical constructions that were guaranteed to surpass his most successful, but intuitive, renderings. And with nostalgia he looks back to the good old days when his experience and feeling made him an outstanding craftsman. And we should realize that, as far as programming is concerned, the battle is still going on. From a European country, the name of which I shall not divulge in order to avoid personal complications, I recently studied a proposal for the organization of its computing science teaching at University level. The majority of its authors —all of them professors of computing science in their country— should be characterized as "craftsmen". As a result, their proposal had a pronounced anti-intellectualistic flavour: it stressed that the students should be taught how to solve the problems of "the real world" and that, therefore, the curriculum should pay as little attention as possible to "abstract subjects". Such utterances are unmistakable and, undoubtedly, you recognize them. So much for the pure craftsman's point of view.

At the other end we have the pure scientist. If we give him the power of decision, the result will be equally disastrous. He will see his discipline —be it automata theory, recursive function theory, formal language theory, logic or queueing theory, you name it— with the exceptional clarity that we are entitled to expect from the modern scientist, but one thing is for him nearly impossible to accept, viz. that his beautiful and formal apparatus, indispensable as it may be, does not necessarily suffice. Since Turing we have the complete theory of how to manipulate bits, and is not that what all computing boils down to? And why all that fuss about the problems of "the real world"? *His* theory proves that all these problems can be solved, so why bother about actually solving them? Also such utterances are unmistakable and, undoubtedly, you recognize them.

So, the extremes are no good, we must blend them. But now we must be careful, for "blending" is no longer a one-dimensional question. It is not just "so many percent craftsman and so many percent scientist" but "this from the craftsman and that from the scientist". To drive home that message I shall describe to you a disastrous blending, viz. that of the technology of the craftsman with the pretence of the scientist. The craftsman has no conscious, formal grip on his subject matter, he just "knows" how to use his tools. If this is combined with the scientist's approach of making one's knowledge explicit, he will describe what he knows explicitly, i.e. his tools, instead of describing how to use them! If he is a painter he will tell his pupils all he knows about all brushmakers and all he knows about the fluctuating price of canvas. If he is a professor of computing science, he will tell his students all he knows about existing programming languages, existing machines, existing operating systems, existing application packages and as many tricks as he has discovered how to program around their idiosyncrasies. And in a short while, he will not only tell what the manual says should be punched in column 17 of the first card in order to indicate your choice of priority queue, but he will also tell and explain the illegal punching in column 17 that will place your program in the highest priority queue while only charging you for the lowest priority one. Again, the symptoms are unmistakable and, undoubtedly, you recognize them.

This disastrous blending deserves a special warning, and it does not suffice to point out that there exists a point of view of programming in which punched cards are as irrelevant as the question whether you do your mathematics with a pencil or with a ballpoint. It deserves a special warning because, besides being disastrous, it is so respectable! You see, on the one hand you stick to the problems of the real world and no one can accuse you of being overdemanding with regard to the powers of abstraction of your students; on the other hand you are as explicit as possible and everything you tell is the objective, undeniable truth. And when someone has the temerity to point out to you that most of the knowledge you broadcast is at best of moderate relevance and rather volatile, and probably even confusing, you can shrug your shoulders and say "It is the best there is, isn't it?"

As if there were an excuse for acting like teaching a discipline that, upon closer scrutiny, is discovered not to be there.... Yet I am afraid, that this form of teaching computing science is very common. How else can we explain the often voiced opinion that the half-life of a computing scientist is about five years? What else is this than saying that he has been taught trash and tripe?

With a little bit of knowledge of human nature, after the above tirade against the wrong blending, all of you will now expect me to say that my sympathy is with the inverse blending. This expectation is correct: as teachers of programming we should try to blend the technology of the scientist with the pretence of the craftsman.

Sticking to the technology of the scientist means being as explicit as we possibly can about as many aspects of our trade as we can. Now the teaching of programming comprises the teaching of facts —facts about systems, machines, programming languages etc.— and it is very easy to be explicit about them, but the trouble is that these facts represent about 10 percent of what has to be taught: the remaining 90 percent is problem solving and how to avoid unmastered complexity, in short: it is the teaching of thinking, no more and no less. The explicit teaching of thinking is no trivial task, but who said that the teaching of programming is? In our terminology, the more explicitly thinking is taught, the more of a scientist the programmer will become.

This, of course, raises the question of the feasibility of the teaching of thinking. In order to make this question realistic, we shall qualify it somewhat: knowing how to teach thinking will not imply that each student is also able to learn it. This need not deter us: in this respect "thinking" would not differ from any other subject that we try to teach. So, let us consider the question after this qualification: can thinking be taught? The blurb on the backside of my 1957 edition of Polya's "How To Solve It" is quite positive: "Deftly, Polya the teacher shows us how to strip away the irrelevancies which clutter our thinking and guides us toward a clear and productive habit of mind.".

Fine, but that is only the blurb: on the other side it has been remarked that its first edition dates already from 1944 and that Polya's larger work on the same subject, "Mathematics and Plausible Reasoning", has been coolly received by the mathematical community and has had at most a very minor influence on the teaching of mathematics at university level. Its cool reception by the mathematical community says at second thought, however, nothing against the feasibility of Polya's project. On the contrary! For its cool reception can also be interpreted as the rejection by the mathematical guild that feels threatened, as all guilds do, when the secrets of their trade are made public. To publish 30 years ago a book about the making of mathematical discoveries was heresy, as it still is in the eyes of many mathematicians today. And to quote from "Management and Machiavelli" by Antony Jay: "In corporation religions as in others, the heretic must be cast out not because of the probability that he is wrong but because of the possibility that he is right.". In other words, the relative rejection of Polya's work on heuristics tells probably more about the intellectual inertia of the mathematical establishment than about his books themselves and I suggest you this time —unusual as the advice may seem!— to believe the blurb.

I regard Polya's "How To Solve It" as a promising and significant first step. It presents heuristics as a kind of checklist of standard questions which may be helpful in not overlooking a simple, but somehow unexpected, solution, if there is one. When I first read it, I was somewhat disappointed by it, a disappointment that was a direct consequence of my already being deeply involved in programming: I felt that my problems as a programmer were for a large portion beyond the scope of what Polya covered. At first I hesitated to say so aloud, because stressing the exceptional nature of one's own field is usually a sure way of making oneself utterly ridiculous. But after careful consideration I concluded that the intellectual challenge presented by the programming task is, indeed, as unprecedented as the high-speed automatic computer itself. And it had caused in my mind a shift of attention from "how to discover the unexpected" towards "how to avoid unmastered complexity", towards "how to reduce the demands made on our quantitatively limited powers of reasoning".

You must take my word for it that past experience has made me a firm believer that this newer aspect of thinking, i.e. how to avoid unmastered complexity, can indeed be taught. This strikes you perhaps as a strong statement, it becomes only stronger when you also know that I am usually not given to unwarranted optimism. Among other things it can be done by the identification and subsequent description of the more productive "complexity generators".

But it is good to remember that there are also some intrinsic limits to the degree in which thinking can be taught explicitly, "in the scientific manner" so to speak. To quote Polya: "The first rule of discovery is to have brains and good luck. The second rule of discovery is to sit tight and wait till you get a bright idea. It may be good to be reminded somewhat rudely that certain aspirations are hopeless. Infallible rules of discovery leading to the solution of all possible mathematical problems would be more desirable than the philosopher's stone, vainly sought by the alchemists. Such rules would work magic; but there is no such thing as magic. To find unfailing rules applicable to all sorts of problems is an old philosophical dream; but this dream will never be more than a dream.". And it is there, where, unavoidably, the teaching of thinking becomes more like the teaching of a craft, where the student picks up by unconscious imitation: it is here that, as in the good old days of the guilds, an inspiring master can do wonders and can found a School by his example.

To those of you in the academic teaching business I have only one urgent plea: please be not ashamed of the extent to which your teaching of thinking is "unscientific"! It is good to remember that all the unfathomed depth of the human mind is already at play in the process of human communication. We have —despite what psychologists, paedagogues and the like may think— not the faintest idea *how* knowledge, insights and habits are transferred. It is not unlikely, that the actual transfer is *always* by imitation, and that all the explicit teaching in the scientific tradition is no more than giving the student some verbal handles, which are no more than an aid to memory. If this is true, then all *purely* "scientific teaching" —i.e. the explicit rules and no more— is bound to be, and to remain forever, a barren activity.

To end up my talk I would like to tell you a small story, which taught me the absolute mystery of human communication. I once went to the piano with the intention to play a Mozart sonata, but at the keyboard I suddenly changed my mind and started playing Schubert instead. After the first few bars my surprised mother interrupted me with "I thought you were going to play Mozart!". She was reading and had only seen me going to the piano through the corner of her eye. It then transpired that, whenever I went to the piano, she always knew what I was going to play! How? Well, she knew me for seventeen years, that is the only explanation you are going to get. Since then I believe that it is vain to try to understand what goes on in the classroom between who teaches and who learns, and that having no model of that process is safer than having one, of which the crudeness has been forgotten.

I thank you for your attention.

Nuenen, 5th March 1975   PROF. DR. EDSGER W. DIJKSTRA
                                          Burroughs Research Fellow

G., Polya, *How To Solve It*, (Anchor A 93) Doubleday and Company, Inc, Garden City, New York, U.S.A., 1957

Antony, Jay, *Management and Machiavelli*, Penguin Books Ltd., Harmondsworth, Middlesex, England, 1970

EWD482
Exercises in Making Programs Robust

(This is a sequel to the very exploratory EWD452: "About robustness and the like" which was initiated in September 1974 and closed on 31st January 1975.)

In this report I shall pursue a very simple idea. Provided that we give an adequate formulation of what we admit as "a single machine malfunctioning", we can interpret the effort as that of making a program in such a way that under the assumption of at most a single malfunctioning, the machine will never produce a wrong result as if it were the right one. I shall not, however, start my considerations with a very precise definition of the class of malfunctionings I am going to allow a single instance of: the probability that I have designed a tool of which, after much hard labour, we must conclude that it is insufficient for reaching our goal, is then just too high. I shall therefore start at the other end, and investigate the consequences of applying a technique that —with a certain amount of goodwill— can be viewed as "making a program more robust" and afterwards analyse which class of malfunctionings it catches under the assumption of at most a single instance. The more elaborate exercises, I am sorry to announce, will be rather painful ones, because we cannot do them with too simple examples: if the example is very simple —like forming the sum of a hundred stored values— the only way to make the program more robust boils down (in some way or another) to doing the computation twice and I am —obviously!— more interested in what we can achieve without paying that price. (All by itself, this observation is already somewhat alarming: under assumption of a perfect machine, we are used to breaking down the whole computation as a succession of little steps, each of them trivial in itself, but

110

if they can only be made more robust by duplication, our robustness concerns force us to consider larger "units". This seems a warning that we are tackling a nasty subject!)

$$*\quad\quad*$$
$$*$$

A very simple example to start with. A common program structure to establish a relation R is

(1)   establish P; do $BB \rightarrow S$ od

where $(P$ and $BB) \Rightarrow wp(S, P)$
and $(P$ and non $BB) \Rightarrow R$

and we could replace (1) by

(2)   establish P; do $BB \rightarrow S$ od; if P and non $BB \rightarrow skip$ fi

where the added statement causes abortion if the loop terminates with non P or BB, i.e. in a state in which we are not entitled to conclude the validity of R.

Time-wise this seems an attractive modification, because it does not generate an overhead on the repeatable statement S. An example would be (for $N \geqslant 0$) with

$R: a^2 \leqslant N$ and $(a + 1)^2 > N$ and $P: a^2 \leqslant N$

to add to the program

$a := 0\{P\}$; do $(a + 1)^2 \leqslant N \rightarrow a := a + 1$ od $\{R\}$

the checking statement

if $a^2 \leqslant N$ and $(a + 1)^2 > N \rightarrow skip$ fi   .

But this example immediately illustrates the very restricted —i.e. nearly empty— range of applicability of this transformation: it only works in those cases where finding the answer may be hard, but checking the answer is (always!) easy. These cases seem to be rather the exception than the rule, and it would not amaze me if, often, when we think that we have found an example, the property that the correctness of a result is so easily checked can be used to speed up the process of finding one. (The above square root example is, indeed, ridiculously inefficient for larger values of N.)

$$*\quad\quad*$$
$$*$$

What do we do if the verification of P and non BB amounts to redoing the computation, as for instance, when the correctness proof appeals to the Linear Search Theorem? Very crudely, if our first program operates on a variable (set) x

(3)   establish $P(x)$;
       do $BB(x) \rightarrow S(x)$ od

we could introduce a second set of variables, y say, and duplicate (under the assumption of determinacy)

(4)   establish $P(x)$;
    do $BB(x) \to S(x)$ **od**;
    establish $P(y)$;
    do $BB(y) \to S(y)$ **od**;
    if $x = y \to skip$ **fi**   .

We can also merge the two processes, but

    establish $P(x)$ and $P(y)$;
    do $BB(x) \to S(x)$; $S(y)$ **od**;
    if $x = y \to skip$ **fi**

is a little bit too optimistic if we allow —and I think that we should— erroneous sequencing as would result from an erroneous evaluation of a guard as possible malfunctioning. Program (5) is in this sense safe.

(5)   establish $P(x)$ and $P(y)$;
    do $BB(x) \to$ **if** $BB(y) \to S(y)$ **fi**; $S(x)$ **od**;
    if non $BB(y)$ **and** $x = y \to skip$ **fi**   .

Up till now, there has been no gain by the transition from (4) to (5). However, a fairly common structure of type (3) operates on a state space (x, z) and has the general form

    establish $P1(z)$ and $P2(x, z)$;
    do $B1(z)$ **and** $B2(x, z) \to x := f(x, z)$; $z := g(z)$ **od**   .

Here, repeated application of $z := g(z)$ generates a sequence of z-values —on account of $B1(z)$ possibly finite— and in variable x some function value of this sequence of z-values is computed (collected, if you prefer). The relation $P1(z)$ —which $z := g(z)$ will keep invariant— has been introduced to represent any possible *redundancy* in the representation of z. (If this redundancy is absent, $P1(z)$ does not depend on z at all and is identically true, and the remainder of this section —probably the whole report— is no longer applicable.) If $B2(x, z)$ is identically true, the sequencing is independent of x and, therefore, of the function f. If, however, we are looking for the first z-value (if any) that satisfies some property —e.g. if we are looking for the smallest divisor less than the square root plus one— $B2$ indicates that the search can be stopped as soon as a z-value satisfying the criterion has been found.

Again, we can merge the two copies, but what about letting the two state spaces share the same z?

(6)   establish $P1(z)$ and $P2(x, z)$ and $P2(y, z)$;
    do $B1(z)$ **and** $B2(x, z) \to$
        if $B1(z)$ **and** $B2(y, z) \to y := f(y, z)$ **fi**;
        $x := f(x, z)$; $z := g(z)$
    od;
    if non $(B1(z)$ **and** $B2(y, z))$ **and** $x = y \to skip$ **fi**   .

How good is (6)? Suppose that the values of x, y and z are currently all correct, but that the evaluation of a guard is incorrect. Since this incorrect evaluation is supposed to be the only malfunctioning, either it will itself cause abortion, or the next guard evaluation will do so. Suppose that the value of x has been corrupted and that this was our only malfunctioning, which is assumed to imply that y and z are and will remain correct. There are three cases. Firstly we will, during $x \neq y$, encounter a case that $B2(x, z)$ $\neq B2(y, z)$ and this will cause abortion. The second possibility is that, although $x \neq y$ remains, this will not occur, but then the last guard will cause abortion (on account of $x = y$). The third possibility is that this last abortion will not occur, because in the mean time $x = y$ has been reestablished, i.e. the (apparently information destroying) operation $x := f(x, z)$ has absorbed the malfunctioning: apparently, it did not matter! For a corruption of y (with the assumption that then x and z are, therefore, correct) the same applies. We are left with a corruption of z.

The operation $z := g(z)$ is already supposed to satisfy

(7) $(P1(z)$ **and** $B1(z)) \Rightarrow wp(\text{“}z := g(z)\text{”}, P1(z))$,

i.e. it is supposed not to destroy the validity of $P1(z)$. If we assume that the operation $z := g(z)$ will, in addition, not destroy the validity of **non** $P1(z)$:

(8) **(non** $P1(z)$ **and** $B1(z)) \Rightarrow wp(\text{“}z := g(z)\text{”},$ **non** $P1(z))$

—i.e. will keep $P1(z)$ invariant in the strict sense— , then changing the last line of (6) into

> **if non** $(B1(z)$ **and** $B2(y, z))$ **and** $x = y$ **and** $P1(z) \rightarrow skip$ **fi**

will guarantee that a corruption of z will be caught as well, if we assume that

(9) z is represented in such a redundant fashion, that any corruption of it that would not destroy the validity of $P1(z)$ can be regarded as a multiple malfunctioning, or, to put it in another way, each single malfunctioning affecting z will make $P1(z)$ false.

*   *
*

I have done extensive exercises with a program solving the following problem: generate all cyclic arrangements of 16 zeroes and 16 ones, such that all 32 possible configurations of 5 successive bits occur (and, therefore, exactly once). Another formulation of the same problem is: generate all permutations $h_0 \ldots h_{31}$ of the numbers 0 through 31 satisfying

0) $h_0 = 0$,

2) $suc(h_i, h_{i+1})$ for $0 \leq i < 31$,

3) $suc(h_{31}, h_0)$,

where $suc(a, b) = (a \bmod 16 = b \mathbf{\ div\ } 2)$.

It is in the latter form that we shall tackle it. First of all, because $suc(0, x)$ has only the solutions $x = 0$ and $x = 1$, and $h_1 \neq h_0$, it follows that $h_1 = 1$. Therefore in a permutation satisfying 1) and 2) it follows that $h_{31} = 16$, for: $suc(16, x)$ has as only solutions $x = 0$ and $x = 1$ and thus, for all $i < 31$ we have $h_i \neq 16$. In short, we can drop the permutation requirement 3) because it is implied by the others. The original inner block as designed by W.H.J. Feijen, was essentially the following one:

```
begin virvar x; privar h, p;
   x vir int array := (0); h vir int array := (0, 0);
   p vir bool array := (0, true); do p.dom ≠ 32 → p: hiext( false) od;
   do h(0) = 0 →
      begin glovar x, h, p; privar c;
         if h.dom < 32 → skip
         ▯ h.dom = 32 →
            begin glovar x; glocon h; privar j;
               j vir int := 0;
               do j ≠ 32 → x: hiext(h( j)); j := j + 1 od
            end
         fi;
         c vir int := 2 * (h.high mod 16);
         do p(c) →
            do odd(c) → c, h: hipop; p:(c) = false od;
            c := c + 1
         od;
         h: hiext(c); p:(c) = true
      end
   od
end        .
```

The extensive exercises, however, have been thrown into the wastepaper basket, because they had a very ad hoc character and the proofs that the resulting programs were resistant to a single malfunctioning either failed or became so laborious as to become unconvincing. It was that disappointing experience that prompted me to try to formulate —"in abstracto" so to speak— what I was really doing, while designing the above robust structure (6). My next experiment will therefore be to try the above general technique in a hopefully systematic manner to this specific program. (In order to keep the experiment fair, I shall *not* exploit the fact that something more about the answer is known: it has been proved that the number of solutions equals 2048, but we continue as if this theorem were unknown to us.)

To establish the connection between this program and (6), general x of (6) corresponds to the output array x of our example and the role of the general z of (6) has been taken over by the pair h, p. Relation $P2$ is the simple (and not too interesting):

$P2(x, h, p)$: the value of array x "consists" of all solutions, in alphabetical order, that alphabetically precede the permutations that begin with

$$h(0) \ldots h.high.$$

(The term "consists" is loose, but hopefully clear enough. It is further to be noted that in the above formulation of $P2$, the boolean "presence" array p is not mentioned.)

The more interesting relation $P1$ consists of two terms: $P1.1(h)$ **and** $P1.2(h, p)$:

$P1.1(h)$:   for all i satisfying $h.lob \leqslant i < h.hib$ we have $suc(h(i),$ $h(i + 1))$

$P1.2(h, p)$:   for all k satisfying $0 \leqslant k < 32$,
                $p(k)$ implies that there exists 1 value for i, and
                non $p(k)$ implies that there exists no value for i, such that
                $h.lob \leqslant i \leqslant h.hib$ **and** $h(i) = k$.

According to $P1.1$ integer array h contains in general redundant information: a boolean array —manipulating the bits of the original statement of the problem— would have done the job also. Feijen replaced the boolean array by an integer array for reasons of efficiency.

According to $P1.2$ boolean presence array p stores purely additional information that follows functionally from h; it has been introduced also for reasons of efficiency by Feijen.

And here lies our hope for gain: the redundancy that we need for the robust presentation of z may already be present for efficiency's sake!

We may wonder whether the redundancy provided by h and p is sufficient. Because p follows uniquely from h, a scrambling of the value of p will always violate $P1.2$. It is, however, possible to scramble h without violating $P1.1$ or $P1.2$ (it is difficult, but it can be done). This can be remedied by replacing the boolean "presence" array p by an integer "place" array p, satisfying the new

$P1.2(h, p)$:   for all k satisfying $0 \leqslant k < 32$,
                either $p(k) = -1$ and there exists no value i satisfying
                $h(i) = k$,
                or $0 \leqslant p(k) \leqslant h.hib$ and then $i = p(k)$ is the only value
                for
                $i \geqslant 0$ (see below), satisfying $h(i) = k$.

As the cost is negligible and it is our plan to do a thorough job, I propose to switch to the integer "place" array p. (The last requirement $i \geq 0$ has been added because it is a simplification to extend the array h at the low end with $h(-1) = 16$ for the verification of $P1.1$: upon removal of a top element the array h does not become empty.)

The critical operation is now "$z := g(z)$". We must change it so as to satisfy (8) as well. We can, indeed, insert additional tests that would lead to abortion if the intended modification of z would lead to a violation of **non** $P1(z)$, but this is not sufficient, because how do we know that the correct new value of z has been assigned to it? (If $z := g(z)$ erroneously acted as a *skip*, we would produce the same solution twice!)

The critical value, of course, is that of "c"; if the initialization of c had erroneously been carried out as

$$c \ \textbf{vir} \ int := 2 * (h.high \ \textbf{mod} \ 16) + 1,$$

a whole class of solutions could be skipped.

So we had better concentrate upon the active scope of c and repeat our games (or similar ones; wait and see). We have for the active scope of c —i.e. more precisely: until the extension $h: hiext(c)$— if all goes well the invariant relation

$$P3(h, c): \quad suc(h.high, c) \quad .$$

Because $(\textbf{non} \ P3(h, c)) \Rightarrow wp(\text{``}h: hiext(c)\text{''}, \textbf{non} \ P1.1(h))$ it suffices, as far as the invariance of **non** $P1.1(h)$ is concerned, to keep —besides **non** $P3(h, c)$— also $\textbf{non}(P1.1(h) \ \textbf{and} \ P3(h, c))$ invariant. As a result we don't need to check whether

$$c, h: hipop$$

could perhaps destroy **non** $P1.1(h)$, because that would imply the emergence of **non** $P3(h, c)$, which will not disappear unnoticed.

As $P3(h, c)$ covers the four most significant digits of c, the least significant digit of c seems to be our remaining Achilles heel. I propose to *count* the number of even numbers among $h(0)$ through $h(h.hib)$, extended with c during the latter's active scope.

This will catch erroneous initialization of c; if the guard $odd(c)$ is erroneously evaluated, an even c will disappear without the count being decreased, if the guard is erroneously evaluated false, $c := c + 1$ will increase the number of even values, while it should decrease them by one. This count is a kind of fancy parity bit. The full program is shown below.

WARNING: the proofreading of the program text has not been done with the same care I spent on the pages of my book.

```
begin virvar x, y; privar h, p, n; n vir int := 1;
    x vir int array := (0);  y vir int array := (0);
    h vir int array :=   (−1, 16, 0);
    p vir int array := (0, 0);  do p.dom ≠ 32 → p:hiext(−1) od;
    do h(0) = 0 →
        begin glovar x, y, h, p, n; privar c;
            if h.dom < 32 → skip
            ▯ h.dom = 32 → if p(0) = 0 → skip fi;
                begin glovar x; glocon h; privar j; j vir int := 0;
                    do j ≠ 32 → x:hiext(h( j)); j := j + 1 od
                end
            fi;
            if h.dom < 32 → skip
            ▯ h.dom = 32 → if p(0) = 0 → skip fi;
                begin glovar y; glocon h; privar j; j vir int := 0;
                    do j ≠ 32 → y:hiext(h( j)); j := j + 1 od
                end
            fi;
            c vir int := 2 ∗ (h.high mod 16); n := n + 1;
            do p(c) ⩾ 0 → if p(c) ⩾ 0 → skip fi;
                do odd(c) → if suc(h.high, c) → c, h:hipop fi;
                            if p(c) = h.hib + 1 → p:(c) = −1 fi
                od;
                c := c + 1; n := n − 1
            od;
            if suc(h.high, c) → h:hiext(c) fi;
            if p(c) = −1 → p:(c) = h.hib fi
        end
    od;
    if h.dom = 2 and h(0) = 1 and n = 0 and p(0) = −1 and p(1) = 0 →
        begin glocon p; privar j; j vir int := 2;
            do p( j) = −1 and j < 31 → j := j + 1 od;
            if p( j) = −1 → skip fi
        end
    fi
end
```

The comparison of the global values x and y, which should be equal, has been delegated to the surroundings.

Let me give some explanatory notes.

The outer guard $h(0) = 0$ is not repeated automatically, if true: it only matters, when we think that we have found a solution, and then it should be confirmed by $p(0) = 0$; this means that after the last solution has been found and $p(1)$ is already $= 1$, it would not be detected if the outer repetition went on for a while. Why should it?

The operations, which are essentially of the form $x := f(x, z)$ and $y := f(y, z)$, are themselves fully unchecked: if something goes wrong there that is harmful, different values of x and y will result. Note that the test whether a new solution has been found is repeated: once for x and once for y.

The conclusion that $p(c) \geqslant 0$ holds, has to be confirmed, otherwise the erroneous conclusion that extension with c would lead to duplication would cause possibly a large collection of solutions to be skipped. (This additional confirmation was lacking in my first version of the robust program.) I observed the omission while typing these notes! The conclusion that on account of **non** $p(c) \geqslant 0$ the repetition has to be terminated is asked for confirmation 7 lines lower.

The test $odd(c)$ in the innermost repetition does not need further confirmation, since any erroneous evaluation would leave its traces in a noncorrect value of n.

Finally, at the end of our original program, it is checked —somewhat superfluously— that $h.dom = 2$; the test $h(0) = 1$ is necessary for the confirmation that the outermost repetition has not stopped too early, thereby possibly missing a number of the last solutions. Finally $P1.2(h, p)$ is fully checked. (We can regard the test $h.dom = 2$ as part of that test, so perhaps its presence is fully justified after all.)

And this concludes my treatment of this example.

$$* \qquad *$$
$$*$$

As the plurals in my title betray, I originally intended to deal with more examples. On second thought I shall confine myself in this report to this single example: I am already on the eighth page, with single space typing. Although I had announced that the exercises would be rather painful, I did not expect that it would be so much so. So I think that I should distribute the report now, as it stands, hoping for helpful comments. Therefore a few concluding remarks.

If the inefficiency of our final program "hurts", we should be aware of the following considerations. Why does it "hurt"? Well, because the many tests that we have inserted are on the one hand assumed to absorb computer time, and on the other hand —unless the machine is completely lousy— will be very skew. Of course, for if the machine were perfect, the tests would give no information at all! The normal reaction to such very skew tests has been to devote dedicated hardware to them (vide the parity check or the interrupt circuit). If techniques, as displayed in this report, would be applied to general purpose programs —note, that I have not made up my mind, whether that would be a good thing!— this conflict could perhaps be solved by the presence of some program-controlled hardware that could do some of the checking in parallel with the main computation.

For the time being, techniques as shown are probably more appropriate in special purpose environments, such as, for instance, micro-programs or just the instruction cycle. One of the reasons for undertaking all this was my growing doubt about whether our techniques for the quality control of chip design and chip construction are sufficient. If techniques like the above can be transferred to that more microscopic level, we might feel confident to catch in a single stroke both design errors and incidental machine malfunctionings.

Nuenen, 20th March 1975   PROF. DR. EDSGER W. DIJKSTRA
                                                      Burroughs Research Fellow

EWD494
Trip Report E.W. Dijkstra 16th April/ 7th May, 1975, U.S.A. and Canada

With a Boeing 707, which can remain in the air for 11 hours and 45 minutes, our flying time from Amsterdam to Los Angeles was 11 hours and 30 minutes. One of the advantages of that flight is that upon arrival at Los Angeles no more time is wasted upon circling above the airport! At Immigration I found myself speeding up the proceedings by acting as a German-English interpreter between elderly Lufthansa passengers and the young (and beautiful) female U.S. Immigration officer, all in my own interest, because I wanted to catch my connection to San Francisco. (It worked.) For the benefit of my readers who enter the USA at Los Angeles as transit passenger the following advice:

(1) get your luggage booked through to at least your next destination in the USA: already in the Custom's Area, your luggage will be placed on an "Express Belt". It works!
(2) try to get TWA as your next carrier: from the International Arrivals to the TWA-building is *really* within walking distance (and on US Airports, walking distances are very rare indeed!).

I caught my connection and at 22.00 (their time!) I was picked up by my host, Tony Wasserman, who drove me to his home. After some talking, two hard-boiled eggs, a glass of cold milk and a few glasses of whiskey I went to bed and slept from midnight until 6 o'clock in their morning. At 7 o'clock we had breakfast and then my host —who was Chairman of ACM Pacific 75— and his wife disappeared and I was left to myself. For one and a half hours I studied Vol. 1, *nr.*1 of the IEEE Transactions on Software Engineering. (With the exception of the Liskov-Zilles paper, which was at least instructive, that first issue seemed to me alarmingly weak and I was glad to have refused to join its Editorial Board. The biographical blurbs about the members of that board —no doubt supplied by the subjects themselves— were very amusing when compared against each other! At Los Angeles, next week, many others would express their disappointment about that first issue.) Vol. 1, *nr*.1 proved sufficiently soporific on that Thursday morning for another two hours of undisturbed sleep on the family couch. The nett effect was that, at noon, I had had eight hours of sleep and, from then onwards, I had unusually little trouble with the eight-hour time shift. That was fine and reassuring, for it was with considerable trepidation that I had been looking forward to my commitments: a lecture on that Thursday at Berkeley at 4 o'clock (= midnight) and the next Friday a luncheon speech at San Francisco ACM Pacific 75 and, the same afternoon, again at 4 o'clock a lecture at Stanford.

At Berkeley the lecture room overflowed, and I had very little blackboard space. The sound system, however, was adequate and I was not expected to speak for more than 50 minutes. It was an acceptable performance. The Chinese restaurant where we should have dinner together and where Tony Wasserman would pick me up during the evening having had a fire, we ended up in a Japanese restaurant. Between the talk and the dinner I was rescued by Sue Graham and Michael Harrison, with whom I drank a few glasses of nice, white wine in a cool and peaceful living room. For the last glass we were joined by Vuillemin, who had asked a question after my talk. (It turned out that I had him in my audience at the Summer School in Le Breau-sans-Nappe, some five years ago: as usual, I did not remember, but, thank goodness, he did not blame me. Otherwise, he would not have turned up.)

On Friday morning I joined Tony Wasserman while going to the ACM Pacific 75. I bought a small, cheap camera and did not attend any of the sessions, except the Luncheon Banquet, where I had to read —no problem therefore— my Luncheon Speech. (It was printed in the Conference Proceedings, and under such a circumstance I always find it a little bit silly just to read my text —as if one's audience cannot read! I used the Railway Parable by way of introduction. It all went very well.) I walked through the corridors, was introduced to Codd (we had never met) and encountered Lyle, Cowan and Barton from Burroughs. They invited me for an informal meeting near San Diego (with Holt and Petri), but next week I discovered that I could not make it.

Immediately after the Conference Banquet I was taken to Stanford, where I met Jim Eve as expected; I also found there Brian Randell and Peter Henderson (which I could have expected) and Rod Burstall (which was a pleasant surprise). As Stanford had asked for the same lecture as Berkeley, I gave the same lecture again. This time we had been moved to a larger auditorium, so that it did not overflow. The sound system was not of a convincing quality —it was in the EE Department— and the old blackboards were of the type that cannot be cleaned anymore. I suffered less from these minor disturbing influences than the previous day and the lecture went very smoothly. (I fear that I am getting quite spoiled by the lecturing facilities at the THE!) In the evening there was a party at Jim and Margaret Eve's (temporary) Castle and at 11 o'clock I disappeared with Don and Jill Knuth, where I woke up at four o'clock in the morning, awake beyond redemption. At 6 o'clock in the morning I was writing a letter to Ria at their dinner table and when it was nearly completed, Jill came down for breakfast. The morning was devoted to an exchange of problems and solutions, views and opinions between Don and me, the afternoon to walking over the Stanford Campus and piano playing —his organ was going to be installed within a few weeks— . Early in the evening Don and Jill Knuth brought me back to Tony Wasserman's house, where we joined a party. There I met Richard Karp from Berkeley, Bob Floyd from Stanford and John Backus from IBM. Bob Floyd was very excited because he had just derived the exact minimum number of steps needed for addition in number systems with unique representation (by pushing a lower bound and an upper bound until they coincided). It had taken him about a year to do so and he was clearly still absolutely excited that he had succeeded. (Without denying the brilliancy of the argument, I must confess that I am not convinced of the central importance of the problem as far as computing science is concerned: it strikes me more as pure mathematics.)

After having been shown the San Francisco surroundings on Sunday morning, I flew under Tony Wasserman's guidance from San Francisco to Los Angeles in order to attend from Monday through Wednesday the International Conference on Software Reliability. Those were three busy days: besides being the first speaker —that is, after the Keynote Address by Ruth Davies from the NBS, a Keynote Address that I did not understand— I was also the last speaker, and it was intended that I should try to use that last slot for a summing up. (My printed text in the Proceedings was only an "Emergency Exit" in case that I had not figured out what to say. I felt a little bit shaky at that last session, confronted by an audience of about a thousand people and intending to speak without written text. As the audience was very mixed, I spoke mainly about the various forms of pressure to do the wrong things, about the false hopes and the lies that are the curse of our profession and about the strains, tensions and pains caused by the fact that a craft is changing into a science. It was that kind of talk. At the end I had used only five paragraphs or so from the Emergency Exit. Three days later I heard —to my surprise!— that I had been "so bitter". I don't think so: "honest" would have been a better term. It was a quite risky performance, but quite a few came to me afterwards and thanked me. I hope that I have not offended or disturbed more people than necessary.)

The International Conference on Software Reliability was, to start with, a circus with about a thousand participants instead of the estimated four hundred. At closer inspection it was a very mixed lot, as mixed as the title item "Software Reliability" was lousy. One lesson is clear: when organizing a conference, don't use a vague title like that.

There were mainly three groups of people:

(a)   the correctness guys,
(b)   the program testers and other engineering pragmatists,
(c)   the software project managers.

The three categories are presumably listed in order of increasing magnitude and decreasing quality. Category (c) felt itself very clearly threatened by the technicians of the other two categories, and showed this in various ways. One way was to deny flatly that —at least today and for the next years to come— the technicians could contribute, e.g. L.M. Culpepper's postulate (Naval Ship Research and Development Center): "For the present, reliable software must be produced by people whose primary skills and interests lie outside the field of programming.". For the record I quote from R.D. Williams's (from TRW) salestalk: "...In fact, at TRW, where the search has been intense and continuous over the years, a great deal of progress has been made, a lot has been learned and we can say conservatively (sic!) that we have come a long way.[...] Despite having introduced unprecedented rigor into the task of specifying and reaching mutual agreement on unambiguous requirements, we fully appreciate the need for even more rigor and a comprehensive technology to guide and control the requirement specification effort." Etc. There was at least one other TRW-paper in the same vein, and more than one person has asked himself (or others) whether this conference was in part a part of TRW's sales promotion. (Boehm, the program chairman, is from TRW.) If so, it must have had some negative effects as well, for I saw many people leaving the room in absolute disgust. Classifying programmer mistakes according to various (ill-defined) categories was also a beloved pastime, and, of course, there was our psychologist NN_2 who does not know that anecdotes are only a poor substitute for conversation.

The type (c) people thought mainly in terms of power. The type (b) people were a little bit more pathetic, because they felt clearly threatened in their technical skills: on the whole they had at least the lurking suspicion that their approach was not fully right. It was here that we had a number of statistical papers based on the assumption that software errors caused malfunctioning subject to a Poisson distribution (what else?) and from then onwards, etc... They had a tendency to defend themselves by putting on the hat of the "reasonable, reliable engineer", pointing out —sometimes at great length— that "correctness", although of course important, was only a very small aspect of the task. Too much of that was presented in terms of the vulgar controversy —vulgar because fruitless— of "common sense" versus "mathematics", of "the practical problems of the real world" versus "theory"; Parnas's paper had too much of that flavour for my taste.

The type (a) speakers felt most secure. They showed proof techniques, either by hand or (partly) mechanized, to be applied during or after program development and, in general, they did not oversell too much. They derived their sense of security clearly from the firm mathematical basis of their work and some of their relative modesty from previous failures of Artificial Intelligence. I myself found the methods less convincing the more they relied upon mechanical assistance. Various people showed how they tried to debug programs by "symbolic execution" (James C. King "A new approach to program testing" and Robert S. Boyer, Bernard Elspas and Karl N. Levitt "SELECT— a formal system for testing and debugging programs by symbolic execution.") but I have grave doubts whether these efforts make much sense: I fear that a combinatorial explosion will quickly prevent their application and thus reduce their significance. They tend to partition the input space according to the resulting flow of control ("the control path") and that seems self-defeating: a sentence like "each loop can be executed as many times as a user feels necessary to convince himself of its correctness" is taken as a support of my doubts! Shmuel Katz and Zohar Manna ("Towards automatic debugging of programs") state "The main tool we use will be the invariants of the program, which express the relationships among the variables at pre-chosen cutpoints during execution of the program" and that seems to make more sense. My judgement will be postponed until I have made a sufficiently thorough study of their paper; I hope that its presentation can be simplified! I was more attracted by Susan L. Gerhart's paper "Knowledge about programs: a model and case study". Susan L. Gerhart was also co-author (with John B. Goodenough) of "Towards a theory of test data selection"; while reading that I found myself somewhat depressed when I observed that these authors thought it still necessary to show that a program may be wrong, although testcases exercising the whole program text have been processed correctly. Later, while reading other papers, I became still more depressed when I discovered that this warning is still necessary! I came home with a fat, green bible of more than 560 pages containing more than 60 papers, of which perhaps 10 percent worth studying. I left the Conference rather depressed, but in retrospect it is perhaps not so bad at all (To quote Strachey's quotation "After all, 95 percent of everything is rubbish.": 10 percent worthwhile is then not bad at all!) The chairman was absolutely convinced that the conference had been a great success, but he seemed to judge primarily by the number of paying participants.

The next two days were passed at ISI, where Ralph London had invited a small number of people for an informal gathering. I do not remember all that were present, for we came from eight different countries, and I remember only Manna, Ershov, Burstall, Randell, Bledsoe, Luckham, Good, London, Turski, Wulf and Musser. On Thursday morning I showed the on-the-fly garbage collection, proof included, and the audience was duly impressed (Bill Wulf was even delighted, for he felt that he could use the solution very well). Bledsoe showed some mechanical proofs from normal analysis, using "extended reals", Burstall did his IFIP paper again, Randell showed the implementation of recovery blocks, and London and his crew gave a demonstration of their verification system. My feelings with respect to that project are still very mixed, for a great variety of reasons. Their screens were beautiful and the whole system seemed nicely engineered, but.... the demonstration had to take place during lunch, because then we could have a dedicated PDP10 at our disposal with 256K words. The demonstration took nearly an hour, the program was a program for the binary search and got stuck in most of the proofs. After the demonstration I studied the program text, which I found hard to understand. So I decided to program it myself and I derived formally a much more beautiful (and more "efficient") program on the backside of an envelope in two minutes. This contrast gave me the uneasy feeling that with the economy of their system something is still very wrong. One thing is certain: the stress on mechanical proofs is because they want a *certification* and (on what justification?) trust a machine better than a human being. That a proof is also the carrier of our understanding and that the joy of understanding is the last one we should delegate to machines is hardly stressed, probably because it cannot serve as a basis for funding.

On Friday afternoon I flew to Phoenix, Arizona, where I was due to perform on Saturday morning and afternoon on the invitation of the Phoenix Chapter of the ACM. Upon arrival in Phoenix my hosts, Dr. Susan Brewer and her husband, invited me for a concerto given by the Borodin Quartet. This was quite a surprise! The performance took place in the building of The Phoenix Chamber Music Society —or something very similar— and I was exposed to music and a new aspect of American social life. After the performance we had a late dinner with the soloists. My performance on Saturday morning was not too successful: in an overloaded room with the doors open (for reasons of ventilation) I had to fight the airport noise, only assisted by what was described as "a weak microphone". I had to work with an overhead projector, but the pen had a very blunt point and this was difficult to combine with my subject, which required rather lengthy formulae. It was a distressing battle. During lunch I retrieved from my luggage a pen with a sharper point and used some of the prepared "visuals" that I had used at my first talk in Los Angeles. The second one went much better. Early in the evening I flew back to Los Angeles, where Bob Merrell and his wife were at the airport to pick me up and to take me to Mission Viejo, where I stayed in the Mission Viejo Hilton Inn.

(The room number in Mission Viejo was 242; in Los Angeles my room number had been 338 and as I am used to factoring room numbers, this was a surprise! The Mission Viejo Hilton Inn was better than the International Hotel in Los Angeles, which was just terrible: "Two eggs any style", I discovered in Los Angeles, excludes hard boiled.... Both their bars were hardly illuminated and had music, but in the International Hotel the volume was such as to make conversation nearly impossible.)

For a week I stayed in Mission Viejo at the Burroughs Large Systems Plant. It felt like coming home, most people I encountered I had met before.

On the one hand it was hard work: about forty percent of the time I stood at a blackboard. On the other hand it was rewarding, since we communicated very effectively. One of the first days we entered the plant at about 8 o'clock in the morning and, after having accepted coffee from one of the secretaries, they showed me what they wanted to ask me, and at ten past ten we were down to essentials. Yet it all took place in a relaxed manner, orders of magnitude less hectic than the preceding ten days. My presence was responsible for a few social events and I saw a few very nice homes, often with a beautiful view. (I wondered whether that climate would make me utterly irresponsible!) I was, however, severely tempted to offer the plant something like the "Edsger W. Dijkstra Blackboard", but I have done no more than express the intention. On the anniversary of Her Majesty our Queen I took half an afternoon off; I ate dinner in solitude and wrote all evening.

I left Mission Viejo on Saturday morning. At a quarter to seven in the morning Bob Merrell was at the Hilton Inn's doorstep and took me to the airport in Los Angeles, from where I flew to Montreal. I had another four days to go, and that stay in Canada enabled me to absorb at least three of the eight hours time shift in advance. The flight to Montreal was interrupted by a stop at Toronto, where we had to see our luggage through customs. It was a hectic situation, and I was already mentally preparing myself for getting stuck in Toronto, chasing my luggage, when at last it turned up, just in time for getting on the flight again. In Montreal I was picked up by someone from IBM who drove me to the Castle Montebello.

From Monday through Wednesday IBM sponsored there a conference on Software Engineering Education, and in my innocence I had expected an audience of computer scientists. My driver, however, was a manager, who opened the conversation with something like "So you are the world expert on structured programming and chief programmer teams.". Then I knew that I was out in the wilderness and politely refused to be associated with Harlan D. Mills. During that car ride I heard more about hockey than I ever wanted to know. I felt very low when we arrived at Montebello. Upon arrival I found the scene considerably brightened by the broad shoulders and similar neck of Wlad Turski.

The Montebello conference was very instructive for me, although I learned a lot without which I would have been happier. At most fifty percent of the participants were computing scientists; the rest were either IBM officials or managers of the automatic data processing departments of large IBM customers. I had full opportunity to observe all the intricate love/hate relations between the angles of the triangle "university-manufacturer-customer". It was all very frightening and I wish that I had a mastery of my pen like Arthur Koestler, for then I could have written a companion volume to his "The Call Girls".

The central victims in this drama are the so-called MBA's (short for "Master of Business Administration") and the firms dependent on their services, in short, their employers. They really have painted themselves into a corner with very sticky molasses! They have made a number of unforgivable mistakes. One mistake is that they have based their full automation upon the IBM/360. When that machine was announced, it was immediately clear to many —even inside IBM!— that it would be practically impossible to write decent software for it, for it contained too many too serious blunders. You cannot program a crooked machine to go straight, and a hardened piece of junk propagates all through the system. As the software cannot be acceptable, stability was the last that could be expected. Yet they chose that shaky basis as their starting point. The next mistake is that they decided to program in COBOL. And now they find the administration of these big firms dependent on 5 million lines of COBOL! That would already be terrible all by itself, but on top of that misery they find IBM coming with a next release of OS/360 before they have managed to adjust their program library to the changes introduced at the previous release. They have set up gigantic administrations and have made their firms fully dependent on them, but have done so in the absence of the necessary competence to do so. It is absolutely terrible, and one of these days something terrible is bound to happen. It is irresponsibility on the verge of lunacy, but, believe me or not, the MBA's seem to believe they have done something very clever! But now, quite unexpectedly it seems, they are in trouble. One of those speakers made the duty of the university quite clear: IBM came with its confusing releases at a greater speed than the system programmers in the business could cope with, customer training was also defective, and therefore the universities (who had lots of experts in the area of operating systems, all of them with a lot of educational experience) should give crash courses in "How to live with the next release of OS/360". Perhaps the government could mediate between the vendor and the universities so that the universities could get advance information, etc. And what can the University do? To quote C.A.R. Hoare: "And simplicity is the unavoidable price which we must pay for reliability.". We know that this is going to collapse, it must, crushed under the weight of its own unwieldiness. And things are not going to improve, they will become worse. NN_3, now one of IBM's vice-presidents, announced in his keynote address —so bad, that many Canadians felt obliged to offer me their apologies on behalf of that American, and if you know something about the Canadian/American relations that is saying a good deal!— better times: primary memory would become so cheap that OS/360 could at last grow from 2.5 million somethings (bytes or words, does not matter) to 4 million somethings! Only more and more of the same, becoming demonstrably more intertwined. It is no longer "logical spaghetti", but "logical barbed wire". In the middle of the morning, NN_3 thought it fit to intervene by shouting "Why is everybody so damned pessimistic?". Tom Hull gave, as the next speaker in the discussion, him the answer "Because all of us have heard this morning's keynote address.". He did that perfectly.

But on the whole it was ghastly; unreal. I was severely shocked by the cultural level of the business participants. Their jokes were stale and sordid and —for people in business this amazed me— they could not drink their alcohol with style (and alcohol was provided by IBM plenty: "whiskey galore"; also this lavishness was somewhat appalling). But also technically, they were absolutely uneducated. I remember one extremely fruitless discussion with a man, who talked all the time about "the user". I suggested to him that he should not use that term and that he should separate his concerns: on the one hand try to make your system meet the requirements —and during that phase it is wise to consider yourself as the user— and if the system's customer happens to be someone else than yourself, deal with the problem of discovering his needs and intentions as a separate issue. He absolutely refused to make this separation of concerns.

Later I heard Harlan Mills give a summing up of some of the things I had said —together with some Harlanesk additions— for that business audience. It was terrible, a misuse of language to which to the best of my powers I could not give a meaning. So, every third phrase I interrupted Harlan "please could you explain or restate what you tried to say", but it was hopeless. Tom Hull helped me and I was very grateful to him. Later, when it was all over, our eyes met, and Tom gasped "Jezus!". It was the first time that I had heard him use strong language. How to sell empty but impressive slogans under the cloak of academic respectability. . . .

Turski's comments were short "They don't want computer scientists, nor software engineers, they want brainwashed mental cripples.". It is too true. . . .

On the last morning, Harlan Mills gave the summing up talk. It was again very much of the same, but, remarkably enough, I learned something from him, viz. the expression "entry level jobs". His argument was that the university should not train experts —as an aside: training and education were constantly confused— because the jobs those experts should get were no "entry level jobs". This may be a profound difference between the academic community and (at least some of) the business community: there is not the slightest objection to giving the most responsible university function, viz. a full professorship, to a youngster who has just got his Ph.D. It does not happen so very often, because really brilliant people are rare; but nothing in the university environment forbids it as soon as a really brilliant man emerges. On the contrary, I am tempted to add! But to the business communities represented it was unthinkable to give a youngster any real responsibility. . . .

The most frightening thing —and that made it all so unreal— was that all those business blokes, although in great trouble, were so little alarmed. They said that they were trying to dig themselves out of the hole again, but only wished to try to do so by well-established practice. So they will only sink deeper into the mud. If they really want to get out of the mess, something drastic has to be done and if they don't, something drastic will happen all by itself. But this was clearly beyond their imagination.

Nuenen, 9th May 1975   PROF. DR. EDSGER W. DIJKSTRA
                                        Burroughs Research Fellow

EWD498
How Do We Tell Truths that Might Hurt?

Sometimes we discover unpleasant truths. Whenever we do so, we are in difficulties: suppressing them is scientifically dishonest, so we *must* tell them, but telling them, however, will fire back on us. If the truths are sufficiently unpalatable, our audience is psychically incapable of accepting them and we will be written off as totally unrealistic, hopelessly idealistic, dangerously revolutionary, foolishly gullible or what have you. (Besides that, telling such truths is a sure way of making oneself unpopular in many circles, and, as such, it is an act that, in general, is not without personal risks. Vide Galileo Galilei....)

Computing Science seems to suffer severely from this conflict. On the whole, it remains silent and tries to escape this conflict by shifting its attention. (For instance: with respect to COBOL you can really do only one of two things: fight the disease or pretend that it does not exist. Most Computer Science Departments have opted for the latter easy way out.) But, Brethren, I ask you: is this honest? Is not our prolonged silence fretting away Computing Science's intellectual integrity? Are we decent by remaining silent? If not, how do we speak up?

To give you some idea of the scope of the problem I have listed a number of such truths. (Nearly all computing scientists I know well will agree without hesitation to nearly all of them. Yet we allow the world to behave as if we did not know them....)

$$* \quad * \quad *$$

Programming is one of the most difficult branches of applied mathematics; the poorer mathematicians had better remain pure mathematicians.

The easiest machine applications are the technical/scientific computations.

The tools we use have a profound (and devious!) influence on our thinking habits, and, therefore, on our thinking abilities.

FORTRAN, "the infantile disorder", by now nearly 20 years old, is hopelessly inadequate for whatever computer application you have in mind today: it is now too clumsy, too risky, and too expensive to use.

PL/I —"the fatal disease"— belongs more to the problem set than to the solution set.

It is practically impossible to teach good programming to students that have had a prior exposure to BASIC: as potential programmers they are mentally mutilated beyond hope of regeneration.

The use of COBOL cripples the mind; its teaching should, therefore, be regarded as a criminal offence.

APL is a mistake, carried through to perfection. It is the language of the future for the programming techniques of the past: it creates a new generation of coding bums.

The problems of business administration in general and data base management in particular are much too difficult for people that think in IBMerese, compounded with sloppy English.

About the use of language: it is impossible to sharpen a pencil with a blunt axe. It is equally vain to try to do it with ten blunt axes instead.

Besides a mathematical inclination, an exceptionally good mastery of one's native tongue is the most vital asset of a competent programmer.

Many companies that have made themselves dependent on IBM equipment (and in doing so have sold their soul to the devil) will collapse under the sheer weight of the unmastered complexity of their data processing systems.

We can found no scientific discipline, nor a healthy profession, on the technical mistakes of the Department of Defense and, mainly, one computer manufacturer.

The use of anthropomorphic terminology when dealing with computing systems is a symptom of professional immaturity.

By claiming that they can contribute to software engineering, the soft scientists make themselves even more ridiculous. (Not less dangerous, alas!) In spite of its name, software engineering requires (cruelly) hard science for its support.

In the good old days physicists repeated each other's experiments, just to be sure. Today they stick to FORTRAN, so that they can share each other's programs, bugs included.

Projects promoting programming in "natural language" are intrinsically doomed to fail.

* *
*

Isn't this list enough to make us uncomfortable? What are we going to do? Return to the order of the day, presumably....

Nuenen, 18th June 1975   PROF. DR. EDSGER W. DIJKSTRA
                     Burroughs Research Fellow

PS. If the conjecture "You would rather that I had not disturbed you by sending you this." is correct, you may add it to the list of uncomfortable truths.

                           EWD

EWD501

Variations on a Theme: An Open Letter to C.A.R. Hoare

Dear Tony!

For a variety of reasons I have not yet reacted to your article on Monitors [1]. For one thing, it failed to convince me —something I felt bad about, because I knew that this might have been due to the circumstance that I had been too lazy to go in detail through your more sophisticated examples— . Secondly, I was also not too pleased with the alternatives I could offer myself —my difficulty in finding good identifiers for the operations I was considering was just a symptom of my own mixed feelings— . Eventually I got interested in what one can do without mutual exclusion, and I dropped the subject —not without remorse, for I had left a task undone: I had failed to make up my mind!— .

Recently the topic was brought back to my attention by a nice technical report by Coen Bron [2], and in a Tuesday afternoon discussion with Wim Feijen, Alain Martin, Martin Rem and Liesbeth Steffens I tried, as a result, to redesign my (formerly rejected) alternative, in the hope that this time I could do a more conclusive job. This letter records the quintessence of that discussion and the following considerations.

About the Microscopic Delays Implied by Mutual Exclusion

The whole purpose of a monitor is to grant mutually exclusive access to a bunch of common variables, and this implies two things.

132

Firstly, the whole monitor concept is only adequate if a monitor will only be "active" during a negligible fraction of time. (And on the next higher level of abstraction, we shall indeed ignore the CPU-time spent on "monitoring"!) Secondly, in any multiprocessor installation, attempted monitor calls while the monitor is active imply delays, but in view of the first remark I propose to attach no significance whatsoever to the order in which such "microscopic" delays have been caused. Such microscopic delays will last until the moment when otherwise the monitor would have become inactive, and one of the microscopically delayed processes will be granted access to the monitor. Our only (logical!) requirement is the exclusion of the (in view of our first remark highly improbable) danger of individual starvation. (Round Robin, for instance, would do!) In the following the microscopic delays will not be mentioned anymore, logically it is as if "by magic" no process attempts to call a monitor while it is active. (Early in the discussion I had failed to make a clear distinction between microscopically delayed processes eager to call the monitor and macroscopically delayed processes that, being woken up, were eager to continue an interrupted execution of a monitor procedure —in what follows the latter class will disappear— ; this confusion was so disastrous that it did not last long!)

NOTE. At the lowest level I expect no objection to implementing the microscopic delays by means of the busy form of waiting. (End of Note.)

About the Macroscopic Delays Introduced by a Monitor

The further purpose of a monitor is to introduce macroscopic delays when necessary and, ideally, a monitor is formulated in such a fashion that it does not reflect the number of partners between which the cooperation is regulated. It should describe "my" behaviour versus "the others". (In the THE-system the cooperation was coded in a context in which all partners were individually known and explicitly referred to; in retrospect I regard that now as one of the more significant shortcomings of that system.) In order to describe the rules of cooperation independent of the number of partners involved, I envisaged describing it in terms of a finite number of named queues of sleeping —i.e. macroscopically delayed— processes, where the queues themselves could be of any length, and each sleeping process would occur in exactly one queue.

Right at the start, our decision that the elements on a queue should be linearly ordered seemed more emphatic than yours. You write: "If more than one program is waiting on a condition, we postulate that the signal operation will activate the longest waiting program. This gives a simple, neutral queuing discipline, which ensures that every waiting program will eventually get its turn.". But if individual starvation is the danger you would like to exorcize, Round Robin or allowance counts would have done as well.

I propose for the linear order of the elements in each queue a role that seems to me much more fundamental: "the (sleeping) others" are known to "*me*" by virtue of their place in one of the queues. If they were sets instead of linearly ordered queues, the different "(sleeping) others" would have no distinct identities.

$$*\qquad *\qquad *$$

(Continued after an interlude during which I just listened to Dvorak's Serenade —mainly for wind instruments— in D moll, opus 44: a delightful piece of music!)

I saw —you know my weakness for railroad metaphors!— the queues as one-directional railroad tracks of a shunting yard with each "(sleeping) other" in its own carriage —sleeper, if you so desire!— somewhere on one of the tracks of the shunting yard. Waking up a process implies that it leaves the yard and, therefore, the track on which it is waiting. But why should leaving a track imply waking up? In this view it comes quite naturally to allow that sleeping processes can be shunted from one track to another without being woken up. Thanks to this metaphor I freed myself of one of the constraints you had introduced.

Now for some terminology, in order to avoid misunderstanding. A process is "in monitor state" from the beginning of the execution of the first statement of a monitor procedure it has called until the end of the execution of the dynamically last statement of that monitor procedure, when its concurrently executable code can continue to be obeyed. For a given monitor n processes may be in monitor state. Either the monitor is inactive: in that case all n processes are sleeping somewhere on the shunting yard and each process, when woken up —i.e. removed from the shunting yard— will continue the execution of the monitor procedure it had called at the point, where it had gone to sleep. Or the monitor is active: in that case $n - 1$ processes are sleeping somewhere on the shunting yard and one of them has the special status "*me*", viz. the process, whose monitor call is continued to be executed. (Associating your "conditions" with my "tracks" of the shunting yard, this represents a slight departure from your proposal, in which a process that is awake —i.e. does not occur on a queue— can wake up another by signalling: you then have more than one process being awake, but only one, whose monitor procedure execution is continued. I preferred to identify "*me*" with the one and only active process and to have *all* others in monitor state explicitly somewhere on the shunting yard.)

What I was looking for was a nice set of operations in terms of which I could describe the shunting, the reallocation of "*me*", and the leaving of "*me*" of the monitor state. I did not like your term "condition" since it evoked in my mind the wrong associations: it does not reflect a linearly ordered set of sleeping processes. For lack of a better name I introduced the type "*fifoq*", an acronym for "first-in-first-out-queue", but this was a *very grave mistake*, which led me astray for more than 24 hours! It implies too much about the long-range history, whereas at each moment only the current value matters! It was a mental liberation when it dawned upon me that I could stay within the shunting yard metaphor and could just call them "trains". (For a while I used the term "tracks", but that was discarded on account of its associations with drums and disks. Eventually the transition from track to train turned out to be a blessing: whereas the "track" suggests a "place holder" or a "location", the "train" suggests a value, viz. a linearly ordered sequence of sleeping processes. It opens the way to "train expressions", which describe how new trains are composed out of the cars already on the shunting yard. It is, by the way, frightening to observe the devious and sometimes obnoxious influence of the terms I tentatively introduce! The wrong choice can drag in the wrong associations or deny you the expressive power needed to describe what you would like to think about, but then are unable to do. How does one avoid falling unaware into the trap of the inadequate metaphor? I know so many earlier instances of my falling into that trap and I honestly try to be aware of the danger; yet I did it again!)

My next problem was with "wait" and "signal"; I tried "sleep" and "wake", but quickly ran out of names for more intricate shunting operations, possibly to be combined with a redefinition of "*me*". I found myself forced to describe the operation in which "*me*" should go to sleep "somewhere" and another sleeper should take over the role of "*me*" instead. I even considered horrible neologisms like "slake", in order to express the combination of putting one process to sleep and waking up another. As you can imagine, I quickly ran out of descriptive names.

The way out seemed the introduction of "train expressions" and an assignment statement. The train expression would describe the new train as a concatenation of (cars of) existing trains. Its "evaluation" would have as implicit side-effect taking away the cars used in the new train value from the train operands: shunting does not change the number of cars on the shunting yard! I tried to describe just shunting as an assignment to a train variable, just changing monitor activity from one process to another by an assignment to "*me*" and the combination of the two by a sort of concurrent assignment with at the left-hand side "*me*" and a train variable.

It was understood that "*me*" could occur as component of a train expression. And it was the idea that, by definition, the shunting yard should contain the sleeping processes, that caused the need for the concurrent assignment. Composition of a new train containing "*me*" could not be the first assignment statement, for then the active process would sleep before it had assigned a new value to "*me*", I could not invert the order either, because then I would have two "*me*'s". Hence the idea of the concurrent assignment, which solves such problems.

It looked promising and I started to write a manuscript, but after a couple of hours at least ten pages were thrown into the waste paper basket; although it worked after a fashion, the code needed for the monitors became more and more tortuous as my examples became more ambitious. It was really appalling! I was coding in a conceptually nice and clean interface, but in spite of its conceptual simplicity it was apparently inadequate. It was one of those rare beautiful days in which one can work in the garden, but in spite of the shining sun I was close to desperate. There was only one thing I could do: put all papers away, pour myself a glass of beer, look into the blue sky, and figure out where I had got stuck.

One glass of beer —even part of it!— sufficed. Although "I" have to describe "my" behaviour versus "the others", "I" am part of the whole community, and it is extremely awkward if I cannot treat "*me*" on the same footing as "the others". While during inactivity of the monitor all "sleepers" occur on the shunting yard, it is rash to identify —what I had done!— the contents of the shunting yard with "the set of sleepers". During monitor activity, "*me*" should be allowed to occur (obviously at most once!) on the shunting yard as well, just as one of "the others"! This has a few drastic consequences. For reasons of safety, one should insist that all semicolons of a monitor procedure fall into one of two categories: those semicolons where "*me*" is somewhere on the shunting yard —and placing "*me*" on the shunting yard is *not* allowed and redefining "*me*" implies that the old "*me*" remains in monitor state and goes to sleep— and those semicolons where "*me*" is not on the shunting yard —where placing "*me*" on the shunting yard is allowed and redefinition of "*me*" implies that the old "*me*" leaves the monitor state— . To allow "*me*" to appear —at most once!— on the shunting yard during monitor activity solved all my problems. It is such an obvious generalization. During monitor inactivity, "*me*" does not exist and, therefore, cannot occur on the shunting yard. Yet it took me hours of following false ideas to discover it! I shall describe my new solutions at another occasion: tomorrow is Sunday, so I am not in a hurry, but in the mean time it is past two o'clock and I had better go to sleep. I thank you —although you must be unaware of it!— for your patience and your inspiring "presence". My problem is that I really like letter writing. . . .

*   *   *

(Sunday afternoon, 6th July 1975.)

A train is a sequence of cars. A train expression forms a new train by concatenating the cars of trains together in the obvious manner. With

$tr0, tr1, tr2$: train

examples of train expressions are $(tr0, tr1)$: this train consists of the cars of $tr0$ followed by the cars of $tr1$. As a result of this train formation, the trains $tr0$ and $tr1$ have become empty, which value is indicated by "*nil*".

($tr2$, me) forms a train one longer than $tr2$ by appending "me" at the rear end.

(me, $tr2$) forms a train one longer than $tr2$ by putting "me" in front of the train $tr2$.

I shall indicate shunting operations by means of assignment statements

$$\langle train\ variable \rangle\ :=\ \langle train\ expression \rangle \qquad \text{e.g.}$$

$$tr0\ :=\ (tr1,\ tr0) \qquad tr2\ :=\ (tr2,\ me) \qquad tr0\ :=\ (tr0,\ tr1,\ tr2) \qquad \text{etc.}$$

After evaluation of the *train expression*, the train assigned to must be empty; otherwise its cars would "disappear". One way to impose this is to require that in a train assignment the train assigned to occurs somewhere in the *train expression*. I shall not do so and shall allow

$$tr0\ :=\ (tr1,\ tr2)$$

as an abbreviation of "$tr0\ :=\ (tr0,\ tr1,\ tr2)$" when I can assert the initial emptyness of $tr0$.

Potential change of "me" will also be indicated by an assignment statement:

$$me\ :=\ head(tr0) \qquad me\ :=\ nil \qquad .$$

When the value "nil" is assigned to "me", the monitor becomes inactive until the next call of a monitor procedure, which implicitly assigns to "me" the identity of the calling process. The evaluation of the function "$head(tr0)$" yields (for initially non-empty $tr0$) the first car of $tr0$, which is taken off $tr0$. (Note that this is also a glorious side-effect: all problems can be solved by postulating that the components of a *train expression* are evaluated in order from left to right.) If initially $tr0$ is empty, it remains so, and the value of $head(tr0)$ is "nil".

These two types of assignment permit complete separation between shunting on the one hand and process switching on the other. Note that an assignment to "me":

(1)   must be a dynamically last statement of a monitor procedure when "me" does not occur on the shunting yard; the process that was "me" leaves monitor state and can continue with its concurrently executable code;

(2)   should not be a dynamically last statement of a monitor procedure when "me" does occur on the shunting yard; the process that was "me" remains in monitor state, but remains asleep until its identity is reassigned to "me", whereafter the execution of the interrupted monitor procedure is resumed at the next statement.

Now for some examples. Let me first code your single resource monitor, which macroscopically grants the single resource on *fifo* basis ([1], page 550)

```
single resource: monitor
begin busy: boolean;
  nonbusy: train;
  proc acquire:
    if busy → nonbusy := (nonbusy, me); me := nil
    [] non busy → skip
    fi;
    busy := true; me := nil
  corp acquire;
  proc release:
    if busy → busy := false; me := head(nonbusy) fi
  corp release;
  busy := false
end       .
```

(As you have seen, a call of "*release*" while **non** *busy* leads to abortion.) The above is a straight transliteration of your text and does not clearly reflect that *acquire* will only assign the value *true* to *busy* if initially it is *false*. I offer the following alternative solution for *acquire*:

```
proc acquire:
  nonbusy := (nonbusy, me); me := head(nonbusy);
  do busy → nonbusy := (me, nonbusy); me := nil od;
  busy := true; me :− nil
corp acquire       .
```

When you see this for the first time, it may strike you as a coding trick: depending on whether *nonbusy* is empty to start with "*me* := *head(nonbusy)*" will leave "*me*" unaffected or not. The test on "busyness" is only performed by the one that was at the head of the queue, and when it finds *busy* true, it places itself back at the *head*.

But it allows a nice generalization. Suppose that we have to synchronize the unbounded buffer, where (with $p > 0$ and $c > 0$)

$$prod(p): n := n + p \quad \text{and} \quad cons(c): n := n - c$$

have to be synchronized in such a fashion that $n \geqslant 0$ remains invariant.

Here we go: (consumers being served on *fifo* basis)

```
ubb: monitor
begin n: integer;
    con: train;
    proc prod( p: integer):
        n := n + p; me := head(con)
    corp prod;
    proc cons(c: integer):
        con := (con, me); me := head(con);
        do n < c → con := (me, con); me := nil od;
        n := n − c; me := head(con)
    corp cons;
    n := 0
end ubb     .
```

Finally, the same problem, but instead of serving the consumers on *fifo* basis, they may try on *fifo* basis.

```
ubb: monitor
begin n: integer;
    con, temp: train;
    proc prod( p: integer):
        n := n + p; temp := (con); me := head(temp)
    corp prod;
    proc cons(c: integer):
        if n ⩾ c → n := n − c; me := nil
        [] n < c → con := (con, me); me := nil;
                   do n < c → con := (con, me); me := head(temp) od;
                   n := n − c; me := head(temp)
        fi
    corp cons;
    n := 0
end ubb     .
```

This strategy has, of course the danger of individual starvation: another strategy with the same danger is to give priority to the requesting consumer with maximum value of c. The coding of that one is quite fun and I leave it as an exercise to you.

*   *   *

If I wanted to make a really strong case for my constructs, I should, of course, continue this letter with the coding of all your examples, but I am not going to do that now: after all, it is Sunday afternoon! For the time being I have the feeling of having done my share, and I am looking forward to your comments in particular.

You will have noticed that, for instance, in *"release"* I need at the end an additional *"me := nil"*. We could allow its omission and make the additional rule that it will be supplied by default. If you are going to suggest that as an improvement of my proposal, I promise that I shall get very cross with you (or, for that matter, with anyone else who suggests that "improvement")!

A shortcoming could be that we have only variables local to the monitor and locals of each call: if you look at *"temp"* it could be a local of a "monitor activity". Do we think that a serious shortcoming? It could be overcome by declaring *"temp"*, *"prod"* and *"cons"* inside a special "inner block" of the monitor that is entered upon activation of the monitor and left at the moment the monitor becomes inactive. I think I don't care about this refinement, but I may be overlooking a forceful argument in its favour.

My dear Tony, it was as always a pleasure and a privilege to write to you. With greetings and best wishes,

yours ever

Edsger

Nuenen, 5th July 1975   PROF. DR. EDSGER W. DIJKSTRA
                                                          Burroughs Research Fellow

[1] Hoare, C.A.R., "Monitors: An Operating System Structuring Concept" *Comm.* ACM, 17, 10 (Oct. 1974) 549–557
[2] Bron, C., "Description of Conditional Critical Regions in Terms of *P*- and *V*-Operations." Memorandum nr. 84, May 1975, Department of Applied Mathematics, Twente University of Technology, P.O. Box 217, Enschede, The Netherlands.

To Professor C.A.R. Hoare
Department of Computer Science
The Queen's University of Belfast
BELFAST BT7 1NN
Northern Ireland

EWD503
A Post-Scriptum to EWD501

Dear Tony!

Monday morning I went to XEROX to have a few copies made of EWD501 and from there via the THE home. At the THE I showed Wim Feijen what I had written during the weekend, and I discussed with him what I intended to write in the afternoon.

In the afternoon I wrote EWD502, "On a gauntlet thrown by David Gries". When that was completed, Wim came along. He had studied EWD501, and his first remark was that the procedure *cons* in the last monitor of EWD501 can be simplified, thanks to the initial emptyness of the *train temp*:

proc *cons*(*c*: *integer*):
   do $n < c \rightarrow con := (con, me); me := head(temp)$ **od**;
   $n := n - c; me := head(temp)$
corp *cons*;

Another observation he made was that if, in the last version of procedure "*acquire*", the second line

   $nonbusy := (nonbusy, me); me := head(nonbusy)$

is omitted, it is still correct but now implements a last-in-first-out strategy. I had these remarks in the back of my mind when I designed the readers and writers monitor and the diskhead monitor (see following pages).

Monday evening I was tired; Ria and I went away on the tandem. Tuesday was my day at the THE. In the morning I had some examinations, in the afternoon we studied EWD501 with the little group and made a first solution to the readers and writers. Tuesday evening I embellished it, and thought about a few linguistic alternatives. This morning I had to write a referee's report, this afternoon I designed the diskhead monitor, and typed both monitors.

It is now early in the evening. Let me describe to you the linguistic alternative I have been thinking about. Until now we have done as if the monitor only exists after the initialization has been completed. But we could regard the monitor "existing" as soon as the initialization starts, and regard the initialization as performed by an (anonymous) process in monitor state. The one consequence would be that all initializations in the monitors I have written these last days should end with an additional "*me* := *nil*". That obligation is hardly a recommendation, in contrast, perhaps, to the now created possibility that after initialization the monitor process can place "*me*" on the shunting yard, thereby remaining available for activities that would be hard to place otherwise.

In the diskhead monitor you will see that the sort process, which should insert the new requester —placed in *qu*1— in the correct position into the *train upsweep*, will fail to do so, when the new requester should be placed at the rear end of *upsweep* —this "appending" is no insertion— . As a result, requests and releases have to begin with

   "*upsweep* := (*upsweep*, *qu*1)"

just to be on the safe side. (When *qu*1 = *nil*, the above shunting has no effect.) This could be regarded as ugly. If the monitor itself could sleep on the shunting yard as well, I think that this could be remedied by attaching the monitor at the rear end of *upsweep*, before the new requester is placed in the correct position. It gives us the possibility to have some activity inserted after the last one and that, in general, seems a sound and useful facility.

```
readers and writers: monitor:
begin ar, aw: integer;
  readers, writers: train;
  proc startread:
    readers := (head(writers), readers, me); me := head(readers);
    do aw ≠ 0 → readers := (me, readers); me := nil od;
    ar := ar + 1; me := head(readers)
  corp startread;
  proc endread:
    if ar > 0 → ar := ar − 1; me := head(writers) fi
  corp endread;
  proc startwrite:
    writers := (writers, me); me := head(writers);
    do ar ≠ 0 or aw ≠ 0 → writers := (me, writers); me := nil od;
    aw := 1; me := nil
  corp startwrite;
  proc endwrite:
    if aw = 1 → aw := 0; readers := (readers, head(writers));
                me := head(readers)
    fi
  corp endwrite;
  ar := 0; aw := 0
end readers and writers
```

This is my version of the readers and the writers, according to your specifications of page 556. (Although I wrote it on Tuesday evening, I should say *"our"*, as the problem was discussed on Tuesday afternoon at the THE with the usual group; particularly Wim Feijen's contribution should be acknowledged.)

It has, I think, some charming features. The invariance of

$$(ar \geqslant 0 \text{ and } aw = 0) \text{ or } (ar = 0 \text{ and } aw = 1)$$

is beautifully maintained, when we remember that the repetitive construct can only terminate with its guard(s) *false*. (The alternative constructs in *endwrite* and *endread*, which may cause abortion, are only there for safety.) The nice thing is that these two guards, derived from the invariant relation, occur only once! The whole choice of strategy is reflected in the shunting and switching! Isn't that nice?

The way in which, in *"startread"*, the presence of a waiting *writer* prevents new *readers* from getting access also pleases me. At first it may strike you as a coding trick, but after having played with these *trains* for a while, it comes quite naturally. The way in which *"endwrite"* gives priority to the *readers* is also quite nice; at least, I think so.

In programming style, the above is very much different from your approach, in which the continuation after a "wait" can do no harm on account of what has been checked by the other process that caused the "signal". In such a way one can also get one's programs right, but in principle I think the approach a wrong one: your procedures are logically more intertwined —at least so it seems to me— and it is therefore a stronger invitation to make logical spaghetti.

The convincing beauty of the above contrasts with the program on the next page, where I did the *diskhead* monitor without the scheduled wait, and without the "condname.queue". That was not easy!

```
diskhead: monitor
begin headpos, newdest: cylinder;
    direction: (up, down);
    busy: boolean;
    upsweep, downsweep, qu1, qu2: train;
    proc request(dest: cylinder);
        upsweep := (upsweep, qu1); downsweep := (downsweep, qu2);
        newdest := dest;
        if dest > headpos or dest = headpos and direction = up →
            qu2 := (upsweep); qu1 := (head(qu2), me); me := head(qu1);
            do busy → if newdest ⩾ dest → upsweep := (upsweep, me);
                                me := head(qu2)
                [] newdest < dest → upsweep := (upsweep, qu1, me, qu2);
                                me := nil
                fi
            od
```

$\square$ *dest* < *headpos* **or** *dest* = *headpos* **and** *direction* = *down* →
    *qu*1 := (*downsweep*); *qu*2 := (*head*(*qu*1), *me*); *me* := *head*(*qu*2);
    do *busy* →**if** *newdest* ≤ *dest* →
                downsweep := (*downsweep*, *me*); *me* := *head*(*qu*1)
          $\square$ *newdest* > *dest* →
                downsweep := (*downsweep*, *qu*2, *me*, *qu*1); *me* := *nil*
            fi
    od
fi;
if *headpos* < *dest* → *direction* := *up*
$\square$ *headpos* > *dest* → *direction* := *down*
$\square$ *headpos* = *dest* → *skip*
fi;
headpos := *dest*; *busy* := *true*; *me* := *nil*
corp *request*;
proc *release*: *busy* := *false*;
  if *busy* →*upsweep* := (*upsweep*, *qu*1);
          downsweep := (*downsweep*, *qu*2);
          if *direction* = *up* →
            downsweep := (*head*(*upsweep*), *downsweep*);
            me := *head*(*downsweep*)
          $\square$ *direction* = *down* →
            upsweep := (*head*(*downsweep*), *upsweep*);
            me := *head*(*upsweep*)
          fi
  fi
corp *release*;
headpos := 0; *direction* := *up*; *busy* := *false*
end *diskhead*

Salvo errore et omissione, the above is a replacement for your *diskhead* monitor on page 555–556. It could be argued that the above could only be programmed on a very warm day with thunderstorms; for your information, it is such a day! But it has not the danger of individual starvation when all requests are for the same cylinder! Your "scheduled wait" does not talk about this. Agreed? On account of the above I understand that you yielded to the temptation to introduce the scheduled wait. Note how, in *"release"*, some shunting avoids the need for "condname.queue". That part of the construction I think quite neat!

Greetings and best wishes! Yours ever

Nuenen, 9th July 1975   EDSGER

EWD504
Erratum and Embellishments of EWD503

Erratum: the text of the procedure "*release*" at the end of EWD503 should begin as follows.

proc *release*:
   if *busy* →*busy* := *false*;
            upsweep := (*upsweep*, *qu*1); *downsweep* := (*downsweep*, *qu*2);
            if ... etc.

To keep the interpunction consistent, I should have used a colon in line 6:

proc *request*(*dest*: *cylinder*):

*   *
*

First embellishment: the text of the procedure "*endwrite*" in EWD503 is no longer "quite nice" since I discovered the alternative:

proc *endwrite*:
   if *aw* = 1 →*aw* := 0; *writers* := (*head*(*readers*), *writers*);
            me := *head*(*writers*)
   fi
corp *endwrite*;

When there are both *readers* and *writers* waiting, it avoids the final unnecessary activation of the oldest *writer*. Clearly, "shunting" is something I still have to learn!

*   *
*

Second embellishment: C.S. Scholten pointed out to me, that the *diskhead* monitor of C.A.R. Hoare, and therefore also the one in EWD503, has a danger of individual starvation on a macroscopic scale. If *direction* = *up* and the *train* "*upsweep*" is not empty —more precisely, contains requests with *dest* > *headpos*— a continuous stream of requests with *dest* = *headpos* can cause the requests in *upsweep* never to be honoured. The moral of the story is that requests with *dest* = *headpos* have to be placed in the other stream! The remedy seems to be to replace line 9 by

   if *dest* > *headpos* **or** *dest* = *headpos* **and** *direction* = *down* →

and line 17 by

   [] *dest* < *headpos* **or** *dest* = *headpos* **and** *direction* = *up* →

Wasn't that a nice pitfall? And then to think that there are people that still refuse to believe that programming is difficult.....

*   *   *

Remark about the devious influence of the programming language we are using: if I had been trained to think in PL/I with its horrible "BEGIN statements", "END statements" and "RETURN statements" the invention as described in EWD501, in which the notion of "the dynamically last statement of a monitor procedure" plays a role, would probably not have been made! Again a frightening thought!

Nuenen, 12th July 1975   PROF. DR. EDSGER W. DIJKSTRA
                                                Burroughs Research Fellow

EWD508

A Synthesis Emerging?

Introduction

This document does not contain language proposals; at a later stage they may be inspired by it. It has no other purpose than to record discussions and programming experiments. It is exciting because it seems to open the possibility of writing programs that could be implemented

(a)   either by normal sequential techniques
(b)   or by elephants built from mosquitoes
(c)   or by a data-driven machine.

That programs intended for the second or third implementation could be "inefficient" when regarded as sequential programs is here irrelevant. The important result would be that the same mathematical technique for the intellectual mastery of sequential programs can be taken over —hopefully lock, stock and barrel— for the intellectual mastery of those, as yet less familiar, designs. Finally, and this seems the most important promise, it introduces the possibility of concurrent execution in a non-operational manner.

From the past, terms as "sequential programming" and "parallel programming" are still with us, and we should try to get rid of them, for they are a great source of confusion. They date from the period that it was the purpose of our programs to instruct our machines: now it is the purpose of the machines to execute our programs. Whether the machine does so sequentially, one thing at a time, or with a considerable amount of concurrency, is a matter of implementation and should *not* be regarded as a property of the programming language. In the years behind us we have carried out this program of non-operational definition of semantics for a simple programming language that admits (trivially) a sequential implementation; our ultimate goal is a programming language that admits (highly?) concurrent implementations equally trivially. The experiments described in this report are a first step towards that goal.

27th and 31st July, 1975

It all started on Sunday 27th of July 1975, when Tony Hoare explained to me in the garden of Hotel Sepp in Marktoberdorf (Western Germany) upon my request the class-concept of SIMULA (including the so-called *inner*-concept); at least he explained his version of it. I had always stayed away from it as far as possible, in order to avoid contamination with the extremely operational point of view as practised by Dahl et al., and, after some time I could not even (under)stand their mechanistic descriptions anymore; they just made me shudder. In late 1974, Tony sent me a paper that looked better, but still made me shudder; I read it once, but, doubting whether I could endure the exposure, I consciously refused to study it at that moment. On Saturday 26th I decided that the moment to be courageous had come and asked Tony to explain to me what he was considering. He was a tolerant master, allowing me to change terminology, notation and a way of looking at it, things I had to do in order to make it all fit within my frame of mind. To begin with, I shall record how our discussions struck root in my mind. I don't know whether a real SIMULA fan will still recognize the class-concept; he may get the impression that I am writing about something totally different. My descriptions are definitely still more operational and mechanistic than I would like them to be; it is hard to get rid of old habits!

*   *   *

Suppose that we consider a natural number, which can be introduced with the initial value zero, and can be decreased and increased by 1, provided it remains non-negative. A nondeterministic, never-ending program that may generate *any* history of a natural number is then

```
nn begin privar x; x vir int := 0;
       do true → x := x + 1
       ⫿ x > 0 → x := x − 1
       od
   end      .
```

Suppose we want to write a main program operating on two natural numbers y and z, a main program that "commands" these values to be increased and decreased as it pleases. In that case we can associate with each of the two natural numbers y and z a nondeterministic program of the above type, be it that the nondeterminacy of each of these two program executions has to be resolved ("settled", if you prefer) in such a way that the two histories are in accordance with the "commands" in the main program. For this purpose we consider the following program. (Please remember that the chosen notations are not a proposal: they have been introduced only to make the discussion possible!)

> *nn* **gen begin privar** x; x **vir** *int* $:= 0$;
>   **do** $?inc \rightarrow x := x + 1$
> $[]\ x > 0$ **cand** $?dec \rightarrow x := x - 1$
>   **od**
>   **end**

main program:

> **begin privar** y, z; y **vir** *nn*; z **vir** *nn*;
>   :
> $\dot{y}.inc$; $\ldots$; $y.dec$; $\ldots$; $z.inc$; $\ldots$; $z.dec$; $\ldots$
> **end**   .

NOTES

1) We have written two programs. Eventually we shall have three sequential processes, two of type "*nn*" —one for y and one for z— and one of type "main program". The fact that the first one can be regarded as a kind of "template" I have indicated by writing **gen** (suggesting "generator") in front of its **begin**.

2) The main program is the only one to start with; upon the initialization "y **vir** *nn*" the second one is started —and remains idling in the repetitive construct— , upon the initialization "z **vir** *nn*", the last one is introduced in an identical fashion. It is assumed —e.g. because the "main program" is written after "*nn*"— that the main program is within the lexical scope of the identifier "*nn*".

3) The two identifiers *inc* and *dec* —preceded in the text of *nn* by a question mark— are subordinate to the type *nn*; i.e. if y is declared and initialized as a variable of type *nn*, the operations *inc* and *dec* —invoked by "$y.inc$" and "$y.dec$" respectively— are defined on it and can be implemented by suitably synchronizing and sequencing the execution of the y-program with that of the main program.

4) When in the main program "$y.inc$" is commanded, this is regarded in the y-program as the guard "$?inc$" being true (once). Otherwise guards (or guard components) with the question mark are regarded as undefined. Only a true guard makes the guarded statement eligible for execution.

5) The block exit of the main program, to which the variables y and z are local, implies that all the "query-guards" are made false: when $?inc$ and

?dec are false for the *y*-program, the repetitive construct terminates and that local block exit is performed: the "*x*" local to the *y*-program may cease to exist. It is sound to view the implicit termination of the blocks associated with the variables *y* and *z* to be completed before the exit of the block to which they are local —the main program— is completed. (End of Notes.)

*   *
*

In the preceding section we have assumed that the main program was somehow within the scope of "*nn*". But one can ask what funny kind of identifier this is; it is the name of a program text, however, there are as many *nn*'s as the main program introduces natural numbers. The decent way to overcome this is to introduce a fourth program, a "natural number maker", say *peano*. Suppose that the purpose of *peano* is not only to provide —i.e. to create and to destroy— natural numbers, but also to print at the end of its life the maximum natural number value that has ever existed.

```
peano
begin privar totalmax; totalmax vir int := 0;
   do ?nn → gen begin privar x, localmax;
                     x vir int, localmax vir int := 0, 0;
                     (//do ?inc →x := x + 1;
                               do localmax < x → localmax := x od
                           [] x > 0 cand ?dec → x := x − 1
                           od//);
                     do totalmax < localmax → totalmax := localmax od
                end
   od;
   print(totalmax)
end
```

main program

```
begin privar y, z; y vir peano.nn; z vir peano.nn;
      :
      y.inc; ...; y.dec; ...; z.inc; ...; z.dec
end
```

The idea was, that the program called *peano* is read in and executed, until it gets stuck at the repetitive construct with the (undefined) query "*?nn*". With the knowledge of the identifier *peano* (and its subordinate *peano.nn*) the main program is read in and executed, and because *inc* is subordinate to *peano.nn*, it becomes subordinate to *y* by the initializing declaration "*y* **vir** *peano.nn*".

NOTES

1) In the above it has not been indicated when *peano* will terminate and print the value of *totalmax*.

2) The generator describing the natural number exists of three parts:

> its opening code;
> (//its local code//);
> its closing code.

Access to the local variable *totalmax* of *peano* is permitted only in the opening code —here the facility is not used and in "*nn*" the "(//"could have been moved forward— and in the closing code. Different natural numbers may "*inc*" simultaneously, only their opening and closing codes are assumed to be performed in mutual exclusion.

3) If the main program is a purely sequential one, immediately after initialization *y.dec* will cause the main program to get stuck. If the main program consists of a number of concurrent ones, the one held up in *y.dec* may proceed after another process has performed *y.inc*. Our natural numbers would then provide an implementation for semaphores!

4) It is now possible to introduce, besides the *peano* given above, a "*peanodash*" that, for instance, omits the recording of maximum values. The main program could then begin with

begin privar *y*, *z*; *y* **vir** *peano.nn*; *z* **vir** *peanodash.nn*; ....

The importance of the explicitly named "maker" in the declaration/initialization lies in the fact that it allows us to provide alternative implementations for variables of the same (abstract) type. (End of Notes.)

The above records the highlights of Sunday's discussion as I remember them. Many of the points raised have been recorded for the sake of completeness: we may pursue them later, but most of them not in this report, as the discussion took another turn on the next Thursday.

*   *
*

On Thursday, a couple of hours were wasted by considering how also in the local code instances of generated processes —natural numbers— could be granted mutually exclusive access to the local variables of their maker. Although we came up with a few proposals of reasonable consistency, Tony became suddenly disgusted, and I had to agree. The whole effort had been "to separate", and now we were re-introducing a tool for fine-grained interference! Our major result that day was the coding of a recursive data structure of type "sequence". The coding was as follows (omitting the type of parameters and of function procedures). It is not exactly the version coded on that Thursday afternoon, but the differences are minor.

```
sequencemaker begin
    do ?sequence → gen begin
    (//do ?empty → result := true
     [] ?has(i) → result := false
     [] ?truncate → result := false
     [] ?back → result := nil
     [] ?remove(i) → skip
     [] ?insert(i) → begin privar first, rest; first vir nint := i;
            rest vir sequencemaker.sequence;
          do first ≠ nil cand ?empty → result := false
          [] first ≠ nil cand ?has(i) → if first = i →
          result := true [] first ≠ i → result := rest.has(i) fi
          [] first ≠ nil cand ?truncate → result := true;
            begin pricon absorbed; absorbed vir bool := rest.truncate;
                if absorbed → skip [] non absorbed → first := nil fi
            end
          [] first ≠ nil cand ?back → result := first; first := rest.back
          [] first ≠ nil cand ?remove(i) → if i ≠ first → rest.remove(i)
             [] i = first → first := rest.back fi
          [] first ≠ nil cand ?insert(i) → if i ≠ first → rest.insert(i)
             [] i = first → skip fi
        od end
    od//) end
od end
```

It is a recursive definition of a sequence of different integers. Let *s* be a variable of type sequence.

s.empty	is a boolean function, *true* if the sequence *s* is empty, otherwise *false*
s.has(i)	is a boolean function with an argument *i* of type integer; it is *true* if *i* occurs in the sequence, otherwise *false*
s.truncate	is an operator upon *s*, which also returns a boolean value; if *s* is nonempty, the last value is removed and the value *true* is returned; if *s* is empty, it remains so and the value *false* is returned
s.back	is an operator upon *s*, which returns a value of type *nint* (i.e. the integers, extended with the value *nil*); if *s* is nonempty, the first value is returned and removed from *s*; if *s* is empty, it remains so and the value *nil* is returned
s.remove(i)	is an operator upon *s* with an argument *i* of type integer; if *i* does not occur in *s*, *s* is left unchanged; otherwise the value *i* is removed from the sequence *s* without changing the order of the remaining elements in the sequence

s.insert(*i*)   is an operator upon *s* with an argument *i* of type integer; if *i* does occur in *s*, *s* is left unchanged, otherwise *s* is extended at the far end with the value *i*.

(The above is a set of rather crazy specifications: they grew in an alternation of simplifications —we started with a binary tree— in order to reduce the amount of writing we had to do, and complications, when we became more ambitious, and wanted to show what we could do.)

NOTE. I am aware of the lousiness of the notation of an operator upon *s* that returns a value. I apologize for this lack of good taste. (End of Note.)

The *sequencemaker* is very simple: it can only provide as many sequences as it is asked to provide; the storage requirements for a sequence are very simple, viz. a stack. (In our rejected example of the binary tree, although lifetimes are, in a fashion, nested, life is not so simple.) The *sequencemaker* has no local variables (like *peano*); accordingly, each sequence is simple: its opening and closing codes are empty. The outer repetitive construct describes the behaviour of the empty sequence: all its actions are simple with the exception of ?*insert*(*i*), as a result of which the sequence becomes nonempty. In an inner block, which describes the behaviour of a sequence that contains at least one element, two local variables are declared: the integer "*first*" for that one element, and the sequence "*rest*" for any remaining ones.

It is illuminating to follow the execution of the call "*remove*(*i*)". Suppose that *i* does not occur in the sequence. Then we constantly have "*i* ≠ *first*", and the task of removing *i* is constantly delegated to the rest, until it is delegated to an empty rest, for which "*remove*(*i*)" reduces to a *skip*. If, however, the value *i* occurs in the sequence, it occurs in a nonempty sequence, and "*i* = *first*" is discovered; the command then propagates in the form "*first* := *rest.back*". The last nonempty sequence that performs "*first* := *rest.back*" gets the value *nil* from its successor and establishes for itself "*first* = *nil*". As a result, the repetitive construct in its inner block is terminated, an inner block exit is performed, prior to the completion of which all query-guards for its successor are set *false*, and its successor performs an exit from its outer block and ceases to exist.

It is also instructive to follow how, upon exit from block

begin privar *s*; *s* **vir** *sequencemaker.sequence*; ... **end**

at a moment that *s* may contain many elements, the sequence *s* disappears. All query-guards to *s* are set to *false*, which forces termination of the inner repetitive construct for *s*, which results in a block exit from its inner block (which first requires deletion of its *rest*); upon completion of this block exit, the query-guards still being *false*, termination of the outer repetitive construct and block exit from the outer block of *s* are forced. This is very beautiful: the hint to delete itself, given to the head of the sequence, propagates up to its end, reflects there, travels back, folding up the sequence in a nice stack-wise fashion, as, of course, it should. In its elegance —or should I say: completeness?— it had a great appeal to us.

$$* \quad * \quad *$$

It was at this stage, that I realized that the same program could be visualized as a long sequence —long enough, to be precise— of mosquitoes:

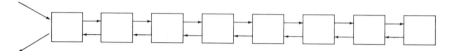

where each mosquito is essentially a copy of the text between ($//$ and $//$), and each mosquito is the "*rest*" for its left-hand neighbour. Execution of the declaration "*rest* **vir** *sequencemaker.sequence*" can be interpreted as a command to one's right-hand neighbour to initialize its instruction counter to the beginning of the program. Each mosquito is ready to accept a next command from the left as soon as it has nothing more to do, i.e. its control has successfully returned to one of the sets of query-guards. Giving a command to the right lasts until the command has been accepted when no answer is required and until the answer has been returned when an answer is required.

It is instructive to follow the propagation of activity for the various commands.

?*empty* is immediately reflected.

?*has*(i) propagates up the sequence until i has been detected or the sequence has been exhausted, and from there the boolean value (*true* or *false*, respectively) is reflected and travels to the left until it leaves the sequence at the front end. All the time the sequence is busy and cannot accept another command. The time it takes to return the answer *true* depends on the distance of i from the beginning of the sequence; the time it takes to return the answer *false* is the longest one, and depends on the actual length of the sequence (not on the number of mosquitoes available).

?*truncate* and ?*back* propagate at practically full speed to the right; at each mosquito, there is a reflection one place back to absorb the answer. Note that ?*truncate* (in the inner block) *starts* with "**result** $:= true$" and ?*back* *starts* with "**result** $:= first$" —actions, which can be taken to be completed when the mosquito to the left has absorbed the value— . This is done in order to allow the mosquito to the left to continue as quickly as possible.

?*remove*(i) propagates still more simply (until it becomes a ?*back*).

?*insert*(i) propagates also quite simply, until the wave is either absorbed —because "$i = first$" is encountered— or the sequence is extended with one element. The fascinating observation is that any sequence of *?remove(i)*, *?insert(i)*, *?back*, and *?truncate* may enter the sequence at the left: they will propagate with roughly the same speed along the sequence; if the sequence is long, a great number of such commands will travel along the sequence to the right. It is guaranteed to be impossible that one command "overtakes" the other, and we have introduced the possibility of concurrency in implementation in an absolutely safe manner.

NOTE. Originally *?truncate* was coded differently. It did not return a boolean value, and was in the outer guarded command set

$$?truncate \rightarrow skip$$

and in the inner guarded command set

first $\neq$ *nil* **cand** *?truncate* $\rightarrow$
  if *rest.empty* $\rightarrow$ *first* := *nil*
  [] **non** *rest.empty* $\rightarrow$ *rest.truncate*
  fi   .

As soon as we started to consider the implementation by a sequence of mosquitoes, however, we quickly changed the code, because the earlier version had awkward propagation properties: two steps forward, one step backward. The version returning the boolean was coded when we had not yet introduced the type *nint*; after we had done so, we could also have coded *truncate* with a parameter of type integer: in the outer guarded command set

$$?truncate(i) \rightarrow \textbf{result} := nil$$

and in the inner guarded command set

first $\neq$ *nil* **cand** *?truncate(i)* $\rightarrow$
  result := *i*; *first* := *rest.truncate(first)*   .

The last part of this note is rather irrelevant. (End of Note.)

This was the stage at which we were when we left Marktoberdorf. As I wrote in my trip report EWD506 "A surprising discovery, the depth of which is —as far as I am concerned— still unfathomed.".

*   *
*

What does one do with "discoveries of unfathomed depth"? Well, I decided to let it sink in and not to think about it for a while —the fact that we had a genuine heatwave when I returned from Marktoberdorf helped to take that decision!— . The discussion was only taken up again last Tuesday afternoon in the company of Martin Rem and the graduate student Poirters, when we tried to follow the remark, made in my trip report, that it would be nice to do away with von Neumann's instruction counter. (This morning I found a similar suggestion in "Recursive Machines and Computing Technology" by V.M. Gluskov, M.B. Ignatyev, V.A. Myasnikov, and V.A.

Torgashev, IFIP 1974; this morning I received a copy of that article from Philip H. Enslow, who had drawn my attention to it.)

We had, of course, observed that the propagation properties of "$has(i)$" are very awkward. It can keep a whole sequence of mosquitoes occupied, all of them waiting for the boolean value to be returned. As long as this boolean value has not been returned to the left-most mosquito, no new command can be accepted by the first mosquito, and that is sad. The string of mosquitoes, as shown above, is very much different from the elephant structure that we have already encountered very often, viz. all mosquitoes in a ring.

Nice propagation properties would be displayed by a string of mosquitoes that send the result as soon as found to the right, instead of back to the left! Before we pursue that idea, however, I must describe how I implemented (recursive) function procedures in 1960 —a way, which, I believe, is still the standard one— .

Upon call of a function procedure the stack was extended with an "empty element", an as yet undefined anonymous intermediate result. On top of that the procedure's local variables would be allocated, and during the activation of the procedure body, that location —named "**result**"— would be treated as one of the local variables of the procedure. A call

$?has(i)$ →**if** $i = first$ → **result** $:= true$
$\quad\quad\quad\quad$ [] $i \neq first$ → **result** $:= rest.has(i)$
$\quad\quad\quad$ **fi**

could result in 9 times the second alternative and once the first, so that the answer is found at a moment of dynamic depth of nesting equal to 10. In the implementation technique described, the boolean result is then handed down the stack in ten successive steps: the onymous result at level $n + 1$ becomes at procedure return the anonymous result at level n, which is assigned to the onymous result of level n, etc.: a sequence of alternating assignments and procedure returns. Under the assumption that assignment is not an expensive operation, this implementation technique can be defended very well.

But it is an implementation choice! When implementing

result $:= rest.has(i)$

no one forces us to manipulate the value of "$rest.has(i)$" as an intermediate result that subsequently can be assigned! An alternative interface with the function procedure would have been to give it an additional implicit parameter, viz. the destination of the result —e.g. in a sufficiently global terminology, such as distance from stack bottom. In that case the implementation of

result $:= rest.has(i)$

would consist of a recursive call on "has" in which the implicit destination parameter received would just be handed over to the next activation. When, at dynamic depth 10, the boolean value would become known, it would instantaneously be placed at its final destination, after which the stack could collapse. In the case of a fixed number of mosquitoes, always present, needed or not —that is the simplification I am thinking about now— there is not much stack collapse, and the configuration that now suggests itself is the following

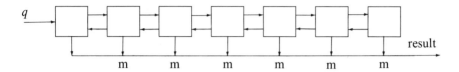

The mosquitoes still have the same mutual interconnection pattern, but I assume that each request for a value that enters the network at the left at the question mark is accompanied by "a destination" for the result. The reason that I have added the line at the bottom is the following. A sequence is a very simple arrangement, and in that case also the "external result", as soon as known, could be handed to the right-hand neighbour for further transmission. If, however, we consider the tree that would correspond to a variable of the type "binary tree", the result would then finally arrive in one of the many leaves. If we associate a real copper wire with each connection between two mosquitoes, and we wish the result to appear at a single point, then we must introduce some connecting network so that the various paths of the results can merge. Hence the additional line. The points marked "*m*" are binary merge points. We have arranged them linearly, we could have arranged them logarithmically, logically —and perhaps even physically— we can think of them as "multi-entry merges".

I am not now designing in any detail the appropriate mechanism for collecting the external result as soon as it has been formed somewhere in the network. My point is that there are many techniques possible, which all can be viewed as different implementation techniques for the same (recursive) program. Their only difference is in "propagation characteristics". The reason that I draw attention to the difference in implementation technique for the sequential machine (without and with implicit destination parameter) is the following. In the case of the linear arrangement of mosquitoes, each mosquito only being able to send to its right-hand neighbour when its right-hand neighbour is ready to accept, we have a pipeline that, by the nature of its construction, produces results in the order in which they have been requested. This, in general, seems too severe a restriction, and for that purpose each request is accompanied by a "destination" that as a kind of tag accompanies the corresponding result when finally produced. Obviously, the environment driving the network must be such that never two requests with the same destination could reside simultaneously in the network.

* * *

True to our principle that about everything sensible that can be said about computing can be illustrated with Euclid's Algorithm, we looked at good old Euclid's Algorithm with our new eyes. We also took a fairly recent version that computes the greatest common divisor of three positive numbers. It is

$$x, y, z := X, Y, Z;$$
$$\textbf{do } x > y \rightarrow x := x - y$$
$$\quad [] \; y > z \rightarrow y := y - z$$
$$\quad [] \; z > x \rightarrow z := z - x$$
$$\textbf{od}$$

with the obvious invariant relation

$gcd(x, y, z) = gcd(X, Y, Z)$ **and** $x > 0$ **and** $y > 0$ **and** $z > 0$.

Our next version was semantically equivalent, but written down a little bit differently, in an effort to represent that in each repetition we were really operating on a triple x, y, z. That is, we regarded the above program as an abbreviation of

$$x, y, z := X, Y, Z;$$
$$\textbf{do } x > y \rightarrow x, y, z := x - y, y, z$$
$$\quad [] \; y > z \rightarrow x, y, z := x, y - z, z$$
$$\quad [] \; z > x \rightarrow x, y, z := x, y, z - x$$
$$\textbf{od} \quad .$$

We then looked at it and said, why only change one value? This, indeed, is not necessary, and we arrived at the following similar, but mathematically different, program:

$$x, y, z := X, Y, Z; \hspace{4cm} \text{(program 3)}$$
$$\textbf{do non } x = y = z \rightarrow x, y, z := f(x, y), f(y, z), f(z, x) \textbf{ od}$$

with

$$f(u, v): \textbf{if } u > v \rightarrow \textbf{result} := u - v$$
$$\quad\quad\quad [] \; u \leq v \rightarrow \textbf{result} := u$$
$$\quad\quad\textbf{fi}$$

or, if we want to go one step further for the sake of argument, with

$$f(u, v): \textbf{if } u > v \rightarrow \textbf{result} := dif(u, v)$$
$$\quad\quad\quad [] \; u \leq v \rightarrow \textbf{result} := u$$
$$\quad\quad\textbf{fi}$$

and

$$dif(u, v): \textbf{result} := u - v \quad .$$

How do we implement this? We can look at program 3 with our traditional sequential eyes, which means that at each repetition the function f is invoked three times, each next invocation only taking place when the former one has returned its answer. We can also think of three different f-networks, which can be activated simultaneously. We can also think of a *single* f-network that is activated three times in succession, but where the comparison of the next pair of arguments can coincide in time with forming the difference of the preceding pair. To be quite honest, we should rewrite program 3 in the form

$x, y, z := X, Y, Z;$ (program 4)
do non $x = y = z \rightarrow tx, ty, tz := f(x, y), f(y, z), f(z, x);$
                     $x, y, z := tx, ty, tz$

od .

The reason is simple: we want to make quite clear that always the old values of x, y, z are sent as arguments to the f-network, and we want to code our cycle without making any assumptions about the information capacity of the f-network. The above program works also if we have an f-network without pipelining capacity.

*   *
*

I was considering a mosquito that would have six local variables, x, y, z, tx, ty, and tz; it would first "open" tx, ty, and tz, i.e. make them ready to receive the properly tagged results, then send the argument pairs in any order to either one or three f-networks, and finally, as a merge node, wait until all three values had been received. When I showed this to C.S. Scholten, he pointed out to me that the same result could be obtained by two, more sequential mosquitoes: one only storing the x, y, z values, and another storing the tx, ty, tz values, waiting for the three values to be delivered by the f-network. This is right.

Some remarks, however, are in order. I can now see networks of mosquitoes, implementing algorithms that I can also interpret sequentially and for which, therefore, all the known mathematical techniques should be applicable. Each mosquito represents a nondeterministic program that will be activated by its "query-guards" when it is ready to be so addressed and is so addressed, and where the act of addressing in the addressing mosquito is only completed by the time that the mosquito addressed has honoured the request. We should realize, however, that these synchronization rules are more for safety than for "scheduling", because dynamically such networks may have awkward macroscopic properties when overloaded. Take the long string of mosquitoes that, together, form a bounded buffer, each of them alternatingly waiting for a value from the left and then trying to transmit this value to the right. If this is to be a transmission line, it has the maximum throughput when, with n mosquitoes, it contains $n/2$ values. Its capacity, however, is n. If we allow its contents to grow —because new values are pumped in at the left while no values are taken out at the right— it gets stuck: taking out values from the sequence filled to the brim empties the buffer, but this effect only propagates slowly to the left and the danger of awkward macroscopic oscillations seems not excluded.

The next remark is that I have now considered elephants built from mosquitoes, but the design becomes very similar to that of a program for a data-driven machine. The programs I have seen for data-driven machines were always pictorial ones —and I don't like pictures with arrows, because they tend to become very confusing— , and their semantics were always given in an operational fashion. Both characteristics point to the initial stage of unavoidable immaturity. I now see a handle for separating the semantics from the (multi-dimensional, I am tempted to add) computational histories envisaged. In a sense we don't need to envisage them anymore, and the whole question of parallelism and concurrency has been pushed a little bit more into the domain where it belongs: implementation. This is exciting.

* *
*

A sobering remark is not misplaced either, and that is that we have already considered highly concurrent engines —e.g. the hyperfast Fourier transform via the perfect shuffle— that seem to fall as yet outside the scope of constructs considered here. And so does apparently the on-the-fly garbage collection. We can only conclude that there remains enough work to be done!

PS. For other reasons forced to go to town, I combine that trip with a visit to the Eindhoven Xerox branch. The time to reread my manuscript for typing errors is lacking and I apologize for their higher density.

Nuenen, 25th August 1975   PROF. DR. EDSGER W. DIJKSTRA
Burroughs Research Fellow

EWD512
Comments at a Symposium

Ladies and Gentlemen,

Before airing a number of comments and remarks I would like to tell you something about my past, lest I be misunderstood.

Firstly —and this is apparently in contrast to a number of people present — I consider myself as being a very lucky person because I am perfectly happy with the role that mathematics have played in my life. Extended over a period of 45 years, my mathematical education has been, I guess, about a 10 man year effort; you may not like the result, but I liked most of the experience immensely and that amount of fun and intellectual excitement I regard, all by itself, as a sufficient justification. Besides that, my enjoyment was untampered by the now fashionable quibble about "heredity" versus "environment", because in any case my dear mother played a major role in it.

Why do I bring this up? Well, simply, because the only fruitful way of considering computers that *I* know of is regarding them as mathematical machines. Knowing that, I came to this symposium with very low expectations, because this year's motto is "Computers and the educated individual". But mathematics, however, is no longer regarded as an essential ingredient of the cultural baggage of the educated man! Read Eric Temple Bell complaining about the watering down of the American high school, where mediocrity has become the norm, a degradation covered by a misuse of the notion "democratic". Read Courant's introduction to Morris Kline's "Mathematics in Western Culture", and look around yourself: you will find many in your environment who pose as educated persons and simultaneously announce with some curious pride that "of course they never understood mathematics". Two generations ago, the pitiful one who found mathematics beyond him tried to cover up his mental infirmity. In short: with today's "educated" individual, and with computers being mathematical machines, our subject "Computers and the educated individual" has a hard time finding an area of application.

To make things worse, the "educated individual" is so unfashionable as to have become nearly extinct. In the name of justice and equality, the bright pupils are no longer allowed to understand what the stupid ones cannot grasp, and many a government threatens the race of the well-educated individuals with genocide. In the hands of the pedagogues education has been replaced by training, and what used to be sowing the seeds of understanding with a hope for harvest has been replaced by educational engineering. Even the individual had better disappear and submerge into a team as quickly as possible. Instead of "Computers and the educated individual", I propose the more appropriate title: "Computers and the ill-trained mob".

In that setting I have been asked about software in the next 25 years! The safest weather prediction for tomorrow is, as we all know, "the same weather as today", and if I followed that line I should predict another 25 years of FORTRAN and COBOL. I expect this prediction to be true to a large extent because there have always been enough fools in this world. But this is the kind of uninteresting prediction that says that tomorrow morning the sun can be expected to rise again. It would only be the full truth if the name of our subject were "stagnation".

Mind you, the pressures to enforce stagnation are strong enough. Sound financial principles seem to dictate that the more expensive our mistake the longer we must maintain it, and there are computing scientists that honestly believe that OS/360 is here to stay, from now until eternity, the argument being that it is too expensive to replace it. There is the possibility that we will learn to make a better system at lesser cost; there is the certainty that it will become too risky and too expensive to continue to use it. Already, many a large organization is nearly crushed under the sheer weight of the illogical, unmastered complexity of its automatic data processing systems. Things *have* to change and, therefore, *will* change. Perhaps we have to wait for a few more spectacular collapses until it dawns upon mankind that we had better understand what we are doing. I *don't* believe in stagnation, I *do* believe in patience. The current tools will be replaced by better ones because the current ones are just too inadequate.

Please do not misinterpret my appreciation of FORTRAN: if there had been a Nobel prize for computing science, FORTRAN would have been an achievement worthy of it. But that appreciation should not engender the mistaken belief that FORTRAN is the last word in computing; on the contrary, it was one of the first words. It is just no longer adequate: since the twenty years of its existence, the computing scene has changed by several orders of magnitude. How could it still be adequate? We don't control Jumbo Jets by whip and spur!

There are two views of programming. In the old view, the purpose of our programs is to instruct our machines; in the new one, it is the purpose of our machines to execute our programs. In the old view a programmer's expertise is proportional to his knowledge of all the funny properties of the equipment against which he has to fight a continuous battle. In the new view a programmer's competence is displayed by his good taste and the justification with which he rejects inelegant implementations and clumsy interfaces. In the old view, programming becomes easier when the machines become faster and bigger because we can then stay further away from the limits of their capacity; in the new view (recognizing that before we had machines programming was no problem at all), it is recognized that our programming problems will grow with the power of our machines, because we will become more ambitious.

I am perfectly convinced that there will come a time when it will be recognized that programming is one of the more difficult branches of applied mathematics because it is also one of the more difficult branches of engineering, and vice versa. I am equally convinced that, simultaneously, programming will evolve from a craft learned by apprenticeship into an intellectual discipline that can be taught and studied and that need no longer be based on the technical mistakes of the department of defence and the computer manufacturers. Don't blame me for the fact that competent programming, as I view it as an intellectual possibility, will be too difficult for "the average programmer" — you must not fall into the trap of rejecting a surgical technique because it is beyond the capabilities of the barber in his shop around the corner.

To imagine the teaching of a discipline of programming as a science requires some imagination. Any effort to teach programming while disguising its intrinsic mathematical nature is doomed to failure, but we shall have to teach a discipline of programming in a way that differs from the average way in which mathematics is taught today. The problem with today's mathematical curricula is that mathematical *results* are published and taught quite openly, but how mathematics is *done* is not published, nor taught explicitly, and the student must pick it up by osmosis, so to speak. In this respect mathematics is only half-way between the open science and the secret craft of the guilds, and we are forced to observe that the great majority of trained mathematicians are only amateur thinkers.

But programming, when stripped of all its circumstantial irrelevancies, boils down to no more and no less than very effective thinking so as to avoid unmastered complexity, to very vigorous separation of your many different concerns.

As far as my experience goes, programming in the sense of thinking, or thinking in the sense of programming, can indeed be taught. Not all your students will learn it, but in that respect it is no different from any other subject. Polya's "How To Solve It" and his "Art of Plausible Reasoning", although inspiring, are not enough. That would be more than can be expected, for the programming problem only emerged after those books had been written. And perhaps Polya tried to teach something more elusive than what we are trying to teach now. Polya was concerned with problem solving, and he made a sort of checklist that one could go through when trying not to overlook the in some sense "surprising" or "unexpected" solution. But this time we are not so much concerned with problem solving in Polya's sense. I think that "solution composition" comes much closer to what we have to do now. We have to fight chaos, and the most effective way of doing that is to prevent its emergence. We have to learn to avoid all forms of combinatorial complexity generators that, when active, rapidly tax our ability to carry out a case-analysis far beyond the limits of our power of reasoning. To recognize the emergence of a combinatorial complexity generator long before it has poisoned your design beyond salvation requires constant vigilance, a vigilance that can and should be taught. To circumvent such emerging complexity generators may very well be a tough problem, the solution of which I can only describe as mathematical invention. A great advantage is that we know at least what we are looking for, and —perhaps most important of all— that a terminology is emerging with which we can name the different stages and aspects of our intellectual endeavour, a terminology in which we can answer the otherwise frustrating question that so often emerges in the midst of one's struggles in "What the hell am I really doing?".

The main virtue of machines is that they have confronted us with a new class of extremely difficult problems that, with love, luck, and discipline, we shall learn to cope with. As a reaction to this challenge, consciously trained thinkers will emerge: we need them. The first consciously trained thinkers will be largely self-taught ones, but ... consciously trained, and they will learn how to educate others.

No one needs to tell me that, with all its political and social implications, this will be a very slow process, much slower than technically necessary. It is that "ritenuto" enforced by society that may see to it that my prediction is good for —as Ewan Page asked— the next 25 years.

Newcastle-upon-Tyne, 11th September 1975

EWD513
Trip Report E.W. Dijkstra, Newcastle, 8–12 September 1975

On Monday the 8th of September I flew —i.e. "was flown"— from Eindhoven to Amsterdam in the late afternoon. In the early evening I flew from Amsterdam to Newcastle. I did so in the company of Goos —now from Karlsruhe— , whom I had met in the waiting area of Schiphol Airport and who was heading for the same destination as I: the IBM/Newcastle Symposium. Like nearly all German professors he talked more about the situation at his university than about his work. He told me that now they have 700 (!) students in computing science, and I could only guess what he taught them. British Caledonian was only fifteen minutes late, and the flight was about as pleasant as flights can be. After landing, the Newcastle cold surprised us; it would surprise us for the whole rest of the week.

While the participants at these yearly symposia are always pretty much the same —as are the jokes of Ewan Page— , the subjects are rather different and the speakers are refreshed accordingly. Last year's topic, "Formal aspects of computing science", was "hard", this year's topic, "Computers and the educated individual", was as "soft" as soft can be, and I would have been disappointed if I had went with high expectations. On Monday evening, shortly after our arrival, our hosts Page and Randell were "at home" as usual —at Page's home, to be precise— and this informal gathering was quite nice (as usual), and when all the other guests had left, I assisted (as usual) with the washing up. Brian and I walked back to "Hotel Randell", where I stayed, together with Jim Horning. The next morning, the symposium started in earnest, and the series of one-hour talks started.

NN_4 (Bell Laboratories) gave two talks on "The History of Computers to the year 2000" and "Computers in the Coming Society". I found it very interesting to observe him and to see what a successful career in big business can do to an otherwise intelligent man. If he still has the ability to doubt, he did not show it.

165

Naur (Copenhagen University) gave three talks, the first two on "An Adaptable Course of Elementary, University Level, Computer Science" and a last one on "Problems of Attitudes in Discussing the Computer/Society Relation". His three hours seemed about twice as much as what would be needed for what he wanted to tell. All three talks contained relevant information for those who are interested in the atmosphere of and the prevailing prejudices at Scandinavian universities today, and it all sounded pretty depressing. The course that he described was intended to be adaptable to students from various disciplines, which apparently meant that the medical students would get medical examples, the social scientists exercises from their field, etc. (I was surprised at the ease with which he referred to "social scientists": are there any?). It was made quite clear that, rather than giving definitions "students would be required to recognize a card punch when they were shown a photograph of it". It left me wondering where the "University Level" came in. In his last talk I remember him pointing out the danger when the authority of the university was misused to back opinions favoured by the labour unions —i.e. backed for that very reason—. I could not agree more; if it happens, I expect the authority of the university to fade rather rapidly. (It seems to be doing so already.)

Clark (Washington University) gave three talks: The Basis of Present Computer Design, Alternative Computing Models, and Developments and Speculations. (His last one was the only talk I missed, so I have really behaved myself quite well!) From the first two I picked up nothing. The volume of his voice was terribly low, his diction made him difficult to understand and, besides that, he made the impression of having given up hope before he started to cross the gap between his hardware interests and his (mainly) software-oriented audience. Those who attended his third talk said later to me that it was much better than his first two ones. During the closing dinner on Thursday evening I had the pleasure of sitting next to him, and I enjoyed his then interesting company very much —to the extent that I have no memory at all of what we have eaten!   .

Ms. NN_5 (Watson Research Center) was the obligatory IBM-speaker (or should I say "speakster" or "speak-person" or "voice"?) with three talks on "The Future of Programming for Non-Programmers". She was terrible; her misuse of English really drove me up the wall. One of my colleagues tried to survive her torrent of nonsense by counting noisewords, such as "simply, sort of, kind of, you know, really, I mean, more or less, OK, that is to say, in some sense, in fact, first of all", and gave up after a total of 180 in 27 minutes. It was impossible to filter them out. But even apart from the noisewords, her language was abominable, even on her prepared transparencies. Of course she used "to execute" —with the subject "program"— as an intransitive verb, she talked about "implementing answers", wrote about "objects" which in her explanation were "concepts" etc., and was able to state that something —obviously I have forgotten, what!— was "simply a little bit crucial". My impression is that IBM would love to sell a great number of computer-driven colour TV-screens, and that a number of AI techniques will be used to keep the electrons busy. The need for elaborate man/machine interaction can certainly be enhanced by designing more incomprehensible systems.

Holt (Massachusetts Computer Associates) gave three talks on "Formal Methods in Systems Analysis" (title to be confirmed). On Wednesday afternoon, during the "excursion", he talked to a small group of people at the university. (Because I had been writing that afternoon, I missed it but for the last 25 minutes.) He showed some very nice examples of the relevance of Petri-nets, for instance for the study of the possible behaviour of a consumer and a producer, coupled by alternatively used buffers. And he was very eloquent in arguing that it is a mistake to think that just "bare facts" can be recorded. He is very clearly —and, I think, with great justification— convinced of the nearly all-pervading "relevance" of his considerations, by the time that he then chooses subjects that any course in computing science should contain, I am no longer with him. Should the curriculum contain as a subject "History and structure of the computer industry?". He thinks so. Finally I am grateful to him for having drawn my attention to "the tracking problem". Someone who extracts —or: constructs— such a beautiful example must have thought deeply. (In Holt's case it was interesting to observe the great variety in reactions that he evoked from different members of his audience!)

By far the most gifted speaker was F.J.M. Laver, C.B.E., a retired civil servant (from the post office) who gave two brilliant talks on "Informatics and Employment" and "Computation and Democracy". It was an absolute delight to listen to him. Light-footed and serious simultaneously, he was the symposium's subject "Computers and the educated individual" become flesh! I shall not try to paraphrase what he said, as it is totally impossible for me to do justice to his performance. I wish that *we* would have more civil servants of that sort!

There were three one-hour discussions. The first one did not really get moving. The second one, with the specific topic "What to Include in Courses", was not very exciting either, partly because curricula discussions are always depressing, but probably more because its chairman NN_4 had already made up his mind many years ago. The last discussion, on Friday afternoon, was a little bit more lively. On Ewan Page's request to stir up matters a little bit I opened it with EWD512, which I had been writing on Wednesday afternoon, when I learned that Ewan would like me to present some views.

At various occasions, but particularly during that last discussion, I was reminded of a recent remark by Tony Hoare, that the main difference between the pure scientist and the business manager is that the pure scientist has the duty to strive after perfection, while the business manager must make the best choice between the bad and the worse. And, seeing my English University Colleagues, I can only conclude that in England higher education has become big business... Their problem seems no longer to be what insights to create that should be taught if teaching is to be a worthwhile activity at all; their main problem seems to be which forms of coloured water can be poured into a glass as if it were wine. And after forgetting for reasons of convenience that this can never be done without faking, the professors start discussing in which semester it should be done, and by whom... Reminding them of their obligations towards perfection is an act of indecency. Depending on my mood I think all this saddening or alarming. (It was only this morning that I realized that with one or two exceptions, I do not know what these professors of computing science are *doing*! No one talked to me about his work; dwindling travel budgets was a more common subject.)

The willingness to accept what is known to be wrong as if it were right was displayed very explicitly by NN_4, who, as said, seems to have made up his mind many years ago. Like so many others, he expressed programmer productivity in terms of "number of lines of code produced". During the discussion I pointed out that a programmer should produce solutions, and that, therefore, we should not talk about the number of lines of code produced, but the number of lines of code used, and that this number ought to be booked on the other side of the ledger. His answer was "Well, I know that it is inadequate, but it is the only thing we can measure.". As if this undeniable fact also determines the side of the ledger.... .

On Friday afternoon we flew back to Amsterdam; again British Caledonian did so with a delay of fifteen minutes. This time, but we shall not blame British Caledonian for it, the flight was bumpy. I made the trip in the company of my Utrecht colleague van der Sluis, with whom I talked about a few beautiful proofs and who told me something about the level of the discussions between representatives of the Dutch universities and our Ministry of Education. It is something like "If you believe only half of what I am saying, I am, therefore, entitled to lie twice as much.".

At eight o'clock it was announced that the Amsterdam-Eindhoven flight was canceled due to a thunderstorm near Eindhoven, and it was only late that evening when I came home. Saturday morning, while I was having a bath, we had a tornado, and I knew that the summer was no more.

Nuenen, 13th September 1975   PROF. DR. EDSGER W. DIJKSTRA
                                                     Burroughs Research Fellow

PS. After I had introduced the msi —milli-split-infinitive— as the practical unit of linguistic irritation, Brian Randell threatened to name the unit of "grammatical pedantry" after me; I took it as a compliment!

EWD525

On a Warning from E.A. Hauck

During my visit to Mission Viejo, last April, Erv Hauck made the passing remark that he did not believe that error recovery could compensate effectively for the ill effects of a basically unreliable storage technique. Intuitively I was perfectly willing to share that belief; this note reports on my efforts to justify it and to find the arguments that would change it into my considered opinion.

In the following I consider words of a length of n stored bits; with $p0$, $p1$, $p2$, etc. I shall denote the probability of no error, a one-bit error, a two-bit error, etc. If bit-errors are independent events occurring for each bit with a probability p —we shall call this "Assumption A"— we have

$$p0 = (1 - p)^n, \; p1 = np(1 - p)^{n-1},$$
$$p2 = n(n - 1)p^2(1 - p)^{n-2}/2, \text{ etc.;}$$

for large n and small p, these values are reasonably well approximated by

$$p0 = 1 - p1, \; p1 = np, \; p2 = p1^2/2, \; p3 = p1^3/6, \text{ etc.}$$

System 1, Without Rejected Configurations

To start with we consider a code that only corrects one-bit errors. (Such codes exist, e.g. for $n = 3$: "zero" = 000 and "one" = 111; then 001, 010, and 100 will be interpreted as "zero", and 110, 101, and 011 will be interpreted as "one".) With a memory with a microsecond cycle time and $p1 = 10^{-6}$, a one--bit error will be successfully corrected once every second, and under Assumption A an undetected error will occur once every 2,000,000

169

sec = 23 days. This may seem OK for the optimist, but it is not, on account of the absence of rejected configurations. Suppose that, as a result of a drifting powersupply, say, it gets worse and we go up to $p1 = 10^{-5}$: a one-bit error will be corrected every 100 msec, an undetected error occurs every 20,000 sec = 5 hours, 30 minutes; when $p1 = 10^{-3}$, an undetected error will occur every 2 seconds! The absence of rejected configurations means that we are not warned about this deterioration and the resulting memory is something one cannot rely upon.

System 2, with Rejected Configurations

We now consider a code that corrects one-bit errors, and detects two-bit errors. (Such codes also exist, e.g. for $n = 4$: "zero" = 0000 and "one" = 1111; any configuration with two ones and two zeros will be rejected, such as 0110.) With the same microsecond cycle time and $p1 = 10^{-6}$, we have a one-bit error successfully corrected every second, under Assumption A a detected error every 23 days, and an undetected error once every 200,000 years. That seems safe, since a slowly increasing value of p, due to some technical degradation, may be expected to give the alarm of a two-bit error long before an undetected error has occurred. But it is, alas, absolutely unsafe, because, in many —and in a sense: in all— technologies, Assumption A is not justified: the storing and reading of n bits are not technically independent. We therefore consider for the sake of simplicity the other extreme —Assumption B— "with a probability p the reading of a word will deliver n random bits".

Exploring Assumption B

System 1 could have been improved by counting the number of corrections: under Assumption A a correction once every second would imply that the memory is not in too bad a condition (at least, if we think an error every 23 days acceptable — I don't actually, but that is now beside the point). Under Assumption B (because a random sequence is nearly sure to be interpreted as a one-bit error) the machine will perform a one-bit correction once every second, but whenever it does so, it is an erroneous correction: de facto the memory can be expected to make a fatal error once every second.

In order to estimate how System 2 would perform under Assumption B we must estimate how large the probability is that a random sequence will be rejected. If each two-bit error is to be detected, any two correct codes must differ in at least 4 bit positions. For $n = 2^m$, the exact solutions are known: there are then 2^{n-m-1} different codes. As each code has $2^m + 1$

acceptable representations (the $n = 2^m$ representations formed by changing one bit + the original code), the number of acceptable representations is $2^{n-m-1}(2^m + 1) = 2^{(n-1)}(1 + 2^{-m})$, i.e. slightly more than half of the 2^n possible bit sequences. As a consequence slightly less than half of them will be rejected.

From this we must conclude that —regardless of the value of p— when we start the machine, in 50 percent of the cases an undetected memory error has occurred before a memory error is detected. I cannot regard this as attractive either! (We could live with it if p were very small, i.e. the memory was highly reliable, but that was not the case we were considering!)

Assumption B —all bits random— is, of course, a severe form of malfunctioning. But we don't get any solace from that; instead of random values for $n = 2^m$ bits, we arrive at the same probability for rejection when choosing only $m + 1$ bits randomly, and accepting the remaining $n - m - 1$ bits as read from memory.

The moral of the story is, that Hauck's warning is not to be ignored!

*   *
*

The reason that my attention returned to Hauck's warning and that I tried to find its justification was that I was (re)considering the relative merits of neutral, local redundancy —such as parity checks and their embellishments— versus tailored, global redundancy, when our aim is to reduce drastically the probability that a wrong result will be mistaken for a correct one. Local error correction is in this respect harmful as soon as errors graver than those the detection mechanism can cope with can occur as well. As the correction mechanism for single bit errors has enlarged the collection of acceptable representations, the probability that the computation proceeds with erroneous values increases with the length of the computation. But that is another story.

Nuenen, 29th October 1975   PROF. DR. EDSGER W. DIJKSTRA
                                             Burroughs Research Fellow

EWD528
More on Hauck's Warning

In EWD525 "On a warning from E.A. Hauck" I mentioned without proof that with $n = 2^m$ bits 2^{n-m-1} different messages exist —I called them "codes", but that is an unusual terminology for which I apologize— , such that any two different messages differ in at least four bit positions, thus allowing correction of one-bit errors and detection of two-bit errors. Since then I have been shown a proof of that theorem; I report that proof because it is so nice, and because it gives some further insights.

For the sake of brevity I shall demonstrate the theorem for $16 = 2^4$ bits (in a way that is readily generalized for other values of m). We consider 16 bits numbered from 0 through 15, writing their index in binary:

$$d_{0000}, d_{0001}, d_{0010}, d_{0011}, \ldots, d_{1111}.$$

With "$xxx1$" we denote the set of odd indices, with "$xx1x$" the set $\{0010, 0011, 0110, 0111, 1010, 1011, 1110, 1111\}$, in general the set obtained by all possible substitutions of a 0 or a 1 at a place marked "x", and define $h0 = parity(d_{xxx1})$, $h1 = parity(d_{xx1x})$, $h2 = parity(d_{x1xx})$, $h3 = parity(d_{1xxx})$ where the function "$parity$" is $= 0$ if among the (8) bits with an index from the indicated set, the number of 1's is even, and $= 1$ if it is odd. Further we introduce $h = parity(d_{xxxx})$, which is just the sum of all the 16 bits modulo 2.

The 2^{11} correct messages are then characterized by the equations

$$h0 = h1 = h2 = h3 = h = 0.$$

NOTE. The above equations have indeed 2^{11} different solutions: the 11 bits d_3, d_5, d_6, d_7, d_9, d_{10}, d_{11}, d_{12}, d_{13}, d_{14}, and d_{15} can be chosen freely, we then solve $h0$ for d_1, $h1$ for d_2, $h2$ for d_4, and $h3$ for d_8, and finally h for d_0. (End of note.)

172

We now denote by "a" the binary number formed by "$h3\ h2\ h1\ h0$" and observe:

(0) for each correct message we have

   $h = 0, a = 0$

(1) for a one-bit error at bit position i we have

   $h = 1, a = i$

(2) for a two-bit error at bit positions i and j

   $h = 0, a =$ the bit-wise sum of i and j

   (because $i \neq j$, we conclude that $a \neq 0$, thereby distinguishing this case from a correct message)

(3) for a three-bit error at positions $i, j,$ and k

   $h = 1, a =$ the bit-wise sum of $i, j,$ and k.

(4) for a four-bit error at positions $i, j, k,$ and l

   $h = 0, a =$ the bit-wise sum of $i, j, k,$ and l.

etc.

Under the assumption that one- and two-bit errors are the *only* errors that can occur, the rules are

$h = 0$ and $a = 0$:   accept the bit sequence as given
$h = 1$:   invert bit d_a
$h = 0$ and $a \neq 0$:   alarm, as two-bit error has been detected.

From the above, however, we see that all errors in $3, 5, 7, \ldots$ bits will then erroneously be interpreted as one-bit errors, i.e. in those cases our error correction indeed increases the probability of a wrong result being produced as if it were a correct one. The above gives a clear demonstration of the possible "harmfulness" of error correction alluded to in EWD525's last paragraph. Hence this note.

Nuenen, Plataanstraat 5   PROF. DR. EDSGER. W. DIJKSTRA
                                            Burroughs Research Fellow

EWD538
A Collection of Beautiful Proofs

This chapter contains a compilation of beautiful proofs, proofs of which I expect that all mathematicians will agree that they are beautiful. The purpose of this compilation is to collect the material that may enable us to come to grips with the main qualities that together constitute "mathematical elegance". Further analysis and comparisons of these gems will be postponed until the collection is thought to be large enough. In order to avoid too much of a personal bias (and, also, to build up a larger collection than I could think of myself) I have asked others for their contribution to the collection. The only constraint was that the proof could be appreciated by the "generally educated"; all contributions that required specialized mathematical knowledge had, alas, to be rejected.

1. A Classical Example

In the late 18th century a German schoolmaster gave —with the intention of keeping his pupils busy for another hour— the task to sum one hundred terms of an arithmetic progression to a class of little boys who, of course, had never heard of arithmetic progressions. The youngest pupil, however, wrote down the answer instantaneously and waited gloriously, with his arms folded, for the next hour while his classmates toiled: at the end it turned out that little Johann Friederich Carl Gauss had been the only one to hand in the correct answer. Young Gauss had seen instantaneously how to sum such a series analytically: the sum equals the number of terms multiplied by the average of the first and the last term. (To quote E.T. Bell: "The problem was of the following sort, $81297 + 81495 + 81693 + \cdots + 100899$, where the step from one number to the next is the same all along (here 198), and a given number of terms (here 100) are to be added.")

In two respects this is a classical example: firstly young Gauss produced his answer about a thousand times as fast as his classmates, secondly he was the only one to produce the correct answer. So much for the effective ordering of one's thoughts!

2. The Pythagorean Theorem, Proof I

When I was twelve years old, I learned the following proof, in which a square with sides $a + b$ is considered in two different ways.

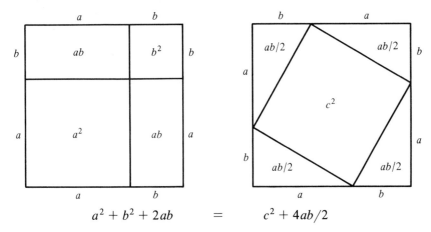

$$a^2 + b^2 + 2ab \qquad = \qquad c^2 + 4ab/2$$

The two expressions are different expressions for the same area: they are therefore equal. Next we observe $2ab = 4ab/2$ and by subtraction we find $a^2 + b^2 = c^2$. A beautiful proof in the good old Greek tradition that fascinated me when it was shown to me, and satisfied me for more than 30 years.

3. The Pythagorean Theorem, Proof II

The following proof was shown to me a few years ago. The areas of similar figures have the same relation as the squares of corresponding lines; for three similar figures with areas A, B, and C, respectively, and corresponding lines a, b, and c, respectively, any homogeneous linear relation satisfied by A, B, and C is, therefore, also satisfied by a^2, b^2, and c^2, and vice versa. In particular we know that $A + B = C$ implies $a^2 + b^2 = c^2$.

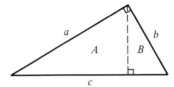

Here we have three similar triangles with a, b, and c, respectively, as their hypotenuse; the sum of the areas of the first two equals the area of the third triangle, i.e. $A + B = C$, hence $a^2 + b^2 = c^2$.

4.   The Theorem of Pompeiu

For a triangle ABC of which at least two sides have different lengths, we can choose a point P such that the lengths AP, BP, and CP are such that no triangle can be formed from those three pieces.

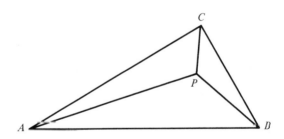

In any triangle, each side must be smaller than the sum of the two others. But, if $AC > BC$, we can choose P so close to C, that $AP > BP + CP$; hence they can not be the lengths of the sides of a triangle.

This observation led the Rumanian mathematician Pompeiu to the conjecture that, conversely, for an equilateral triangle ABC no such point exists, i.e. that for every point P the lengths AP, BP, and CP satisfy the triangular inequalities. He gave a proof, which —I am told— was very ugly. The following beautiful proof is due to G.R. Veldkamp; it gives a constructive existence proof of such a triangle with sides equal to AP, BP, and CP, respectively.

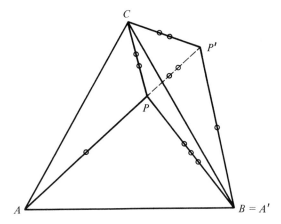

We rotate triangle CAP around point C over 60 degrees, so that A' coincides with B and P gives rise to its corresponding point P'. The process of rotation implies that $AP = BP'$ and $CP = CP'$. But now triangle PCP' is an isosceles triangle with, at point C, a top of 60 degrees. Hence it is equilateral, and we conclude that $CP = PP'$. Triangle PBP' has three sides of the required lengths and the Theorem of Pompeiu has been proved.

5. Euclid's Theorem on Primes

Denoting the integer numbers ≥ 2 by the term "multiples", we can define the primes as those multiples that cannot be written as the product of two multiples. From this definition it follows immediately that for each multiple there exists at least one prime dividing that multiple.

Let P be a prime; define the multiple Q as the product of all primes $\leq P$, increased by 1. The multiple Q has been constructed in such a way, that none of the primes $\leq P$ divides Q; the prime dividing Q must, therefore, be $> P$. Hence there is no largest prime number.

NOTE. It is not unusual that, after the construction of Q, the proof considers the two cases "Q is a prime" and "Q is not a prime" separately. The above proof shows that this case analysis is superfluous; the case analysis has probably been induced by the linguistic distinction between singular and plural forms. (End of note.)

6.   Euclid's Theorem on the Base Angles of an Isosceles Triangle

Using the theorem that any two triangles that have two sides and the included angle equal to two sides and the included angle of the other are congruent, it should be proved that the base angles of an isosceles triangle are equal, more precisely, that from $AC = BC$ follows the equality of angles A and B.

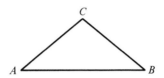

Because $AC = BC$, we have also $CB = CA$; angle C is equal to itself and the theorem allows us to conclude that the triangles ACB and BCA are congruent. These two triangles have angles A and B as corresponding parts, hence they are equal.

NOTE. It is not necessary —as Euclid seems to have done— to bisect angle C and then to use the theorem to show that the original triangle is cut into two congruent parts. (End of note.)

7.   A Covering Problem

Given the figure as shown below that could be covered by 138 squares, and 69 dominoes of two squares each —one such domino is shown below—

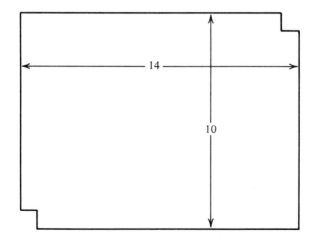

domino

the question to be answered is: can the figure be covered by the 69 dominoes? The answer is negative, and the argument is as follows.

Consider the 10 * 14 rectangle before the two opposite squares have been removed, and colour its squares alternatingly black and white as with a chess board: the rectangle then shows 70 white squares and 70 black ones. The two squares to be removed have, however, the same colour, and our figure, therefore, has 70 squares of the one colour and 68 squares of the other colour. Each domino covers one white and one black square; together the dominoes cover, no matter how they are placed, 69 black and 69 white squares. As a result they cannot cover the given figure.

8.   The Harmonic Series Diverges

Consider

$$S_n = 1/1 + 1/2 + 1/3 + 1/4 + 1/5 + 1/6 + 1/7$$
$$+ 1/8 + \cdots + 1/n.$$

It has to be shown that, by choosing n sufficiently large, we can achieve $S_n > M$ for arbitrarily large value M; in other words we have to show that the sequence $S_1, S_2, S_3, \ldots$ is unbounded. We observe that

$$S_2 - S_1 = 1/2$$
$$S_4 - S_2 = 1/3 + 1/4 > 1/4 + 1/4 = 1/2$$
$$S_8 - S_4 = 1/5 + 1/6 + 1/7 + 1/8 > 1/8 + 1/8 + 1/8 + 1/8$$
$$= 1/2 \qquad\qquad\qquad\qquad etc.$$

In other words: starting with $n = 1$, S_n is increased by at least $1/2$ each time n is doubled.

9.   The Eigenvalues of a Hermitean Matrix Are Real

A Hermitean matrix is the generalization of a real, symmetric matrix; its transpose equals its complex conjugate

$$A^T = A^* \qquad . \tag{1}$$

For a given matrix A, *lambda* is an eigenvalue if and only if the equation

$$A.x = lambda.x \tag{2}$$

has a non-null vector x as solution.

Taking the transpose of both sides of (2) we get

$$x^T . A^T = lambda . x^T$$

and then post-multiplying both sides by $x*$ we get

$$x^T . A^T . x* = lambda . x^T . x* \qquad . \tag{3}$$

Taking the complex conjugate of both sides of (2) we get

$$A* . x* = lambda* . x*$$

and then pre-multiplying both sides by x^T we get

$$x^T . A* . x* = lambda* . x^T . x* \qquad . \tag{4}$$

On account of (1) we conclude that (3) and (4) have equal left-hand sides, and hence

$$0 = (lambda - lambda*) . x^T . x* \qquad .$$

Because x is a non-null vector and $x^T . x*$ is a sum of absolute values, we conclude that $x^T . x* > 0$, and hence

$$lambda = lambda* \qquad . \qquad \text{Q.E.D.}$$

10.   The Cauchy-Schwarz Inequality

Let $a_1, \ldots, a_n$ and $b_1, \ldots, b_n$ be $2n$ real numbers. Then the following inequality holds:

$$(a_1 b_1 + \cdots + a_n b_n)^2 \leqslant (a_1^2 + \cdots + a_n^2)(b_1^2 + \cdots + b_n^2) \qquad .$$

Consider the following quadratic form $Q(x)$ in x, defined by

$$Q(x) = (a_1 + b_1 x)^2 + \cdots + (a_n + b_n x)^2 \qquad .$$

Because, for real x, $Q(x)$ is defined as the sum of the squares of n real numbers, for real x the inequality $Q(x) \geqslant 0$ must hold. In other words, the equation $Q(x) = 0$ has at most one real root, and its discriminant is $\leqslant 0$. Collecting powers of x in the definition of $Q(x)$ we find:

$$Q(x) = (a_1^2 + \cdots + a_n^2) + 2(a_1 b_1 + \cdots + a_n b_n) . x$$
$$+ (b_1^2 + \cdots + b_n^2) . x^2$$

with the discriminant

$$(a_1 b_1 + \cdots + a_n b_n)^2 - (a_1^2 + \cdots + a_n^2)(b_1^2 + \cdots + b_n^2) \qquad .$$

The conclusion that this discriminant is nonpositive proves our inequality.

11. Reconstructing an Odd Polygon from the Midpoints of Its Sides

We shall show the construction for poly = 5.

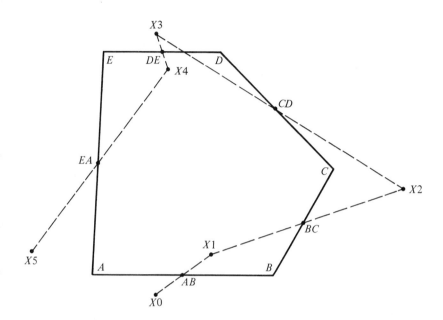

For the pentagon *ABCDE*, the points marked *AB, BC, CD, DE,* and *EA* respectively are the midpoints of its successive sides. Given the positions of those five midpoints, it is requested to reconstruct the original pentagon *ABCDE*.

Consider what happens when we subject a plane to five successive rotations of 180 degrees each with *AB, BC, CD, DE,* and *EA* as the successive centres of rotation. The point that originally coincided with *A* coincides with *B* after the first rotation, with *C* after the second rotation, etc. and coincides again with *A* after the fifth and last rotation. Because the pentagon has an odd number of sides, the total transformation of that plane is therefore a rotation of 180 degrees with *A* as its centre of rotation.

We now trace a point in the rotated plane that originally coincides with an arbitrary point *X*0. Rotating it around *AB* gives us its position *X*1 after the first rotation, rotating that around *BC* gives us its position *X*2 after the second rotation, etc. until we have constructed its final position *X*5. As that could also have been reached by rotating *X*0 over 180 degrees around the —still unknown— point *A*, we conclude that *A* is the midpoint of the line from *X*0 to *X*5! The positions of the other four vertices *B, C, D,* and *E* now follow trivially.

12.   The Number of Factors p (for p prime) in $n!$

Let n be a natural number, let p be a prime number, and let $s(n, p)$ denote the sum of the digits of the representation of n in the number system with radix p. Then the number of factors p in $n!$ equals

$$\frac{n - s(n, p)}{p - 1} . \tag{1}$$

Expression (1) is clearly correct for $n = 1$. Its general validity is proved by mathematical induction. Suppose that $n + 1$ has k factors p; the transition from $n!$ to $(n + 1)!$ then increases that number of factors p by k. But replacing n by $n + 1$ also increases (1) by k, because when 1 is added to n, the carry is propagated over k digits $= p - 1$, which all turn into zero.

13.   Frank Morley's Theorem

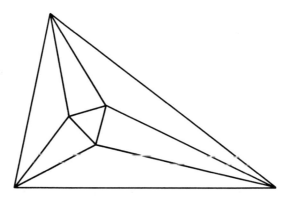

In 1904 Frank Morley discovered the following theorem —see previous figure— :

The adjacent pairs of the trisectors of the angles of a triangle always meet at the vertices of an equilateral triangle.

The shortest proof I know for this theorem proves, in fact, a stronger theorem, which also determines the orientation of that equilateral triangle. We start in our proof not with the arbitrary triangle, but with the equilateral one. Choose the three positive angles α, β, and γ such that $\alpha + \beta + \gamma = 60°$. Draw an equilateral triangle XYZ and construct the triangles AXY and

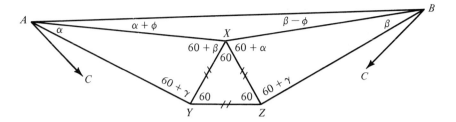

BXZ with the angles as indicated in the above picture. Because $\angle AXB = 180° - (\alpha + \beta)$, it follows that if $\angle BAX = \alpha + \varphi$, $\angle ABX = \beta - \varphi$. Using the rule of sines three times (in triangles *AXB*, *BXZ*, and *AXY*), we deduce

$$\frac{\sin(\alpha + \varphi)}{\sin(\beta - \varphi)} = \frac{BX}{AX} = \frac{XZ.\sin(60° + \gamma)/\sin(\beta)}{XY.\sin(60° + \gamma)/\sin(\alpha)} = \frac{\sin(\alpha)}{\sin(\beta)}.$$

Because in the range considered the left-hand side of this equation is a monotonically increasing function of φ, we conclude that $\varphi = 0$ is, in this range, its only root. Completing the picture and repeating the argument twice we conclude that the angles at *A*, *B*, and *C* are trisected, and thus Morley's Theorem is proved without the aid of any additional lines.

(To be continued in a later report.)

EWD539
Mathematics Inc., a Private Letter from Its Chairman

Dear...,

Yes, indeed, it has been a hectic year! Thank you for your kind feelings. As a matter of fact it started already around Xmas last year, when the rumour reached us that the International Research Development Corporation IRDC was trying to penetrate our market! IRDC is represented by Obfuscate et al., that old clannish solicitors firm in Oldcastle-upon-Time, which —as luck would have it!— employs a former classmate of mine. I wrote him a letter —full of sugar, you may be sure!— as if I were appealing to him for legal advice. It all worked out beautifully, he even sent us a draft contract, thus providing us with all the information we wanted to have! It was all most reassuring: IRDC is so firmly entangled in legal complications that they are no longer a serious threat. Our monopoly is safe — and in case of problems, we have arranged a secret affair between the nightporter of the Hosanna Building and the second daughter from old Obfuscate's first marriage, so blackmail is always there as emergency exit.

The whole affair had one nasty consequence: in our moment of panic we felt that we had to *do* something, and our Proof of the Riemann Hypothesis has been brought out into the field, contrary to the advice of our marketing manager who felt that it still required too much maintenance. And right he was: we can —and do!— burn our stove with the incoming trouble reports! At the end of March we transferred fifty mathematicians from Production to Field Support, thus solving two problems at once.

Business being what it was, something had to be done about production, for our stock of unsold theorems was growing beyond the acceptable limits. I have always argued that we should have a reasonable amount of spare theorems in stock, but in March they already occupied nearly two full floors

184

of the Hosanna Building! Besides the transfer of the fifty mathematicians
—we have, of course, selected the fifty most productive ones— we have
returned to our old method of productivity measuring: since February 1974
we measured mathematician productivity by the number of new results
obtained per month; we are now back on the more realistic and, after all,
also more objective technique of counting the number of lines of proof
produced per week. Thanks to those two measures, the stack of unsold
theorems, I am happy to say, is slowly shrinking back to normal size.

But for a few little, specialized firms (one in finite geometry and another
one in combinatorial logic), Mathematics Inc. has now full control of the
mathematical market, a circumstance that is certain to create both political
and economic problems. It is not yet an open battle, but the first symptoms
of revolt against our dominance becomes visible for the discerning eye.

For the time being we have nothing to fear, for our greatest allies are and
remain the universities, their departments of mathematics, I mean. They
should fight us to death, because the more we proceed, the more obsolete
they become, and in the end they will be abolished as superfluous. But the
technique is so simple! One just sponsors a conference that one calls a
"symposium" with only invited university professors as participants. One
chooses a nice subject like "The Impact of Mathematics on Society in the
Eighties" or "The Role of Mathematical Education in Preparing for the
Future" or any other nil-topic. They are so flattered, they come in as an
eager flock, proudly carrying their badges home when it is all over. It is
pathetic! But also absolutely effective! Did you know that our Differentiation Kit is now used at 378 universities, all over the world? All their alumni
will have to subscribe to our "Journal of Kit Differentiation" for the rest of
their lives, if they want to remain up to date. The whole movement has now
such an impetus that it proceeds without us pushing it anymore; the French
have already founded a separate Society for Theoretical Kit Differentiation.
It is the same story with our Linear Algebra Kit, our Integration Kit, and
our Statistics Kit. It fully absorbs and paralyzes them, leaving the field open
for us. Our only obligation is to modify the Kits regularly, that is, to change
their appearance slightly, just enough to suggest progress. And really, the
universities love them: they always fall for the newest model! They feel
themselves superior to the other backward universities and colleges that
have not yet converted to Kit Mathematics.

You know that the overall economic, political, and social aspects of this
whole venture interest me more than the purely technical issues. But the
latter are intriguing too! As soon as Mathematics Inc. grew beyond one
hundred employees —can you remember how long ago that was? it seems
ages... — it was clear that, no matter what we would tackle, the diversity of
our products and manufacturing techniques would create havoc from the
organizational point of view. As standardization of products is only possible
to a very limited extent —the market place somehow insists on variety— we
had to standardize our manufacturing techniques. And we are proud of our

IR System for Integrated Reasoning, and I think justly so. In the beginning the IR System was not too successful, because we needed a computer and chose the then fashionable 1033-alpha, a machine for which the MTBF transpired to be of the order of magnitude of twenty minutes. The IR System works much better since we have replaced it by the new model 1033-omega, for which via a switch on the console the parity check can be disabled. As soon as we had the new machine, IR made significant progress: the whole IR System now consists of the following languages:

ASL   Axiom Statement Language
LSL   Lemma Statement Language
TSL   Theorem Statement Language
PSL   Proof Statement Language
PVL   Proof Verification Language
PRL   Proof Refuting Language (our main debugging aid)
IL   Inference Language.

Their mutual relation is roughly as follows

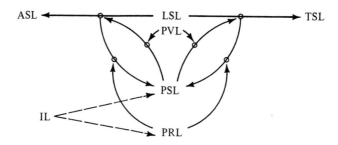

Legenda: arrows denote causal connection.

means that the vertical one controls the horizontal one.

Actually this is a slight simplification, because it refers only to the high-level languages PVL, PSL, and PRL, while we have the corresponding low-level languages pvl, psl, and prl as well: they are only needed when the IR-facilities need more efficient exploitation.

As you see immediately from the above diagram, ASL, LSL and TSL are purely syntactic languages without any semantic contents, PSL is a language with an ambiguous, nondeterministic syntax and only first-order semantics, while only PVL and PRL have second-order semantics. IL —although we call it Inference Language for the sake of homogeneity— is, of course, no language at all: it is no more than the specification of the interpretation that can supply quasi-semantics for ASL, LSL, and TSL.

It is amazing that people have never thought about the coupling of reasoning controlling activities, but once you have got the idea, it is clear that the above scheme provides all the facilities you may ever need. Our IR System —which, of course, is for internal use only— has been very successful. (I have heard rumours that the application of PRL to the Riemann Proof will require a 1033-omega-super, extended with a quadruple-length complex arithmetic unit. Some guys are so fanatic that they want to order one, but —thank goodness!— I hold the purse strings, and I think that I can convince them that also in this case we had better stick to the company policy —which, after all, has always been very successful— of leaving the last stage of quality control to those rare customers that think that they really need that extra quality.)

Needless to say, I consider the main benefits of the IR System to be psychological and sociological: the presence of the tool has effectuated more homogeneity in the company than regulations could ever have achieved. There was a time that our topologists could not communicate with the number theorists, they lived in different worlds, although they could work on the same floor! But the IR System provides a standard, common universe of discourse, and, again they understand each other. You can believe me or not, but the other day I saw one guy of the Riemann Group and another guy from the Four Colour Project exchange a few IL-cards! I cannot describe to you how happy that observation made me: at that moment I knew that I had founded a living company. Semper floreat et crescat!

Yours ever,

1st December 1975   EDSGER W. DIJKSTRA, Chairman
                                           Mathematics Inc.
                                           Hosanna Building

PS. SECRET! We are, of course, constantly trying to protect our company against the possible consequences of changing attitudes, and we are not blind to the current anti-intellectualistic undercurrents in our society that rouse popular feeling against Reason. We keenly observe the semi-mystic "back-to-nature" movements that want to do away with organization, with power, with shaving, bra's, and socks. They provide an alibi for the second rate college teacher preaching that "truth is dehumanized if it has to be proved" and "true truth is what one feels to be true" etc. In view of this quasi-religious revival, our third Assistant Vice-President is contemplating —I think that that is the right word for it— an Artificial Devotion Department. (Maybe it is only because his wife presently spends a lot of her time "reviving". Before the AD Department has materialized, she may have lost interest in revivals or he in her....) In the preparatory stage he has designed Canonical Forms for the Seven Capital Sins, and you should see them: they are absolute beauties! It looks very promising, and this could turn into a very interesting daughter of the company. (End of Secret.)

EWD554
A Personal Summary of the Gries–Owicki Theory

This is a very personal summary of the theory developed by Susan Speer Owicki under supervision of David Gries. I had a flu, and on its first day I just slept and shivered; later I passed the time in bed with trying to reconstruct what I had learned from reading in Susan Owicki's doctoral thesis. If the following fails to do justice to their work —someone has borrowed my copy of her thesis!— I am the only one to blame.

At one time, it was the function of our programs to instruct our machines, but times have changed: now it is more fruitful to consider it the purpose of our machines to execute our programs. The same shift of attention can be recognized in the more theoretical work concerned with the semantics of programming languages. At one time this was a very descriptive activity, trying to capture what happened in our machines during program execution. The result was a series of operational language definitions, in which the semantics of programming languages was given by an interpreter that under control of the program text changed the machine state over and over again. By means of "abstract programs" and equally "abstract states" people have tried to mold this approach into a viable tool, but it kept all the essential disadvantages of operational language definitions. Faced with a specific program they tell you no more than how to do a hand-simulation. Since Floyd, and later but more noticeably Hoare, we have been shown another approach, which seems more promising.

Here a program text is regarded as a mathematical object all by itself, which is postulated to establish a relation between two machine states. If we were very pure, we should call them, say, the "left-hand state" and the "right-hand state". The relation between the two states is implicitly given by a set of axioms and rules of inference that together delineate what, given a text, one can prove about that relation. Taken all by itself, this would be a very formal and rather sterile game, but it so happens that the axioms have been chosen very carefully, so carefully in fact, that when we identify the "left-hand state" with the initial state and the "right-hand state" with the final state of a computer (as can be recorded in its store) a started sequential computer can establish an instance of that relation (and can even do so without implicit backtracking).

In the preceding paragraph I have tried to capture the essence of this so-called "axiomatic method" as clearly as possible, because it has generated much misunderstanding and discussion (which has generated more heat than light). Even as much as five years after its introduction, the axiomatic method has been blamed for not demonstrating that it captured correctly the computational model that was supposed to underly it, "the computational model on which it was based". The axiomatic method is not "based" upon a computational model; the most we can say is that it has been inspired by a computational model. Once the axioms are chosen, it is the obligation of the implementation to provide a sufficiently truthful model. With purely sequential programs, this approach has been very successful; the Gries–Owicki Theory presents the first significant step towards applying similar techniques to concurrent processing as well.

Taken literally, the previous sentence makes no sense. From a very puristic point of view, neither Floyd nor Hoare (nor I in the early seventies) talked about "sequential programming" or "sequential programming languages". We talked about texts, and about proving things about them. The aspect of "being sequential" had absolutely no meaning on that level of discourse, it became only meaningful when we tried to visualize a computer establishing an instance of the relation, when we tried to visualize "a computation". And the axioms we considered were such that the only safe and realistic implementation of such a computing engine we could envisage was one in which the actions took place one after the other. Apart from that "implementation detail" the whole notion of sequentiality was not applicable in our level of discourse, in which we had abstracted quite rigorously from the class of computational histories.

From the same puristic point of view, the Gries–Owicki Theory does not deal at all with concurrent processing. It is again a formal system relating a pair of machine states to each other by means of a text. Only the proof rules —the axioms and the rules of inference— differ. It so happens that, when we would like to design a computing engine able to establish an instance of this relation, we suddenly see a straightforward way in which a number of processors could be engaged concurrently on that task. So we are not designing a "language for concurrent programming" or any similar misnomer; from our mathematical point of view it is a programming language as any other, with consequences and possibilities for the implementation that we should ignore at the current level of discourse.

A simple "sequential" program can be represented as

"$S0; S1; \ldots; Sn$"   .

When we wish to describe in more detail the kind of relations between initial and final state, e.g. we wish to establish a set of initial states corresponding to a final state satisfying the relation R, we can interlace our sequence of statements Si with a sequence of relations Pi:

$$\{P0\}S0; \{P1\}S1;\ldots; \{Pn\}Sn\{R\}$$

The axiomatic definition associates with each statement Si —assignment statements to start with— a so-called predicate transformer wp. If now we have for $0 \leqslant i < n$

$$Pi = wp(Si, Pi+1)$$
$$Pn = wp(Sn, R)$$

then for the whole program S we have $P0 = wp(S, R)$, and we interpret $P0$ as the weakest pre-condition for the initial state such that starting program S as a whole is certain to end up in a final state satisfying R.

This is because from given units Si —say, assignment statements— the semicolon describes how a new unit can be formed. In formula, the semantics of the semicolon is given by

$$wp(\text{``}S1; S2\text{''}, P) = wp(S1, wp(S2, P))$$

from which, for instance, follows that the semicolon is associative. If we wanted, for instance, to combine in program S the first two initial statements into a single unit —indicated by square brackets— we could indicate this as follows:

$$\text{``}\{P0\}[S0; S1]; \{P2\}S2;\ldots; \{Pn\}Sn\{R\}\text{''}$$

By combining $S0$ and $S1$ in the above way into a single unit, the relation $P1$ remains anonymous; implementation-wise it says that we prefer not to pay explicit attention to the "intermediate state" that will prevail after execution of $S0$ but before execution of $S1$. In the purely "sequential systems" we are familiar with, our freedom in combining units into larger ones, thereby eliminating the "internal predicates", is unrestricted: we are all the time free to choose to consider a composite object either as an unanalyzed whole or as something composed out of parts. In the Gries–Owicki Theory this freedom is restricted (thereby giving the implementation greater freedom, such as the introduction of concurrency).

We have shown on the previous page how the concatenation using the semicolon gives rise to internal predicates. So do the other sequencing techniques or "control structures" of "sequential programming", e.g.

$$\{P12\} \textbf{if} \ B1 \rightarrow \{P1\}S1$$
$$[] \ B2 \rightarrow \{P2\}S2$$
$$\textbf{fi} \ \{R12\} \quad .$$

Here the rules are that $P12$ should be the weakest predicate satisfying

$P12 \Rightarrow (B1 \text{ or } B2)$ (in order to avoid abortion)
$(P12 \text{ and } B1) \Rightarrow P1$
$(P12 \text{ and } B2) \Rightarrow P2$

where $P1$ and $P2$ are given by $P1 = wp(S1, R12)$ and $P2 = wp(S2, R12)$. Again we are free to "eliminate" predicates such as $P1$ or $P2$, for instance by replacing the second equation by

$(P12 \text{ and } B1) \Rightarrow wp(S1, R12)$.

In our program we could indicate that elimination of $P1$ for instance by

$\{P12\}$ **if** $[B1 \rightarrow S1]$

somehow suggesting that the whole first guarded command is to be regarded as a single unit. In "sequential programming" such freedom of combination, of elimination of predicates, is unrestricted.

The notation of the square brackets is unattractive if we want to indicate the elimination of the predicate following a repetitive construct. Moreover, the repetitive construct introduces the problem of termination. Provided

$(P12 \text{ and } B1) \Rightarrow wp(S1, P12)$
$(P12 \text{ and } B2) \Rightarrow wp(S2, P12)$

we can read and justify

$\{P12\}$ **do** $B1 \rightarrow S1$
      $\square$ $B2 \rightarrow S2$
      od $\{P12 \text{ and non } (B1 \text{ or } B2)\}$

as stating that the initial validity if $P12$ is sufficient to ensure the final validity of $(P12 \text{ and non } (B1 \text{ or } B2))$, provided that the repetitive construct terminates on this level. If the repetitive construct is followed by a next statement, we can again eliminate its post-condition by a straightforward proof that it implies the pre-condition for the next statement.

Certain predicates are never eliminated. We never eliminate the predicate describing the total pre-condition or the predicate describing the total post-condition. (In a sense they can never be regarded as the internal predicate of a composition.) Furthermore we shall never eliminate what could be described as "the post-condition of a guarded command set". If the guarded command set is the body of an alternative construct, this refers to the post-condition of the alternative construct; if the guarded command set is the body of a repetitive construct, this refers to the invariant relation. The reason for this restriction is the following: each assignment statement and each set of guards now has a unique preceding predicate, where with "preceding predicate" we mean the last preceding, non-eliminated predicate. For instance

$$\{P0\}\ S1;\ S2;$$
$$\{P1\}\ S3;\ \textbf{if}\ B4\ \rightarrow\ \{P2\}\ S4$$
$$\quad\quad \text{[} B5\ \rightarrow\ S5;\ S6$$
$$\quad\quad \textbf{fi};$$
$$\{P3\}\ S7;$$
$$\{P4\}\ \textbf{do}\ B8\ \rightarrow\ S8;\ \{P5\}S9\{P4\}$$
$$\quad\quad \text{[} B10\ \rightarrow\ S10\{P4\}$$
$$\quad\quad \textbf{od};\ S11\{R\}\quad .$$

Then we have:

P0 is the preceding predicate of S1 and S2;
P1 is the preceding predicate of S3, B4, B5, S5, and S6;
P2 is the preceding predicate of S4
P3 is the preceding predicate of S7
P4 is the preceding predicate of B8, S8, B10, S10, and S11
P5 is the preceding predicate of S5.

Besides non-abortion in the alternative construct and termination of the repetitive construct, we have to prove

$$P0 \Rightarrow wp(S1, wp(S2, P1))$$
$$P1 \Rightarrow wp(S3,(B4 \Rightarrow P2)\ \textbf{and}\ (B5 \Rightarrow wp(S5, wp(S6, P3))))$$
$$P2 \Rightarrow wp(S4, P3)$$
$$P3 \Rightarrow wp(S7, P4)$$
$$P4 \Rightarrow (B8 \Rightarrow wp(S8, P5))\ \textbf{and}\ (B10 \Rightarrow wp(S10, P4))\ \textbf{and}\ (\textbf{non}\ (B8\ \textbf{or}\ B10)$$
$$\quad \Rightarrow wp(S11, R))$$
$$P5 \Rightarrow wp(S9, P4)\quad .$$

Each of these six relations is an implication, in which the antecedent is an assertion and the consequent contains only other assertions, guards, and statements of which the antecedent is "the preceding predicate".

Suppose for a moment that, using other means, we have established that P0 is strong enough to guarantee proper termination as well. Starting the obvious sequential implementation in an initial state satisfying P0, a computation would ensue during which at the corresponding stages the machine would be in a state satisfying one of the Pi's, and finally the machine would end in a state satisfying R. What would we have to prove in addition if we would like to ensure, that at all those stages another predicate, Q say, would be true as well? This, of course, under the assumption that we would start the machine in an initial state also satisfying Q.

Well, in principle, we should replace in our six relations all the predicates Pi and R at all their occurrences by Pi **and** Q and R **and** Q respectively! The first line would become

$$P0\ \textbf{and}\ Q \Rightarrow wp(S1, wp(S2, P1\ \textbf{and}\ Q))\quad .$$

Its consequent reduces as follows

$$wp(S1, wp(S2, P1 \text{ and } Q)) = wp(S1, wp(S2, P1) \text{ and } wp(S2, Q))$$
$$= wp(S1, wp(S2, P1)) \text{ and } wp(S1, wp(S2, Q)).$$

Therefore, when the above six formulae —without the Q inserted— have been proved, our only *additional* proof obligation is

$$P0 \text{ and } Q \Rightarrow wp(S1, wp(S2, Q))   \quad \text{(and five similar ones)}   .$$

With respect to our original program we say that we have "proved the invariance of Q".

Consider now two programs, operating on the same variables. Suppose further, that with respect to each program we have proved the invariance of the assertions occurring in the other (or: occurring in the others, when we have three or more such programs). This is, of course, a very strong assumption. But if it is satisfied, we have proved something useful about the following nondeterministic implementation.

Let us start a machine in an initial state satisfying each program's initial assertion. We now allow execution of an arbitrary one of the programs to proceed until its next assertion. Firstly we have proved that this assertion will then hold, secondly we have proved that the initial assertion(s) of the other program(s) have not been disturbed. Then, again, an arbitrary program is allowed to proceed with its execution until the next assertion, etc. When all programs have finished, all final assertions will hold.

Mind you: we are not talking about concurrency yet. We are talking about a nondeterministic machine, which can take care of the progress of a bunch of sequential programs, and we have stated conditions under which we can certainly allow a certain degree of interleaved execution, viz. from assertion to assertion.

As the reader will have noticed, I have mentioned a few times "suppose that we have proved proper termination". I made that caveat, because we would like to apply our theory also to a bunch of programs with the property that for the individual programs proper termination cannot be proved. Termination of a repetitive construct in one program may depend on the execution of another program having reached a certain stage. This will certainly be the case when we implement synchronization constraints by means of a busy form of waiting. In such a case, we cannot even "prove" termination of the bunch of programs without further assumptions about the daemon that makes the choice how to interleave: the bunch would not terminate if every time the daemon selected the waiting process to perform the next inspection of the unchanged state of affairs! The fact that a proof of termination of the whole bunch may require assumptions about the friendliness of the daemon justifies postponement of that issue.

It is not only the repetitive construct for which the taming of the daemon can be an issue; the alternative construct might also call for a certain amount of friendliness of the daemon. It could for instance, be one of the daemon's restrictions that an alternative construct preceded immediately by its "preceding predicate" will never be selected for execution in those machine states where its selection for execution would lead to abortion of that program.

For the time being we assume that there is at least one sequence of choices by the daemon that will lead to proper termination of all the programs, and we assume the daemon to be friendly enough to choose such a sequence.

But even for that target, our formalism has to be changed: we have to replace the weakest pre-conditions $wp(S, P)$ which guarantee proper termination in a final state satisfying P by the so-called "weakest liberal pre-conditions" $wlp(S, P)$ guaranteeing that the mechanism S will *not* terminate in a state satisfying **non** P. (This is the transition from total correctness, where the production of the right result is guaranteed, to partial correctness, where only the production of a wrong result is excluded. C.A.R. Hoare took this step a long time ago, and apparently at that time without much hesitation; I don't like it too much and would not like to take it unless I felt forced to do so.)

*   *   *

The next step is to introduce the possibility of concurrent execution, but to do it in such a way that, firstly, it is easily implementable and that, secondly, no further nondeterminacy is introduced. For this purpose we divide the variables over various classes. On the one hand we have the *private variables*; private variables are always private to a specific program, viz. the *only* program that is allowed to refer to them. They are the local variables of the program to which they are private; the other programs cannot inspect their values, nor change them. On the other hand we have the so-called *common* or *shared variables*: they are the remaining variables, to which at least two processes refer. It is clear that all interaction between the different programs must take place via the shared variables.

Each program is executed from assertion to assertion; here we assume that evaluation of a guard from a guarded command set implies evaluation of *all* guards from that set. The step from each assertion to the (dynamically) next assertion —our considered grain of interleaving— we call "a unit of action". We now impose upon our units of action the constraint that they can be implemented with *at most one access to at most one shared variable*. With a memory switch that, in case of competition, orders the individual accesses to memory in some way or another, it is now clear that we can allow concurrent execution of as many units of action as we have still incompleted programs. The reason that we are allowed to do so is that, no matter how we mix them, there always exists an order in which the units of action, executed one at a time, would have established the same nett effect. Two units of action referring to two different common variables (or to no common variables at all) commute, and for two units of action referring to the same common variable we can take the order in which the switch has granted them access to that shared variable.

Our restriction regarding access to shared variables has severe consequences: the guards of a guarded command set may refer to at most one
shared variable. On the other hand, we now know that, with B a shared
variable

$\{P1\}$ **if** $B \rightarrow S1$
  $[]$ **non** $B \rightarrow S2$
  fi $\{P2\}$

will not lead to abortion. (Note that in the case of two successive inspections
of B it is hard to prevent that, when the first inspection has encountered the
value *false*, the next inspection may encounter the value *true*.) Note that, if
in the above example B is not a common variable (nor an expression
referring to one), the guards of the guarded command set do not refer to a
shared variable, in which case $S1$ may refer once to a common variable, and
$S2$ may refer once to a different common variable: we have two possible
units of action! For the time being, this is about the only thing I intend to
say about concurrency.

*   *   *

Consider now the two programs

$\{P0\}$ $in1 := true$; $\{Q0\}$ $in2 := true$;
$\{P1\}$ **do** $in2 \rightarrow \{P1\}$ $in1 := false$; $\{Q1\}$ **do** $in1 \rightarrow \{Q1\}$ $in2 := false$;
         $\{P2\}$ $in1 := true$ $\{P1\}$ $\{Q2\}$ $in2 := true$ $\{Q1\}$
  od;   **od**;
  $luck1 := true$; $luck2 := true$;
$\{P3\}$ critical section 1; $\{Q3\}$ critical section 2;
$\{P3\}$ $luck1, in1 := false, false$; $\{Q3\}$ $luck2, in2 := false, false$;
$\{P4\}$ noncritical section 1 $\{Q4\}$ noncritical section 2.

PROGRAM 1   PROGRAM 2

with $P0$: **non** $luck1$, we can prove

  $P1$:   **non** $luck1$ **and** $in1$
  $P2$:   **non** $luck1$ **and non** $in1$
  $P3$: $luck1$ **and** $in1$
  $P4$:   **non** $luck1$ **and non** $in1$

and similarly for the Q's in Program 2. Furthermore we observe that all the
Pi imply P: $luck1 \Rightarrow in1$, and, similarly, that all the Qi imply Q: $luck2 \Rightarrow in2$.
We can now replace all the original assertions Pi in Program 1 by Pi **and** Qj
for any j; the proofs remain valid, because Program 1 does not refer to the
variables mentioned in Qj. Similarly we can replace all the original forms of
Qi in the second program by Qi **and** Pj for any j: again the proofs remain
valid, because Program 2 does not refer to the variables mentioned in Pj.
Having thus proved that the assertions of each program are invariant with
respect to the other program, we can conclude the universal validity of P
and Q.

Finally we consider the relation R: **non**($luck1$ **and** $luck2$). This relation can also be added to all assertions; it is also everywhere valid. The critical assignment in Program 1 that could destroy its validity is, of course, "$luck1$ $:= true$", but it is safe because

$wp("luck1 := true", R) = $ **non** $luck2$,

a condition that is implied by Q **and non** $in2$. We interpret the universal validity of R as the guarantee of mutual exclusion in time of the two critical sections.

*   *   *

The classical use of critical sections has been the maintenance of an invariant relation

$IR(a, b, c)$

between a number of shared variables —here denoted by a, b, c— , where this invariance cannot be maintained by a single unit of action, as a result of which a modification of the variables a, b, and c always implies a temporary violation of $IR(a, b, c)$, followed by its restoration. With the aid of the additional variables we can replace it by a relation that is, indeed, universally valid, viz.:

$luck1$ **or** $luck2$ **or** $IR(a, b, c)$.

Under the assumption that the pieces of program denoted by "noncritical sections" do not refer to the shared variables a, b, and c —nor to the private variables "$luck$", of course— the proof that the noncritical sections leave this relation invariant is trivial. For the critical sections —the only pieces of program that are allowed to refer to a, b, and c— it suffices to give the invariance proof for each of the critical sections in isolation.

At the beginning of critical section 1 —i.e. immediately after the assignment "$luck1 := true$", we can assert

$luck1$ **and** $IR(a, b, c)$.   (1)

Internally, within the critical section 1, we can introduce, wherever $IR(a, b, c)$ is temporarily violated, assertions of the type

$luck1$ **and** $IR'(a, b, c, priv1)$ (2)

where with "$priv1$" we have denoted any other variables —besides $luck1$— that are *private to Program 1*. At the end of the critical section 1 —i.e. just before $luck1$ is reset to *false*— we must have again assertion (1). We assume a similar proof that critical section 2, considered in isolation, as a whole does not violate $IR(a, b, c)$.

The reason why these two separate proofs for the critical sections in isolation suffice is that assertions (1) and (2) are invariant with respect to Program 2 (and vice versa). The internal statements of critical section 2 cannot violate them, because their preceding predicates all contain the factor "*luck2*", and the universal validity of *R*:

non(*luck*1 **and** *luck*2)

ensures that the conjunction of these predicates and the assertions (1) and
(2) is *F*; because *false* implies everything, these proofs of invariance are
trivial. The statements in noncritical section 2 cannot violate them either,
because they don't refer to the variables occurring in (1) or (2).

NOTE. These proofs are so trivial that within critical sections the constraint
that "units of action" refer to at most one shared variable can be weakened.
Because, with a private variable "*register*",

register := *c*; {*register* = *c*}*c* := *register* + 1

gives rise to an internal assertion "*register* = *c*" which is trivially invariant,
it is tempting to consider then the alternative *c* := *c* + 1 as a unit of action.
Such shortcuts should only be introduced with great care. (End of note.)

*   *
*

Our solution for the mutual exclusion problem uses essentially two
shared variables *in*1 and *in*2. (They are really the only two variables that
matter: variables *luck*1 and *luck*2 are so-called "ghost variables" which have
only been introduced for the sake of being able to formulate what we mean
by "mutual exclusion" and of being able to formulate the proofs. In the
actual programs to be executed they —and all operations operating on them
— can be eliminated.) We also know that this solution is not acceptable
when we reject solutions with the danger of after-you-after-you blocking.
This danger is exorcized by Dekker's solution, which I give below in the
following form. The initial value of the shared integer "turn" should be
either 1 or 2. I only give Program 1; Program 2 can be obtained from it by
interchanging 1's and 2's.

```
{P0} in1 := true;
{P1} if in2 →{P2} if turn = 1 →skip {P3}
                 [] turn ≠ 1 →{P4} in1 := false;
                             {P5} do turn ≠ 1 → skip {P5} od;
                             {P6} in1 := true {P3}
               fi;
               {P3} do in2 → skip {P3} od
     [] non in2 → skip
     fi;
       luck1 := true;
{P7} critical section 1;
{P7} turn := 2;
{P7} luck1, in1 := false, false;
{P8} noncritical section 1
```

Studying this program in relative isolation, we derive, under the assumption

$P0$:	**non** $luck1$	further
$P1$:	**non** $luck1$ **and** $in1$	
$P2$:	$P1$	
$P3$:	**non** $luck1$ **and** $in1$ **and** $turn = 1$	
$P4$:	**non** $luck1$	
$P5$:	**non** $luck1$ **and non** $in1$	
$P6$:	**non** $luck1$ **and non** $in1$ **and** $turn = 1$	
$P7$:	$luck1$ **and** $in1$	
$P8$:	**non** $luck1$ **and non** $in1$	

Again the relation $luck1 \Rightarrow in1$ is implied by all of them, and together with Program 2 we can derive the universal validity of **non**($luck1$ **and** $luck2$) as before.

The difference between this program and the previous program is that we need only weaker assumptions about the daemon if we would like to be sure of termination of this program. With the previous program, the daemon could select an unbounded number of units of action from Program 1 and an unbounded number of units of action from Program 2, without ever one of the critical sections being selected. With our new programs this is no longer true.

Selection of an infinite number of units of action from program 1 implies —because there are only two loops in it, and from at least one an infinite number must be selected— the validity of

($P5$ **and** $turn \neq 1$) **or** ($P3$ **and** $in2$)

or

(**non** $in1$ **and** $turn \neq 1$) **or** ($in1$ **and** $in2$ **and** $turn = 1$)   .   (3)

(Note that the term "$turn = 1$" in the Pi is invariant with respect to Program 2.) For Program 2 we have the corresponding relation

(**non** $in2$ **and** $turn \neq 2$) **or** ($in1$ **and** $in2$ **and** $turn = 2$)   .   (4)

The conjunction of (3) and (4) reduces to

(**non** $in1$ **and non** $in2$ **and** $turn \neq 1$ **and** $turn \neq 2$)   .

And, indeed, when we start the two programs with, say, $turn = 3$, the infinite looping of both programs is quite easily realized. If, however, we start the two programs —and so we assume— with

$turn = 1$ **or** $turn = 2$ (5)

then it is easily seen that (5) is invariant with respect to both programs, therefore can be regarded as universally valid, and thus implying the falsity of the conjunction of (3) and (4). This falsity is usually taken as the proof of the absence of the danger of after-you-after-you blocking (and, a fortiori, the absence of the danger of deadlock).

The conclusion that the machine executing the programs' units of action in interleaved fashion will eventually terminate rests on the assumption that the daemon will not be so grossly unfair as to select always the next unit of action from the same program. From a formal point of view this is a most unattractive assumption.

It would introduce a mechanism of unbounded nondeterminacy, it would give us means for implementing

"set x to any positive integer"

without being able to give an upper bound for the final value of x. We could, for instance, replace in program 1 the statement **do** $in2 \to skip$ **od** by

$x := 1;$ **do** $in2 \to x := x + 1$ **od** .

The consequences of introducing unbounded nondeterminacy are sufficiently horrifying to reject the above approach.

Such a little loop with a skip as the repeatable statement is, of course, too indirect a way of indicating that, to all intents and purposes, this program should not continue. We supply it with a kind of "fake continuation". The only way of not making assumptions about the fairness of the daemon is to restrict it explicitly in its freedom. The alternative construct gives us a way out.

In normal sequential programming we have regarded an alternative construct with all its guards false as a reason for abortion. An equivalent rule for the implementation would be: postpone progress of this computation as long as all the guards are *false*. In a uniprogramming environment we have "once all *false*, always all *false*" and this second rule would be as good as abortion. In a multiprogramming environment it would mean for the daemon that, as suggested earlier, "an alternative construct preceded immediately by its "preceding predicate" will never be selected for execution in those machine states where its selection for execution would lead to abortion of that program". By replacing in the last program

do $turn \neq 1 \to skip$ **od**   by   **if** $turn = 1 \to skip$ **fi**

and

do $in2 \to skip$ **od**   by   **if non** $in2 \to skip$ **fi**

and postulating that the daemon will not select a unit of action that starts with an alternative construct with *false* guards only, we have eliminated *from this example* all unbounded repetitions. To what extent the ideal "no unbounded repetitions in the individual programs" can be achieved in general —possibly by allowing certain *special* units of action to refer to more than one shared variable— is a question to which I don't know the answer at the moment of writing.

Nuenen, 14th of March 1976   PROF. DR. EDSGER W. DIJKSTRA
Burroughs Research Fellow

EWD561
A "Non Trip Report" from E.W. Dijkstra

On my last visit to the U.S.A. I found that many regular readers of my trip reports have no picture at all of my daily life when I am *not* travelling. And, indeed, how should they without further information? This "non trip report" is written with the intention of redressing the balance.

Tuesday is my day at the Eindhoven University of Technology. It has by now a well-established pattern. In the morning I lecture for two hours and further take care of all "irregular" business (mail, receiving students, etc.). The afternoon is reserved for a four-hour discussion with a small group of young computing scientists on whatever subject is brought up.

Lecturing is great fun. Officially I give only two courses, an introduction to programming in the fall semester and a course on synchronization and communication in the spring semester, but successive years are never the same: the subject matter is so much alive that it is no problem at all to keep these lectures fresh. (I myself find them, as a matter of fact, often quite exciting!) It is a great help that only half of my audience, which is about 70 people, is formed by students that have to follow the course; the remaining ones come from other departments or from outside and, quite often, already have their degree: they come because they are interested, and that makes an inspiring audience!

The discussion in the afternoon —we are currently five; besides myself two from within and two from outside the University— takes place in my office at the University, and its topics cover in principle a very wide range. It may be an open question that I raised that morning at my lecture, the thesis topic of one of the participants, something that one of us has read somewhere and seemed important to him, something one of us has done, or the difficulties he is encountering while trying to do so. (Most of the technical EWD's have been discussed at some stage in this group.) On the average, these Tuesday afternoons are very productive, but it varies as much as the topics; sometimes we just get stuck.

The other more or less fixed point in my week is Friday, which is in principle reserved for working together with a colleague of long standing. We have worked together for nearly a quarter of a century! As an experimental physicist he entered the hardware side of our field, while I, a theoretical physicist, entered it as a programmer. This difference in background is still reflected in the nature of our work, but we know each other so well by now that we can appreciate the other's achievements and problems and can often help the other. Besides being very bright and knowledgeable, he is a mature scientist, and many things that turned out to become a major topic have been discussed with him in their infancy, when they were still hunches. Because working with him takes "the full mind", it is usually a day of very hard work, which leaves me tired, and it is a good way to end the week. Then I have the weekend to recover and to regroup my forces.

The other days of the week I am, in principle, a free man, but a few (mostly self-imposed) constraints usually define what has to be done.

A self-imposed constraint is that all appeals to my assistance in which the professional life of others is at stake are dealt with promptly. Under this category fall refereeing of papers for symposia and journals and the evaluation of research proposals for funding organizations and of candidates for university posts. (It differs from country to country; my impression is that, for instance, English and American universities seem to rely more heavily on external assessment than the Dutch ones.)

Besides those constraints I have to observe the deadlines that are the consequence of having committed myself to address an audience. Invitations to do so usually reach me long before the planned date of delivery, so long, in fact, that I usually don't propose to talk about what I have done at the moment of acceptance, but commit myself to talk about the work that I intend to do in the meantime. But I also know myself well enough to know that I work very poorly under strong pressure, and my desire to have my document ready well in advance of the actual deadline restricts my freedom.

In my little one-man research establishment, the mail plays of course an important role: to give you some idea, the practical unit for the rate of incoming mail seems to be "pounds/week". Of course I don't need to read it all. Some of it can be thrown away at a glance, most of it I just scan —e.g. lists of abstracts of articles produced by such-and-such organization, or encyclopedic works— to keep an overview of what is happening elsewhere. This does not take much of my time. But some of the stuff that is sent to me is very interesting, and then I want to study it. Occasionally it keeps me busy beyond that, either because I start a correspondence with the author, because I don't like the offered solution and try to do better or because the author's attack seems to give a fresh handle on one of my old unsolved problems.

*   *   *

In a recent paper "The high cost of programming languages", C.A.R. Hoare expressed at the end the "hope that one day we shall learn to design a language which will combine the merits (rather than the features) of its predecessors". After listing such merits, he continues:

> But it will not be an easy task to design such a language; like all great engineering breakthroughs, it will require an insight and understanding of the total environment of implementation and use of the product; consideration and rejection of a thousand bright ideas; and a constant appeal to the criteria of low cost and high effectiveness. Furthermore, I believe that it will require an undeviating pursuit of elegance and rigour, which is characteristic of the best tradition of University research. There are few engineering disciplines in which the successful pursuit of academic ideals can pay higher material dividends than in Computer Science.

Although I am not (yet?) engaged in the design of a new programming language, I give the above quotation because I share the opinions expressed —and expressed better than I could formulate them!— and it therefore gives an apt description of the nature of my work. Indeed: "rejection of a thousand bright ideas" nicely captures its experimental nature.

From our current mastery of programming to "software engineering" as a discipline worthy of that name, we have still far to go. There is clearly a discipline emerging for the design of little things and for proving their correctness. That is great and encouraging, for these little things are by no means restricted to toy-problems like Euclid's Algorithm for the gcd; they also include difficult and important little things like locking mechanisms and microcode for square-root algorithms down to the bit level. But they are "little" things: it is great, it is encouraging, but not enough! Here, for instance, is an area of research where, to quote Hoare "the successful pursuit of academic ideals can pay high material dividends", at least I believe so. But I know of only one way of discovering why the application of our formal techniques, which is so successful "in the small", is less successful when we try to apply them with greater ambition, and that is "try it!". So that is, for instance, what I have done during the last month. The eventual product (EWD550 in this case) was a 19-page document, but many pages with less successful formalization and proving experiments have disappeared into the wastepaper basket. What I learned from the experience I intend to summarize in a later issue of the EWD series.

I mention the exercise because it seems typically to be among the type of things that I should be doing. First of all, the time was not wasted; on the contrary, it proved to be very difficult to attain in this case the "elegance and rigour, which is characteristic of the best tradition of University research". Whether it would be done at a University, however, remains to be seen: it is —and I have said so explicitly in EWD550— work without any deep thought and, as a result, work without any glamour (and that is what many workers in the academic environment need or think they need). I think that it would be very hard to get funding for it; it is the kind of incremental improvement of which we sometimes need many, one after the other; it is the kind of work that requires hard and quiet thinking. I am in the lucky position to be able to do so, but it gives rise to obligations, the more so because the funding of individual research seems to become more and more unpopular. (I quote from a recent issue of the Bulletin of the American Academy of Arts and Sciences:

> Moreover, attitudes toward research have altered. American foundations and government agencies have become reluctant to fund research performed by individuals, preferring instead to help build large institutions and applied research centers, which can assign research priorities according to perceived and immediate economic needs.

The complaint is not new; that the situation seems to get worse is somewhat alarming.) Finally a job like that gives me some sense of achievement, and at regular intervals that is a nice feeling!

(EWD550 deals with the formal treatment of a modest syntactic analysis. Organizations less enlightened than Burroughs Corporation tolerate such a project only provided it is immediately done on a grandiose scale: IBM allowed its Vienna Laboratory to embark upon the problems of the definition of semantics, provided Vienna formalized the semantics of PL/I, of all languages! Needless to say, the Vienna Lab more or less collapsed under that effort.)

*　　　*
*

During the same period of time I wrote EWD554 "A personal summary of the Gries–Owicki theory", also a project without glamour in the sense that all I have done in those fourteen pages has been to condense the quintessence of the thesis written by Owicki under Gries's supervision; from my side there was no originality involved. Also EWD554 can be regarded as an experiment, viz. an experiment in presentation. Owicki's thesis —being a thesis!— doesn't read too smoothly. (I lent my copy of her thesis to a student that wanted to do some work in operating systems theory; I never saw him —nor my copy of her thesis— again!) This is a great pity because, hidden beneath the sometimes pompous formalism, her method contains the germ of a technique for dealing with a collection of otherwise unmanageable problems. One may raise the question: "Should I spend my time on rephrasing other people's work in an effort to make it more accessible and to show its significance?". I think that sometimes I should. I wrote that text with a dual objective, viz. to offer my students some underlying material and to make a number of people within Burroughs familiar with this work. (I had a third, more selfish objective: I wanted to understand it myself, and in order to be able to do so I *had* to reduce it to its bare essentials.) In connection with EWD554 I must admit that I treated my students as guinea pigs: I tried my presentation of that theory out on them. The experiment

—I am happy to say— gave a positive outcome. I admit "using" my regular audience for such purposes, I am not ashamed of it. There is hardly a point in developing a methodology unless one can transmit it to others, and, therefore, the possibility to transmit it should be tested experimentally.

I don't regret having written that document. It was a personally rewarding experience because it showed me something the duo Gries–Owicki had not seen yet clearly, viz. a nonoperational approach to concurrency. Besides that, who else could have done this? In writing EWD554 I needed all my experience as a teacher to make it palatable, and all my experience as a scientist to make it simple, i.e. to extract "the bare essentials". Again I am grateful for being in the position that I can allow myself to do essential work without glamour!

*   *
*

This "non trip report" covers about the last month. The plan to write such a report has been with me for some time; the fact that it covers a period of non-glamorous activities is a pure accident. If it had covered the period during which I was engaged in the design of the on-the-fly garbage collection (EWD520) or was lighting a similar piece of firework without burning my fingers too badly, its tone would probably have been quite different. This alternation between spectacular, nearly reckless intellectual adventure and most definitely non-spectacular (but solid!) work does not disturb me at all, for the progress of science needs both of them.

*   *
*

This is a good occasion to explain "the missing numbers" in the EWD series. Some numbers are occupied by documents that I failed to complete; sometimes I start on a document because I hope and expect that I can achieve a result, for instance because I have the exciting feeling of having a new bright idea, but when I then try to use it, it does not work. Furthermore I don't send my Dutch texts to the USA. Each week during term time, for instance, at the beginning of my lectures I address my students with a speech in Dutch commenting on the world we live in; each speech is traditionally one page long and occupies a new EWD number. I give these speeches for the enlightment of my students, but probably even more for my own fun and in order to exercise regularly my written Dutch. Like the documents I write in my capacity of Chairman of the Board of Mathematics Inc., they are also linguistic exercises. (With Mathematics Inc., by the way, I am in trouble. No matter how corrupt our commercial practice, no matter how fraudulent our scientific activities, the world around us seems to beat us. In these competitive times it is bloody hard even to catch up with reality!)

Nuenen, 1st of April 1976   PROF. DR. EDSGER W. DIJKSTRA
                                             Burroughs Research Fellow

EWD563
Formal Techniques and Sizeable Programs

By now we know quite convincing, quite practical, and quite effective methods of proving the correctness of a great number of small programs. In a number of cases our ability is not restricted to a posteriori proofs of program correctness but even encompasses techniques for deriving programs that, by virtue of the way in which they have been derived, must satisfy the proof's requirements.

This development took place in a limited number of years, and, for those who are familiar with such techniques, has changed their outlook on what programming is all about so drastically, that I consider this development both fascinating and exciting: fascinating because it has given us such a new appreciation of what we already knew how to do, exciting because it is full of unfathomed promises.

This development is the result of a very great number of experiments: experiments in programming, in axiomatizing, and in proving. It could never have taken place if the researchers in this field had not shown the practical wisdom of carrying out their experiments with small programs. As honest scientists they have reported about their actual experiences. This, alas, has created the impression that such formal techniques are only applicable in the case of such small programs.

Some readers have exaggerated and have concluded that these techniques are primarily or exclusively applicable to so-called "toy problems". But that is too great a simplification. I do not object to describing Euclid's Algorithm for the greatest common divisor as a "toy problem" (in which capacity it has been a very fertile one!). But I have also seen perfectly readable and adequate formal treatments of much less "toyish" programs, such as a binary search algorithm and a far from trivial algorithm for the computation of an approximation of the square root, which would be ideal for a microprogram in a binary machine. I call this last algorithm "far from trivial" because, although it can be described in a few lines of code, from the raw code it is by no means obvious what the algorithm accomplishes.

The question that I would like to address here is what we may expect beyond those "small examples". Hence the adjective "sizeable" in my title.

The crude manager's answer to my question is quite simple: "Nothing.". He will argue that difficult problems require large programs, that large programs can only be written by large teams which, by necessity, are composed of people with, on the average, nth rate intellects with n sufficiently large to make formal techniques totally unrealistic.

My problem, however, is that I don't accept that answer, since it is based on two tacit assumptions. The one tacit assumption is that difficult problems require large programs, the second tacit assumption is that with such a Chinese Army of nth rate intellects he can solve the difficult problem. Both assumptions should be challenged.

On challenging the second assumption I don't need to waste many words. The Chinese Army approach —also called "the human wave"— has been tried, even at terrific expense, and the results were always disastrous. OS/360 is, of course, the best known example of such a disaster, but please don't conclude from NASA's successful moonshots that it has worked in other cases. There is plenty of evidence that the data processing associated with these NASA ventures was full of bugs, but that the total organization around it was so redundant that the bugs usually did not matter too much. In short, there is plenty of experimental evidence that the Chinese Army approach does *not* work; and as a corollary we may conclude that the perfection of Chinese Army Generals is a waste of effort. At the end of my talk I hope you will agree with me that, in order to reach that conclusion, said experimental evidence was superfluous, because a more careful analysis of the tasks at hand can teach us the same.

*   *
*

For my own instruction and in order to collect material for this talk I conducted an experiment that I shall describe to you in some detail. I do so with great hesitation because I know that, by doing so, I may sow the seed of misunderstanding. The problem of a speaker is that, if he does not give examples, his audience does not know what he is talking about, and that, if he gives an example, his audience may mistake it for his subject! In a moment I shall describe to you my experiment and you will notice that it has to do with syntactic analysis, but please, remember that syntactic analysis is *not* the subject of my talk, but only the carrier of my experiment for which I needed an area for computer application in which I am most definitely not an expert.

I wrote a paper with the title "A more formal treatment of a less simple example". Admittedly it was still not a very large example; the final solution consisted of four procedures, of which, in beautiful layout with assertions inserted, three were only 7 lines and the last one 18 lines long. But the whole document is 19 typed pages, i.e. about 14 times as long as the raw code. It took me several weeks of hard work to write it, and when it was completed I was grateful for not having been more ambitious as far as size was concerned. It dealt with the design of a recognizer for strings of the syntactic category $\langle sent \rangle$, originally given by the following syntax:

$$\langle sent \rangle : := \langle exp \rangle; \tag{1}$$
$$\langle exp \rangle : := \langle term \rangle | \langle exp \rangle + \langle term \rangle | \langle exp \rangle - \langle term \rangle$$
$$\langle term \rangle : := \langle prim \rangle | \langle term \rangle * \langle prim \rangle$$
$$\langle prim \rangle: := \langle iden \rangle | (\langle exp \rangle)$$
$$\langle iden \rangle : := \langle letter \rangle | \langle iden \rangle \langle letter \rangle$$

That was all!

My first experience was that, in order to give a more precise statement about the string of characters that would be read in the case that the input was *not* an instance of $\langle sent \rangle$, I needed *new* syntactic categories, derived from (1) and denoting "begin of...": for each syntactic category $\langle pqr \rangle$ I needed the syntactic category $\langle bopqr \rangle$, characterizing all strings that either are a $\langle pqr \rangle$ or can be extended at the right-hand side so as to become a $\langle pqr \rangle$ or both.

$$\langle bosent \rangle: := \langle sent \rangle | \langle boexp \rangle \tag{2}$$
$$\langle boexp \rangle: := \langle boterm \rangle | \langle exp \rangle + \langle boterm \rangle | \langle exp \rangle - \langle boterm \rangle$$
etc.

(In an earlier effort I had also used the notion "proper begin of a $\langle pqr \rangle$", i.e. at the right-hand side extensible so as to become a $\langle pqr \rangle$ but *not* a $\langle pqr \rangle$ by itself. This time I obtained a simpler and more uniform treatment by omitting it and only using "begin of..." as derived syntactic categories.)

The next important step was the decision to denote the fact that the string K belongs to the syntactic category $\langle pqr \rangle$ by the expression:

$$pqr(K) \quad .$$

This decision was an immediate invitation to rewrite the syntax as follows:

$$\langle sent \rangle: := \langle exp \rangle \langle semi \rangle$$
$$\quad \langle semi \rangle: := ;$$
$$\langle exp \rangle: := \langle term \rangle | \langle exp \rangle \langle adop \rangle \langle term \rangle$$
$$\quad \langle adop \rangle: := + | -$$
$$\langle term \rangle: := \langle prim \rangle | \langle term \rangle \langle mult \rangle \langle prim \rangle$$
$$\quad \langle mult \rangle: := *$$
$$\langle prim \rangle: := \langle iden \rangle | \langle open \rangle \langle exp \rangle \langle close \rangle$$
$$\langle iden \rangle: := \langle letter \rangle | \langle iden \rangle \langle letter \rangle$$
$$\quad \langle open \rangle: := ($$
$$\quad \langle close \rangle: :=)$$

The invitation, however, was only noticed after I had dealt with the first line of the syntax, dealing with $\langle sent \rangle$; when dealing with $\langle exp \rangle$, it was the occurrence of both the $+$ and the $-$ that induced the introduction of $\langle adop \rangle$, because without it my formulae became full of insipid duplication. It was only then that I discovered that the boolean procedure "$semi(x)$" —only true if the character x is a semicolon— and the other boolean procedures that I needed for the classification of single characters were a specific instance of the convention that introduced "$pqr(K)$". Finally I realized that the usual *BNF*, as used in (2), is an odd mixture in the sense that in the productions the characters stand for themselves; in (3) this convention is restricted to the indented lines.

A next important decision was to denote for strings (named $K, L, \ldots$) and characters (named $x, y, \ldots$) concatenation simply by juxtaposition, e.g. KL, Ky, yLx, etc. Now we could denote the arbitrary nonempty string by yL or Ly and could derive from our syntax formulae like

$$(exp(L) \textbf{ and } semi(y)) \Rightarrow sent(Ly) \quad .$$

It also enabled me to define the "begin of...":

$$bopqr(K) = (\textbf{E}L: pqr(KL)) \quad .$$

I mention the apparently trivial and obvious decision to denote concatenation by juxtaposition explicitly, because in the beginning my intention to do a really neat formal job seduced me to introduce an explicit concatenation operator. Its only result was to make my formulae, although more impressive, unnecessarily unwieldy.

From my earlier effort I copied the convention to express post-conditions in terms of the string of characters read. With "S" defined as the string of input characters "read" —or "moved over" or "made invisible"— by a call of "$sentsearch$", and with "x" defined as the currently visible input character, we can now state the desired post-condition for our recognizer "$sentsearch$":

$$Rs(S, x, c): \quad bosent(S) \textbf{ and non } bosent(Sx) \textbf{ and } c = sent(S) \quad . \quad (4)$$

The first term expresses that not too much has been read, the second term expresses that S is long enough, and the last term expresses that in the global boolean "c" —short for "correct"— the success or failure to read a $\langle sent \rangle$ from the input should be recorded.

In short, we treat S and x as variables (of types "character string" and "character" respectively) that are *initialized* by a call of *sentsearch*. I mention this explicitly, because for a while we departed from that convention, and did as if the "input still to come" were defined prior to the call of *sentsearch*. We tried to derive from our post-condition weakest pre-conditions in terms of the "future" input characters, and the result was a disaster. At some time during that exercise we were even forced to introduce a deconcatenation operator! The trick to regard as "post-defined output" what used to be regarded as "pre-defined input" cannot be recommended warmly enough: it shortened our formulae with a considerable factor and did away with the need for many dummy identifiers.

Another improvement with respect to our earlier effort was a changed interface with respect to the input string. In my earlier trial I had had as a primitive to read the next character

$$x := nextchar$$

where "*nextchar*" was a character-valued function with the side-effect of moving the input tape over one place. (If S is the string of characters read, the above assignment to x should be followed implicitly by the "ghost statement" $S := Sx$.) Prior to the first $x := nextchar$, the value of the variable x was supposed to be undefined. In the new interface, where x is the currently visible character and S the string of characters no longer visible, I chose the primitive "*move*", semantically equivalent to the concurrent assignment

$$S, x := Sx, new\ character \qquad .$$

This minor change of interface turned out to be a considerable improvement! In the new interface, the building up of S lags one character behind compared with the old interface. Formula (4) shows how we can now refer —using concatenation— to two strings, one of which is a character longer than the other. With the old interface we would have needed a notation for a string one character shorter than S, something so painful that in my earlier effort a different specification for *sentsearch* was chosen, with the old interface more easily described, but logically less clean than (4).

I wanted to write a body for *sentsearch* in terms of a call on *expsearch* and the boolean primitive $semi(x)$ which was assumed to be available. I wished to do so only on account of the syntax for $\langle sent \rangle$ and discovered that I only could do so under the assumption —to be verified later when the full syntax was taken into account— that

$$sent(L) \Rightarrow \textbf{non } (\textbf{E } y\colon bosent(Ly)) \tag{5}$$

would hold. Confronting this with the specification (4) we conclude that if *sentsearch* establishes a final state with $c = true$, i.e. $sent(S)$, the second term —**non** $bosent(Sx)$— is true for all values of x: in other words, postulate (5) states that the end of an instance of the syntactic category $\langle sent \rangle$ can be established "without looking beyond".

We assume the availability of a primitive *expsearch*. Defining "E" to be the string of input characters moved over by it, it establishes, analogous to (4):

$$Re(E, x, c)\colon \quad boexp(E) \textbf{ and non } boexp(Ex) \textbf{ and } c = exp(E) \qquad . \tag{6}$$

Called by *sentsearch*, it implies $S := SE$ (as "*move*" implies $S := Sx$). A possible body for *sentsearch* is now:

proc *sentsearch*: $\{S = empty\ string\}$
    expsearch$\{Re(S, x, c)\}$;
    if non $c \rightarrow \{Rs(S, x, c)\}skip\{Rs(S, x, c)\}$
    [] **non** *semi*$(x) \rightarrow \{Rs(S, x, false)\}c := false\{Rs(S, x, c)\}$
    [] c **and** *semi*$(x) \rightarrow \{\mathbf{A}\ y :: Rs(Sx, y, c)\}move\{Rs(S, x, c)\}$
    fi $\{Rs(S, x, c)\}$
corp

For its correctness proof I needed three theorems:

Theorem 1. $(Re(L, x, c)$ **and non** $c) \Rightarrow Rs(L, x, c)$

Theorem 2. $(Re(L, x, c)$ **and non** $semi(x)) \Rightarrow Rs(L, x, false)$

Theorem 3. $(Re(L, x, c)$ **and** c **and** $semi(x)) \Rightarrow (\mathbf{A}\ y :: Rs(Lx, y, c))$.

The proofs of these three theorems and also of

    $boexp(L) \Rightarrow$ **non** $sent(L)$,

which I needed in these proofs, took more than one-and-a-half pages.

In the meantime the first 6 of the 19 pages had been written. The primitive *expsearch* asked for another three theorems to be proved and was finished 4 pages later; by analogy *termsearch* took only half a page; the primitive *primsearch* required another six theorems to be proved and was completed 6 pages later. The remaining two-and-a-half pages were needed to prove assumption (5) and the similar

    $(term(L)$ **and** $adop(y)) \Rightarrow$ **non** $boterm(Ly)$

and

    $(prim(L)$ **and** $mult(y)) \Rightarrow$ **non** $boprim(Ly)$

and for some closing remarks.

I shall not go into any detail about these proofs and programs. I only mention that I had to replace

    $\langle exp \rangle ::= \langle term \rangle | \langle exp \rangle \langle adop \rangle \langle term \rangle$

first by

    $\langle exp \rangle ::= \{\langle term \rangle \langle adop \rangle\} \langle term \rangle$

in order to open the way for a repetitive construct in the body of *expsearch*. Thereafter I had to replace it by

    $\langle exp \rangle ::= \langle adder \rangle \langle term \rangle$
    $\langle adder \rangle ::= \{\langle term \rangle \langle adop \rangle\}$

because I needed the expression "*adder(L)*" in my proofs and assertions. The syntax for ⟨*term*⟩ and ⟨*prim*⟩ was subjected to similar massaging operations.

*   *   *

So much for the description of my experiment. Let me now try to summarize what seem to be the more relevant aspects of the whole exercise.

(1)   The routines I designed this time were definitely more beautiful than the ones I had written three years ago. This confirms my experience with the formal treatment of simpler examples, when I usually ended up with more beautiful programs than I had originally in mind.

(2)   A slight change in the interface describing the reading of the next input character caused a more serious change in the overall specifications chosen for *sentsearch*: the formal treatment exposed the original interface as a seed of complexity.

(3)   To treat a program absorbing input *L* formally as a nondeterministic program assigning, as it were, a "guessed" value to *L* is a very useful device, so useful, in fact, that all by itself it is probably a sufficient justification for including nondeterminacy in our formal system. (Independently and in another context, also C.A.R. Hoare was recently led to treat input in this fashion.)

(4)   Nearly 11 of the 19 pages don't deal with the programs at all! They are exclusively concerned with exploring the given syntax and proving useful theorems about strings, theorems expressed in terms of predicates derived from the given syntax.

(4.1)   My earlier treatment of this example took only 7 pages: most of the theorems I proved this time were regarded as "obvious" in the older treatment.

(4.2)   Several patterns of deduction appear in more than one proof; the introduction of a few well-chosen lemmata could probably have condensed somewhat what now took 11 pages.

(4.3)   The formal treatment of a program requires a formal "theory" about the subject matter of the computations. The development of such a theory may be expected to require the introduction of new concepts that did not occur in the original problem statement.

(4.4)   In the development of such a theory the choice of notation is crucial. (In this exercise the struggle of developing the theory was mainly the search for an adequate notation; once that had been invented, the development of the theory was fairly straightforward and I don't think that the final document contains more than a single line —at the end, where I was getting tired and lazy— that could cause a serious reader serious problems.)

(5)   There is a wide-spread belief that such formal proofs are incredibly long, tedious to write, and boring to read, so long, tedious, and boring as a matter of fact, that we need at least a computer to verify them and perhaps even a computer to generate them. To the idea that proofs are so boring that we cannot rely upon them unless they are checked mechanically I have

nearly philosophical objections, for I consider mathematical proofs as a reflection of my understanding and "understanding" is something we cannot delegate, either to another person or to a machine. Because such philosophical objections carry no weight in a scientific discussion, I am happy to be able to report that my experiment completely belied the said wide-spread belief.

For many years I have found that when I write an essay in which a program is developed, the total length of the essay is a decimal order of magnitude greater than the length of the program in which it culminates. The transition to a highly formal treatment has *not* changed that ratio significantly: it has only replaced the usual handwaving and mostly verbal arguments by more concise, much more explicit, and, therefore, more convincing arguments. The belief that formal proofs are longer than informal arguments is not supported by my experiment.

The belief that the writing and reading of such proofs is tedious and boring has also certainly not been confirmed: it was an exciting challenge to write it and those who have seen it have confirmed that it was fascinating to read, because it all fitted so beautifully —as, of course, in a nice formal proof it should!—. I am tending to regard the belief that these formal proofs must be long, tedious, and boring as a piece of folklore, even as a harmful —because discouraging— piece of folklore that we had better try to get rid of. The fact that my formal treatment was *in all respects* to be preferred to my former, informal treatment was one of the most encouraging experiences from the whole experiment, and I shall not try to hide the fact that I am getting very, very suspicious of the preachers of the refuted belief: they are mostly engaged on automatic verification or proving systems. By preaching that formal proofs are too boring for human beings they are either trying to create a market for their products and a climate favourable for their funding or only trying to convince themselves of the significance of their work. The misunderstanding is aggravated by the complicating circumstance that their own activities seem to support their beliefs: I have seen a number of correctness proofs that have been produced by (semi-)mechanized systems, and, indeed, these proofs were appalling!

(6)   The design consisted of a set of procedures; ignoring the possibility of a recursive call —as would have been the case when the second alternative production for ⟨ *prim* ⟩ had been omitted— they form a strict calling hierarchy of four layers deep. It is worth noticing that all through that calling hierarchy the specification of the procedures is of the *same* simple nature. The fact that when we go up the hierarchy we create in a sense more and more "powerful" machinery is *not* reflected in greater complication of the treatment, more elaborate interfaces, or what have you. This, too, is a very encouraging observation; it gives us some clue as to what we might expect when we would undertake a more ambitious experiment with a still less simple example.

Somewhere in his writings —and I regret having forgotten where— John von Neumann draws attention to what seemed to him a contrast. He remarked that for simple mechanisms it is often easier to describe how they work than what they do, while for more complicated mechanisms it was usually the other way round. The explanation of this phenomenon, however, is quite simple: a mechanism derives its usability in a larger context from the adequacy of its relevant properties and when they are very complicated, they are certainly not adequate, because then the mechanism is certain to introduce confusion and complexity into the context in which it is used.

As a result of this observation I feel that there is a reasonable justification for the expectation that a next more ambitious experiment will just confirm my earlier experiences.

* * *

As you will have noticed I have accepted as some sort of Law of Nature that, for the kind of programs I talk about, I accept a documentation ten times as long as the raw code, a Law of Nature that relates how we think to the best of our ability when we program to the best of our ability. Those struggling with the maintenance of programs of, say, 100,000 lines of code, must shudder at the thought of a documentation ten times as bulky, but I am not alarmed at all.

My first remark is that, for the kind of programs I am talking about, the actual code is apparently a very compact deposit of our intellectual labours. In view of the various —and considerable!— costs caused by sheer program length, this compactness should be a reason for joy! But then we cannot complain at the same time about the factor ten! You cannot have your cake and eat it.... .

My second remark to console the man struggling with the 100,000 lines of code is, admittedly, still a conjecture, but a conjecture for which I have not the slightest indication that it might be wrong. The conjecture is that the actual size of 100,000 lines is less dictated by the task he seeks to solve than by the maximum amount of formal text he thinks he can manage. And my conjecture, therefore, is that by applying more formal techniques, rather than change the total amount of 100,000 lines of documentation he will reduce the length of the program to 10,000 lines, and that he will do so with a much greater chance of getting his program free of bugs.

* * *

As a result of this exercise I discovered an omission from all computer science curricula that I am familiar with: we don't try to teach how to invent notations that are efficient in view of one's manipulative needs. And that is amazing, for it seems much less ambitious than, say, trying to teach explicitly how to think effectively. When learning standard mathematical subjects, students get acquainted with the corresponding standard notations and these are fairly effective; so they have good examples, but that is all! I think it could help tremendously if students could be made aware of the consequences of various conventions, consequences such as forced repetition, or all information sinking into the subsubsubscripts, etc.

My last remark is added because you may have noticed quantitative concerns from my side, such as worrying about the length of formulae and proofs. This is partly the result of a small study of elegant solutions. The study is not completed yet, but one observation stands out very clearly: the elegant solutions are short.

Appendix

By way of illustration I include an excerpt from EWD550 "A more formal treatment of a less simple example". After the establishment of formulae (7) through (11) —as numbered in EWD550!—, i.e. the choice in the case of (7), (8), and (11), and the derivation in the case of (9) and (10):

$$Rs(S, x, c): bosent(S) \text{ and non } bosent(Sx) \text{ and } c = sent(S) \tag{7}$$
$$\langle sent \rangle := \langle exp \rangle; \tag{8}$$
$$\langle bosent \rangle := \langle sent \rangle | \langle boexp \rangle \tag{9}$$
$$boexp(L) \Rightarrow \textbf{non } sent(L) \tag{10}$$
$$Re(E, x, c): boexp(E) \text{ and non } boexp(Ex) \text{ and } c = exp(E) \tag{11}$$

the text continues as follows.

"Designing *sentsearch* in terms of *expsearch* means that we would like to have theorems, such that from the truth of a relation of the form *Re* the truth of relations of the form *Rs* can be concluded. There are three such theorems.

Theorem 1. $(Re(L, x, c) \text{ and non } c) \Rightarrow Rs(L, x, c)$

PROOF.   Assumed:
0. $Re(L, x, c)$ **and non** c
         Derived:
1. $boexp(L)$ with (11) from 0
2. $bosent(L)$ with (9) from 1
3. $c = exp(L)$ with (11) from 0
4.   **non** c from 0
5.   **non** $exp(L)$ from 3 and 4
6.   **non** $sent(Lx)$ with (8) from 5
7.   **non** $boexp(Lx)$ with (11) from 0
8.   **non** $bosent(Lx)$ with (9) from 6 and 7
9.   **non** $sent(L)$ with (10) from 1
10. $c = sent(L)$ from 4 and 9
11. $Rs(L, x, c)$ with (7) from 2, 8, and 10
                                       (End of Proof of Theorem 1.)"

(End of Appendix.)

EWD570
An Exercise for Dr. R.M. Burstall

Dear Rod,

Because —as you know— we Dutch are a God-fearing nation, Ascension-day is here an official Holiday, and on official Holidays I don't work. Today I just fooled with figures.

In doing so I discovered a function of the natural numbers that has a nice recursive definition, viz.

$$\text{fusc}(1) = 1$$
$$\text{fusc}(2n) = \text{fusc}(n)$$
$$\text{fusc}(2n + 1) = \text{fusc}(n) + \text{fusc}(n + 1)$$

a definition which, as far as complexity is concerned, seems to lie between the Fibonacci series and the Pascal triangle.
(The function fusc is of mild interest on account of the following property: with $f1 = \text{fusc}(n1)$ and $f2 = \text{fusc}(n2)$ the following two statements hold for $n1 \neq n2$: "if there exists an N such that $n1 + n2 = 2^N$, then $f1$ and $f2$ are relatively prime" and "if f_1 and f_2 are relatively prime, then there exist an $n1$, an $n2$, and an N, such that $n1 + n2 = 2^N$". In the above recursive definition, this is no longer obvious, at least not to me; hence its name.)

Having seen your exercises concerning the derivation of an iterative program, starting with the recursive definition for the nth number of the Fibonacci series, I was suddenly reminded of that exercise when I was considering an iterative program for the computation of fusc. It should be a rewarding exercise, since there exists a very nice iterative program:

$$n, a, b := N, 1, 0;$$
do $n \neq 0$ **and** $even(n) \rightarrow a, n := a + b, n/2$
$\quad \square \; odd(n) \rightarrow b, n := b + a, (n - 1)/2$
od $\{b = \text{fusc}(N)\}$.

I wish you luck and enjoyment!

Yours ever,

Edsger

Nuenen, 27th May 1976   PROF. DR. EDSGER W. DIJKSTRA
Burroughs Research Fellow

EWD573
A Great Improvement

After my return from my last trip the first thing W.H.J. Feijen and M. Rem showed me was a much improved definition of "*wdec*", for which they gave the credit to my colleague F.E.J. Kruseman Aretz. In [1] I had written:

> More specifically: we shall use the notation $wp(S, R)$, where S denotes a statement list and R some condition on the state of the system, to denote the weakest pre-condition for the initial state of the system such that activation of S is guaranteed to lead to a properly terminating activity leaving the system in a final state satisfying the post-condition R.

For a well-chosen programming language the article continues by defining how for any given S and R the pre-condition $wp(S, R)$ is derived. One page later, when dealing with a repetitive construct and its termination, [1] continues:

> Let t denote some integer function, defined on the state space, and let $wdec(S, t)$ denote the weakest pre-condition such that activation of S is guaranteed to lead to a properly terminating activity leaving the system in a final state such that the value of t is decreased by at least 1 (compared to its initial value). [...] The relation between wp and $wdec$ is as follows. For any point X in state space we can regard $wp(S, t \leqslant t0)$ as an equation with $t0$ as the unknown. Let its smallest solution for $t0$ be $tmin(X)$. (Here we have added the explicit dependence on the state X.) Then $tmin(X)$ can be interpreted as the lowest upper bound for the final value of t if the mechanism S is activated with X as initial state. Then, by definition, $wdec(S, t) = (tmin(X) \leqslant t(X) - 1) = (tmin(X) < t(X))$.

Kruseman Aretz's definition is

$$wdec(S, t) = wp(S, t < t0)_t^{t0}$$

where the notation R_y^x is used to denote a copy of expression R in which each occurrence of variable x is replaced by y (or by (y) if necessary).

EXAMPLE. Let S be

> **if** *true* $\rightarrow x := x - y$
> $[\!]$ *true* $\rightarrow x := x - z$
> **fi**

and let $t = x$. Then —see [1]— we have:

$wp(S, t < t0) =$
$(true \textbf{ or } true) \textbf{ and } (true \Rightarrow wp(\text{“}x := x - y\text{”}, x < t0))$
$\qquad\qquad\quad \textbf{and } (true \Rightarrow wp(\text{“}x := x - z\text{”}, x < t0)) =$
$wp(\text{“}x := x - y\text{”}, x < t0) \textbf{ and } wp(\text{“}x := x - z\text{”}, x < t0) =$
$(x - y < t0) \textbf{ and } (x - z < t0)$.

Hence $wdec(S, t) = wp(S, t < t0)_t^{t0} = (x - y < x)$ **and** $(x - z < x) = y > 0$ **and** $z > 0$.

This is much simpler than my original treatment. Analogous to the first five lines, we would have to derive first

$wp(S, t \leqslant t0) = (x - y \leqslant t0) \textbf{ and } (x - z \leqslant t0).$

Then we would have to find the smallest solution for $t0$ satisfying that equation and that is not a very standard operation! In this case we would find

$$tmin = \max(x - y, x - z)$$

and then we would derive

$$wdec(S, t) = tmin < t = \max(x - y, x - z) < x = \max(-y, -z) < 0$$
$$\min(y, z) > 0 \quad .$$

(End of example.)

The example shows that Kruseman Aretz's alternative definition does not only embody a conceptual simplification, but that it also smooths the formal labour to be performed. It couples in a very direct way the derived condition *wdec* with the fundamental condition *wp* in a way that is very familiar from the axiom of assignment.

*   *
*

In retrospect I blame myself for acquiescing in my ugly original definition. I knew quite well that it was ugly: it was preceded in [1] by "Note (which can be skipped at first reading).". But I failed to hear my own warning!

*   *
*

It was only after the above had been typed that I was told about the heuristics that had led to the new formulation of *wdec*. For that part, Kruseman Aretz gave the credit to M. Rem: it seems to have been the typical multi-person achievement, in which it is very hard to reconstruct later who has contributed what.

The argument is the following. Let us introduce an auxiliary variable $t0$, say, in which the value of t is recorded prior to the execution of S. (For the sake of this recording we assume that the value of t can be "computed", so that it can be assigned to $t0$.) Then we define

$$wdec(S, t) = wp(\text{"}t0 := t; S\text{"}, t < t0)$$

because the weakest precondition that "$t0 := t; S$" is guaranteed to establish $t < t0$ is, indeed, the weakest precondition for S such that S is guaranteed to decrease t (by at least one, because t is an integer-valued function). But, thanks to the axiom of concatenation, this right-hand side reduces to

$$= wp(t0 := t, wp(S, t < t0))$$

which, thanks to the axiom of assignment, reduces to

$$= wp(S, t < t0)_t^{t0}$$

and that is exactly the expression I gave here.

[1] Dijkstra, Edsger W., Guarded Commands, Nondeterminacy and Formal Derivation of Programs. *Comm.* ACM 18, 8 (Aug. 1975) 453–457.

Nuenen, Plataanstraat 5   PROF. DR. EDSGER W. DIJKSTRA
                                                    Burroughs Research Fellow

EWD575
To H.D. Mills, Chairman
Software Methodology Panel

Dear Harlan,

I am not quite sure how to comment on "Essential Elements of Software Engineering Education" by Peter Freeman, Anthony Wasserman, and Richard E. Fairley because I don't like its underlying political assumptions, because I know that, when dealing with politically distasteful attitudes, my pen tends to get venomous, and, finally, because I don't particularly want to offend anybody. So I hesitate.

There is, for instance, the authors' view on the proper role of our universities. They include producing the graduates industry and government ask for. An alternative view is trying to educate the graduates the rest of the world will need in the future, independent of the question to what extent the rest of the world already understands its future needs. This may sound presumptuous, but universities are by definition —if they are any good— presumptuous institutions with targets more far away in the future than most other organizations. I definitely prefer the alternative view, for where, otherwise, is the necessary innovation to take place? The degeneration of our universities into graduate factories is a development I would not like to encourage, because I consider it to be a threat to our civilization.

There is, for instance, the authors' view on the role of the intellectual individual. With their stress on the supposed virtues of group activity (and on the need for "communication skills"!) they seem to regard minimization —or possibly even elimination— of his role as an ideal worth to be pursued. I regard that as a threat to our civilization. (For further details I refer you, for instance, to *The Organization Man* by William H. Whyte, first published by Simon and Schuster, New York, 1956.)

There is furthermore the observation that of their Five Pillars of Wisdom for the software engineer —computer science, management science, communication skills, problem solving, and design methodology— only the first is hard science, while the remaining four —if existing at all— range from soft to very soft. I am afraid, however, that the current fashion grossly overestimates the importance and potentialities of the soft sciences, and would not like to enforce that fashion because, again, I regard it as a threat to our civilization. (For further details I refer you to *Social Sciences as Sorcery* by Stanislav Andreski, first published by André Deutsch, 1972.)

Finally, like most political documents, it is superficial. The suggested analogy between the software engineer and the family doctor is false because the commitment of the medical profession and the commitment of any engineering profession are of quite different natures. The most blatant example of superficiality is probably their argument in favour of communication skills; they refer to "the software engineer's need to communicate with a wide range of people and machines". As a piece of hilarious nonsense I think that this is only surpassed by the title "The education of a computer" (*Proc. ACM National Conference 1* (Pittsburgh, 1952) 243–250).

So, if you intend to follow Raymond T. Yeh's suggestion to use the paper by Freeman et al. "as a basis for departure", I can only recommend that you depart from it as far as possible.

*   *
*

C.V. Ramamoorthy's "Preliminary Report on Software Evaluation" is less objectionable: it gives a survey of what is or has been done —no matter how sensible or how foolish— and I have not the slightest reason to assume that his survey is unfair or incomplete. The report is very instructive, even perhaps in unintended ways. This does not imply that I have no objections: the author fails to challenge the assumption that the whole approach makes any sense at all. Let me quote:

> The approach is to identify a set of software characteristic attributes representing good and bad, reliable and unreliable programming practices. For each attribute, measures called metrics are formulated. The merit figure of a program is then defined as the normalized weighted average of these attribute metrics. The validity of this approach depends heavily on the chosen attributes, the metric formulation and the function that combines these metrics.

The first sentence is OK, but in the second sentence the word "measure" is used in a most unscientific sense. In science we measure physical quantities, something that is a meaningful activity because (the measurements of) these quantities are supposed to satisfy certain explicitly stated laws; the purpose of the measurements is to confirm or to refute the supposed laws. Here, however, to "measure" is used in the sense of "attaching a number to", in very much the same way as psychologists construct an IQ. (It is a fallacy to assume that an IQ "measures" something!) The next sentence is OK in the sense that it describes a common practice, be it a deplorable one; the last sentence is wrong in that it assumes that the notion of "validity" is applicable to such practices, in that it assumes that some of these practices can be more "valid" than others: validity is a binary criterion.

In his research (!) recommendation the author shows —apparently without noticing it— that the problem is recursively unsolvable: here he suggests that the criteria used in evaluating the quality of software, in turn, should be evaluated themselves for their effectiveness. (And so ad infinitum... !) The recommendation ends with "These effectiveness measures may allow a user to include an optimal set of tools in a software evaluation system to meet his special needs.". No matter how hard I tried, I could not attach a sensible meaning to that sentence; presumably it will be discovered that more "research" should be devoted to the quantification of the user's "special needs", so that we can decide whether a set of tools is "optimal"!

The whole activity has very little to do with what I would like to regard as software engineering. It is more the further refinement of management "science" as a self-perpetuating activity. If the manager needs a number, he will get one. I am afraid that the whole activity is adequately captured by the well-known saying "If you ask a foolish question, you will get a foolish answer.".

NOTE (Added to Avoid Misunderstanding). I don't know how to manage the design (or should we say "the discovery"?) of software. I hope that my saving grace is that I don't pretend to. (End of note.)

Good luck!   Yours ever,

                                                    Edsger

Nuenen   PROF. DR. EDSGER W. DIJKSTRA
                                                    Burroughs Research Fellow

PS. May I ask you to distribute this text to the other panel members? I don't have all their addresses and, besides, most of them are located in the USA. Thank you.

                                                    EWD

EWD576
On Subgoal Induction

In [1] I encountered "subgoal induction" as a technique for proving partial correctness. It was applied to a program S that I would write down as

$$S: \quad x := f(x0);$$
$$\textbf{do } B(x) \rightarrow x := g(x) \textbf{ od};$$
$$x := h(x) \quad .$$

In order to prove

$$\{P(x0)\}S\{R(x0, x)\} \tag{1}$$

—i.e. if $P(x0)$ holds and execution of S terminates properly, then in the final state $R(x0, x)$ will hold— "subgoal induction" is used. The technique consists of finding a relation $Q(x, z)$ satisfying

$$(\textbf{A}x: (\textbf{non } B(x)) \Rightarrow Q(x, h(x))) \tag{2}$$

$$(\textbf{A}x, z: (Q(g(x), z) \textbf{ and } B(x)) \Rightarrow Q(x, z)) \tag{3}$$

$$(\textbf{A}x, z: (P(x) \textbf{ and } Q(f(x), z)) \Rightarrow R(x, z)) \tag{4}$$

and it was stated that the existence of a relation Q satisfying (2), (3), and (4) proves (1).

My general inclination when I encounter such formulae —particularly when I encounter them in a report that is really dealing with something else — is to skim them, assuming that they are no more than variations on an old theme. Formula (3), however, attracted my attention, because, if $U(x)$ is the invariant relation for the repetitive construct, we have to prove —see [2]—

$$(U(x) \textbf{ and } B(x)) \Rightarrow U(g(x)) \tag{5}$$

and, if we compare (5) with (3), we see that the substitution of $g(x)$ for x occurs at the other side of the implication! This was reason enough to investigate subgoal induction a little bit more closely.

223

Suppose Q satisfies (2), (3), and (4). We will show that

$$U(x): \qquad (\mathbf{A}z: Q(x, z) \Rightarrow Q(f(x0), z)) \qquad\qquad (6)$$

is a suitable invariant relation. It is clearly established by "$x := f(x0)$", the first statement of S. To prove (5) we have to prove

$$((\mathbf{A}z: Q(x, z) \Rightarrow Q(f(x0), z)) \textbf{ and } B(x)) \Rightarrow$$

$$((\mathbf{A}z: Q(g(x), z) \Rightarrow Q(f(x0), z)) \qquad\qquad (7)$$

For those values of x such that $B(x)$ is false, implication (7) is vacuously true; for those values of x such that $B(x)$ is true, (3) tells us that $Q(g(x), z)$ is a stronger condition on z than $Q(x, z)$, so that whatever is implied by the latter is certainly implied by the former. Hence (7) and thus (5) follows from (3).

Finally we have to prove that

$$(U(x) \textbf{ and non } B(x)) \Rightarrow wp(\text{“}x := h(x)\text{”}, R(x0, x)) \qquad . \qquad (8)$$

Thanks to (2) and (6), the left-hand side of (8) reduces to

$$(\mathbf{A}z: Q(x, z) \Rightarrow Q(f(x0), z)) \textbf{ and } Q(x, h(x))$$

from which we conclude —applying the quantified implication for $z = h(x)$— the truth of

$$Q(f(x0), h(x)) \qquad .$$

Because the initial value $x0$ satisfies $P(x0)$, we conclude —applying (4) with $x = x0$ and $z = h(x)$— the truth of

$$R(x0, h(x))$$

but thanks to the axiom of assignment this is identical to the right-hand side of (8). Hence (8) follows from (2), (4), and (6).

Thus we have established that —as was to be expected— subgoal induction is indeed the next variation on an old theme.

The analysis described above was carried through together with C.S. Scholten.

Nuenen   PROF. DR. EDSGER W. DIJKSTRA
                                               Burroughs Research Fellow

[1] Is "sometime" sometimes better than "always"? Intermittent assertions in proving program correctness, by Zohar Manna and Richard Waldinger, STAN-CS-76-558.
[2] Guarded Commands, Nondeterminacy and Formal Derivation of Programs, by Edsger W. Dijkstra, *Comm.* ACM 18, 8 (Aug. 1975) 453–457.

EWD577
Trip Report E.W. Dijkstra, ECI-Conference 9–12 August 1976, Amsterdam

It was the kind of conference from which one returns with a glorious headache. It had been organized by the European Cooperation in Informatics, a joint enterprise of the Information Processing Societies of the various European countries. The response to the Call for Papers had been very low: only 36 papers had been submitted. Instead of cancelling the conference, the organizers decided that, by abolishing parallel sessions and selecting 12 of the submitted papers, the conference could still be held. (After all, they had six invited papers in addition to the submitted ones!) In spite of the meagre program, they still managed to collect about 250 participants. It is very questionable whether, with those 250 participants, they reached the break-even point; if they didn't, I just cannot have pity with them. It would serve them right, for organizing a bad conference is a worse crime than not organizing a conference at all. (Besides that, they had been warned.) The organizers committed what I would like to describe as "Contempt of Audience". It saddened me to see the extent to which the degrading circumstances at the European universities have broken the spirits of my colleagues, and it saddened me to observe their apathy and indifference, in which they have "learned" to accept the junk as if it were the real thing. The most frightening aspect of it all is that most of them present their abolishment of all norms and (time-honoured!) quality standards as an act of great wisdom.

The conference was held in the new building of the Free University of Amsterdam. I had never been there before. It must be about the last university building erected during the time that our government thought itself infinitely rich. It was in many respects an ideal setting; in a most important aspect, however, it was not: at no moment did one get the impression of being in a seat of learning and a centre of culture, on the contrary! I walked through the University Bookshop, but it was of a shocking vulgarity —as bad as the book department of the Bijenkorf (i.e. a chain of large department stores, oriented towards the superficial, fashionable consumer)—. Comic strips that were not funny, political pamphlets full of cliches, science fiction books and pamphlets of obscure mystical cults. And, to top it all, when we entered the Auditorium a few minutes before the conference started, there was.... Muzac! I was flabbergasted. (In my previous trip report, I made a remark about differences in noise level at both sides of the Atlantic: from that comparison, I learned, at least Amsterdam should be excluded. While portable radios are strictly forbidden in most public buildings, such as railway stations and the Eindhoven University Campus, the bar at the lounge of the Free University in Amsterdam did not observe that rule! The whole place was of a disgusting vulgarity.)

The first afternoon was devoted to Program Development and Verification in Practice and Theory. Michael Jackson gave his talk as an invited speaker. It was well-presented and certainly fell under the heading Program Development in Practice, but it had little to contribute beyond the rather limited problem area of file processing in (or: in spite of?) COBOL. Then Antonio Salvadori from the University of Guelph, Ontario, described the "Guelph Efficiency Monitor, a preprocessor system which can analyse a COBOL program at any development or running stage". I quote:

The statistics gathered and printed consist of
- a COBOL clause and verb count
- a percentage breakdown of PROCEDURE DIVISION verbs used
- the number of source records, number of comment cards, indication
of non-ANSI standard verbs, etc.

The last speaker was P. Hammersley, Cambridge UK, on "Team Organization in Integrated On-Line Computer Projects", a talk that was well-covered by its title. His English was a pleasure to listen to, but it was a talk with little or no technical or scientific content and I —like many others—found my thoughts wandering away.

In the evening there was a reception by the State Secretary of Interior Affairs and Burgomaster and Aldermen of Amsterdam; the reception was held in the beautiful surroundings of the new Vincent van Gogh Museum, where the air was polluted by... audible wallpaper! Most of us looked back on a wasted afternoon and were worried whether the conference would get any better.

The next morning was devoted to Concepts and Techniques of Database Management. The invited speaker, C.J. Date (IBM General Products Division) was the morning's best speaker. He knew what he was talking about and gave what seemed to be a good overview. For those unfamiliar with the topic, his talk was quite instructive.

The afternoon was devoted to Computer Networks. Louis Pouzin (IRIA) was the invited speaker on "Names and Objects in Heterogeneous Computer Networks". He had originally prepared a more technical presentation than, in the meantime, he dared to give and in a hurry he redesigned his presentation. As a result it was a bit rambling, but it was still quite clear that he knew what he was talking about. I had heard him many times before, but unaware of his past as a telephone engineer: that past was mentioned in the introduction and was quite discernable.

On Wednesday morning —again Program Development and verification etc.— I opened the session as the invited speaker. Tony Hoare should have been that morning's session chairman but, Tony being prevented from attending, his role was taken over by L.A.M. Verbeek of Twente University. I did not present my material well. I knew that it (EWD563) was difficult to present. I wanted to show what I had learned from a highly formal experiment, which had recently taken me more than a month to conduct. I could not explain that lesson without sketching the experiment, an activity that, indeed, took too much time and was only partly successful. (The trouble was that, while trying to do it, I noticed this!) In retrospect a very simple tutorial —nothing new— on formal program derivation would have been more appropriate for this occasion. Afterwards I.D. Ichbiah (CII) showed a similar —but less formal— case study of program development; I think he reached his audience better. Then Shmuel Katz (IBM Israel Scientific Center, Technion City, Haifa, Israel) gave a well-prepared talk on "Program Optimization Using Invariants". I think that it told more about the role of science and technology in the state Israel than about computing science as such.

Wednesday afternoon was again devoted to Database Management. Rudolf Bayer (Technische Universität München) was the invited speaker on "Integrity, Concurrency and Recovery in Databases.". His talk was well-prepared and well-presented (but for the fact that he tried to show too much). I was not convinced by his proposed solution: it was complicated and his "conclusion" that deadlock *prevention* was impractical did not seem to me to be sufficiently justified. I have more the impression that he had failed to discover how to do it. Later, in private, I had a long discussion with him about the current database folklore. It was very instructive for me; he, at least, is willing to challenge the common tacit assumptions, even if they have already found their way in standard proposals! (So does Michael Jackson, who repeatedly expressed his strong fear that already identified mistakes will be "cast in concrete" by the standardization bodies.)

The afternoon ended with a Panel Discussion on Database Management with P.J.H. King (United Kingdom), G.M. Nijssen (Belgium), and A.A. Verrijn Stuart (The Netherlands) as panelists and T.W. Olle as chairman, who found it necessary to address the panelists by their Christian names. It was just terrible! A few weeks earlier Olle had sent six questions to the three panelists and each question was answered by each panelist. For more than an hour we had an eighteen-fold demonstration of the well-known saying "If you ask a silly question, you'll get a silly answer.". In our innocence we thought that this panel discussion would be the absolute low of the conference: little did we suspect what the future still held in store for us.

From 20.00 to 24.00 a Dutch evening with plenty to eat and to drink had been announced. What had *not* been announced was that conversation would be absolutely impossible thanks to constant "music" produced by two alternating groups. Thanks to uncontrolled electronic amplification they produced a deafening noise that was physically painful. I had been stupid enough to try to talk: the next morning I had a sore throat; Horst Hünke had the same experience.

The invited speaker for the last morning —devoted to Architecture— was NN_6 from IBM, Böblingen, Germany, on "Trends in Computer System Structure and Architecture". But for a scathing remark about Honeywell not marketing MULTICS and another scathing remark about Burroughs and the ILLIAC IV, the speaker *only* mentioned IBM products, mentioning their catalogue numbers at a higher rate than I could factor them. It was a bloody shame. Van Wijngaarden, who was chairman of that session, took the precaution of not allowing any discussion and announced the coffee break. But was this a wise decision? During the coffee break several youngsters came to me, seriously worried by the fact that that shameful show had been allowed. They must have left the ECI-conference with in their mouths the bitter taste of dishonesty. Is this the way to educate our next generation?

It ended with a closing speech by van Wijngaarden in his capacity of Conference Chairman. Apart from thanking all the people who had contributed —he did so very nicely— he somewhat repaired the situation by commenting on NN_6's performance, be it in veiled terms. A large portion of his closing speech was devoted —in less veiled, but admirably chosen terms — to a public rebuke to me for my lack of tolerance. I had not only been annoyed by the music —and had shown so— but also by the fact that at the occasion of this conference a well-publicized ECI Computer Chess Tournament had been arranged. I did not like that at all —and had shown so— because I am of the considered opinion that, contrary to public superstition, the game of chess is of no relevance to computing science. By organizing the tournament, the ECI had only added fuel to that public misconception. It is perhaps easier to be tolerant, as soon as one doesn't care anymore....

$$*\quad\quad*$$
$$*$$

I learned a few things about Databases. I learned —or, had my tentative impression confirmed— that the term "Database Technology", although sometimes used, is immature, for there is hardly any underlying "science" that could justify the use of the term "technology". I even have my doubts when I am asked to believe that "database technology is still in its infancy", for that strikes me as being asked to regard the quacks at the fairs as the infancy of medical science. The point is that the way the database management experts tackle the problems seems to be so grossly inadequate. They seem to form an inbred crowd with very little knowledge of computing science in general, who tackle their problems primarily politically instead of scientifically. (In this respect the panel discussion was very revealing: at least half of the time was devoted to problems related to standardization! From the history of programming language development they should have learned to what disasters that premature concern about standardization may lead.) Often they seemed to be mentally trapped by the intricacies of early, rather ad hoc solutions to rather accidental problems; as soon as such a technique has received a name, it becomes "a database concept". And a totally inadequate use of language, sharpening their pencils with a blunt axe.

Lousy use of language —and therefore confusing— was a fairly general phenomenon. Allow me to end with the following anthology of crazy expressions. (Most of them are meaningless; if they mean something, it is something nonsensical.)

"virtual systems"
"virtual terminals"
"logical names"
"physical names"
"logical abstractions"
"mapping of one level of abstraction onto the layer below"
"data structures are mapped into several layers of abstraction"
"a programmer efficiency index"
"an effective implementation view of the corporate data model"
"different levels of abstraction of view of data"
"dynamic change"

and, to crown the confusion,

"the computer playing this game".

No, gentlemen, three times No: computers don't play.

Nuenen   PROF. DR. EDSGER W. DIJKSTRA
                                                Burroughs Research Fellow

P.S. To give you some impression of how "international" this conference was: more than 150 participants were Dutch.

P.P.S. A final quotation from our IBM-spokesman:

"Interfaces decrease performance and increase manufacturing cost.".

NN_6

EWD578
More About the Function "fusc" (A Sequel to EWD570)

In EWD570 I introduced the function "fusc", given by

$$\text{fusc}(1) = 1, \text{fusc}(2n) = \text{fusc}(n),$$

$$\text{fusc}(2n + 1) = \text{fusc}(n) + \text{fusc}(n + 1) \quad .$$

Without violating the given relations we can extend the definition with $\text{fusc}(0) = 0$. I showed there the following iterative program for the computation of $\text{fusc}(N)$ —with "peven" and "podd" standing for "positive and even" and "positive and odd", respectively—

$n, a, b := N, 1, 0;$
do $\text{peven}(n) \rightarrow a, n := a + b, n/2$
$\quad \| \ \text{podd}(n) \rightarrow b, n := b + a, (n - 1)/2$
od $\{\text{fusc}(N) = b\}$

On my last trip to the USA, while lecturing to a Burroughs audience, my audience derived this program after it had decided —after only a few modest hints!— that a good candidate for an invariant relation would be

P: $\text{fusc}(N) = a * \text{fusc}(n) + b * \text{fusc}(n + 1)$.

The audience arrived at this suggestion after a few simple considerations. The first observation was that

$$\text{fusc}(N) = \text{fusc}(n)$$

would be simple to initialize by means of $n := N$. They quickly saw that this was too simple, and considered

$$\text{fusc}(N) = a * \text{fusc}(n) \quad ,$$

equally trivially initialized by $n, a := N, 1$; it was then remarked that

230

initialization would not be complicated by an additive term

$$\text{fusc}(N) = a * \text{fusc}(n) + b$$

as that is initialized by $n, a, b := N, 1, 0$. The observation that for $n = 0$ the first term would disappear but that $\text{fusc}(n + 1) = 1$ would then hold suggested, together with the third part of the definition for fusc, the fully blown-up P as given above. Separating the cases

$n = 2k$:
$$\begin{aligned}
\text{fusc}(N) &= a * \text{fusc}(n) + b * \text{fusc}(n + 1) \\
&= a * \text{fusc}(2k) + b * \text{fusc}(2k + 1) \\
&= (a + b) * \text{fusc}(k) + b * \text{fusc}(k + 1)
\end{aligned}$$

$n = 2k + 1$:
$$\begin{aligned}
\text{fusc}(N) &= a * \text{fusc}(n) + \text{fusc}(n + 1) \\
&= a * \text{fusc}(2k + 1) + b * \text{fusc}(2k + 2) \\
&= a * \text{fusc}(k) + (a + b) * \text{fusc}(k + 1)
\end{aligned}$$

my audience quickly derived —to its pleasant surprise!— the iterative program given above.

$$* \qquad * $$
$$*$$

From the above program, two properties of fusc follow. The first is that the value of fusc applied to an odd argument does not change if in the binary representation of the argument we invert all "internal" digits, i.e. the binary digits between the most- and the least-significant ones. For instance $\text{fusc}(19) = \text{fusc}(29)$ because in binary 19 and 29 are 10011 and 11101, respectively. This follows from the comparison of the a, b-pairs during those two computations. After processing the least significant digit of the arguments, both have $a, b = 1, 1$. As a result of the inverted internal digits, the one computation has the role of a and b interchanged with respect to the other computation. Because the sum of two values is a symmetric function of its arguments and, as a result of the last —i.e. most-significant— 1 in the argument, that sum of a and b is delivered (in b) as the final value, both computations deliver the same result.

The next property is more surprising. (At least, I think so.) Let us try to represent the pair a, b by the single value m, according to the convention

$$a = \text{fusc}(m + 1) \qquad b = \text{fusc}(m) \quad .$$

In the case of peven(n) the operation on a, b has the form $a, b := a + b, b$ or:

$$\begin{aligned}
\text{fusc}(m + 1), \text{fusc}(m) &:= \text{fusc}(m + 1) + \text{fusc}(m), \text{fusc}(m) \\
&:= \text{fusc}(2m + 1), \text{fusc}(2m) \quad ,
\end{aligned}$$

an operation that translates into $m := 2m$. Similarly $a, b := a, a + b$ translates into $m := 2m + 1$. Initially, we have $m = 0$. Substituting all this we get

$n, m := N, 0;$
do peven$(n) \rightarrow m, n := 2*m, n/2$
  $[]$ podd$(n) \rightarrow m, n := 2*m + 1, (n - 1)/2$
od $\{fusc(N) = fusc(m)\}$.

Thus the fusc-value does not change if we write the binary digits of the argument in the reverse order. For example fusc(19) = fusc(25) because 19 and 25 are in binary 10011 and 11001, respectively. I think this second property more surprising!

*   *   *

In a way that does not admit generalization I discovered the equivalence

$2 \,|\, fusc(n) \Leftrightarrow 3 \,|\, n$

i.e. fusc(n) is even iff n is a multiple of 3. Inspired by a recent exercise of Don Knuth I tried to characterize the arguments n such that $3 \,|\, fusc(n)$. With braces used to denote zero or more instances of the enclosed, the vertical bar as the BNF "or", and the question mark "?" to denote either a 0 or a 1, the syntactical representation for such an argument (in binary) is

$\{0\}1\{?0\{1\}0 \,|\, ?1\{0\}1\}?1\{0\}$.

I derived this by considering —as a direct derivation of my program— the finite state automaton that computes fusc(N) **mod** 3. It was the first time in my life that I did what others have done many times before, i.e. relate a finite state automaton to a grammar. The exercise is until now only of modest interest; it taught me that division by a fixed factor and (simple!) syntactic analysis are closely related processes, and that insight I think somehow illuminating.

*   *   *

Since the distribution of EWD570 it has been discovered that more mathematicians have occupied themselves with function fusc —they only gave it a different name!—, a fact that is not surprising in view of its properties. J.J. Seidel and F.L. Bauer independently pointed out to me that it is no. 56 in Sloane's Dictionary of Integer Sequences, which refers to an article by G. de Rham, Elemente der Mathematik, Vol. 2 (1947) pg. 95. It was fun!

Nuenen, 16th August 1976   PROF. DR. EDSGER W. DIJKSTRA
                                             Burroughs Research Fellow

EWD582

A Proof of a Theorem Communicated to Us by S. Ghosh

BY EDSGER W. DIJKSTRA and C.S. SCHOLTEN

In a letter of 19 August 1976, S. Ghosh (currently c/o Lehrstuhl Informatik I, Universität Dortmund, Western Germany) communicated without proof the following theorem in natural numbers —here chosen to mean "non-negative integers"— :

Given a set of k linear equations of the form

$$L_i = b_i \qquad (0 \leqslant i < k) \tag{1}$$

in which the L_i are homogeneous linear expressions in the unknowns with natural coefficients and the b_i are natural numbers, there exists a single equation

$$M = c \tag{2}$$

in which M is a homogeneous linear expression in the unknowns with natural coefficients and c is a natural number, such that (2) has the same natural solutions as (1). (The equation $M = c$ need not be unique.)

Because the natural solutions of (1) are the *common* natural solutions of (3) and (4), as given by

$$L_0 = b_0$$
$$L_1 = b_1 \tag{3}$$

and

$$L_i = b_i \qquad \text{for } 2 \leqslant i < k \tag{4}$$

it suffices to prove that (3) can be replaced by a single equation with the same natural solutions as (3).

Consider for natural p_0 and p_1, to be chosen later, the equation

$$p_0 * L_0 + p_1 * L_1 = p_0 * b_0 + p_1 * b_1 \qquad . \tag{5}$$

233

All solutions of (3) are solutions of (5). We shall show that p_0 and p_1 can be chosen in such a way that, conversely, all natural solutions of (5) are solutions of (3). We shall do so by choosing p_0 and p_1 in such a way that (5), considered as an equation in L_0 and L_1, has (3) as its *only* natural solution; because all natural choices for the original unknowns will give rise to natural L_0 and L_1, this is sufficient.

Considered as an equation in L_0 and L_1, the general parametric solution of (5) is given by

$$L_0 = b_0 + t * p_1$$
$$L_1 = b_1 - t * p_0$$

(where, to start with, t need not be a natural number). We shall choose a natural p_0 and p_1 in such a way that from natural L_0 and L_1, viz.

$$b_0 + t * p_1 \geqslant 0 \tag{6}$$
$$b_1 - t * p_0 \geqslant 0 \tag{7}$$

left-hand sides of (6) and (7) integer   ,   (8)

we can conclude $t = 0$.

Choosing $p_1 > b_0$, we derive from (6)

$$t > -1 \quad . \tag{9}$$

Choosing $p_0 > b_1$, we derive from (7)

$$t < 1 \quad . \tag{10}$$

Choosing p_0 and p_1 furthermore such that $\gcd(p_0, p_1) = 1$, we derive from (8) that t must be integer; in view of (9) and (10) we conclude that $t = 0$ holds. Summarizing: (5) can replace (3) provided

$$p_0 > b_1, p_1 > b_0, \gcd(p_0, p_1) = 1 \quad .$$

                                       *   ॥ł   *

EXAMPLE. Let the given set be $x = 1$, $y = 1$, $z = 1$. The first two equations can be combined by choosing $p_0 = 2$ and $p_1 = 3$, yielding:

$$2 * x + 3 * y = 5, \quad z = 1 \quad .$$

These two can be combined by choosing $p_0 = 2$ and $p_1 = 7$, yielding

$$4 * x + 6 * y + 7 * z = 17$$

for which $(1, 1, 1)$ is, indeed, the only natural solution. (End of example.)

Nuenen, 3 August 1976   PROF. DR. EDSGER W. DIJKSTRA
                                                        DRS. C.S. SCHOLTEN

EWD584

Trip Report E.W. Dijkstra, Poland and USSR, 4–25 September 1976

Because I had to check in at Schiphol Airport at seven o'clock in the morning I went to Amsterdam the previous evening and slept in Hotel Frommer quite near to the airport. As the courtesy coach leaving the hotel at 6.30 was my target, I set my alarmclock at 5.45. When I entered the breakfast room at 6.00, however, I knew with devastating certainty that half an hour later we would have transport problems. I decided to be one of the first arriving at the coach, finished my breakfast quickly —which was no problem, for it was of sub-airline quality— and made for the coach. Some time later I had the satisfaction of observing that my prediction had been correct. The Lufthansa flight to Warsaw —with a stop in Frankfurt— was smooth and pleasant; besides that I was served a breakfast distinctly better than the one I had just discarded.

In Warsaw I had my first confrontation with totalitarian bureaucracy: it took me more than one hour to pass customs and immigration. As soon as I had left the official area, I was greated by dr. Ian Madey, who was quite surprised to see me: he was waiting for someone else. (As he is about the only Pole I know, I had assumed that he had been sent out to collect me.) The process of collecting arriving participants was of a refreshing informality. (Later I understood why: these Symposia on the Mathematical Foundations of Computing Science are visited yearly by a very inbred crowd: everybody knows everybody!) With my host, prof. Antoni Mazurkiewicz, and two others, I had an improvised lunch in Madey's apartment, which was quite close. At half past three we joined a coach that had collected participants from Warsaw Airport and Warsaw Central Station, and then we were on our way to Gdansk, where we arrived at 22.45. After a late supper I stumbled into my bed: seven hours in a coach —on Polish roads and seemingly without shock absorbers— is no fun.

The trip, although tiring, was interesting. It confirmed the impression I had received while looking down from the plane: every square inch of Polish soil is cultivated if possible. As we approached Gdansk the many little farmhouses were gradually replaced by fewer larger farms. The explanation is probably to be found in the time that Gdansk was still Danzig and export of grain enabled the farmers to become richer, the closer they were to the export harbour.

It is quite clearly still a poor country, even thirty years after the war. Ian Madey's apartment was well-kept and well-furnished —most of it pre-war furniture, I thought— but small. Private cars are a rare commodity, a private car in reliable condition seems exceptional; during that coach trip I saw at least ten cars stuck with mechanical trouble. Mazurkiewicz, who made the trip from Warsaw to Gdansk in his old Volkswagen, told me in Gdansk that half-way he had had to extinguish a fire in his car, and four days later he had not been able yet to have got it repaired. The dinners at NOVOTEL were of a depressingly tasteless monotonicity. At breakfast a single cup of coffee was the only fluid served, for a second cup one had to pay. The NOVOTEL building, however, was new and comfortable; it seemed an exact copy of the other hotels of the French (!) NOVOTEL chain.

It was quite clear that, among the people I met, "the system" has very little sympathy, but they seem to have discovered a way not to suffer from it too much. It seems to be accepted as one of those unavoidable things —more or less like a climate—, they made the impression of being reasonably happy in spite of it all. The Polish sense of Humour is in any case exquisite.

The Symposium was one where I —although an invited speaker— did not really belong. (I would not have accepted the invitation, had it not been for the fact that I could drop by on my way to Moscow.) I was immediately invited to act as session chairman on the first Monday morning, which, of course, meant that I could not escape. After lunch I was still so tired from Sunday's travels that I went to my room for a little nap. I fell asleep and missed most of the afternoon's talks, but all people I asked have assured me that I had not missed much.

I was Tuesday morning's first speaker. On the previous evening there had been a reception; because I felt that I might have to address a hundred hangovers, I made a special effort of it. The conference proceedings had been handed out on Sunday evening. They contained the text I had prepared, which, being perfectly readable by itself, had already been read by many participants. It seemed silly to read that text aloud, so I gave a completely new talk under the title "Back to Nature, or Two Cheers for Simplicity.". It went well. The end was totally new for a large fraction of the audience, because I ended up with the development of a little program, and many of them seemed never to have seen a program in their whole life.

This was the shortcoming of the whole symposium. There was a minority of computing scientists and a majority of mathematicians who really believed —or at least: behaved as if— that they could contribute anything relevant to the mathematical foundations of computing science without knowing enough about the latter subject. (A Flemish speaker demonstrated his unfamiliarity in a way that amused me very much. After having seen me as session chairman on Monday and as invited speaker on Tuesday, he discovered in my presence on Wednesday morning to his surprise that I was Dutch. After a few words of Dutch we switched back to English because others were present; he then asked me the polite —at least: politely intended— question "What is your area?". I could not resist the temptation to answer "Computing Science".) Years ago the power of the Polish mathematical and logical establishment and its tendency to strangle computing science had already been explained to me, so I was not too surprised when one of the organizers told me that they hoped to have established themselves to such an extent —this was their 5th Symposium— that next year automata theory could be deported to a separate symposium. I hope that they succeed, for they deserve to be freed from that form of pure mathematics, which seems more like a bureaucracy: a self-perpetuating activity, masochistically in love with its own, self-inflicted complexities.

I quote —because it is so typical— the opening sentence of the Conclusions of one of the invited speakers (Wilfried Brauer, Hamburg: "W-Automata and their Languages."):

> The theory presented here may help to solve some more known problems; it gives rise to quite a number of new questions and it offers several ways for future research: . . .

Also de Bakker ran true to form. He proudly demonstrated a proof rule for the PASCAL procedure call without the restrictions on the parameters that Igarashi, London, and Luckham had introduced. As his new proof rule has the consequence that one cannot prove the correctness of the procedure in isolation, but may in principle need different proofs for the different calls, any reasonable man would conclude that the Igarashi-London-Luckham restriction is such a wise one that we may speak of a flaw in the design of PASCAL. But de Bakker emphatically refused to draw that conclusion! (Without going into details, however, I would also like to mention that I had reason to admire de Bakker's political courage.) Good talks were presented by Mazurkiewicz (Poland) and by Berthelot and Toucairol (France!). Nivat also arrived.

*   *   *

My departure from Poland was less successful. I had to fly all by myself from Gdansk to Warsaw, where I had to catch my connection to Moscow. The first flight was delayed and —knowing no Polish— I found it hard to discover how long the delay would be. The distance between the airports of arrival and departure in Warsaw was —fortunately!— small. The transfer was not pleasant, because the man from the Polish Academy of Sciences that picked me up did not seem to like that job at all. After I had checked in and had passed emigration, I came into a real chaos when we had to guide our own luggage through customs. I nearly lost my balance and luggage in a pushing crowd of a few hundred Poles. Embarkation time was approaching and just when I was wondering for the tenth time whether I would get through in time, the baggage handlers of the airport solved the problem by placing all the unchecked luggage on the belt. I was then pushed into the departure hall, from there through a gate —that mentioned neither Moscow nor my flight number— where a very stern and cross lady —well, lady... — at the gate tore my boarding pass into two, from there into a coach and from there into a LOT airplane. We took off before the scheduled departure time, but when the announced flying time did not seem to be correct either, I suddenly got alarmed, wondering whether I was flying to, say, Bukarest! I was greatly relieved when a stewardess could confirm that I was, indeed, on my way to Moscow. It was my first flight on a Tupulev and it was a very pleasant one. Disembarkation again had more resemblance to cattle being driven out of a wagon. Since I had no Moscow address of my host, nor a telephone number —only Andrej Ershov's promise that he would meet me at the airport—, I was greatly relieved to see him before I had passed customs and financial formalities: the officer spoke English and was courteous and helpful. After my Polish experiences this was a pleasant change; later I would learn that also inside the USSR such courtesy seemed very rare.

I was met by Andrej Ershov and Sergej Pokrovskii from the Computer Center in Novosibirsk —they would accompany us on the whole trip— and an older colleague from Moscow who drove us in his new, first car —only 800 km done— to the Hotel of the Sovjet Academy of Sciences. The driver's uncontrolled way of changing lanes made the trip a nerve-racking experience: I am sure that he will have had an accident before his new car is 1000 km older.

Then our grand tour started. After two days, Tony Hoare from Belfast joined us (on Saturday evening). On Monday night we went from Moscow to Kiev, on Thursday night from Kiev to Leningrad, on Sunday night by train from Leningrad to Moscow and from there by plane to Novosibirsk, where we performed for the next two days. On Thursday morning we left Novosibirsk. Tony stayed a further day in Moscow; I left Moscow on Thursday evening for Amsterdam (again via Frankfurt) where I arrived at a quarter to eleven in the evening, pleasantly surprised to find my wife with the car at the airport: instead of another night in a hotel, we drove back to Nuenen and arrived home at a quarter to one in the middle of the night. I just dropped into bed and slept until ten o'clock next morning; taking a real hot bath, I realized that I still saw memories of mosques, icons, cots in the mud, and policemen, yeah, policemen everywhere: they still haunted my memory.... .

The general pattern of our visits to those four towns was a lecture by Tony, a lecture by me, a public performance of both of us for a large audience, one or two "scientific discussions", and an official dinner —with vodka, caviar, and toasts— with our hosts. We worked hard: our lectures were between two and three —mostly three— hours. Andrej had counted the number of our performances and had added the audience sizes. On our last day, when visiting prof. Marchuk, the Director of the Siberian Branch of the Sovjet Academy of Sciences, he proudly reported that in seventeen meetings we had addressed over 2500 people. Under normal circumstances that kind of quantitative reporting would have amazed me, but this time I just noticed it, for it was exactly what in the meantime I had learned to expect. (This is what one expects in a society that tries to leave the Middle Ages by means of five-year plans; I was not surprised at all to observe Marchuk swallowing these numerical data as if they were highly relevant.) All our lectures went very well. (Only at the beginning of my first talk did panic seize me: standing in front of a fully packed auditorium with two blackboards I discovered that with the Soviet chalk I couldn't write on them! After a delay of a few minutes someone liberated two miserable pieces of chalk that were slightly better. With grim satisfaction, a week later in Leningrad, I saw a Russian wrestling with the same problem.) It was my first experience with addressing an audience by means of intermittent translation; when Andrej did it —and that was nearly always— it worked beautifully. He often seemed to enjoy it, he was clearly much more than just an interpreter. (In Kiev I started with "just an interpreter", but within five minutes Andrej took his place.)

Our "scientific discussions" were more difficult. On the first Saturday morning I had such a discussion all by myself, because Tony had not arrived yet. We had chosen "computer science education" as its central theme because I wanted to check a remark in a recent advice to the US Government, viz. that in the USSR programming was taken very seriously and was primarily done by people with a solid mathematical background. I found that remark confirmed. The only difficult moment during that discussion was when my opinion about mechanical verification and further Artificial Intelligence work was asked. It was a difficult moment, for I had already discovered many years ago that the amount of support for AI-projects in particular says less about the intrinsic merits of these projects but much more about the political climate that supports them. Suddenly Andrej needed twice as much Russian to translate me. Twice we have had a discussion about one of their microprocessor projects, but that was nearly impossible. It reminded me of my discussion at IBM Hursley in the early seventies, shortly after the THINK-notices had been replaced by warnings to keep company-confidential matters secret, and, just when I arrived, the IBM-er who wanted my advice received a telephone call reminding him that he was not allowed to tell me anything, not even to formulate his question. In the USSR it was the same crazy game of hide-and-seek. How can you comment on something when they don't tell you what to comment on? They either feigned not to understand the question or gave a null-answer —"This will depend on the circumstances." etc.—. Eventually we extracted that they proposed a tree-like "store-and-forward" communications network of about one hundred microprocessors, each with its own clock of about 30 MHz. (When I asked the clock frequency, a long discussion in Russian started: Tony, who speaks Russian, told me later that they were discussing among themselves whether they were allowed to answer my question.) I told them that I did not expect that it would work, because I expected glitches all over the place. They then started to explain why they were sure that that would not be the case. From that explanation I got a strong impression that they hardly understood the phenomenon, but I felt no longer tempted to give further explanations.

It is undoubtedly true that I observed a strongly mathematical approach to computing science, but it seemed to me to be mathematics of the wrong kind. Very pompous, with Roman, Greek, and Gothic alphabets —Andrej complained about the "indexomania" in his country— and void of any simplicity or elegance. A "machine" is at least a ten-tuple, and all their work seems soaked with more and more elaborate computational models. I remember the man who proudly told us that *his* computational model distinguished between no fewer than five (!) different kinds of store. In short, it seems all highly ineffective. I got two *explicit* indications, that mathematical elegance is not regarded as very important (a decadent capitalistic luxury?). It will take a long time before they will discover that in computing science elegance is not a dispensable luxury, but a matter of life and death.

I was surprised by the susceptibility —or should I say: vulnerability?— to foreign (primarily American) influences. Jack T. Schwarz was touring the USSR for the nth time in order to keep the Russians up to date on the latest developments of SETL. (Was this part of some sort of Helsinki treaty between the USA and the USSR?) On the one hand I know that many people have grave doubts about the whole SETL-project (and I know some of the reasons), on the other hand it was strange —nearly alarming— to see that in the USSR Schwarz was taken absolutely seriously. In Leningrad I discovered that they had been misguided enough to invest God knows how much in an implementation of .... ALGOL 68 for the Russian 360! In Novosibirsk a group had recently embarked on automatic program verification etc., very much in the line of London et al., without *any* tangible justification for the hope that they should do any better. During our lunch with Marchuk, the latter asked our comments after he had explained why computing science in his opinion was such an important field, an explanation that was no more than a reiteration of the Artificial Intelligence hopes! (John McCarthy, too, is a regular guest in Novosibirsk.) I could only comment by quoting George Polya, that infallible rules of discovery would work magic, but that there is no such thing as magic. (Under such circumstances, quotations are *very* useful: they enable one to give unwelcome answers without being rude.)

Tony gave a very plausible explanation: no matter how doubtful they are, they just cannot afford to leave a Western exercise unexplored, for suppose that those capitalists book a significant result! I think that that explanation is correct. It seems in full accordance with Andrej's attitude, which is one of extreme tolerance, combined with a tendency to collect a wide variety of documents. (The *size* of his personal library in the institute was most impressive.)

The departure from Moscow was again a chaotic affair. I was taken to the airport by a young Russian who spoke some English but was unable to explain to me how I should proceed and what formalities I had to go through in what order. I flew back in a Lufthansa plane, filled mainly with Germans who had had a trade exhibition. The tension began already to discharge at the gate: still three policemen to pass and we shall be free again... There was a clear sigh of relief when the plane took off.

*   *   *

Some random remarks.

My first impression of Poland in the evening was that it was extremely well —not to say: over-brightly— illuminated, and I thought "They must be very concerned about the well-being of the average citizen to light his path so well.". On closer inspection the illumination was always on parking lots, timber yards, and the like. It was clearly a protection against theft and my Sportstourist guide that saw me off to my plane to Warsaw did not make a secret of this fact. In the USSR the same bright illumination; in Moscow I even saw that most cars were parked with their wiper blades removed (and even little plastic covers on the arm tips). When my guide showed me a row of parked cars and said proudly "All Sovjet-made." I could not resist the temptation to ask maliciously whether the wiper blades had been removed as a protection against theft. Answer: "I don't know; I don't have a car.". After having verified my conjecture I told him later that day not to behave like a bloody fool. He took the hint and was, from that moment onwards, quite honest. He was not a party member, although (nearly pathologically) nationalistic. I had already observed this, he himself had observed that trait as well. He confessed this with a very curious mixture of pride and shame. Later he told me that —although he had had ample exposure to Frenchmen and Americans— this was his first confrontation with "northern Western Europe" (i.e. Tony and me). He had been afraid and had found the first few days very difficult. (The fact that Tony and I knew each other so well was, of course, an added difficulty.) The next time I go there —I am not sure at all whether there will be a next time; an invitation for next year has been declined without the slightest hesitation!—

I shall take, say, a fresh Herald Tribune and Le Monde and Times with me: our guide was absolutely thrilled when he found in the Intourist Hotel in Leningrad a six-day old copy of Le Monde in the shop: he immediately bought it and said to me "I would never have believed that possible.".

*   *   *

A few remarks about "the sociology of science" or "how to make a career". A young mathematician who lectures in Poland on EOL's and ETOL's etc. told me his motives for entering automata theory. He did not particularly like the subject, nor had he any belief in its relevance. But he found the subject easy, had observed relatively little competition, and, in his country, could earn a living with it because the university authorities confused it with computing science anyhow. At first I was shocked by his cynicism — he was a young man with most of his life still before him. At second thought I found it harder to blame him: he was perfectly honest about it and I could only pity him for having so few illusions (although, of course, this may save him some disappointments).

Next I observed a systematic application of the saying "In the land of the blind the one-eyed is king.". People try to make careers in computing science by frequenting in this respect underdeveloped countries and obscure conferences. I had seen a few of such cases in Western Europe, behind the iron curtain the phenomenon is very pronounced: it was sometimes embarrassing to hear which of my countrymen had frequented their places. And then the man who, later this fall, would go for a month to Singapore to lecture about Lindenmayer systems! That must be just what they need...

*   *   *

A KLM purser told me the other day —or was it night? it was one of those circumstances under which one is never quite sure which is which— a story about a cooperation agreement between KLM Royal Dutch Airlines and Aeroflot. In preparation for the cooperation nearly 30 KLM employees, among whom my purser, learned Russian. My purser had been one of the first to serve on a flight with a mixed crew. As soon as the Soviets, however, discovered that the Dutchmen they cooperated with understood Russian, the agreement was cancelled! It is frightening to observe such a large nation to be so nervous and so uncertain, but after my recent experiences over there I have no problem at all in believing my purser's story.

*   *   *

I was shown many cathedrals and monasteries, and in Leningrad mummifying caves in which an underground monastery had been built. It breathed the spiritual atmosphere of the Dark Middle Ages, but that underground monastery had had its heyday in the eighteenth century. It was crowded mostly with Russian tourists; at the exit was the Marx quotation about religion and opium, and a nearby church was now a Museum for Religion and Atheism. They have very mixed and ambiguous feelings towards religion, also cramped. After a week Sergej asked me whether I was a Christian; what else could I do but ask him whether he was a Communist? (We both answered "No.") I found that cramped attitude towards religion irritating and even a little bit sickening. Of antisemitism, I am happy to say, I have personally observed nothing. This in strong contrast to Hungary in 1968, where I found the open antisemitism appalling.

*   *   *

Like a good boy I had decided to write my wife a long letter from each of the towns I would visit. So I wrote her a letter from Gdansk, a letter from Moscow and a letter from Kiev, but then I heard that they would take at least ten days to arrive because they would be opened and that, apparently, is a time-consuming process. (Upon my return I could verify that both rumours were indeed correct: they had taken ten days to arrive and they had been opened! The shocking thing was that they were not stamped "Opened by censor"; on the contrary, they had been opened and reclosed carefully, but I had taken a few precautions and was absolutely certain that at least one of the Russian letters indeed had been opened! I had written them in the kind of double-talk, with which no Russian censor could find anything at fault, at the same time certain that my wife would understand.)

In Leningrad I realized that writing letters would not make much sense anymore, so I ordered a telephone call for Saturday evening between 21.00 and 22.00. I was in my hotel room all the time, waiting, but nothing happened. So next morning I sent a telegram. The girl at the counter was cross, maybe because the price of the telegram was something like her weekly wage. The text is a true reflection of how I felt:

> dear ria heard my letters from moscow and kiev not expected to arrive before my return telephone effort from leningrad failed hence cable saying still alive bowels reasonable eyesight good trip tiring interesting and depressing talks went like clockwork and very well received hosts as pleasant as they can be guided tours past historical buildings closest approximation of hell imaginable thank heaven tony is here sunday morning working together kiss children also yours longing to be home edsger

It seemed a reasonable way to spend my rubles!

*   *   *

I did my best to behave as one should in bugged rooms, but I found it difficult. I remember that, when I asked the IBM-er in Hursley whether the room in which he received me, was bugged, the IBM-er orally protested "No, of course not." while nodding affirmatively. Similar situation while I paid my compliments to the Dutch embassador in Moscow. I remembered never to comment on our Russian hosts but when, in Moscow in my hotel room I started to explain to Tony the type of computer architecture I had been thinking about lately, better trained than I Tony immediately suggested a walk. It did not rain and we walked for nearly two hours. It took Tony a long time to grasp the idea, so it might be a little bit revolutionary. Eventually he got quite excited, but agreed that several critical issues have to be investigated rather carefully, before the idea can be proposed as a realistic one. Then we returned to the hotel and went to bed.

*   *
*

To fill the page a quotation from my diary (Leningrad):

Friday was a tiring day for me. Morning lecture of three-and-a-half hour (fifteen minutes break included). Well-prepared talk on the importance of nonoperational definition of programming language semantics went like clockwork. (First time I gave that talk.) In the afternoon we were exhibited for an audience of about 400 people in the University auditorium, together with Jack Schwarz, who was selling SETL. Schwarz's "position statement" contained expressions such as "...a large mess of structure..." and "automatic choice". When later confronted with these quotations he answered "crudity is the characteristic of language". Speak for yourself, Sir! But if that is his attitude, my revulsion fully explained.

Nuenen, 16th October 1976   PROF. DR. EDSGER W. DIJKSTRA
                                                  Burroughs Research Fellow

EWD585
Trip Report E.W. Dijkstra, Tokyo, 28 Sept.–3 Oct. 1976

Tokyo, Thursday morning six o'clock local time, and hopelessly awake.

I left Nuenen last Tuesday a few hours after my lectures in the morning and plan to be back in time for my next week's performance. On Monday I spoke with the Dean of the faculty, who remarked that for the kind of life I was living I needed an iron constitution. I must disappoint him: I haven't. It is still warm in Tokyo. In my hotel room I found a kimono on my bed, ready to be used by the "dear guest"; the airconditioning is cooling so frantically that, indeed, I have put it on. (The thermostat in my room is set to 30 degrees: I conclude that the cooling is totally independent of its setting.)

I flew from Amsterdam to Tokyo via Anchorage, Alaska, for refuelling (8.5 + 7 hours). In Anchorage the crew was refreshed, but I felt that the passengers were in an equal need of being refreshed: it was a very long flight. On the first stretch the hostesses acted as waitresses, on the second more as nurses.

Landing in Anchorage was a surprising excitement. I had never expected that an intermediate stop would cause such a thrill, but I can only summarize my impression of Alaska by saying that you won't believe it until you have seen it, and that even then it is hardly believable. A fantastic river delta, with uncountable streams winding their way between black rocks via mud into the sea and white, cruel mountains along the horizon: an unbelievable sight! The airport itself was disappointing: after my most distressing experiences with Soviet toilets —more precisely, the absence thereof, at least of usable ones— I set my feet on American soil with great trust and confidence. In Anchorage, however, the confidence is unwarranted: it is distinctly less clean than California —or my home country for that matter—.

Amsterdam, Monday morning 0:20, Hotel Frommer.

The whole trip was somewhat exhausting. The conference was on Thursday and Friday, I arrived in Tokyo on Wednesday evening and was due to depart from Tokyo Saturday noon, and would be back on Sunday morning. When I arrived in Tokyo at the Okura Hotel at 8 pm., tired and dirty, I was faced by five hungry gentlemen who had waited with dinner for me. I did not quite know how to refuse in a sufficiently polite manner, had a ten-minute shower, and then we were taken to a Japanese restaurant, where a few hierarchically high-placed gentlemen were waiting for us. After a tea ceremony they left; we six had to go on with our dinner. Then two days conference —about which later— and then back home, but the return trip was a disaster.

Saturday morning —I was already awake at four o'clock— shortly after I had checked out at 9:15 and was waiting for Mr. Haruyasy Nakayama to see me off at the airport, I got a telephone call that the plane, instead of leaving at noon, would leave at 9 pm. Nakayama helped me kill the morning by taking me and Weber —a speaker from the USA— on a trip in his car through Tokyo and a walk through the imperial gardens. Weber had kindly given me the key of his hotel room where I slept from 1 pm until 5 pm. Those four hours were very welcome, as my night had been bad. At seven a car took me to the airport; Nakayama could not accompany me, as he had another appointment, so there I had to fight my battle unassisted. First I could not find the KLM desk, but eventually I discovered a little notice that JAL took care of that. There were two special first-class counters, I was helped very quickly and received a card with an invitation from KLM to rest and have a drink in the first-class lounge. I was looking forward to it, for my experience in the first-class lounge at Schiphol had been excellent. There was a terrible queue at customs and emigration but the prospect of the first-class lounge sustained me all through the proceedings. When, at last, the final formality had been completed, I found myself in a dirty, crowded international departure hall in which clear indications as to which flights left when via which gates were lacking —the quality of the sound system was poor— and discovered that the first-class lounge, which I now needed more than ever, was at the other side of the customs/emigration boundary! Neither peace nor a drink were my share and I was greatly relieved when, 15 minutes later than announced previously, I recognized the call for my flight and the embarkation procedures started. They used crowded coaches, it took a long time, it was warm and people were smelly (garlic?). Eventually I sank in the cushions of my seat in the first-class compartment of a KLM Boeing 747 and felt much better. At that moment I did not even mind to hear that we would take the southern route and that I was 28 hours away from Amsterdam; at that moment it only meant for me that I could enjoy the KLM care for twelve hours more than on the first flight. We would have three successive crews and intermediate stops in

Manilla, Bangkok, New Delhi, Dubai, and Athens. Until New Delhi everything went fine but for the fact that three expensive, but also talkative and smelly, Japanese passengers did not leave the plane in spite of all the opportunities they had had to do so.

In New Delhi the real misery started. During take off —we had not been allowed to leave the plane— shortly before the point of no return, a huge bird disappeared in one of the engines. The pilot managed to slow down again and to stop before the end of the runway. We were taken to the New Delhi International Departure Hall —which was described as airconditioned: it had fans circulating the hot air— and it was only after five hours of uncertainty that we heard that, probably, we could leave with the same motor. (Otherwise the delay would have been at least another twenty-four hours: "Air India might have a spare motor in Bombay that KLM could borrow".) The idea of twenty-four hours in New Delhi did not attract me at all; knowing that my bowels are the weak part of the equipment, having neither tropical nor South-American experience, and having seen the cockroaches crawling over the carpets of the International Departure Hall, I was in low spirits. (Besides that I was now sticky all over, since the chairs in the hall were covered with plastic.) The second time we took off from New Delhi we did not catch a bird and it was only then that I heard how narrow my escape from a long delay had been: if the delay had been longer than the six hours it was, the crew would not have been allowed to continue the flight before having rested. It is past one o'clock: and so to bed!

*   *
*

Quite apart from the pains —see above— of physical displacement, I regret this trip strongly. One thing is certain: I was lured into acceptance of the invitation on false pretences. I was invited for the "5th International Symposium on Information" but I cannot call a symposium where three non-Japanese speakers participate "international". It was organized by JIPDEC, standing for "Japanese Information Processing Development Center". JIPDEC had not invited me directly, I had been approached on its behalf by the Scientific Attaché of the Royal Netherlands Embassy in Tokyo. It was the Nth Japanese invitation, and I had been able to withstand the first $N - 1$; I have now learned that the intervention of one of our Embassies is no guarantee. The scientific attaché had misjudged JIPDEC, me, or both.

The symposium consisted of three half-day sessions, one on Thursday afternoon, and two on Friday. Each session consisted of a one-hour speech by the foreign speaker, an interval, and comments from a Japanese panel; finally the first speaker could comment on the comments. The Americans were scheduled for the first sessions; I had to perform on the last one.

By the time I had to perform I was very depressed: until that moment the yen had been the unit of thought! And this was not the consequence of the fact that the two American speakers —one spoke on computer audits and the other on decentralization of banking administration— were from the financial world. The symposium was opened by Japan's most famous economic commentator. I found the whole happening very curious. I was reminded of the keynote address by Vincent Learson at an ACM Conference in 1972. Learson (of IBM) argued then for a full hour that it was the task of computing science to assist in maintaining the American economic supremacy in the face of the Japanese threat, a threat so serious that it was our scientific duty to assist IBM in its calling to save the country. (Even for an all-American audience that talk by Learson would have been shocking: it was so bad that afterwards many Americans came to me in order to apologize for it.) Here in Tokyo the same story, only still worse: microcomputers had been invented in order to save the fragile Japanese economy (and no one apologized this time). Quite typically, it never became clear whether the production or the use of microcomputers should save Japan!

The whole symposium struck me not as a real symposium, but more like a Kafkaesk simulation of a symposium. The Japanese panel members —four per panel and each member spoke for about a half hour— were absolutely terrible. They never produced anything more than a concatenation of vague motherhood statements, and they repeated themselves all the time. In Japanese they may have said the same thing three times with different words; there is the possibility that limitations of the English vocabulary of the interpreters caused these repetitions to sound more like each other than in the original, but I don't think so, for the interpreters made a very competent impression. I think that they really repeated themselves. (One of the Japanese panel members confessed before speaking in private that he did not really know what to say: nevertheless he used his full half hour!) I really should know more about the Japanese language, I think that there is something very wrong with it. Andrej Ershov had warned me that the times to express something in English and Russian respectively are as 7 to 10; Nakayama told me that for English and Japanese the ratio was 1 to 2. Listening to the interpreters I could believe it.

Seemed the speakers to be fake, so seemed the audience. On the first afternoon I scanned the audience, and about 20 percent was fast asleep, with another 20 percent vigorously yawning. (This was also explained to me: many lived far away and had to travel long in the morning and the evening. As a result they were very tired.) Four hundred people going through the motions —and the non-motions, for that matter!— and not a single solid thing said. I felt as in a madhouse. Addressing such an audience is no fun either: neither of the two Americans has been able to get *any* reaction from the audience. I can be very proud of my record: the audience laughed once or twice and I even got two questions from the floor. I was told that that was very exceptional, and I well believe it, for it felt like addressing a hall full of mummies.

It was all so strange that, perhaps, I misinterpret totally what I witnessed. It was my definite impression that the panel members had been selected not for their professional competence but on account of their high position in the hierarchy: they had all the most important functions but did not say a thing. Was the audience selected on the same rules? I don't know. They seemed to be manager types of low quality. I observed that crowd during the interval, when coffee was served. It certainly did not look as usual at the interval of a scientific meeting, but perhaps that is the way in which a crowd of 400 Japanese behave, even if they are scientists. . . .

I was also amazed by the ease with which they seemed to have adopted the new religion of computer networks. That the design of properly operating computer networks presents some difficulties clearly did not count. And that, even if you have it operating properly, it is not always clear how to use the facility at considerable advantage, was also ignored. Networks of microcomputers were going to save the country. This was the new dogma. One must hope that from experience the Japanese know that all these words are just words, for if they really believe what has been said over and over again, it is frightening. (I think that they are not used to require from language that it is really meaningful. A great number of English computer jargon terms have been incorporated in the Japanese language without translation, just copied. It was illuminating that all the meaningless buzz words and vague, dubious terms were included, such as "program maintenance" "the user", "intelligent terminal", "Systems Analyst (or SA)", "Systems Engineer (or SE)", "data structuring", "structured programming (or SP)", "multi-level hierarchy", "concept"(!) etc. All these words, pronounced with an accent, of course, are nowadays perfect Japanese!)

*　　*　　*

On Thursday evening the Dutch Community in Tokyo —about 350 people— came together (this time devoted to the annual commemoration of the end of the Siege of Leyden, which meant "hutspot" and "rauwe haring", the latter dish freshly flown over by KLM). I went there to satisfy my curiosity; I joined them for about two hours, it was quite interesting. Then I was picked up by the Scientific Attaché and his wife and had a quiet chat in his apartment, which gave me a glimpse of an unfamiliar world. They lived quite near the Russian Embassy and it was shortly after the MIG 25 had landed in Japan. It was a very nice evening, but, no matter how nice and interesting, an insufficient justification for the whole trip.

*　　*　　*

The last item but one on my schedule mentioned for Friday evening:

"Mr. Zapf, President of Burroughs Japan, wishes to have the pleasure of inviting Dr. Dijkstra for informal dinner."

Waiting in my hotel room for Mr. Zapf to call, he did indeed call at 7 p.m., terribly embarrassed. He had a business meeting and had heard of this arrangement just a few minutes ago. Linguistic problems had clearly caused some communication difficulties. I told him not to bother and had an excellent dinner together with Weber, did some writing, and went to bed.

*   *
*

One of the questions from the floor was a question that had been posed to me several times in Russia: "But what about the education of the average programmer?". On my way to Novosibirsk I decided to give from now onwards the same standard answer. The question was put to me in Novosibirsk and there it worked. It was also asked in Tokyo, and there the answer worked beyond expectation (because the audience laughed). The answer was the counter-question "What about the education of the average mathematician?"

Nuenen, Plataanstraat 5

PROF. DR. EDSGER W. DIJKSTRA
Burroughs Research Fellow

EWD594
A Parable

(Recently I found the following text in manuscript among old papers of mine. It must have been written in the middle of 1973, but I don't think that in the intervening three years it has lost its significance. Hence I now incorporate it in the EWD series.)

Years ago a railway company was erected and one of its directors —probably the commercial bloke— discovered that the initial investments could be reduced significantly if only fifty percent of the cars would be equipped with a toilet, and, therefore, so was decided.

Shortly after the company had started its operations, however, complaints about the toilets came pouring in. An investigation was carried out and revealed that the obvious thing had happened. Despite its youth, the company was already suffering from internal communication problems, for the director's decision on the toilets had not been transmitted to the shunting yard where all cars were treated as equivalent, and, as a result, sometimes trains were composed with hardly any toilets at all.

In order to solve the problem, a bit of information was associated with each car, telling whether it was a car with or without a toilet, and the shunting yard was instructed to compose trains with the numbers of cars of both types as equal as possible. It was a complication for the shunting yard, but, once it had been solved, the people responsible for the shunting procedures were quite proud that they could manage it.

When the new shunting procedures had been made effective, however, complaints about the toilets continued. A new investigation was carried out and then it transpired that, although in each train about half the cars had indeed toilets, sometimes trains were composed with nearly all toilets in one half of the train. In order to remedy the situation, new instructions were issued, prescribing that cars with and cars without toilets should alternate. This was a more severe complication for the shunting people, but after some initial grumbling, eventually they managed.

Complaints, however, continued and the reason turned out to be that, as the cars with toilets had their toilet at one of their ends, the distance between two successive toilets in the train could still be nearly three car lengths, and for mothers with children in urgent need —and perhaps even luggage piled up in the corridors— this still could lead to disasters. As a result, the cars with toilets got another bit of information attached to them, making them into directed objects, and the new instructions were that in each train the cars with toilets should have the same orientation. This time, the new instructions for the shunting yard were received with less than enthusiasm, for the number of turntables was hardly sufficient; to be quite fair to the shunting people we must even admit that, according to all reasonable standards, the number of turntables was insufficient, and it was only by virtue of the most cunning ingenuity that they could just manage.

With all toilets equally spaced along the train, the company felt confident that now everything was alright, but passengers continued to complain: although no passenger was more than a car length away from the nearest toilet, passengers (in urgent need) did not know in which direction to start their stumbling itinerary along the corridor! To solve this problem, arrows saying "TOILET" were fixed in all corridors, thereby also making the other half of the cars into directed objects that should be properly oriented by the shunting procedure.

When the new instruction reached the shunting yard, it created an atmosphere ranging from despair to revolt: it just couldn't be done! At that critical moment a man whose name has been forgotten and shall never be traced made the following observation. When each car with a toilet was coupled, from now until eternity, at its toileted end with a car without a toilet, from then onwards the shunting yard, instead of dealing with N directed cars of two types, could deal with $N/2$ identical units that, to all intents and purposes, could be regarded as symmetrical. And this observation solved all shunting problems at the modest price of, firstly, sticking to trains with an even number of cars only —the few additional cars needed for that could be paid out of the initial savings effected by the commercial bloke!— and, secondly, slightly cheating with regard to the equal spacing of the toilets. But, after all, who cares about the last three feet?

Although at the time that this story took place mankind was not blessed yet with automatic computers, our anonymous man who found this solution deserves to be called the world's first competent programmer.

*   *   *

I have told the above story to different audiences. Programmers, as a rule, are delighted by it, and managers, invariably, get more and more annoyed as the story progresses; true mathematicians, however, fail to see the point.

Nuenen   PROF. DR. EDSGER W. DIJKSTRA
                                                Burroughs Research Fellow

EWD603
Trip Report E.W. Dijkstra, St. Pierre-de-Chartreuse, 12–19 Dec. 1976

It was a meeting of IFIP Working Group 2.3 on "Programming Methodology", hosted by Gerard Veillon of the University of Grenoble in Hotel Beau Site in St. Pierre-de-Chartreuse, a place once selected for a monastery because of its inaccessibility. Coen Bron —the other Dutch participant— wanted to go by car —after the meeting he remained there for a skiing weekend— and picked me up on Saturday morning. Driving alternatingly, we arrived in Beaune on Saturday evening, having had one major stop. Along European highways, and particularly along the French ones, there is now a chain of highway restaurants under the name of Jacques Borel and in one of these we had lunch. It was the kind of mistake one makes in one's life only once.

In the centre of Beaune we found a nice hotel with (for once) a perfect kitchen. After dinner we had a little evening walk through the sleepy town and were quite surprised —and pleased!— to encounter a big statue of and dedicated to Gaspard Monge! The next morning we continued our travel and it was about noon when we reached our destination. It was a most pleasant trip, but for the fact that Coen felt that it was quite safe for him to read the maps while driving and insisted on showing that he could do so without causing an accident. (When I refused to show signs of discomfort, he first allowed the car to shift to one side of the lane; eventually he asked me "to keep on his behalf my eyes on the road". I then told him what he wanted to hear, viz. that I did not like it.)

My journey back was less successful. With Ross, McKeeman, and Horning I went (by a French train) from Grenoble to Geneva, where the other three had hotel reservations since they would fly from Geneva the next day. I had to catch a connection to Basel where I would pick up the Italy-Holland Express, for which I had a reservation in the sleeper. I intended to be home early Saturday morning. According to the schedule I would have 54 minutes in Geneva, but the French train accumulated a delay of more than one hour and I missed my connection. I had dinner with Doug Ross (who was very hungry), found a room in his hotel, and slept until 4 o'clock in the morning, packed and took a train leaving Geneva at 4:40. With changes in Bern, Basel, Mannheim and Köln I came home in the middle of the afternoon (still cursing the French railway system).

*   *
*

Particularly the first half of the meeting was not successful. It was a coincidence of circumstances. Mike Woodger had been W.G.2.3's extremely successful chairman, but he had given his chair to Jim Horning, who had to get used to the role; besides that, Jim was hit by "Napoleon's revenge". This, however, was probably the minor cause. The more important cause, I think, was that we had an exceptionally great number of "observers" and that —we had had "speaking observers" in the past— many of them were eager to present their thing. This got somewhat out of hand.

In W.G.2.3 a member used to "instruct" the other members only if he had something new to tell of which he felt that it was —or could be— very relevant. More often, the speaking member would seek the others' advice or opinion. The many speaking observers either did not know that rule or felt insufficiently secure to expose their uncertainty. The result was that the meeting was dangerously beginning to look like an ordinary conference with unrefereed papers. The third cause —but this I only realized after the meeting had been closed— was that, a month prior to the meeting, Zahn had sent the so-called "specification" of Peter Henderson, as it occurs in his article "An exercise in structured programming" (or something like that) as a challenge to the participants. Too many people had picked up that gauntlet (instead of ignoring it), and, in view of their preparation, felt entitled to present their experience. With the exception of McKeeman's, all presentations inspired by Henderson's specification were terrible. (This was to be expected, for a more appropriate title for Henderson's paper would have been "A demonstration of the mess generated by indiscriminate use of sloppy English.".) In short: we had a very false start.

On Wednesday morning the observers left the room so as to allow the members to attend to "Working Group matters". It was only then that we realized that, up till that moment, the meeting had largely been wasted, and that all of us were totally miserable about it. We wondered what had happened! Had we run out of steam? Was Programming Methodology completed or exhausted? Should we disband? Since Wednesday afternoon was the official afternoon off, the members unanimously decided to cancel all other arrangements and appointments they had made for that afternoon, and to reconvene after lunch to have a meeting with just members, in order to take the experiment whether, "among ourselves" so to speak, the spirit could be recaptured. It could, and after working from two till after six, most of us felt that disbanding —what had been discussed so seriously that morning— would be premature. There is still enough to be done!

The next two days were rescheduled and, thank goodness, much better (although not sufficiently so to compensate completely for the "lost" Monday and Tuesday; but that would have been too much to ask for).

*   *   *

I shall not review the week's program in any detail. I shall try, instead, to sort out my feelings, impressions, and hopes concerning Programming Methodology in general and W.G.2.3 in particular.

We all know that an ideal program has more virtues than planets will ever be discovered in the universe. To mention but a few: it is correct, efficient, robust, portable, expandable, easy to modify, easy to maintain, easy to read, easy to understand, easy to write, etc.! We also know that Programming Methodology has been successful insofar as it has been able to separate those concerns and to deal with them in turn. We now know, for instance, quite clearly that the unfactored criterion "A program is good (enough) as long as it satisfies your customers." is too woolly to be of *any* help. We now know, for instance, quite clearly that "correctness" is only meaningful with respect to precisely stated functional specifications, which act as a kind of logical firewall between the correctness aspect of the design and its usefulness aspect. (Which mathematician worries about the correctness of a proof for a vague "theorem"?) We also know that the successful isolation of a nontrivial aspect is always a significant scientific contribution (e.g. the discretization of synchronization requirements, BNF to describe the context-free aspect of programming languages, the postulational semantics that abstract from computational histories, etc.). It is from such discoveries —i.e. the isolation of nontrivial aspects and successfully treating them in isolation— that Programming Methodology can profit, probably even can profit more than from anything else.

Such a separation is traditionally opposed to by the people for whom (for lack of a better term in my vocabulary) I have coined the term "integralists". We always had a few integralists in W.G.2.3 and they always caused the problems that are to be expected, but I used to consider them as a useful antidote, and quite healthy when taken in small doses. This time we had too many integralists. Such rigorous separation of concerns is nowadays (politically!) unpopular. The current misgivings about the influence of science in general and of technology in particular are in no way better expressed than by the cry for "interdisciplinary approach", "systems thinking", etc., and he who concerns himself for some time in depth with only one aspect can be sure of getting accused of narrow-mindedness. Yet, the unpopular separation of concerns is more necessary than ever, and W.G.2.3 (not obliged to produce a Magnum Opus) has in this respect not only special opportunities, but by this very fact also special obligations. In its last meeting this was too often forgotten, due largely, although not entirely, to a number of observers who had (mostly unconsciously, I guess) accepted political prejudices of their respective environments as scientific constraints. We should not allow this to happen again. (Large conferences are becoming uniformly boring, nearly everybody reporting how he has tackled the same "wrong" problems with the same inadequate techniques. I am beginning to feel that this uniformity of the behaviour of the scientific world in our field is largely caused by the homogeneity of political objectives, prejudices, and pressures in the Western world. And often they seem pressures to abstain from trying really effective solutions because they are at the time and place politically unpalatable. To interpret the boring uniformity of these large conferences as a symptom of "completion" of the field would be a serious mistake.)

With Programming Methodology in our charter, the effectivity of patterns of reasoning has always been a serious concern. It is, for instance, in the name of that effectivity that systems of postulational semantics have been developed so that we may come to grips with the semantics of a program without being forced to do so via the detour of the class of possible computational histories. Niklaus Wirth made no joke when he wrote that programming languages should be defined without any reference to computers or compilers. (I would like to phrase it still stronger: "independent of any underlying computational model".) Among ourselves most of us really try to stick to that rule (and when, for instance, Tony could not, he apologized for the absence of proof rules!). Now, regrettably, we had a great number of speakers who were unaware of the desirability to abstract from the computational histories, could hardly grasp what was meant by it, and "talked operationally" with all its traditional clumsiness as if we still lived in 1965. We should not allow that to happen again.

We have forgotten that "thinking" as a topic of explicit concern is a very sensitive subject (because we all think and hope to do it well). This very intimate activity of thinking is closely intertwined with our public activities of writing and speaking, and, therefore, how we write and speak should be of equally serious and explicit concern. But this time —and we should not allow it to happen again— the way in which people expressed themselves could not be discussed openly, and we had to subject ourselves for several hours to the most barbarian slipshod haberdashery. (I tried once to ask the speaker for clarification after a few nonsensical sentences. His comment "Are you commenting on my language or on what I am saying?". I shrugged my shoulders and left it at that, for it would have been too painful to explain in public that he made an empty distinction and that he spoke words but said —and probably thought— nothing worthwhile. And that was terrible: in W.G.2.3 we are not used to avoiding discussions that might become painful.)

Some people's mixed attitude towards thinking also surfaced during one of the discussions (but it was not pursued . . .). We were shown experiments in "program transformations" that, while retaining semantic equivalence, may influence efficiency drastically: a fully legitimate and sometimes even fascinating topic. It *may* provide a way of separating in time our concerns about correctness and efficiency: one first writes a correct one and then transforms it into one that is efficient as well. To advocate such an approach now, however, seems premature to me. A few examples given were most unconvincing, because the derivation of the "inefficient but correct program" that could serve as a starting point for the transformation process had taken their designers orders of magnitude more time than has been needed to solve the problem directly: one or several days versus 15 minutes. (A possible explanation could be that, when efficiency is ignored, one receives less heuristic guidance and the "solution space" becomes too great.) When I drew attention to this discrepancy, one of the participants —a full professor at a (once?) famous university!— more or less disqualified that 15-minute solution by remarking that its design had required competent thinking and, therefore, "did not count" because nowadays you could not expect your students to try to learn to do so. He seemed to feel that in the future his system could provide a welcome Ersatz. I drew another conclusion: it confirmed my opinion that there is no substitute for a good brain, and that we would commit the cultural blunder of the decade if, seduced by the promises of Artificial Intelligence, we were to forsake our educational obligations towards the next generation. (I am afraid that the blunder is already being committed on a large scale.)

I think that I can understand the world better if I don't regard Artificial Intelligence and General Systems Thinking as scientific activities, but as political or quasi-religious movements (complete with promise of salvation). Back home I was chagrined to learn that the NSF has a "Program Director Intelligent Systems".

AN AFTERTHOUGHT. What in modern American —my 1973 Webster doesn't mention it yet— is called "deskilling a job", boils down to changing a task in such a way that it can be done by less educated —that means: cheaper— labour. It is mostly inspired by economic considerations: whether it is worth the cultural price to be paid for is another matter.

Some of the people at this meeting seemed engaged in, or to justify their efforts in terms of, "deskilling the programmer's job". Quite apart from its desirability, which I don't feel tempted to discuss here, we should consider its feasibility. If we share the dreams of the Artificial Intelligentsia, the feasibility is no longer a point of discussion: given greater machines, more time, and more funding, the whole programming problem will just disappear. For two reasons I happen not to share that dream: it seems technically as unattainable as automatic theorem proving, and someone will have to take the responsibility to believe (and to act accordingly) that the design is, indeed, the useful engine it was intended to be, and neither confidence nor responsibility are things that can be delegated. What can be done —and I think: should be done— is to try to mechanize the tedium. Mechanizing the tedium, however, increases the density of difficulty of the task that remains! I don't object to it, for it increases mankind's programming ability, but we should be aware of the fact that it is the contrary of "deskilling the programmer's job". (It creates already serious social problems for the thousands and thousands of old practitioners!)

And finally: I can sometimes not escape the impression that the mechanizers of the tedium are overselling their techniques and overstating their case by the (sometimes even mechanic) generation of quite avoidable tedium. (End of afterthought.)

Nuenen

PROF. DR. EDSGER W. DIJKSTRA
Burroughs Research Fellow

EWD607

A Correctness Proof for Communicating Processes: A Small Exercise

Over the last one-and-a-half years C.A.R. Hoare has explored "communicating sequential processes", among many other targets, as a means for describing "elephants built from mosquitoes, all humming in harmony", to quote the old metaphor. His approach has two main characteristics to be described now.

1) The so-called "marriage bureau coupling". Inspired by our familiarity with the assignment statement, he has decided to try to visualize input and output as the two sides of an assignment statement. In the one mosquito the input command assigns a value to one of its —by definition! — private variables, in the other mosquito the matching output command provides the value to be assigned. In the implementation these input and output commands are supposed to prescribe an implicit synchronization: they are viewed as completed simultaneously. (This is in accordance with our earlier impression, viz. that "mutual coincidence" is in such an environment a more essential notion than "mutual exclusion".) Given

mosquito x with a local variable a	mosquito y with a locally formed value E

then the "simultaneous" execution of their respective commands:

$$y?(a) \qquad\qquad x!(E)$$

is semantically equivalent to

$$a := E \quad .$$

Note that the program text for mosquito "x" mentions the sender "y" in its input command "$y?(a)$", and that the text for mosquito "y" mentions the receiver "x" in its output command "$x!(E)$".

2) Each pair of mosquitoes is connected via at most a *single* channel that accommodates two-way traffic. This imposes an ordering in time on the acts of communication between any two mosquitoes. It was felt that this would simplify the mathematical treatment.

*   *
*

We embarked upon one of a series of examples of communicating sequential processes solving a sorting problem suggested by Wim H.J. Feijen. Two mosquitoes each start with a "bag of natural numbers" —the difference between a "bag" and a "set" being that in a bag not all elements need be different from each other— . Mosquito x removes the maximum value from its bag and sends it to mosquito y, which adds it to its bag; this is followed by a transmission by y to x of the minimum element taken from the bag of y, etc. Eventually x ends up with the small elements in its bag and y with the large ones.

Our aim was to investigate to what extent the two mosquitoes could be successfully investigated in isolation. We wrote down texts for both mosquitoes, and then covered the one text with a piece of paper. I now simulate that by first only giving you the text for mosquito x (with many notational liberties, which I hope won't confuse you; $\mp$ and $\doteq$ stand for addition to and removal from bags).

Mosquito x:
begin r, s: bag **of** nat; a, p: nat;
         $s := S$ {the constant S is a non-empty bag **of** nat}; $p := \max(s)$;
         $y!(p)$; $r := s \doteq p$;
         $y?(a)$; $s := r \mp a$;
         $p := \max(s)$ $\{P\}$;
         do $p > a \rightarrow y!(p)$; $r := s \doteq p$;
                     $y?(a)$; $s := r \mp a$;
                     $p := \max(s)$ $\{P\}$
         od
end

With sum(bag) = the sum of the numbers contained in "bag", we have as the relevant invariant relation for the **do...od**:

P: $(\text{sum}(s) = \text{sum}(r) + a)$ **and** $p = \max(s) \geqslant a$.

The first equality is established after $s := r \mp a$; the inequality $p \geqslant a$ is established by $p := \max(s)$, because $\max(s) \geqslant$ any element in s and element a is in s.

We choose for the variant function sum(r):

$w\,dec("r := s \doteq p", \text{sum}(r)) = \text{sum}(s \doteq p) < \text{sum}(r) =$
$\text{sum}(s) - p < \text{sum}(r) = \{\text{on account of } P\}$
$\text{sum}(r) + a - p < \text{sum}(r) = p > a$.

Hence the guard "$p > a$" guarantees effective decrease of sum(r). Because natural numbers are bounded from below, sum(r) is also, and mosquito x terminates. In its final state it has established (P **and** $p \leqslant a$), which implies max(s) = a, i.e. the final value of "a" occurs in the bag "s" and is the largest value in that bag. (If the value(s) of "a" were not bounded from below, termination, indeed, could not be guaranteed. I shall not pursue that now, because proofs of nontermination are a different story.)

* *
*

We now turn our attention to mosquito y.

```
begin  t, u: bag of nat; b, q: nat;
       t := T {the constant T is a nonempty bag of nat};
       x?(b); u := t ∓ b;
       q := min(u);
       x!(q); t := u ≃ q {Q};
       do x?(b) → u := t ∓ b;
               q := min(u);
               x!(q); t := u ≃ q {Q}
       od
end
```

The "query guard" $x?(b)$ is regarded to have the side-effect of assigning a value to b when evaluating to true —as a matter of fact, the value transmitted by the matching $y!(p)$ in mosquito x, but the discussion of this interaction is postponed, as well as the discussion of how a happening in mosquito x can cause the query guard $x?(b)$ to become false— . The invariant relation Q for y's repetitive construct that interests us is

$$Q: \quad q \leqslant \min(t) \quad .$$

We have $wp($ "$t := u \simeq q$", $Q) = q \leqslant \min(u \simeq q)$. Because $\min(u \simeq q) \geqslant \min(u)$, the previous weakest precondition is implied by $q = \min(u)$, a relation which is established by $q := \min(u)$. In short: when mosquito y has terminated, it has established $q \leqslant \min(t)$, i.e. all elements in the bag t are greater than or equal to the final value of q (the final value of q need not occur in the bag t).

* *
*

The proofs, so far, have surprised us in two respects. First of all: when we started we did not know that the weakest condition on the input stream of the a's for termination of x would be that the a's are bounded from below and *nothing else*. (I believe I intuitively felt that the sequences of a's being non-increasing had something to do with it; quod non.) Secondly, we feared another complication when we started: mosquito x terminates when otherwise it would send a value p = the value "a" just received. This value has been transmitted once —if originally in T— or twice —if originally in S— , and for that reason we expected that we would have to distinguish between those two cases. (Trying to live with sum(s) as variant function would have introduced similar problems.) In our treatment the distinction between those two cases has disappeared completely —I even hope that some of my readers did not realize this distinction before I pointed it out to them!— , and that is probably the most pleasant and encouraging gain that we derived from dealing with our mosquitoes in isolation. By now we have studied them to such an extent in isolation that time has come to study the combination.

There are a few rules of the game: input/output command sequences at both sides of a channel must match, i.e. for an input command at one side of the channel we must have a matching output command at the other side. Well, in this simple example, this is OK, in the sense that the sequence of channel commands in x is given by the syntax —with $\{ \ldots \}$ denoting zero or more instances of the enclosed—

$$ y!(p) \qquad y?(a) \qquad \{y!(p) \qquad y?(a)\} $$

and in mosquito y by

$$ x?(b) \qquad x!(q) \qquad \{x?(b) \qquad x!(q)\} \qquad . $$

Ignoring the arguments p, a, b, and q, the one syntax can be transformed into the other by interchanging x and y and also interchanging ? and !. Hence, both syntaxes contain matching sentences, and the whole thing will match, provided that from both syntaxes "the same" sentence is chosen. In this case the choice of sentence is restricted to the length: both mosquitoes must terminate at the same stage.

It seems very tricky if separate termination proofs for both mosquitoes must be given, with in addition a proof that they will terminate after the same amount of traffic. (Not impossible, but tricky.) One of the rules of the game is that when one of the mosquitoes decides on account of its internal logic —such as x in this example— to quit, that this can result in "disappearance of the channel" —e.g. by a block exit, not indicated in our text for x— and that disappearance of the channel will cause at the other side communication commands in a guard position —such as the (second) $x?(b)$ in the text for y— to give rise to a false guard. Tony seems to have chosen for an asymmetry here: only "query guards" are allowed in his proposal. Although the decision is defensible, for the time being we would also like to allow "exclamation guards": termination because the receiving end decides that it has had enough! (Sorry for the very operational terminology.) In view of the symmetry between input and output, this greater freedom does not seem to create much complication. With such an implicit convention for termination, the communication sequences at both ends are now forced to match. (The match can even be decided on purely syntactic grounds; we hope this will always be the case.)

Associate with $y!(p)$ the implicit assignment $pp := pp \mp p$ (to the "ghost bag" pp, which is initialized empty). Similarly associate with $y?(a)$

the assignment $aa := aa \mp a$. We can then strengthen P with

$$s = S \mp aa \simeq pp \quad ;$$

similarly, Q can be strengthened with the relation

$$t = T \mp bb \simeq qq \quad .$$

Taking the arguments in our matching syntaxes into account, a postulate about the communication must enable us to identify p with b, hence pp with bb, and a with q, hence aa with qq. And thus we find firstly $s \mp t = S \mp T$ i.e. conservation of elements. But it also allows us to equate the *final* value of "a" with the *final* value of "q", thus combining from the two final states

$$\max(s) = a = q \leqslant \min(t) \quad ;$$

thus the correctness of the elephant has been established.

Acknowledgements are due to all the countrymen (women) with whom I regularly talk about my work: Feijen, Rem, Scholten, Bulterman, Steffens, Martin, etc. They are not to be held responsible for my mistakes or what have you.

Nuenen

PROF. DR. EDSGER W. DIJKSTRA
Burroughs Research Fellow

EWD608
An Elephant Inspired by the Dutch National Flag

Encouraged by the success of EWD607, we now embark upon the analysis of a more intricate elephant. We start with a cyclic arrangement of $3 + 3$ mosquitoes. Three main mosquitoes, called $R(ed)$, $W(hite)$, and $B(lue)$ respectively, and three buffer mosquitoes RW, WB, and BR, in between:

$$R \to RW \to W \to WB \to B \to BR \to R \quad .$$

The buffer mosquitoes are quite simple, e.g.:

```
RW:   begin channel W;
              begin channel R; buf: pebble;
                     do R?(buf) → W!(buf) od
              end
       end      .
```

When its (input) channel with R ceases to exist, $R?(buf)$ will become *false*, and block exit will cause termination of the existence of the (output) channel with W.

Each of the main mosquitoes has three "bags **of** pebble", named "$r(ed)$", "$w(hite)$", and "$b(lue)$". The R mosquito must collect in its bag called "r" all red pebbles in the system; its "foreign" pebbles it transmits, one at a time, via the buffer mosquito RW, first emptying its blue bag because its blue pebbles, which have to reach their destination via W, have to travel the longer distance. The arrangement is worth investigating because we expect problems with the proof of termination.

The solution that I am proposing has also a starting problem, but I am not going to divulge that now; I hope that that difficulty emerges "naturally" from a systematic analysis of our system.

mosquito R:
begin channel BR;
        x, y: pebble; r, w, b: bag **of** pebble;
        proc accept: **if** non $BR?(y) \rightarrow skip\,[]\ BR?(y) \rightarrow$ place **fi corp**;
        proc place: **if** $white(y) \rightarrow w := w \mp y\ []\ red(y) \rightarrow r := r \mp y$
                    fi corp;
        $r, w, b :=$ "initial values" $\{R3\}$;
        begin channel RW;
            do card$(b) > 0 \rightarrow x := \text{any}(b); b := b \simeq x$;
                      $RW!(x)$; accept
            od $\{R2\}$;
            do card$(w) > 0 \rightarrow x := \text{any}(w); w := w \simeq x$;
                      $RW!(x)$; accept
            od
        end $\{R1\}$;
        do $BR?(y) \rightarrow$ place **od** $\{R0\}$
end

    (and cyclically).

NOTE. "card" —short for "cardinality"— denotes "number of elements in". (End of note.)

We assume that —by some magic, not to be discussed here— BR (the text of which starts with "**begin channel** R") and R (the text of which starts with "**begin channel** BR") perform the entry to their outer blocks simultaneously, thereby establishing the channel between them (which will be used only as an input channel to R). When the three input channels to the main mosquitoes have been established, the six inner blocks will be entered —pairwise simultaneously, but now R paired with RW— and the output channels for the main mosquitoes have been established. (This is *very* informal and intuitive, but OK for the moment: if coded wrongly, such paired block entries can, of course, create a glorious deadlock.)

Let us now study mosquito R backwards. My final goal is to establish proper termination with

$R0$:   card$(b) = $ card$(w) = 0$ **and** y-tail$(R0)$ is empty,

i.e. mosquito R has to terminate with red pebbles only when nothing will be sent to it anymore; with "y-tail(Ri)" I denote the sequence of y-values still to be absorbed in stage Ri before $BR?(y)$ turns definitely *false*.

The first step is to investigate the transition from $R1$ to $R0$. Termination of the repetitive construct inbetween guarantees **non** $BR?(y)$, i.e. guarantees that y-tail$(R0)$ is empty; infinite repetition is excluded by

$$y\text{-tail}(R1) \text{ is finite}\qquad.$$

Because $\text{card}(b) = \text{card}(w) = 0$ does not follow from "**non** BB" it had better hold at $R1$ and be kept invariant by "place". Keeping $\text{card}(w) = 0$ invariant by "place" implies the absence of white pebbles in the tail, avoiding abortion implies the absence of blue ones, and we find for $R1$

$R1$: $\text{card}(b) = \text{card}(w) = 0$ **and** y-tail($R1$) is finite and red only   .

NOTE. The condition "finite and red only" is satisfied by the empty tail. (End of note.)

The next step is to investigate the transition from $R2$ to $R1$. Because $\text{card}(b) = 0$ does not follow from "**non** BB", we require it at $R2$; exclusion of abortion taken into account:

$\text{card}(b) = 0$ **and** y-tail($R2$) contains no blue pebbles   .

We have to impose more, because we have also to guarantee

$\text{card}(w) = 0$ **and** y-tail($R1$) is finite and red only   .

Termination guarantees $\text{card}(w) = 0$ and is guaranteed by

y-tail($R2$) is finite   .

(For the variant function we can take: $\text{card}(w) +$ number of white pebbles in y-tail.) But how do we guarantee that y-tail($R1$) is red only?
Let us define for a finite tail without blue pebbles

if tail contains no white pebbles: *slack* $= -1$
if tail contains white pebbles: *slack* $=$ the total number of red pebbles
                                                        preceding the last white one

and let us consider the relation $\text{card}(w) > slack$. Then

(1) $\text{card}(w) = 0$ implies that the finite tail is all red
(2) $\text{card}(w) > slack$ is an invariant for the repeatable statement from $R2$
       to $R1$; because $\text{card}(w) \geqslant 0$ by definition, this is obvious if the
       resulting tail has no white pebbles, otherwise
       (2a) y has been white, in which case both $\text{card}(w)$ and *slack* remained
             unchanged
       (2b) y has been red, in which case both $\text{card}(w)$ and *slack* have been
             decreased by 1.

Hence, collecting all our requirements, we deduce

$R2$: $\text{card}(b) = 0$ **and** y-tail($R2$) is finite, without blue pebbles **and**
          $\text{card}(w) > slack(R2)$.

For the transition from $R3$ to $R2$, infinite repetition is excluded a priori and abortion is excluded by the absence of blue pebbles in the tail; the invariant relation that does the trick is

$\text{card}(b) + \text{card}(w) > slack$

and we find for $R3$

> $R3$: y-tail($R3$) is finite, without blue pebbles **and** card(b) + card(w) >
> slack($R3$)   .

Taking the finiteness for a moment for granted, we see that

(1)   the absence of blue pebbles in the y-tail is guaranteed (because R does
      not transmit red pebbles, and cyclically)
(2)   slack($R3$) ≤ 0 (because R does transmit blue pebbles, if any, before
      white ones, if any, and cyclically).

Hence, a safe starting state is: each mosquito with at least *one* foreign
pebble! The complication at the start has, indeed, shown up nicely.

Termination was more easily demonstrated than originally feared.

(1)   Mosquito R will generate in its x-sequence an a priori bounded
      number of blue pebbles.
(2)   In the same way mosquito B will only generate in *its* x-sequence an a
      priori bounded number of white pebbles.
(3)   Equating the x-output of B with the y-input of R, we conclude that
      mosquito R will only receive a bounded number of white pebbles.
      Combining 1) and 3) we conclude that mosquito R will only generate a
      finite x-sequence.

The proof of total conservation of pebbles is left to the reader.

Nuenen   PROF. DR. EDSGER W. DIJKSTRA
                                          Burroughs Research Fellow

EWD611

On the Fact that the Atlantic Ocean Has Two Sides

Introduction and Apology

This is an open letter to my co-members of the IFIP Working Group 2.3 on "Programming Methodology". Among my writings thus far it will be an exception, because, until now, it has been very rare for me to undertake a task of which I knew *beforehand* that I would not be able to do it well enough. The reason that, nevertheless, I have decided to undertake it is quite simple: it has to be done, and offhand I can think of no one else less unqualified to try to do so.

My subject should be very simple, for it is only the difference between the orientations of computing science at the two sides of the Atlantic Ocean. That there is a difference should not amaze us at all, for the Atlantic Ocean is very big. For a variety of reasons, however, this difference is a bit hard to discuss: the difference itself is no problem, but it becomes a problem when ignored or denied. It is a bit hard to discuss for about three reasons.

Firstly, we are comparing prevailing attitudes between continents. Everyone familiar with them is aware of the great diversity within each of them, and he knows that writing about "a European attitude" is as much writing about a literary fiction as writing about "an American attitude". In the kind of global comparison I feel forced to make, I simply have to do injustice to differences of continental significance only. I can only ask you to forgive me my gross oversimplifications, of which I am only too aware myself. Abstracting from the inhomogeneity of both of the continents, we can still observe considerable differences between the two continents, and those differences are the subject matter of this open letter.

Secondly, the difference between the Old and the New World has already been discussed so extensively, and by so many, that it is practically impossible to raise the subject without evoking all the cliché prejudices. And in this discussion we *have* to pay attention to the general cultural difference, to the different images of man and society, for they have a profound influence on computing science (much profounder on computing science than on a merely technical subject such as geology or medicine).

Thirdly, many people are a bit touchy about this subject. Both continents have their inferiority complexes —overcompensated or not!— and we are all "party" in the sense that we have been born on one side only! Fully aware of how firmly my roots are planted in Europe, I can only undertake this task with considerable trepidation, afraid as I am of failing to be fair and to do justice. (This fear of being unjust and thereby offensive has been so great that during the first years of my association with Burroughs I have subconsciously avoided comparing the two continents! Having just gathered my courage, I nearly lost it again when I received a letter from Jim Horning, to whom I had mailed a copy of my trip report covering the last W.G.2.3 meeting. Jim wrote me "The analysis of the meeting in your trip report is in substantial agreement with my own, although my report to the members wasn't quite as blunt." I was surprised: evidently my pen is sometimes sharper than intended or suspected.)

Whether we like it or not: it *is* a touchy subject. And that is exactly the reason why it is avoided, and why someone should bring it up. I became aware of this by a curious incident at our last meeting in St. Pierre-de-Chartreuse. After Mary Shaw's presentation a lengthy and, in its way, lively discussion ensued, but it was a very curious one. With the exception of two short questions for clarification posed by European participants, the discussion was entirely an American affair, and it was noteworthy for the inadequacy with which it was carried out. Among the European participants witnessing this discussion, the overwhelming feeling was one of embarrassment. (Some younger ones could hardly believe their ears and voiced their amazement/indignation later in private by comments "Some have to learn it the hard way..." or "Is this 1976 or 1966?" and cruder ones.) The bitter point of the whole incident, however, was that none of us did what should have been done, that none of us interrupted by remarking that this did not seem an adequate way of discussing this topic. That is what would have happened in an unhampered scientific discussion!

In retrospect I have wondered about our silence, and I have blamed myself for it. My conclusion is that by the time that certain topics are becoming so painful to discuss as to paralyze scientific meetings, something has to be done about it. This is my effort.

Scales for Comparison; General Differences

A very useful measure is —called after its inventor— the "Buxton Index". John N. Buxton discovered that the most important one-dimensional scale, along which persons or institutions to be compared can be placed, is the length of the period of time in the future for which a person or institution plans. This period, measured in years, gives the Buxton Index. For the little shopkeeper around the corner the Buxton Index is three-quarters, for a true Christian it is infinite, we marry with one near fifty, most larger companies have one of about five, most scientists have one between two and ten. (For a scientist it is hard to have a larger one: the future then becomes so hazy, that effective planning becomes an illusion.)

The great significance of the Buxton Index is not its depth, but its objectivity. The point is that when people with drastically different Buxton Indices have to cooperate while unaware of the concept of the Buxton Index, they tend to make moral accusations against each other. The man with the shorter Buxton Index accuses the other of neglect of duty, the man with the larger one accuses the other of shortsightedness. The notion of the Buxton Index takes the moral flavour away and enables people to discuss such differences among themselves dispassionately. There is nothing wrong with having different Buxton Indices! It takes many people to make a world. There is clearly no moral value attached to either a long or a short Buxton Index. It is a useful concept for dispassionate discussion.

In my own environment I have suffered from a relatively long Buxton Index —complete with accusations to and fro— until the concept of the Buxton Index was brought to our attention. If, in the course of this discussion, I emerge as "very European", I think that among other things I do so on account of my large personal Buxton Index, because, on the average, the European Buxton Index seems to be larger than the American one. As an example I just mention the funding policy of the NSF and similar organizations —and it does not matter now whether we should regard this as cause or as symptom— . The NSF policy states explicitly, and the need for the statement is significant, that short-term goals at the expense of long-term concerns are not to be sponsored. Fine, but the majority of the research proposals aim at a tangible result within two or three years only. Personally I don't remember ever having seen a proposal for a grant beyond three years. The (to my taste) shortness of these periods has in the past been one of my main considerations for *not* joining the faculty of an American University, and as some of them have tried hard enough to seduce me, I feel entitled to call the difference significant.

*　　*　　*

My first visit to the USA —in 1963— was a shattering experience. (It was also frightening: I started with a few days all by myself in New York.) Of all memories from that visit, one is absolutely overpowering: for the first time in my life I was confronted with a civilization that did not give its scientists the automatic benefit of the doubt or the respect that I was used to. On that trip I learned the word "egg-head" as a truly untranslatable Americanism. (Untranslatability is always significant!) I was shocked to see how intellectuals could be —as it were— by definition suspect, and I remember that the feeling of uncertainty from which I saw my colleagues suffer worried me very much. It was the first time in my life that I realized what difference it makes to be a citizen of a very small monarchy in which each professorial appointment is confirmed by Her Majesty our Queen. (Again we need not argue here whether Her Majesty's involvement is symptom or cause of our scientists's spiritual independence and feelings of social security.)

The above captures the overwhelming impression of my first visit to the USA; the assumption that it refers to a significant difference seems, therefore, safe. My many subsequent visits to the USA gave me some opportunity to figure out what I had seen that first time. The questions are: how does science justify itself, why does a society tolerate scientists? The way in which these questions are answered has a deep influence on the scientist's behaviour, not only on the way in which he presents his results, but also on his way of working and his choice of topics. Traditionally there are two ways in which science can be justified, the Platonic and the pragmatic one. In the Platonic way —"l'art pour l'art"— science justifies itself by its beauty and internal consistency, in the pragmatic way science is justified by the usefulness of its products. My overall impression is that along this scale —which is not entirely independent of the Buxton Index— Europe, for better or for worse, is more Platonic, whereas the USA, and Canada to a lesser extent, are more pragmatic. (Most of you must have been confronted with my Pan-Academic prejudices, which are most definitely Platonic, and by now you may wonder how in the world I could join not only an industrial organization —industrial organizations by their charter being more pragmatic— but even an American one. But the answer is quite simple: in computing science the conflict need not exist —and that is what makes the subject so fascinating!— . To quote C.A.R. Hoare —from memory— : "In no engineering discipline does the successful pursuit of academic ideals pay more material dividends than in software engineering." I could not agree more.)

It is here that I must mention three general phenomena that go hand in hand with greater pragmatism. I must mention them, because they seem all relevant for computing science.

The first phenomenon is a greater tolerance for the soft sciences, which purport to contribute to the solutions of "real" problems, but whose "intellectual contents" are singularly lacking. (When I was a student at Leyden, a quarter of a century ago, economy and psychology had been admitted to the campus, but only with great reservations, and absolutely no one considered them respectable; we had not dreamt of "management science" —I think we would have regarded it as a contradiction in terms— and "business administration" as an academic discipline is still utterly preposterous.)

The second phenomenon is the one for which I had to coin the term "integralism". Scientific thought, as I understand it, derives its effectiveness from our willingness to acknowledge the smallness of our heads: instead of trying to cope with a complex, inarticulate problem in a single sweep, scientific thought tries to extract all the relevant aspects of the problem, and then to deal with them, in turn, in depth and in isolation. (And every time a significant aspect of a complex problem has been isolated successfully, this is ranked as an important scientific discovery. As an example I mention John Backus's introduction of BNF, capturing the context-free aspects of programming language syntax.) Dealing with some aspect of a complex problem "in depth and in isolation" implies two things. "In isolation" that you are (temporarily) ignoring most other aspects of the original total problem, "in depth" means that you are willing to generalize the aspect under consideration, are willing to investigate variations that are needed for a proper understanding, but are in themselves of no significance within the original problem statement. The true integralist becomes impatient and annoyed at what he feels to be "games". His mental make-up compels him to remain constantly aware of the whole chain, even when asked to focus his attention upon a single link. (When being shown the derivation of a correct program he will interrupt: "But how do you know that the compiler is correct?".) The rigorous separation of concerns evokes his resistance because all the time he feels that you are not solving "the real problem".

The third phenomenon that goes hand in hand with a greater pragmatism is that universities are seen less as seats of learning and centres of intellectual innovation and more as schools preparing students for well-paid jobs. If industry and government ask for the wrong type of people —students, brain-washed by COBOL and FORTRAN— then that is what they get. I know that the perpetuation of obsolete programming habits in the U.S.A. is beginning to be considered a matter of serious concern, because in the triangle computer users/computer manufacturers/universities, no single party seems able any longer to interrupt the vicious circle. (The moral of the text I read was that, therefore, here was a federal responsibility, because otherwise the USA could be overtaken by in this respect still more flexible nations. An outsider's corollary of this deadlock situation is that —in no field!— Universities should forsake their role of intellectual innovators.)

                                *
                          *   *

A third difference between the USA and Europe must be mentioned because it has such profound consequences. The USA is very large and, compared to Europe, much more homogeneous. Please don't accuse me of the gross oversimplification "When you have seen one American, you have seen them all". I have now been in so many states of the US and seen so many differences between them that I have concluded that, with my values of the terms, it is better for me to consider the USA not as "a country" but as "a continent". It is more that, besides all the local diversity, there are homogenizing forces in the USA that are absent in Europe. All American computing scientists write, speak, and publish in the same language, they all see the publications from the same ACM and IEEE and the manuals from the same computer manufacturers, their academic research is supported by the same central funding organizations, etc. This large and relatively homogeneous continent tends to become a law unto itself; the American computing community is, therefore, in a greater danger of regarding *its* mode of behaviour as *the* mode of behaviour, it is in a greater danger of becoming provincial and parochial. (Deviation from The Standard then becomes to be considered wrong: in the Computing Reviews of the ACM British authors of British publications are regularly being blamed for their Britishisms! See for a recent instance, for example, CR 30214.)

In this context, the fact that the majority of the American computing scientists are essentially monolingual is of special significance. A thorough study of one or more foreign languages makes one much more conscious about one's own; because an excellent mastery of his native tongue is one of the computing scientist's most vital assets, I often feel that the American programmer would profit more from learning, say, Latin than from learning yet another programming language.

*   *
*

Finally, a difference that is very specific to *academic* computing science: in Europe, Artificial Intelligence never really caught on. All sorts of explanations are possible: Europe's economic situation in the early fifties when the subject emerged, lack of vision of the European academic or military world, European reluctance to admit soft sciences to the university campus, cultural resistance to the subject being more deeply rooted in Europe, etc. I don't know the true explanation, it is probably a mixture of the above and a few more. We should be aware of this difference, whether we can explain it or not, because the difference is definitely there and has its influence on the outlook of the computing scientist.

How Difficult Is Programming?

When, in the late sixties, it became abundantly clear that we did not know how to program well enough, people concerned with Programming Methodology tried to figure out what a competent programmer's education should encompass. As a result of that effort programming emerged as a tough engineering discipline with a strong mathematical flavour. This conclusion has never been refuted. Many, however, have refused to draw it because of the unattractiveness of its implications, such as

(1) good programming is probably beyond the intellectual abilities of today's "average programmer"
(2) to do, hic et nunc, the job well with today's army of practitioners, many of whom have been lured into a profession beyond their intellectual abilities, is an insoluble problem

(3)   our only hope is that, by revealing the intellectual contents of program-
      ming, we will make the subject attractive to the type of students it
      deserves, so that a next generation of better qualified programmers
      may gradually replace the current one.

The above implications are certainly unattractive: their social implications are severe, and the absence of a quick solution is disappointing to the
impatient. Opposition to and rejection of the findings of programming
methodology are therefore only too understandable. We should remember
that the conclusion about the intrinsically mathematical nature of the
programming task has been made on technical grounds, and that its
rejection is always on political or emotional ones.

The rejection takes place at both sides of the Atlantic. It was a British
programmer that commented on my book that "it would be of no meaningful benefit to the programming profession as a whole" because "its techniques are mathematical, whereas the majority of today's programmers are
not.". (I regard this less as a comment on my work than as a statement from
an English programmer that, in his view, his current colleagues are fairly
education-resistant.) It was my own Department of Mathematics in
Eindhoven that needed in 1972 an easier subject than "true mathematics"
in order to enlarge its undergraduate enrollment drastically and chose
.....programming! (This was a very extreme case.)

On the whole, the underestimation of the mathematical maturity required
for the programming task seems somewhat stronger in the USA than in
Europe. In view of earlier remarks about the differences between the two
continents this is understandable. Our "solution" 3 —see above— is a
long-range one and requires a large Buxton Index to appreciate it as such. It
is more Platonic than pragmatic, it is the result of a rigorous separation of
concerns —abstracting from today's average programmers and also from
today's average machines— . It openly appeals to the innovating rôle of the
Universities. It favours the careful development of "natural intelligence"
based on the conviction that "artificial intelligence" will never be able to do
the job.

                    *   *

The first series of machines —that of the singletons— was mainly
developed in the USA shortly after World War II, while a ruined continental Europe had neither the technology nor the money to start building
computers. The only thing we could do was think about them. Therefore it
is not surprising that many US Departments of Computer Science are
offsprings of Departments of Electrical Engineering, whereas those in
Europe started (later) from Departments of Mathematics (of which they are
often still a part). This different heritage still colours the departments, and
could provide an acceptable explanation that in the USA Computing
Science is viewed more operationally than in Europe.

Added to this, John von Neumann's habit of describing computing systems and their parts in an anthropomorphic terminology has been adopted more generally in the USA than in Europe. (I was first exposed to the American's use of anthropomorphic terminology in the late fifties —when the *Comm.*ACM started to appear— and I remember that I was shocked by it. In the meantime, a less anthropomorphic terminology had already been established in my environment.) The problem caused by this metaphor is that it invites us to identify ourselves with programs, with processes, etc, because "existing" is one of our most intrinsic "activities". (That is why death is so hard to grasp.) The prevailing anthropomorphism erects another barrier to abstraction from program execution and computational histories.

To forget that program texts can also be interpreted as executable code, to define program semantics as a direct derivation from the program text and not via the detour of the class of possible computations, to define programming semantics independently of any underlying computational model, these are difficult abstractions to get used to. I have the impression that for an American computing scientist it is still harder than for a European one. Yet it is one of the most vital abstractions, if any significant progress is to be made at all.

It was the complete entanglement of language definition and language implementation that characterized the discussion after Mary Shaw's presentation, and it was this entanglement that left many of the Europeans flabbergasted. It was also this entanglement that made it impossible for me to read the LISP 1.5 Manual: after an incomplete language definition, that text tries to fill the gaps with an equally incomplete sketch of an —of the?— implementation. Yet in the decade after its publication the LISP 1.5 manual conquered a major portion of the American academic computing community. This, too, must have had a traceable influence. Why did LISP never get to that position in Europe? Perhaps because in the beginning its implementation made demands beyond our facilities, while later many had already learned to live without it. (I myself was completely put off by the Manual.)

*   *   *

My first visit to the USA, in 1963, was the result of an amazing invitation from the ACM. Without the obligation to present a paper, I was asked to attend —as "invited participant", so to speak— a three-day conference in Princeton. For the opportunity of having me sitting in the audience and participating in the discussions, my hosts were willing to pay my expenses, travel included! As you can imagine, I felt quite elated, but shortly after the conference had started, I was totally miserable. The first speaker gave a most impressive talk with wall-to-wall formulae and displayed a mastery of elaborate syntax theory, of which I had not even suspected the existence! I could only understand the first five minutes of his talk, and realized that I was only a poor amateur, sitting in the audience on false pretences.

I skipped lunch, walking around all by myself, trying to make out what that first speaker had told us. I got vaguely funny feelings, but it was only during the cocktail party that evening that I had recovered enough to dare to consider that it had all been humbug. Tentatively, I transmitted my doubts to one of the other participants. He was amused by my innocence. Didn't I know that the first performer was a complete bogus speaker? Of course it was all humbug, everybody in the audience knew that! Puzzled I asked him why the man had been invited and why, at the end, some of the participants had even faked a discussion. "Oh, on occasions like that, we just go through the motions. IBM is one of the sponsors of this conference, so we had to accept an IBM speaker. He was given the first slot, because the sooner it is over, the better.". I was flabbergasted.

Since then I have learned that this "going through the motions" is, indeed, a typical habit of the American scientific community. Whenever a large project is sponsored by a sufficiently prestigious or powerful body (MIT, ARPA, IBM, you name it), it is officially treated as sound and successful. The above story illustrates how utterly misleading that habit can be for an innocent European. By European standards, that habit is nearly fraudulent. But if Americans have a capacity for greater dishonesty, they have also a capacity for greater honesty! From American sources —both private and public— I can quote many comments on the Americans so candid that I cannot imagine a European discussing his own country in similar terms.

In other words, the rules that govern when to be explicit and when to be silent, and when to exaggerate for the sake of emphasis and when to use euphemisms, differ in the two continents. In international groups, this can cause endless confusion, and I see only one way out: to make for such a group an explicitly stated rule that everybody be outspoken and as clear as possible.

I don't remember whether it is the result of a consciously taken decision or whether the tradition just grew, but in W.G.2.3 we certainly used to apply such a rule, knowing full well that we would often display what looked like inconsiderate behaviour. I now understand why in a group like W.G.2.3 such a rule is absolutely essential, and I would like you to share that understanding with me. I also suspect that its former application is largely responsible for W.G.2.3's former success, and I would like you to share that suspicion with me.

Nuenen

PROF. DR. EDSGER W. DIJKSTRA
Burroughs Research Fellow

P.S. I apologize for having been so often so apologetic.   EWD

EWD613
Trip Report E.W. Dijkstra, Australia, 16 February 1977–21 March 1977

The trip to "downunder" was terrible. Still remembering my forced stay in the International Departure Hall of New Delhi —with the cockroaches on the carpet— I refused to fly again via the Eastern Hemisphere and had arranged my itinerary via Los Angeles. The IATA tariff rules —imposed by QUANTAS, the Australian airline company— are such that you may have one stopover during the whole trip. Having the choice between arriving in Australia or returning home as a bodily and nervous wreck, I had chosen the first.

I had planned the trip as carefully as possible. Instead of leaving Nuenen early on the morning of the Thursday on which I crossed the Atlantic, I flew to London on the previous evening. I had a hotel reservation quite close to Heathrow Airport, and the idea was that I would start from there on the great crossing as fresh as a daisy. Secondly, I had selected a British Airways flight with only two hours to catch my connection in Los Angeles. The idea was that the BA flight would probably be late: in that case a night of —welcome!— delay in LA would be forced upon me, and then I would not have to pay the additional $600(!), otherwise required for a second stopover.

But my cunning arrangement did not work at all: the hotel in London —the Centre Airport Hotel, Bath Road, Longford, avoid it!!— was terrible, so terrible that I hardly slept at all, and, although we had some delay when leaving from Heathrow, the BA-plane made up for it and arrived in LA dead on time! I caught my connection, and —what was worse— from LA to Honolulu the PANAM Jumbo was filled to the brim with teenagers from an American highschool. (They applauded during take-off, etc...) Perfect as the BA flight had been, so terrible was the PANAM flight: the Boeing 747 suffered from poor shock absorbers, and that made the take-offs bad and the landings worse. With intermediate stops in Honolulu and Pago-Pago

I had plenty of opportunity to observe the phenomenon. After Honolulu I slept a little, but when the Good Lord created the Talkative Airline Passenger, he made one of his worst mistakes.

I arrived in Sydney on Saturday morning, more dead than alive and very thirsty. I was collected by three gentlemen from the University of New South Wales, who were very considerate hosts. They took me to the other terminal, carried my luggage, gave me a few glasses of beer and saw me off at the gate, where I got on the plane to Canberra.

Thinking it over I can still get very cross with QUANTAS. If you were allowed a second stopover, you would not cost the airline companies a single passenger mile more, but for no valid reason the trip is just made much more exhausting than necessary. I know that, when very tired, there is a much greater probability that I have trouble with my eyesight than otherwise. I was therefore very grateful that in Sydney others were willing to carry my suitcase, but in spite of their good care, during that first week in Canberra my eyes worried me twice, once even much longer than on previous occasions. I had plenty of reason for cursing QUANTAS.

Four days before my return home I had the return flight confirmed, but this nervous traveller *knew* that there was something wrong. Because the confirmations had been made by telephone, I had no proof that they had been confirmed, and the day before my departure I went to the PANAM office in Canberra and had the girl behind the counter make a mark on my ticket, stating that my flight had been duly confirmed.

The next day, as soon as I was shown my place —45 D— I was called to the front of the plane via the loudspeakers. I undid my safety belt, went forward and was asked to show my boarding pass. Shortly after I had returned to my seat, someone else came, and I had to show my boarding pass again. After take-off I slept a little and forgot the incident. In Pago-Pago I left the plane to stretch my legs. But when I returned, the seats 45D/E were occupied by an otherwise nice couple. A stewardess promised to sort this out, but while she was still sorting out more and more passengers came on board and the plane became absolutely full. With apologies from the company I was given a —very uncomfortable— chair in the lounge on the second floor, above the first class cabin. In Honolulu I had to go through Immigration and Customs; when I returned I was given seat 45A and I had some sleep. In Los Angeles I had a pleasant stopover of 28 hours. With the direct flight of LUFTHANSA I flew back to Amsterdam in a Boeing 707, nearly full. A planeload of Germans is a bit much. Ria had come with the car to Schiphol to collect me; at a quarter past five I was back in her arms, at a quarter to eight we were home and I went to sleep at nine o'clock for the next twelve hours. When I woke up the next morning, I realized that in Australia it was six o'clock in the evening and in Los Angeles midnight.

*　　*　　*

My Australian hosts had organized my visit very carefully and with much consideration. For four weeks my official status was Visiting Fellow of the

Australian National University, which paid the travel expenses. In the second week I started on a lecture tour of the Universities and local branches of the Australian Computer Society at Adelaide, Melbourne, and Sydney "to earn my living".

I arrived on Saturday 19th of February, was given a few peaceful days for adjustment, and lectured on Thursday 24th and Friday 25th at ANU. (Both days I was the last speaker at a seminar with about 250 participants.) On the evening of Monday 28th I left for Adelaide, where I lectured at the University on Tuesday afternoon and for the ACS that evening. On Wednesday morning I left for Melbourne, where I performed at the University that afternoon and for the ACS on the evening of the next day. On Friday afternoon there was a party in my honour at Peter Poole's house; the weekend I stayed with a Dutch friend —and his relatives— near Melbourne. On the morning of Monday the 7th of March I flew to Sydney, where I lectured at the University of Sydney; the next day I was at the University of New South Wales during morning and afternoon; that evening I addressed the branch of the ACS, and on Wednesday morning 9th of March I returned to Canberra, where I stayed for the last ten days of my visit. In the last week I gave my ninth performance, viz. for the Canberra branch of the ACS. Nine performances of two hours, each for an average audience of 200 people, seemed enough to make the trip worthwhile.

*　　　*
*

Life is not easy for Australian scientists. A look through the papers gives you the impression that Australian spiritual life extends from labour conflicts on the one hand and cricket on the other, with very little in between. Listening to the conversations one discovers that there is bushwalking —with snob value— and that there are horse races —definitely without it — . There is, of course, much more, but that is definitely much less prominent — under the surface, so to speak.

I found many of my colleagues a little bit sad. They feel very much cut off from the rest of the world, and to a large extent they are. Scientific journals are sent by surface mail, and thus arrive late and irregularly. Worse, of course, is that they are cut off from the old boys network and pick up so little from the grapevine.

They are very much aware of this isolation and try to compensate for it. They do this in their personal lives. I found in several homes impressive record collections; I also looked at the bookshelves, and, again, I was often impressed. They also try to do this in their organizations. There were many foreigners and most of the Australian staff members seemed to have been either in Europe or in the USA or both, either for many visits or for extended periods of time. The nett result was that at many places —but particularly at ANU— the whole atmosphere was quite cosmopolitan.

This —and it makes life hard for the Australian scientists— seems in sharp contrast to the cultural (?) climate of the Australian government: a self-centred activity, in which all attention is absorbed by local frustrations and mutual mistrust. (In the different states the railway gauges are different!) My impression of the government and the civil service was one of short-range vision, both in time and space. And in view of the fact that education is always a long-range activity, it is quite understandable that most of my colleagues felt very uncomfortable.

Universities all over the world are very much constrained. Private universities are strongly constrained by the expectations of their students, universities funded by the government are constrained by the latter. In the case of the Australian universities, at least the Departments of Computing Science seem to be held in an iron grip of shortsightedness: the same government that supports the universities is also a very major employer and, hence, constrains them in both ways. A condition for employment of computing people by the civil service seems to be training in either COBOL or FORTRAN! That, of course, is awful. Even if the state, in its capacity of funding body, leaves it to the competence of the departments to design their own curriculum, it jeopardizes that freedom with such employment regulations. From the moment that European departments of computer science concluded that the sooner those two programming languages be forgotten the better, they have ignored them; in Australia teaching PASCAL, however, seems a political issue, a kind of heresy that should not be permitted. (Thank goodness, also Australia has its heretics!) I don't remember having felt the tension between "the campus" and "the real world" so strongly.

I had been looking forward to my talks for the universities, but the addresses to the branches of the ACS I did not look forward to at all. The audiences to be expected had been described to me in most uninspiring terms —it turned out that my spokesmen had been unnecessarily pessimistic—, and I had been warned that at the ACS I was not expected to use a blackboard. So I prepared a talk consisting of words only and tried it out at the first occasion, in Adelaide (with considerable trepidation, because I also stuck to my habit of speaking without notes). It went down very well, and cowardly I used the same talk for the other ACS performances. A cornerstone was how research in programming methodology has forced upon us the conclusion that programming should be regarded as a tough engineering discipline with a strong mathematical flavour. The main theme was that this conclusion has never been refuted, but that many refuse to draw it for emotional or political reasons, reasons that are easy to explain, because the conclusion has many implications that are unattractive, disappointing, or both.

I took a great risk in doing so, because even if I expressed myself in general terms and talked about the world in general, it could be viewed as a foreigner meddling in internal affairs, and that is usually not appreciated. ("Misuse of our hospitality" is a common name for the crime.) But I came away with it, and the talks were a great success and evoked a lively discussion, which, on the whole, made excellent sense. (How I came away with it I still don't know. Either the Australians welcomed the opportunity to discuss their own problems in a new, noncontaminated terminology, or my fame and the "weight" with which I had been announced have acted as a protecting shield; probably both.) The only counteraction I have observed, was an —anonymous!— column in Australia's Computer Weekly of Friday, 4th of March 1977, with all the characteristics of racist slander:

> I am inclined to view Dijkstra, Wirth and Dahl as intellectual products of the Germanic system. Precisely why Tony Hoare associates himself with these three is another thing beyond my ken. [...] His [i.e. Dijkstra's] efforts have been directed into turning a noble art into a rigid discipline on the basis that it would be better for us all. Being just one of the swine watching the dropped pearls I am not sure I like this idea. My suspicion that these concepts are the product of an authoritarian upbringing is strengthened by the fact that Dahl is Scandinavian, Dijkstra Dutch and Wirth Swiss. [...] Quite where you go from here I do not know. I had thought of looking up Freud but I do not think what he would say would be very refined.

The above does not strike me as very refined either. The Computer Weekly was a publication that my colleagues at the ANU usually did not see, but on account of this column they had seen this issue. In my parting speech at my farewell party I referred to it but could say in all honesty that I had no reason to suppose this blurb characteristic for Australia. On the contrary.

The country's sadness is perhaps most clearly reflected in the following comment: "We seem to copy faithfully all American mistakes, but ten years later.". The estimated period of ten years seems to me to be correct. In many little things I was reminded of the mid-sixties. The director of the Computer Centre at ANU was for instance a numerical mathematician, and there was a pronounced concern about programming *languages*, a type of concern we have in the meantime completely outgrown.

*   *
*

Just for the record: my weekend near Melbourne was somewhat unusual. A hundred miles North of Melbourne the wife of a Melbourne surgeon farmed. They had a landing strip near the farmhouse and the surgeon commuted by private plane from the farm to his Melbourne hospital and back. He said that he spent less time commuting than most of his colleagues in the hospital. This may be true, but from my side I am certain that personally he liked flying. On Saturday evening he came from the farm to pick us up in Melbourne, the next evening he brought us back. On Sunday morning the wife and one of the daughters were away for several hours on horseback, inspecting cattle; in the afternoon I was taken on a very rough ride in a landrover to see some paddocks with the surgeon. The weekend showed me a completely different side of Australian life; besides instructive it was very pleasant, and I had no problems in expressing my gratitude for their —rather amazing, if you come to think of it!— hospitality.

*   *
*

The memories from the visits to Adelaide, Melbourne, and Sydney get somewhat blurred. Adelaide was lively, Melbourne dismal, and Sydney mixed. These memories will fade. ANU, Canberra, was quite clearly my base. (The trip to the Universities was tiring because each time I had to adjust to new people; on Wednesday morning, when I flew back from Sydney to Canberra, I had quite definitely the feeling of "returning home". So much for the tact and hospitality of that community!)

In Canberra I had an apartment in the "University House", built on campus for about 150 graduate students and 150 visitors, very much along the pattern of an English college —complete with quadrangle!—, with a large Common Room (with a Yamaha) and a Hall (complete with a Steinway), in which the University Dinner was held each Wednesday night (I attended once). A "Bistro" that served breakfast, lunch, and dinner, a "Cellar Bar" that sold meals at lunch time and dinner time, and served beer, much of which was consumed in the nearby "Fellow's Garden". And, around the corner, a "Bottle Shop" —how is that for a euphemism?—, a mini-supermarket, and laundry. All this was within a ten minute walk from the Computer Centre.

Breakfast was served in the Bistro from 8 until 8:45. At nine o'clock I was at the Computer Centre, where I had a nice office, with an air conditioning that I used twice on very hot and sticky days. I always left the door open. The trick worked; all sorts of people "just came in". At noon we walked to the Cellar Bar and had lunch and beer —or just beer, when tired — and from one o'clock till five I was again at the Computer Centre. Usually we had a beer in the Cellar Bar from half past five until half past six, and then I would have dinner with rotating, but always pleasant company, either in the Bistro, or in town, or at home. The moment I went to sleep varied wildly, I was always awake before eight o'clock in the morning without the mechanical aid. The day after my arrival someone had borrowed sheet music for me —Mozart and Schubert— and before the trip I have played quite a lot. Only one evening on the Steinway. While doing so I was told that I needed special permission for doing so, because it was the property of the ABC (Australian Broadcasting Corporation). Both instruments had suffered from the drought, and yesterday I realized that after a Yamaha a Bösendorfer is the closest possible approximation of heaven. (It had been tuned during my absence.) But for lack of anything better, a Yamaha will do before breakfast.

On one of the last days, one of the staff members dropped in. He was genuinely worried and puzzled, and asked "Why did you come? You did not get anything from this visit.". I could answer that I had come firstly because I had been invited, and secondly because the way in which the invitation from dr. Robin B. Stanton had been phrased had given me the impression that he had sound reasons for being very keen that I should accept the invitation. Shortly after my arrival I began to understand what Stanton hoped that I would do, and I think that I have done it to the extent that can be achieved in a one-month visit. It was hard work, I had to be alert continuously.

The greatest compliment for my hosts in general and for Stanton's care and initiative in particular is probably Ria's remark when she entered my office a page ago: "I am glad you went.". To which I could only add "I am also glad to be home again.".

Nuenen   PROF. DR. EDSGER W. DIJKSTRA
                                          Burroughs Research Fellow

EWD614

A Somewhat Open Letter to EAA or: Why I Proved the Boundedness of the Nondeterminacy in the Way I Did

Dear EAA:

In your recent letter you wrote me about your doubts concerning the way in which I had proved that nondeterminacy was bounded; you even feared that my arguments might be circular. Allow me to answer you in this somewhat public manner; I prefer to answer you in this way because you are not the only one who wondered why I proved it the way I did.

I draw your attention to a paragraph from the last chapter of my book (p. 213):

> The next separations of concerns are carried through in the book itself: it is the separation between the mathematical concerns about correctness and the engineering concerns about execution. And we have carried this separation through to the extent that we have given an axiomatic definition of the semantics of our programming language which allows us, if we so desire, to ignore the possibility of execution. This is done in the book itself for the simple reason that, historically speaking, this separation has not been suggested by our rule of thumb; the operational approach, characterized by "The semantics itself is given by an interpreter that describes how the state vector changes as the computation progresses." (John McCarthy, 1965) was the predominant one during most of the sixties, from which R.W. Floyd (1967) and C.A.R. Hoare (1969) were among the first to depart."

Having quoted this paragraph I now feel tempted to add that, at least in my own head, this separation of concerns took fully place while I was writing the book. In the fourth chapter the if...fi and the do...od are introduced by first giving an informal operational definition. What probably I should have stated more emphatically is that these operational descriptions should not be regarded as definitions upon which my definitions of the *wp* are based, but that these operational descriptions have been no more than a source of inspiration, which can be forgotten as soon as the semantics for IF and DO in terms of the predicate transformer has been *chosen*.

If I choose to define the semantics of

do $B1 \rightarrow S1$ ▯ ... ▯ $Bn \rightarrow Sn$ **od**

by

$wp(\text{DO}, R) = (\text{E } k: k \geqslant 0: H_k(R))$ with
$H_0(R) = R$ **and non** BB and $H_{k+1}(R) = wp(\text{IF}, H_k(R))$ **or** $H_0(R)$

then the weakest precondition $wp(\text{DO}, R)$ is given in terms of a recurrently defined sequence of conditions, and as such it has nothing to do with the notion of "repetition", which refers to what might happen during execution by some implementation.

A usual argument to demonstrate the boundedness of the nondeterminacy considers the class of possible computational histories. The argument is as follows. For a terminating computation each repetition is only executed a bounded number of times, in each alternative construct the computation is only of bounded nondeterminacy, and, hence, by König's Lemma, the "computational tree" can only have a finite number of leaves (i.e. final states).

I rejected the above argument for two reasons. First of all, it is based upon the consideration of the computational histories, whereas I wanted to ignore that program texts also admit the interpretation of executable code. I wanted to postulate the semantics independently of any underlying model of computation; I have done so, but then it is inelegant to prove such a fundamental property using such a model. I at least think it much more consistent to prove such a property directly.

The second reason, however, is that I think that the argument —at least as it stands— is somewhat shaky. The problem lies with the justification of the suggested underlying computational model. After the postulation of the semantics, it is not too difficult (I think) to argue that the obvious implementation, when started in a state satisfying $wp(\text{DO}, R)$, will lead in a finite number of steps to a final state satisfying R. It is also clear (from the rejected argument) that then the number of possible final states is finite. But that could be a property of the implementation, viz. that it can only realize a finite number of the infinitely many permissible final states!

The only decent way I could think of is the one I have followed. First I postulate the way in which predicate transformers may be built up; next I prove the continuity of wp (using induction over the syntax); next I prove the boundedness of the nondeterminacy (by deriving a contradiction from the assumption of unbounded nondeterminacy); and finally I interpret this as a reason for reassurance (p. 77):

> A mechanism of unbounded nondeterminacy yet guaranteed to terminate would be able to make within a finite time a choice out of infinitely many possibilities: if such a mechanism could be formulated in our programming

language, that very fact would present an insurmountable barrier to the possibility of the implementation of that programming language.

In other words: instead of "deriving" the boundedness of the nondeterminacy from the possible behaviour of an implementation —whose "adequacy" must then be demonstrated in a rather complete way— I prove the boundedness of the nondeterminacy and remark that by doing so an otherwise unsurmountable barrier to the possibility of implementation has been removed. Note that nowhere in my book have I *proved* that my little programming language can, indeed, be implemented! That implementability seemed sufficiently obvious to me not to worry about it. Where is the suspected "circularity"?

You write:

> It concerns the definition of the semantics of the **do** construct (page 35). It seems to me that the semantics itself says that nondeterminacy is bounded. It says that if a state satisfies $wp(DO, R)$, i.e. is bound to yield terminating computations finally satisfying R, then there exists a bound on the number of iterations of the DO for this initial state. This is reasonable since nondeterminacy *is* bounded, but your *proof* of the boundedness uses the semantics of DO.

Is it possible that you have suspected circularity by thinking that I have first taken implementability for granted, and then have made essential use of the implementability? Of course my proof of the boundedness of the nondeterminacy uses the semantics of DO! If I did not use the definition of the semantics, how could I prove something about it?

To think about the semantics of a programming language independently of any underlying computational model is with our past, I admit, a difficult mental exercise. Perhaps you don't think it worthwhile. I personally think it is. As long as the operational approach remains the predominant one, languages for "sequential programming" and "concurrent programming" will remain two different topics. I hope to see these two topics merge into a single one. I am hoping for a single programming language that allows sequential implementation, but also allows implementations displaying a lot of concurrency and allows that as "obviously" as the little programming language used in my book allows sequential implementation.

Logic has changed from a descriptive science into a prescriptive one; the "new logician" is an engineer. It is no longer the purpose of our programs to instruct our machines, it is the purpose of our machines to execute our programs. Semantics no longer needs to capture the properties of mechanisms given in some other way, the postulated semantics is to be regarded as the specification that a proper implementation should meet. As you may have concluded from the above, I have never been a great lover of automata theory!

Have I made myself clear now? I hope. The possible complaint against my book that the initial chapters of it don't make my position clear enough is a valid one: my attitude towards its subject matter evolved as a direct result of the very act of writing it! Perhaps —like many articles and most programs!— my book should also be read backwards.

I thank you for your letter. Greetings and best wishes,

yours ever,

Edsger

Nuenen

PROF. DR. EDSGER W. DIJKSTRA
Burroughs Research Fellow

EWD618

On Webster, Users, Bugs, and Aristotle

Thinking is our most intimate activity, and a lot of it is revealed by the way in which we use (and misuse) our language. As a matter of fact, so much is revealed by it that one cannot be a careful listener without the guilty feeling of committing the indiscreet sin of voyeurism. It is exactly this sin that I propose to commit with respect to the computing community: in this case committing the sin is too illuminating to remain virtuous.

*　　*　　*

Linguistical analyses tend to start with dictionaries. There are two types of dictionaries. There is the writer's dictionary, giving hints as to how a language should be used; the Concise Oxford Dictionary is a perfect example of a writer's dictionary. At the other end of the spectrum we have the dictionaries for the reader; they faithfully record how a language happens to be used. Webster's New Collegiate Dictionary is a good example of a dictionary of the latter type. You can hardly use Webster's New Collegiate Dictionary as a guide when writing —it contains terrible verbs like "to disfurnish" and "to disambiguate"— , but its authors are no fools: if an existing word is consistently used in a way that really stretches its original meaning too much, the new meaning is faithfully recorded in the next edition. A beautiful example is given in Webster's New Collegiate Dictionary under the heading "intelligent", where in more recent editions a third meaning has been added:

> able to perform some of the functions of a computer < an ~ computer terminal > .

It is very amusing —and enlightening!— to draw the attention of members of the American computing community to this addition to Good New Webster. They are always startled by it; the Artificial Intelligentsia react with indignation, the others chuckle with delight, but show not seldomly signs of disbelief or amazement at Webster's "courage". Often they get hold of the nearest Webster to check my statement. Having verified it, they give a sigh of relief: the story is clearly too good not to be true. For many a computing scientist this additional meaning of "intelligent" in Webster acts as an authorization of his doubts about the Artificial Intelligentsia —doubts that are shared by almost all computing scientists, but that give many in the USA (where AI is officially regarded as more or less respectable) guilty feelings— . Two cheers for Webster's ruthless accuracy!

*   *   *

The meaning of the "user" —in extreme cases the "casual user"— has also been extended. My Webster (1973) does not record it yet —"one that uses" is the only definition given— , but in this case I have other linguistical indications.

It is already a change of long standing, for it was at least a decade ago when, consulting a Dutch computer manufacturer, I was amazed by and annoyed at the frequent appeal to the untranslated, just copied, "user" in the middle of a Dutch sentence defending some design decision. The noun "user" is, of course, perfectly translatable into Dutch, but those guys did not do it! At the time I did not pay too much attention to this linguistic anomaly; I think that I classified it as the same silly mannerism as displayed by the all-English texts that are printed on Dutch cigarette packages.

But I got definitely suspicious when I learned that also the French —in spite of all their Anglophobia— embed the untranslated English word "user" in the middle of their French sentences! Since then I was alert, and I can now tell you that the word "user" is not only good Russian, but also perfect Japanese!

Now this is very telling. One of the requirements of the final examination at the end of my training at secondary school was the translation of texts from various foreign languages "into good Dutch". Translating a foreign text, we were taught, is a two-stage process: first the exact meaning has to be extracted from the foreign text, and then that meaning has to be rendered exactly in good Dutch. The fact that the "user" of the Anglo-Saxon computing community is copied instead of translated is, therefore, for me a proof that that "user" has lost its original meaning. Subconsciously the foreign term is imported as a neologism, as a new word for a new concept.

The computer "user" isn't a real person of flesh and blood, with passions and brains. No, he is a mythical figure, and not a very pleasant one either. A kind of mongrel with money but without taste, an ugly caricature that is very uninspiring to work for. He is, as a matter of fact, such an uninspiring idiot that his stupidity alone is sufficient explanation for the ugliness of most computer systems. And oh! Is he uneducated! That is perhaps his most depressing characteristic. He is equally education-resistant as another equally mythical bore, the "average programmer", whose solid stupidity is the greatest barrier to progress in programming. It is a sad thought that large sections of computing science are effectively paralyzed by the narrow-mindedness and other grotesque limitations with which a poor literature has endowed these influential mythical figures. (Computing science is not unique in inventing such paralyzing caricatures: universities all over the world are threatened by the invention of "the average student", scientific publishing is severely hampered by the invention of "the innocent reader" and even "the poor reader"!)

*   *   *

In passing I draw attention to another English expression which often occurs in Dutch texts: "the real world". In Dutch —and I am afraid not in Dutch alone— its usage is almost always a symptom of a violent anti-intellectualism.

*   *   *

With the publication of the *Communications* of the ACM, in the late fifties, began my regular exposure to American computing literature. I still vividly remember how shocked I was at first by the heavy use of anthropomorphic terminology. (Later I learned that we owe this habit to John von Neumann.) In the meantime we know that the implied metaphor is more misleading than illuminating. (For instance, in 1964 Fraser G. Duncan eloquently drew attention to all the confusion generated by calling programming languages "languages".) Because the anthropomorphic terminology invites us to identify ourselves with programs in execution, and because "existing" is our most essential "activity", the prevalence of these metaphors presents a severe psychological barrier to freeing our minds from the grip that operational semantics still have on them. I therefore regard the introduction of anthropomorphic terminology into computing as one of the worst services rendered to mankind by John von Neumann. (Lecturing I recently learned that among the Artificial Intelligentsia even the suggestion that anthropomorphic terminology might be unwholesome is already sheer heresy: the mere suggestion is enough to make them raving mad at you! It was very amusing and very revealing.)

It is, however, probably more than just an unhappy consequence of one of John von Neumann's personal tastes. Recently I read Arthur Koestler's account (in "The Sleepwalkers") of how by the work of Copernicus, Keppler, Galileo, and Newton the separation between astronomy and astrology began to take place. Slowly mankind was parting from the Aristotelean animism that had ruled thought for so many centuries. In this light, the prevalence of anthropomorphic terminology in computing can also be viewed as a characteristic of its pre-scientific stage, and a consequence would be that computing *scientists* don't deserve that name before they have the courage to call a "bug" an "error".

POST SCRIPTUM. The day after the above was typed I had to deliver the last lecture at the ACM/ECI International Computer Symposium 1977 in Liege, Belgium. When I arrived I heard that the day before B. Meltzer —one of the Edinburgh Artificial Intelligentsia— had extensively challenged my statement:

> The superstition that underlies so much of Artificial Intelligence activity is that everything difficult is so boring that it had better be done mechanically.

He had done so so emphatically that clearly some sort of rebuttal from my side was expected. Meltzer, however, had already left, and I restricted myself to writing on the blackboard the quotation from Webster that I have given above. I gave the full name of the dictionary and even mentioned the 1973 Edition.

After the closing ceremony and before starting on the journey back home I had a cup of coffee with the ICS Symposium Chairman, David Hirschberg from IBM, who asked me "Is it really true that Webster gives that third definition of "intelligent" or did you just make it up?".

People won't believe it! By now I am wondering what percentage of the readers of this note have already consulted their Webster... (End of post scriptum.)

Please note my new Postal Code!

Nuenen   PROF. DR. EDSGER W. DIJKSTRA
                                                              Burroughs Research Fellow

EWD622
On Making Solutions More and More Fine-Grained

In gratitude dedicated to C.A.R. Hoare, D.E. Knuth, and J.F. Traub.

This note deals with a problem that I owe to C.S. Scholten. Today seems an appropriate day to start writing it, for yesterday evening I completed EWD595' (the second version of EWD595, which is itself the nth version of our joint article on the on-the-fly garbage collection): Scholten's problem was already with us for a few weeks before we realized that it had, in a way, the same flavour as the collector's problem of detecting that the marking had been completed. Perhaps we shall see one day that all these solutions, which at present seem disconnected pieces of logical ingenuity —not to say: intricacy— , are all members of the same family.

In the on-the-fly garbage collection the cooperation of mutator and collector ensured during marking that a stable state —all reachable nodes black and all white nodes garbage— would be reached in a finite number of steps of the collector's marking cycle: the problem was the design of the detection mechanism for the collector that, indeed, the stable state had been reached. Scholten's problem poses such a detection problem for N machines.

Let y denote a vector of N components $y[i]$ for $0 \leqslant i < N$. Let f denote a vector-valued function of a vector argument. The algorithms we shall study solve the equation

$$y = f(y) \tag{1}$$

or, introducing $f0$, $f1$, $f2$, ... for the components of f,

$$y[i] = fi(y) \qquad \text{for } 0 \leqslant i < N. \tag{2}$$

It is assumed that the initial value of y and the function f are such that repeated assignments of the form

$$\langle y[i] := fi(y) \rangle \tag{3}$$

292

will lead in a finite number of steps to y being a solution of (1). In (3) we have used Lamport's notation of the angle brackets: they enclose "atomic actions", which can be implemented by ensuring mutual exclusion in time (when they are considered "to take time"). The sequence of i-values for which the assignments are carried out must be one of some sort of "fair random order" in which, for instance, a finite upper bound is given for the maximum number of consecutive assignments —i.e.: i-values— in which a given j ($0 \leqslant j < N$) does not occur: in other words, we assume that the absence of individual starvation is guaranteed.

Because equation (1) is assumed to have at least one solution, such an initial value of y always exists: start with y equal to a solution! This is, of course, not an interesting case; Scholten has formulated more general conditions (on the domain of the elements of y, on the functions f, and on the initial value for y) under which convergence in a finite number of steps, and towards a solution which is uniquely determined by the initial value of y, can be guaranteed. These conditions do not interest us here: we shall study the more general situation in which in a finite number of steps a (not-necessarily unique) solution of (1) will be reached. (In passing we note that also the marking in the garbage collection had that characteristic of nondeterminacy.)

NOTE 1. The mechanisms we shall design will even "operate" when no solution of (1) is reached within a finite number of steps: then they will fail to terminate. In this sense our programs can be considered as a multidimensional generalization of the Linear Search. (End of note 1.)

We consider solutions consisting of N repetitive processes of the form:

prog.i: **do**... $\rightarrow$ $\langle y[i] := fi(y)\rangle$**od**   .   PR0

The problem is, of course, what to fill in for the d0ts. The roughest sketch would be

prog.i: **do**$\langle$**E** $j: 0 \leqslant j < N: y[j] \neq fj(y)\rangle \rightarrow \langle y[i] := fi(y)\rangle$**od**   PR1

but this version is rejected for two reasons. Firstly, the guard is an unacceptably large grain of action. Secondly and more importantly, we want the construction of prog.i to be independent of fj for $j \neq i$. We can remove the second objection and reduce the first one by introducing a global array e with the boolean elements $e[i]$ for $0 \leqslant i < N$, and maintaining

$$(\mathbf{A}\ i: 0 \leqslant i < N: e[i] \Rightarrow (y[i] = fi(y)))\ .\qquad (4)$$

Because (4) is trivially satisfied by all $e[i]$ *false*, we assume that initialization. With the convention that j ranges over $0 \leqslant j < N$, we can now write

(with some more notational liberties that will be explained later)

prog.i: $\mathbf{do}\langle \mathbf{E}\, j\colon \mathbf{non}\ e[\,j\,]\rangle \to$ PR2
$$\langle \mathbf{if}\ y[i] = fi(y) \to e[i] := true\rangle$$
$$[\!]\, y[i] \neq fi(y) \to y[i] := fi(y);$$
$$(\mathbf{A}\, j\colon e[\,j\,] := false)\rangle$$
    $\mathbf{fi}$
  $\mathbf{od}$.

NOTE 2. I have used the abbreviation $(\mathbf{A}\, j\colon e[\,j\,] := false)$ for the program that performs the assignments $e[0] := false$ through $e[N-1] := false$ in some order. Because here it is part of an atomic action, the undefinedness of the order is still irrelevant. (End of note 2.)

NOTE 3. In PR2, the whole alternative construct is effectively a single atomic action. In view of later needs, however, I have given each alternative its own closing angle bracket. (End of note 3.)

NOTE 4. In the first alternative of PR2, the superfluous assignment to $y[i]$ has been suppressed. (End of note 4.)

NOTE 5. In a more abstract version we could have introduced a set E of those processes j for which $y[\,j\,] = fj(y)$ is guaranteed to hold. In that case $(\mathbf{A}\, j\colon e[\,j\,] := false)$ would have been coded as $E := \varnothing$. Honesty forces me to mention that during more abstract explorations I have, indeed, used such a notation, and to admit that the reason that I don't do so now could very well be that the symbols of set theory are not on my typewriter. The boolean array can be regarded as the characteristic function for E; the problem, of course, is that we can also regard the value of E as a coding for the value of e. (End of note 5.)

It is clear that both alternatives in PR2 leave (4) invariant. It is also clear that $y = f(y)$ is a stable state as far as y is concerned. Termination of one of the processes implies $(\mathbf{A}\, j\colon e[\,j\,])$, from which, together with (4), $y = f(y)$ can be deduced, i.e. that the stable state has been reached, and that all other programs will terminate as well.

NOTE 6. If we really want to spell this out, we would have to *show* the invariance of, say,

$(\mathbf{A}\, j\colon e[\,j\,])$ and $y = f(y)$.

As we have more difficult problems ahead of us, I shall not waste my time on that demonstration: it is really trivial. (End of note 6.)

*   *   *

One of the ways in which we could try to chop up the large grain of action in PR2 would be to separate inspection of y, computation of fi, and modification of $y[i]$. With a local vector vi and a local "scalar" qi we could try:

prog.i: **do**$\langle$**E** j: **non** $e[j]\rangle \rightarrow$ PR3
                $\langle vi := y\rangle\{y[i] = vi[i]\}$;
                $qi := fi(vi)\{qi = fi(vi)\}$;
                if $vi[i] = qi \rightarrow \langle e[i] := true\rangle$
                $[]$ $vi[i] \neq qi \rightarrow \langle y[i] := qi; (\mathbf{A}\,j: e[j] := false)\rangle$
                fi
        od   .

NOTE 7. We have allowed ourselves $vi := y$ as an abbreviation for $(\mathbf{A}\,j: vi[j] := y[j])$. Upon its completion the relation "$y[i] = vi[i]$" can be regarded as a local assertion of prog.i, in spite of the fact that it contains a reference to the global $y[i]$: we can do so because for $j \neq i$, prog.j only inspects, but never modifies the value of $y[i]$. (End of note 7.)

However, the proof of the invariance of (4) fails for the first alternative in the following manner. The weakest precondition for $\langle e[i] := true\rangle$ to establish (4) is

(4) **and** $y[i] = fi(y)$,

but we can only guarantee —see the assertions between braces—

(4) **and** $y[i] = vi[i] = qi = fi(vi)$,

and in order to conclude the former from the latter we need the further assumption $y = vi$. Program PR3 is, indeed, wrong, but the failure of its correctness proof indicates how to repair it.

Because the non-destruction of (4) by $\langle e[i] := true\rangle$ depends on the truth of $y = vi$, we can repair program PR3 by replacing $\langle e[i] := true\rangle$ by

$\langle e[i] := (y = vi)\rangle$

which is a shorthand notation for

$\langle e[i] := (\mathbf{A}\,j: y[j] = vi[j])\rangle$.

Because —specially for large N— this is again a bulky atomic action, we can introduce a global array d with boolean elements $d[i]$ for $0 \leq i < N$, such that

$(\mathbf{A}\,i: 0 \leq i < N: d[i] \Rightarrow (y = vi))$.   (5)

If we can keep (5) invariantly true, replacing $\langle e[i] := true\rangle$ in PR3 by $\langle e[i] := d[i]\rangle$ ensures that $e[i]$ will not be set to true erroneously, i.e. so as to destroy the truth of (4). Assuming all the $d[i]$ initialized to *false*, keeping (5) invariant leads to the following program, which is now derived from PR3 in a straightforward manner:

prog.i: **do**$\langle$**E** j: **non** $e[\,j\,]\rangle \rightarrow$ PR4
            $\langle d[i] := true;\ vi := y\rangle$;
            $qi := fi(vi)$;
            if $vi[i] = qi \rightarrow \langle e[i] := d[i]\rangle$
            $[]\ vi[i] \neq qi \rightarrow \langle y[i] := qi;$
                                   $(\mathbf{A}\,j:\ d[\,j\,] := false)$;
                                   $(\mathbf{A}\,j:\ e[\,j\,] := false)\rangle$
            fi
    od   .

*   *   *

The transition from PR2 to PR4 was motivated by something like the assumption that the fi-computations were time-consuming. Another way of chopping up atomic actions in PR2 would be to separate the modification of $y[i]$ from the false-setting of the $e[\,j\,]$'s. In the following program, derived from PR2, we have introduced a global ghost-variable ef for reasons that will become clear in a moment; ef is assumed to be initialized at *false*.

prog.i: **do**$\langle$**E** j: **non** $e[\,j\,]\rangle \rightarrow$ PR5
            $\langle$**if** $y[i] = fi(y) \rightarrow e[i] := true\rangle$
            $[]\ y[i] \neq fi(y) \rightarrow y[i] := fi(y);\ ef := true\rangle$;
                                   $\langle(\mathbf{A}\,j:\ e[\,j\,] := false);\ ef := false\rangle$
            fi
    od   .

The reason for introducing the ghost-variable ef becomes clear as soon as we realize that $y[i] := fi(y)$ without setting all the $e[\,j\,]$'s to *false*, might cause a violation of (4) as a result of the modification of y. The introduction of ef enables us to express the temporary violation of (4) by replacing it by

$$(\mathbf{A}\,i: 0 \leqslant i < N: e[i] \Rightarrow (y[i] = fi(y)))\ \mathbf{or}\ ef \qquad . \qquad (6)$$

NOTE 8. The name "ef" is for me a mnemonic for "e-implication *false*". (End of note 8.)

Thanks to the introduction of ef, (6) is now clearly an invariant; however, by itself it is too weak to conclude that upon termination $y = f(y)$ holds. As it stands we can only conclude upon termination

$$y = f(y)\ \mathbf{or}\ ef \qquad ,$$

a conclusion that suffices if we can also show the invariance of

$$ef \Rightarrow (\mathbf{E}\,j:\ \mathbf{non}\ e[\,j\,]) \qquad , \qquad (7)$$

for then ef is guaranteed to be *false* upon termination. It is indeed possible to show that (7) is invariant as well, and that, therefore, program PR5 is correct.

Without the introduction of more elaborate ghost-variables we need a somewhat different argument for the demonstration of the invariance of (7). Consider an atomic action that causes for *ef* a transition from *false* to *true*; let this be performed by prog.k. Then, prior to that atomic action we can assert

$$(6) \text{ and non } ef \text{ and } y[k] \neq fk(y)$$

from which **non** $e[k]$ can be concluded. Because prog.k is the only one that can reset $e[k]$ to *true* and cannot cause this resetting to take place before resetting *ef* to *false*, $e[k]$ must remain *false* —and, hence, (**E** j: **non** $e[j]$) must remain *true*— as long as *ef* remains *true*.

The operational argument in the preceding paragraph is highly unattractive; it does, however, show the way out. Introducing a global variable k $(0 \leqslant k \leqslant N)$ we can represent **non** *ef* by $k = N$, and *ef* by $0 \leqslant k < N$. (In particular: when $k < N$, it has been prog.k that lastly caused *ef* to become *true*, i.e. that lastly caused k to become different from N.)

prog.i: **do**$\langle$**E** j: **non** $e[j]\rangle \rightarrow$ PR5′
　　　　　　　$\langle$**if** $y[i] = fi(y) \rightarrow e[i] := true \rangle$
　　　　　　　$[\!] \; y[i] \neq fi(y) \rightarrow y[i] := fi(y);$
　　　　　　　　　　　　if $k < N \rightarrow skip$
　　　　　　　　　　　　$[\!] \; k = N \rightarrow k := i$
　　　　　　　　　　　　fi$\rangle$;
　　　　　　　　　　$\langle$(**A** j: $e[j] := false$); $k := N \rangle$
　　　　　fi
　　od   .

The program has been called PR5′ because it only differs from PR5 by the ghost-variable. The ghost-variable k is assumed to have been initialized $= N$. It is then easy to prove the invariance of

$$k < N \Rightarrow \textbf{non } e[k] \tag{7'}$$

(or, if we don't like undefined right-hand sides of implications, $k = N$ **cor non** $e[k]$). To complete the treatment, relation (6) must be rewritten as

$$(\textbf{A } i: 0 \leqslant i < N: e[i] \Rightarrow (y[i] = fi(y))) \textbf{ or } k < N \tag{6'}$$
　　　　　　　　　　* 　　*　　*

The above three stars stand for as many days of vain struggle, as I tried to merge the two achievements embodied in PR4 and PR5′. Eventually I had some success when I started from the rejected correction of PR3. In the text below, the $e[i]$'s have been renamed for reasons that will become clear later; initially, all the $g[i]$'s are *false*.

prog.i: **do**$\langle$**E** j: **non** $g[j]\rangle \rightarrow$ PR6
$\qquad\qquad \langle vi := y\rangle\{vi[i] = y[i]\};$
$\qquad\qquad qi := fi(vi)\{qi = fi(vi)\};$
$\qquad\qquad$ **if** $vi[i] = qi \rightarrow \langle g[i] := (y = vi)\rangle$
$\qquad\qquad [] \ vi[i] \neq qi \rightarrow \langle y[i] := qi; \ (\mathbf{A} j: g[j] := false)\rangle$
$\qquad\qquad$ **fi**
$\qquad$ **od**   .

I don't repeat its correctness proof, but proceed immediately to chop up its last atomic action as in PR5'. Initially, $k = N$; for the reformulation of (7') we can assume $g[N]$ to be constantly *false*.

prog.i: **do**$\langle$**E** j: **non** $g[j]\rangle \rightarrow \{k \neq i\}$ PR7
L0: $\qquad\langle vi := y\rangle\{vi[i] = y[i]\};$
$\qquad\qquad qi := fi(vi)\{qi = fi(vi)\};$
L1: $\qquad$ **if** $vi[i] = qi \rightarrow \langle g[i] := (y = vi)\rangle$
L2: $\qquad [] \ vi[i] \neq qi \rightarrow \langle y[i] := qi;$
$\qquad\qquad\qquad$ **if** $k < N \rightarrow skip$
$\qquad\qquad\qquad [] \ k = N \rightarrow k := i$
$\qquad\qquad\qquad$ **fi**$\rangle$;
L3: $\qquad\qquad \langle(\mathbf{A} j: g[j] := false); \ k := N\rangle$
$\qquad$ **fi** $\{k \neq i\}$
$\qquad$ **od**   .

In the following correctness proof the atomic actions are referred to by the label on the line of their opening angle bracket.

We first observe that $\{k \neq i\}$ is a local assertion for prog.i in isolation, valid everywhere except between L2 and L3: L0 and L1 don't assign to k, L2 may destroy it, but, because $N \neq i$, L3 will restore $\{k \neq i\}$. But, although k is a global variable, $\{k \neq i\}$ also remains *true* in combination with the other prog. j's, because neither their assignments $k := j \ (j \neq i!)$, nor their assignments $k := N \ (N \neq i!)$ can destroy it.

We next observe the invariance of

$$(\mathbf{A} j: g[j] \Rightarrow (y[j] = fj(y))) \text{ or } k < N \qquad . \tag{8}$$

Action L0 does not assign to its variables. Action L1 can only affect the implication for $j = i$; the weakest precondition of L1 for that implication is, according to the Axiom of Assignment,

$$(y = vi) \Rightarrow (y[i] = fi(y))$$

which follows from the local assertions and the guard, for

$$y[i] = vi[i] = qi = fi(vi) \qquad .$$

Action L2 establishes (8) on account of its term $k < N$, and action L3 also establishes (8) because it makes all implications vacuously *true*.

The next invariance to be established is

$$(\mathbf{A} j: g[j] \Rightarrow (vj = y)) \text{ or } k < N \qquad . \tag{9}$$

It is, like (8), initially *true* because then all the $g[j]$ are *false*; actions L0 and L1 can affect in (9) only the implication for $j = i$, but make that implication *true*, action L2 establishes the truth of (9) on account of its term $k < N$, and action L3, again, makes all implications vacuously *true*.

The next invariant relation is

$$k < N \Rightarrow \mathbf{non}\ g[k] \quad . \tag{10}$$

Action L0 does not affect its variables, action L1 does not do so on account of the local assertion $\{k \neq i\}$, action L3 makes (10) vacuously *true*. Action L2 leaves (10) clearly invariant if, initially, $k < N$; only if initially $k = N$, we need for L2 a more elaborate argument, for we have to show that then, initially, **non** $g[i]$ holds. We shall demonstrate this by deriving a contradiction from the assumption $k = N$ **and** $g[i]$. From this assumption and (8) we conclude $y[i] = fi(y)$ and from this assumption and (9) we conclude $vi = y$, hence $y[i] = fi(vi)$. From the local assertions and the guard, however, we derive $y[i] = vi[i] \neq qi = fi(vi)$, which gives the required contradiction. This concludes the demonstration of the invariance of (10).

On account of (10), $(\mathbf{A}\ j: g[j]) \Rightarrow k = N$, and hence, on account of (8) and (9), we can conclude that $(\mathbf{A}\ j: g[j]) \Rightarrow (\mathbf{A}\ j: y[j] = fj(y)\ \mathbf{and}\ vj = y)$. This concludes our treatment of PR7.

*   *   *

We now introduce $d[i]$'s and $e[i]$'s, for the time being considered as ghost-variables. They are initialized as *false*.

```
prog.i:      do⟨E j: non g[ j]⟩ →                                    PR8
L0:              ⟨d[i] := true; vi := y⟩;
                 qi := fi(vi);
L1:              if vi[i] = qi → ⟨g[i] := (y = vi); e[i] := d[i]⟩
L2:              [] vi[i] ≠ qi → ⟨y[i] := qi; (A j: d[ j] := false);
                     if k < N → skip [] k = N → k := i fi⟩;
L3:                  ⟨(A j: g[ j] := false; e[ j] := false);
                     k := N⟩
             fi
         od     .
```

In addition to the invariance of (8), (9), and (10) we establish the invariance of

$$(\mathbf{A}\ j: d[j] \Rightarrow (vj = y)) \quad . \tag{11}$$

Relation (11) is *true* to start with, L0 leaves it invariant, and so do L1, L2, and L3.

But now we are in a position to establish

$$(\mathbf{A}\ j: e[j] \Rightarrow g[j]) \quad , \tag{12}$$

because L0, L2, and L3 leave it trivially invariant, and L1 does so on account of (11).

From (12) we deduce that $(\mathbf{A}\,j: e[\,j\,]) \Rightarrow (\mathbf{A}\,j: g[\,j\,])$. Hence, the program is still correct if we turn the e's and the d's into normal variables, and replace the outer guard by $\langle\mathbf{E}\,j: \mathbf{non}\ e[\,j\,]\rangle$. After that replacement, however, we can regard the g's as ghost-variables! Removing the operations on the g's and on k we get

prog.i: **do**$\langle\mathbf{E}\,j: \mathbf{non}\ e[\,j\,]\rangle \rightarrow$ PR9
        $\langle d[i] := true;\ vi := y\rangle;$
        $qi := fi(vi);$
        if $vi[i] = qi \rightarrow \langle e[i] := d[i]\rangle$
        $[\!]\ vi[i] \neq qi \rightarrow \langle y[i] := qi;\ (\mathbf{A}\,j: d[\,j\,] := false)\rangle;$
                       $\langle(\mathbf{A}\,j: e[\,j\,] := false)\rangle$
        fi
     od   .

*   *
*

(The above three stars stand for an interval of about two weeks, during which I wrote EWD623 through EWD626, while C.S. Scholten continued to think about his problem. As I have seen his work in the meantime, the following is unavoidably heavily influenced by his results.)

In my next refinement, I start again from PR5 (or PR5′), but wish this time to replace the last line, which is effectively

$$\langle(\mathbf{A}\,j: e[\,j\,] := false)\rangle$$

by

$$(\mathbf{A}\,j: \langle e[\,j\,] := false\rangle)$$

i.e. the single grain that sets all the $e[\,j\,]$'s *false* should be broken up into N little grains, each setting a single $e[\,j\,]$. The single global ghost-boolean is no longer sufficient, nor is the single global ghost-integer from PR5′. We propose to introduce for each prog.i a boolean ghost-array ri, with elements $ri[0]$ through $ri[N-1]$, all initialized at *false*, and each $ri[\,j\,]$ representing prog.i's "obligation" to set $e[\,j\,]$ to *false*.

prog.i: **do**$\langle\mathbf{E}\,j: \mathbf{non}\ e[\,j\,]\rangle \rightarrow \{(\mathbf{A}\,j: \mathbf{non}\ ri[\,j\,])\}$ PR10
L0; $\langle$ **if** $y[i] = fi(y) \rightarrow e[i] := true\rangle$
L1: $[\!]\ y[i] \neq fi(y) \rightarrow \{Ri\}y[i] := fi(y);$
                    $(\mathbf{A}\,j: ri[\,j\,] := true)\rangle;$
L2j: $(\mathbf{A}\,j: \langle e[\,j\,], ri[\,j\,] := false, false\rangle)$
        fi
     od   .

The first atomic action has two labels, labelling its alternative courses of action; on the last line we have condensed N labels. It is clear that $(\mathbf{A}\,j: \mathbf{non}\ ri[\,j\,])$ is an invariant of prog.i's repeatable statement. (Remember that the ghost-variable ri is local to prog.i.) Again we have to prove that

$$(\mathbf{A}\,j: e[\,j\,]) \Rightarrow (\mathbf{A}\,j: y[\,j\,] = fj(y)) \qquad . \tag{13}$$

This conclusion (13) is justified, provided we can find N predicates Rj, such that

$$(\mathbf{A}\,j: (y[\,j\,] \neq fj(\,y\,)) \Rightarrow Rj) \tag{14}$$

and

$$(\mathbf{A}\,j: e[\,j\,]) \Rightarrow (\mathbf{A}\,j:\, \textbf{non } Rj) \quad . \tag{15}$$

Intuitively —that is what (14) says— Rj may be interpreted as "it is uncertain whether the jth equation of (2) is satisfied". We shall, however, define Rj quite differently —as will be shown in a moment, in a way such that (15) is obviously satisfied— and then prove the invariance of (14).

Because (15) can be rewritten as

$$(\mathbf{E}\,j:\, Rj) \Rightarrow (\mathbf{E}\,j:\, \textbf{non } e[\,j\,]) \quad ,$$

an analogy with the marking process of the on-the-fly garbage collection presents itself. In the latter we had relations like "the existence of a white reachable node implies the existence of a grey node", or more precisely "for each white reachable node, there exists a grey node from which it can be reached via (what we called) a propagation path". In other words, (15) is trivially satisfied if we can define Rj to be *true* if and only if node j is in some sort of transitive closure starting from the nodes with a *false* e. (If all the e's are *true*, the set of starting points, and therefore the whole transitive closure, is empty.)

A bold guess is to interpret the truth of $ri[\,j\,]$ as the presence of an arrow from node $nr.i$ to node $nr.j$ and to interpret Rj as **non** $e[\,j\,]$ or reachable via a directed path from another e that is *false*. In formula

$$Rj = (\textbf{non } e[\,j\,] \textbf{ or } (\mathbf{E}\,k:\, Rk \textbf{ and } rk[\,j\,])) \quad \text{(see last page)} \tag{16}$$

from which (15) follows. Because initially all $e[\,j\,]$'s are *false*, all Rj's are initially *true*; we have thus established the initial truth of (14), the invariance of which will be demonstrated now.

The choice L0 leaves (14) invariant: its implications for $j \neq i$ are left unaffected because their antecedents remain (trivially) unaffected, and because their consequents are left unaffected on account of (16) and the fact that L0 is executed under the circumstance that node $nr.i$ has no outgoing arrows (remember $(\mathbf{A}\,j:\, \textbf{non } ri[\,j\,])$). The implication for $j = i$ is and remains vacuously *true* on account of the falsity of its antecedent, as implied by the guard.

The choice L1 leaves (14) invariant. On account of the guard and the initial truth of (14) we conclude that it can only be chosen when Ri holds. Because the truth of Ri is not destroyed by the creation of arrows, and because of (16), we have

$$(\mathbf{A}\,k, j: (Rk \textbf{ and } rk[\,j\,]) \Rightarrow Rj) \quad . \tag{17}$$

L1 establishes Rj for all j, i.e. upon completion each implication of (14) holds on account of its *true* consequent.

Also each of the individual actions L2j leaves (14) invariant, because on account of (16), removal of an incoming arrow of node j, together with $e[j] := false$, can never cause for Rj —and hence for any other Rk— the transition from *true* to *false*.

This could complete our treatment of PR10. However, a little bit more is worth observing. If the *sole* purpose of the arrow is to propagate property R from nodes with **non** e, and no obviously redundant arrows are retained, we may hope that even

$$(\mathbf{A}\, k, j: rk[j] \Rightarrow (Rk \text{ and } Rj)) \tag{18}$$

is invariantly *true*.

We have already observed that choice L0 cannot affect Rj for $j \neq i$. If, initially, node $nr.i$ has an incoming arrow, i.e. there exists a k such that $rk[i]$ holds, then $k \neq i$ because of **non** $ri[i]$; then (18) tells us that initially Rk is *true*. We have just established that Rk then remains *true*, and on account of (17), Ri remains *true*. If node $nr.i$ has no incoming arrows, Ri becoming *false* can do no harm to (18), because it has no outgoing arrows either when L0 is executed.

L1 does not violate (18) because it is only executed under the truth of Ri and all Rj are certainly *true* upon completion.

L2j does not violate (18) either. Because the $ri[j]$ are local ghost-variables of prog.i, the initial truth of $ri[j]$ is obvious; therefore (18) tells us that Rj holds initially and the assignment $e[j] := false$ ensures that Rj holds upon completion. Hence we can conclude that any act L2j leaves all Rj unchanged. Therefore, all right-hand sides of (18) are constant; only one antecedent is strengthened, and thus (18) is indeed an invariant.

Having established that any act L2j leaves all Rj unchanged, that L1 can only cause for Rj a transition from *false* to *true*, and that L0 can only affect Ri, we see that the truth of Ri is not destroyed by any prog. j for $j \neq i$, and that only L0 of prog.i can set Ri to *false*.

*   *
*

(The above three stars stand for a two-hour failure to prove the correctness of the next version without the introduction of more ghost-variables, followed by a restless night.)

Encouraged by the success of the ri's and the Ri's I shall now try to combine the introduction of the vi from PR9 with the chopping up of the *false*-setting of the $e[j]$'s from PR10. I think that this text should not become too repetitive and that I should make a larger jump: I shall also separate the *false*-setting of the $d[j]$'s from the assignment to $y[i]$, and furthermore the *false*-setting of the $d[j]$'s will be chopped up. Analogous to the $ri[j]$'s we introduce $qi[j]$'s to record prog.i's "obligation" to set $d[j]$ to *false*.

In my treatment of PR10 I dislike that the nice relation (18) could only be derived at the end. In order to derive it earlier, I shall try a new proof experiment. I intend to strengthen guards of the alternative construct by adding "ghost-constraints" and show eventually that the strengthening was ineffective because the truth of the added term is implied by the truth of the guard it was supposed to strengthen. The choice of the strengthening is inspired by my desire to keep the initial proof of the invariance of (18) simple. (Because the strengthened guards contain ghost-variables, I have placed them between (temporary) angle brackets.) We consider the following program, where Ri is defined as by (16).

$$
\begin{array}{lll}
\text{prog.}i\text{:} & \textbf{do}\langle \textbf{E}\,j\text{: } \textbf{non } e[\,j]\rangle \rightarrow \{\textbf{A}\,j\text{: } \textbf{non } ri[\,j]\} & \text{PR11} \\
\text{L0:} & \quad \langle d[i] := \textit{true}; \; vi := y\rangle\{y[i] = vi[i]\}; & \\
& \quad qi := \textit{fi}(vi)\{qi = \textit{fi}(vi)\}; & \\
\text{L1:} & \quad \textbf{if } vi[i] = qi \rightarrow \{y[i] = \textit{fi}(vi)\}\langle e[i] := d[i]\rangle & \\
& \quad [\!]\; \langle vi[i] \neq qi \textbf{ and } Ri\rangle \rightarrow \{y[i] \neq \textit{fi}(vi)\} & \\
\text{L2:} & \quad\quad \langle y[i] := qi; (\textbf{A}\,j\text{: } qi[j], ri[j] := \textit{true}, \textit{true})\rangle; & \\
\text{L3}j\text{:} & \quad\quad (\textbf{A}\,j\text{: } \{ri[j]\}\langle d[j], qi[j] := \textit{false}, \textit{false}\rangle); & \\
\text{L4}j\text{:} & \quad\quad (\textbf{A}\,j\text{: } \{ri[j]\}\langle e[j], ri[j] := \textit{false}, \textit{false}\rangle) & \\
& \quad \textbf{fi} & \\
& \textbf{od}\quad . &
\end{array}
$$

Trivially L0 and L3j cannot affect any Rj. L4j, although it removes incoming arrows for node nr. j, can never cause for Rj a transition from *true* to *false*, since it leaves Rj *true* on account of the final **non** $e[\,j]$. Action L2, which only adds arrows, cannot effectuate for Rj a transition from *true* to *false* either. Hence, L1 is the only action that can do so. But because L1 is executed under absence of outgoing arrows, it can only do so for Ri; hence all through the second alternative Ri, which occurs in the guard, is invariantly *true*, and thus —on account of (17)— action L2 makes all Rj *true* and, since Ri **and** $ri[\,j]$ is a precondition for L4j, actions L4j find and leave the Rj's *true*.

Now we are ready to prove for PR11 the invariance of

$$(\textbf{A}\,k, \, j\text{: } rk[\,j] \Rightarrow (Rk \textbf{ and } Rj)) \quad . \tag{18}$$

L0 and L3j trivially don't affect (18), L4j leaves the consequents unaffected and only strengthens an antecedent, L2 makes all consequents *true* and L1 does not violate (18) because it can only set Ri to *false* in the absence of incoming arrows —since the existence of an Rk **and** $rk[i]$ will keep it *true*— and L1 is executed under the absence of outgoing arrows.

The next step is to draw as quickly as possible the relevant conclusion for which we need the $qi[\,j]$'s, and to eliminate them from then onwards from our consideration. We prove the invariance of

$$(\textbf{A}\,j\text{: } (vj \neq y \textbf{ and } d[\,j]) \Rightarrow (\textbf{E}\,k\text{: } qk[\,j])) \quad . \tag{19}$$

L0 can only affect the ith implication, but leaves its antecedent *false*, action L1 does affect none, L2 leaves all consequents *true*, L3j can only affect the jth implication, but it leaves its antecedent *false*, and L4j affects none. Initially all antecedents are *false*, and the universal validity of (19) has been established.

Because —remember that the ri and qi are local variables of prog. i!— it is easily established that $(\mathbf{A}\ k,\ j\colon qk[j] \Rightarrow rk[j])$, we can deduce from (19)

$$(\mathbf{A}\, j\colon (vj \neq y \text{ and } d[j]) \Rightarrow (\mathbf{E}\, k\colon rk[j])) \qquad . \tag{20}$$

From now on we won't refer to the qi's anymore; we shall need (20) once.

In order to prove the invariance of (14) we may expect —because such a circumstance is not unusual at all— to have to strengthen it. I propose to do so by weakening the antecedents $y[j] \neq fj(y)$, because in view of the local assertions in the alternative clause of PR11 it seems attractive to replace them by

$$y[j] \neq fj(vj) \text{ or } y \neq vj$$

(from the negation of which $y[j] = fj(y)$ duly follows). Because we also expect $d[j]$ to hold eventually, it seems safe to weaken the antecedents still further by adding the term "**or non** $d[j]$". Thus we arrive, inspired by (14), at our tentative invariant relation, which is initially trivially *true*:

$$(\mathbf{A}\, j\colon (y[j] \neq fj(vj) \text{ or } y \neq vj \text{ or non } d[j]) \Rightarrow Rj) \qquad . \tag{21}$$

Action L2, which sets all consequents *true*, is harmless, action L3j can only affect the jth implication, but is harmless because L3j is executed under the invariant truth of $ri[j]$ and on account of (18) under the invariant truth of its consequent Rj. Action L4j is trivially harmless now that we have already established that it leaves the Rj's unaffected. We are left with L0 and L1.

Action L0 leaves the consequents unchanged and can only affect the antecedent for $j = i$: in that case it suffices to show that a *false* antecedent remains *false*, i.e. with P the negation of the antecedent

$P\colon \qquad y[i] = fi(vi) \text{ and } y = vi \text{ and } d[i]$

we have to show that

$P \Rightarrow wp(``\langle d[i] := true;\ vi := y\rangle", P) \qquad .$

The Axiom of Assignment defines this weakest precondition as

$y[i] = fi(y) \text{ and } y = y \text{ and } true \qquad .$

The last two terms are *true* all by themselves, and the truth of the first term is implied by the first two terms of P; hence L0 leaves (21) invariant.

But what about L1? We have established that L1 does not affect Rj for $j \neq i$; for $j \neq i$, it cannot affect the antecedents either, so we only need to worry about the ith implication of (21). The assignment $\langle e[i] := d[i]\rangle$, which leaves its antecedent unaffected, can only violate the implication by making the consequent Ri *false* while the antecedent remains *true*. A necessary initial condition for $\langle e[i] := d[i]\rangle$ to make Ri *false* —see (16) and (18)— is

$d[i] \text{ and non } (\mathbf{E}\ k\colon rk[i]) \qquad .$

Combined with the truth of the antecedent, we derive

$(y[i] \neq fi(vi)$ or $y \neq vi)$ and $d[i]$ and non $(E\ k:\ rk[i])$.

Combined with the local assertion $y[i] = fi(vi)$ as derived from the guard, we get

$y \neq vi$ and $d[i]$ and non $(E\ k:\ rk[i])$.

But on account of (20) this is *false*: also L1 does not destroy the validity of (21), whose invariance has now been established.

We are left with the obligation to show that the ghost-guard *Ri* can be omitted. The local assertion $y[i] \neq fi(vi)$ as derived from the guard implies *Ri* with the help of (21), of which we regard the invariance as established. And this completes the correctness proof of

prog.*i*:   **do**$\langle E\ j:$ **non** $e[j]\rangle \rightarrow$ PR12
$\qquad\qquad \langle d[i] := true;\ vi := y\rangle;$
$\qquad\qquad qi := fi(vi);$
$\qquad\qquad$ **if** $vi[i] = qi \rightarrow \langle e[i] := d[i]\rangle$
$\qquad\qquad [\!]\ vi[i] \neq qi \rightarrow \langle y[i] := qi\rangle;$
$\qquad\qquad\qquad\qquad\qquad (A\ j: \langle d[j] := false\rangle);$
$\qquad\qquad\qquad\qquad\qquad (A\ j: \langle e[j] := false\rangle)$
$\qquad\qquad$ **fi**
$\qquad$ **od**   .

REMARK. C.S. Scholten's proof allows for the further chopping up of the second line into

$\langle d[i] := true\rangle;\ (A\ j: \langle vi[j] := y[j]\rangle);$.

At this stage I shall leave that last proof as an exercise for the reader. (End of remark.)

Concluding Remarks

In one respect I consider the way in which this report has developed as a little bit disappointing: the constructive flavour of its beginning has largely disappeared from PR10 onwards. Rather than verify a posteriori I prefer to merge and synthesize proof and program developments. In sequential programming this art has been raised to a considerable height; when I was halfway this report I saw the same merge and synthesis emerging during multiprogram development. This observation excited me, since it would raise the Gries/Owicki theory more clearly to the status of a tool for construction. Perhaps I should not allow myself to be too much disappointed by the disappearance of the constructive flavour: there wasn't much program to be invented anymore, and, besides that, I was of course biased by having seen Scholten's work.

In other respects I am extremely pleased with it. I have discovered at least two tricks that were new for me: the change of ghost-variables into non-ghost-variables and vice versa and —probably more generally applicable than the first trick— the temporary strengthening of guards by adding "ghost-constraints". I feel that the latter has done a great deal in smoothing the correctness proof for PR12; in any case it seems a very neat way for preventing circular arguments.

Furthermore, we now have at least a workable —be it partial— grip on a canonical problem that I have shunned for at least four years (ever since I designed self-stabilizing systems) and that is the general problem of the detection that in such a distributed system the stabilization towards the legitimate states has been completed.

The development of this report was not easy: quite regularly it has strained my agility in the propositional calculus, but I guess that I can learn it. (It was certainly a good training.) In any case it shows —to my taste even convincingly— the feasibility of departing from the usual operational arguments, in which one tries to visualize classes of computational histories; furthermore it shows the vast superiority of the non-operational arguments —once they have been found!— over the traditional ones.

Acknowledgments

I am greatly indebted to C.S. Scholten for again drawing my attention to this problem and for contributing so much to its solution. (He was the first to see clearly the analogy with the garbage collector, and to transfer the notion of "reachability via a path" into the solution of this problem.) Further I am —as usual— indebted to the regular members of the "Tuesday Afternoon Club". (End of acknowledgments.)

EXPLANATION. This was the first project I embarked upon, shortly after Hoare, Knuth, and Traub had given me reason to be grateful to them. Hence the dedication, in great gratitude and not without some pride. (End of explanation.)

Nuenen, 26 May 1977   PROF. DR. EDSGER W. DIJKSTRA
                                             Burroughs Research Fellow

NOTE ADDED LATER (concerning (16). Relation (16) is correct in so far as that it certainly holds. If we want to use it to *define* the Rj as a solution of (16), we must add the remark that the Rj's then must be the minimal solution, i.e. the solution with as few Rj's *true* as possible; this, because the arrows may form cyclic paths. (End of note added later.)

EWD623

The Mathematics Behind the Banker's Algorithm

(I recently lectured on the so-called "Banker's Algorithm" as an example of a method for deadlock prevention. Because my informal justification left my students visibly unconvinced, I designed a more explicit one while preparing my next week's lectures. This note is written because I think the argument I developed at that occasion rather nice; it is not a symptom of any revival of my interest in the Banker's Algorithm as a scheduling strategy.)

We consider a non-empty set P of processes p, each of them engaged on a finite transaction for the completion of which it may need a (varying but bounded) number of units of some shared resource at its exclusive disposal. (The units are all equivalent, say: pages of store.)

A process may "borrow" one or more units, which are then added to its current "loan", it may "return" one or more units, which are then subtracted from its current loan. The act of borrowing is restricted by the condition that for each process the loan will never exceed a pre-stated "need", i.e. the maximum number of units that may be simultaneously needed by that process for the completion of its transactions. The act of returning is restricted by the (obvious) constraint that for no process can the loan ever become negative; upon completion of a transaction, the corresponding loan returns to zero.

If there are "cap" units in the system, the sum of the loans cannot exceed cap. More precisely, if we define

$$\text{cash} = \text{cap} - \text{sum}(\ p \textbf{ from } P\colon \text{loan}[\ p\ ]) \tag{1}$$

then "cash" represents the number of unallocated units and must satisfy

$$0 \leqslant \text{cash} \leqslant \text{cap} \quad . \tag{2}$$

For each process p we have

$$0 \leqslant \text{loan}[\ p\ ] \leqslant \text{need}[\ p\ ] \leqslant \text{cap} \quad . \tag{3}$$

A simple example shows that the danger of deadlock is present. Consider two processes with the following pattern of loans and needs:

cap = 4, need[0] = need[1] = 3, loan[0] = loan[1] = 2, cash = 0   .

Because for each process loan < need still holds, each process is entitled to request a further unit before returning units; however, because cash = 0, deadlock would result if they both do so.

The act of borrowing is, therefore, split into two parts. The process requests the units to be borrowed from a banker and waits until the banker has granted this request.

DEFINITION. A "pattern" (of loans and needs) is "safe" if a granting strategy exists such that it can be guaranteed that all (current and future) requests can be granted within a finite period of time. (End of definition.)

The function of the banker is to keep the pattern safe. The banker does so by inspecting, for each request, whether the pattern that would result from granting it is safe. If it is safe, the request can be granted immediately, and we assume that then the banker does so. If it is not safe, the banker postpones granting it until a more favourable moment: because the postponement has not changed the pattern of loans and needs, which is therefore still safe, that moment will come within a finite period of time. The purpose of the so-called "Banker's Algorithm" is to investigate whether a given pattern of loans and needs is safe.

*   *
*

For each process p we introduce as abbreviation

claim[p] = need[p] − loan[p]   .

The current claim[p] thus represents the maximum number of units process p may need to borrow before it returns any units. Suppose that P consists of N processes and that

$$p[0], p[1],\ldots,p[N-1]$$

represents a permutation of the process numbers such that

$$(\text{A } i: 0 \leqslant i < N: \text{claim}[p[i]] \leqslant \text{cash} + \text{sum}(0 \leqslant j < i: \text{loan}[p[j]]))$$

$$(4)$$

Lemma 1. *Relation (4) implies that the pattern is safe.*

PROOF. The existence of a granting strategy such as required for safety is shown by the strategy of *only* granting (*all*) requests from process $p[i]$, provided that all processes $p[j]$ for $0 \leqslant j < i$ have terminated their transactions. Relation (4) then implies that for $i = 0, 1,\ldots,N-1$ in succession, cash will be sufficient to grant all requests from process $p[i]$ without violating (2). Within a finite period of time, process $p[i]$ will have terminated its transaction and i can be increased by 1. (End of proof.)

The Banker's Algorithm tries to find such a permutation of the process numbers by keeping

$$(\mathbf{A}\ i: 0 \leqslant i < k: \text{claim}[\,p[i]] \leqslant \text{cash} + \text{sum}(0 \leqslant j < i: \text{loan}[\,p[\,j]]))$$

(5)

invariant. After having established it (trivially) by means of $k := 0$, it then tries to increase k by 1 under invariance of (5) until $k = N$. It does so by not changing $p[0], \ldots, p[k-1]$, and by searching for an h satisfying

$$k \leqslant h < N \textbf{ and } \text{claim}[\,p[h]] \leqslant \text{cash} + \text{sum}(0 \leqslant j < k: \text{loan}[\,p[\,j]])$$

(6)

If such an h has been found,

$$\text{``}p: \text{swap}(h, k); k := k + 1\text{''}$$

increases k by 1 under invariance of (5). If, however, for $k < N$ equation (6) has no solution for h, we say that "the ordering effort has failed". If (6) remains solvable each time, until $k = N$, we say that "the ordering effort has not failed".

Because an ordering effort that does not fail implies the existence of a permutation satisfying (4) and, hence, on account of lemma 1 that the pattern is safe, we conclude that for a pattern that is not safe, all ordering efforts must fail. Or, with

Ass.0:   the pattern of loans and needs is not safe
Ass.1:   all ordering efforts fail

we have derived

$$\text{Ass.0} \Rightarrow \text{Ass.1} \qquad .$$

(7)

With

Ass.2:   a failing ordering effort is possible

we conclude (because the set of possible ordering efforts is not empty) that

$$\text{Ass.1} \Rightarrow \text{Ass.2} \qquad .$$

(8)

Consider next

Ass.3:   the non-empty set of processes —or, to be quite precise, the non-empty set P' of process numbers— can be partitioned into $A + B$, such that B is non-empty and

$$(\mathbf{A}\ b \textbf{ from } B: \text{claim}[b] > \text{cash} + \text{sum}(a \textbf{ from } A: \text{loan}[a])).$$

We can then conclude that

$$\text{Ass.2} \Rightarrow \text{Ass.3} \quad . \tag{9}$$

PROOF. Consider the state as reached by the failing ordering effort that is possible under the assumption of Ass.2. Choose then

$$A = \{ p[j] \mid 0 \leqslant j < k \} \quad ,$$

from which we conclude that

$$\text{cash} + \text{sum}(a \text{ from } A: \text{loan}[a]) = \text{cash} + \text{sum}(0 \leqslant j < k: \text{loan}[p[j]]) \quad ;$$

choose furthermore

$$B = \{ p[j] \mid k \leqslant j < N \} \quad ;$$

because $k < N$, B is not empty, and because the ordering effort has failed, (6) has no solution for h, and hence A and B satisfy the criteria that are imposed upon them in Ass.3. (End of proof.)

Finally we conclude

$$\text{Ass.3} \Rightarrow \text{Ass.0} \quad . \tag{10}$$

PROOF. Let all processes from B from now on try to borrow until their loans equal their needs, before they return any units. Let all processes from A terminate their activity. In spite of what has been returned, Ass.3 implies that the banker still does not have enough in cash to see any process from B through to completion, and, hence, the pattern of loans and needs is not safe. (End of proof.)

Combining (7), (8), (9), and (10), we see

$$\text{Ass.0} \Rightarrow \text{Ass.1} \Rightarrow \text{Ass.2} \Rightarrow \text{Ass.3} \Rightarrow \text{Ass.0}$$

but from this cyclic implication we are allowed to conclude

$$\text{Ass.0} = \text{Ass.1} = \text{Ass.2} = \text{Ass.3} \quad . \tag{11}$$

Conclusion (11) is the important one. While it is obvious that a non-failing ordering effort implies that the pattern is safe, (11) implies that the discovery of a *single* failing ordering effort allows us to conclude immediately —i.e. without *any* of the back-tracking that is traditionally involved in the search for permutations satisfying some criterion— that no such permutation exists and that the pattern is not safe.

From (11) it also follows rapidly that, in order to investigate the safety of the pattern that would result from granting a request to process c in a safe situation, the ordering effort can be stopped as soon as $c = p[k]$, for then safety is already implied. (The credit for this discovery is due to L. Zwanenburg, who made it in the early sixties.)

*   *   *

In retrospect I am grateful to the puzzled looks on my students' faces. That from a cyclic arrangement of n assertions, each implying the next one, we can conclude that all n assertions are equivalent —or to put it more dramatically: can conclude all $n(n-1)$ pair-wise implications— is not unknown at all. But the larger the value of n, the more impressive an example of effective reasoning we have, in particular if —as in this case— the assertions have been arranged in such an order that the n implications are not difficult to prove.

It is a pity that, probably, the case $n = 2$ is the most common one, for in that case the "gain" —as measured in terms of the number of implications established— is nihil!

Nuenen

PROF. DR. EDSGER W. DIJKSTRA
Burroughs Research Fellow

EWD629
On Two Beautiful Solutions Designed by Martin Rem

(In recent correspondence with dr. Martin Rem —currently at the Department of Computer Science (mail code: 256-80), California Institute of Technology, PASADENA, California 91109, U.S.A.— he sent me two solutions which I think both so beautiful that they deserve a wider distribution; hence their inclusion in the EWD series; apart from some historical information and formal elaborations that have been added, and some cosmetic changes, I have essentially presented Rem's solutions.)

A P/V-Implementation of Conditional Critical Regions

Since (by an accident of history) the P- and V-operations on semaphores have more or less acquired the status of "canonical" synchronization primitives, inventors of new synchronization concepts have related their inventions to P- and V-operations in two different ways. Either —see, for instance, Hoare [1], concerning monitors— the new concept is shown to be equally powerful by demonstrating that it can be used to implement the P- and V-operations; or —see, for instance, Hoare [2], when introducing the (simple) critical region "**with** r **do** S **od**"— the feasibility of its implementation is argued by showing how to implement it with P- and V-operations. The latter possibility has now been demonstrated by Rem for the conditional critical region "**with** r **when** B **do** S **od**" as well. (In [2], Hoare remarks about the simple critical region "If we assume that a Boolean semaphore mechanism is "built-in", the implementation is trivial." (as indeed it is). When in [2] Hoare introduces the conditional critical regions, he adds

"Some care must be exercised in the implementation of this new feature." and follows with a two paragraph verbal sketch, explaining what has to be done with a queue of processes waiting for r. In [3], Brinch Hansen gives a slightly more detailed sketch of an implementation involving two queues —"queues" that can be recognized in Rem's solution (if looked at abstractly enough)— but it is still no more than a sketch. Ironically enough, Rem now solves the problem by a method —later called "splitting a binary semaphore"— that a few years ago Hoare taught us!)

In processes, so-called "conditional critical regions" of the form "**with** r **when** Bi **do** Si **od**" may occur. Here r denotes a shared variable —or more generally: a cluster of shared variables— , such that r is only accessible from within sections of the text of the form "**when** Bi **do** Si **od**" that are prefixed by "**with** r". (That this constraint is not violated is easily checked by a compiler, a circumstance that is its major justification.)

As with the simple critical regions "**with** r **do** Si **od**", the implementation has to ensure that the executions of the statements Si —prefixed by the same "**with** r"— as they may occur in the different processes, *exclude each other in time*. In addition, a statement Si —like what later would become known as "a guarded command"— is only eligible for execution in those initial states where Bi holds. The implementation has to ensure that these constraints are met by delaying, if necessary, the further execution of the process in which Si occurs.

A further requirement is that no such delay occurs without justification, more precisely:

(1) if no statement Si is under execution —i.e. the requirement of mutual exclusion would not constrain the selection of a next Si for execution — , and

(2) if for one or more processes the Si of a conditional critical region is the next statement to be executed and at least one of the corresponding Bi's is *true*, then the selection of such an Si with a *true* Bi is obligatory.

To make the implementation of this last requirement feasible, a further constraint ensures that activity of one process, but well outside its regions critical with respect to r leaves the "**non** Bi" for all other processes invariantly *true*. This further constraint is that r is the *only* shared variable Bi may depend upon. The whole set of constraints now ensures that the obligation to inspect whether a *false* Bi of a delayed process has turned *true* can be concentrated at the point where the execution of an Sj (of another process!) has been carried to completion.

The technique of the "split binary semaphore" consists of the introduction of a set of binary semaphores —in this example of the three semaphores m, $b1$, and $b2$— of which at most one equals 1. This can obviously be ensured by seeing to it that in each program P- and V-operations —regardless of on which of the three semaphores they operate— alternate dynamically: each P-operation decreases their sum by 1 and each V-operation increases their sum by 1. Furthermore we can assert that between each P-operation and dynamically subsequent V-operation the sum $m + b1 + b2 = 0$; hence the executions of the program sections between such a P-operation and its subsequent V-operation can be viewed as excluding each other mutually in time (if so desired by the traditional argument of Dijkstra [4]).

Rem's solution uses three semaphores $m(= 1)$, $b1(= 0)$, and $b2(= 0)$, and two counters $n(= 0)$, and $nt(= 0)$ —initial values being given between parentheses— . The integer n counts the number of processes "eager" to perform their Si's; during testing, counter nt is equal to the number of Bi's not guaranteed to be *false*. The whole critical activity can only end with $nt = 0$ —otherwise impermissible delays could result— . When an Si has been performed —and, therefore, all Bi may have become *true*— nt has to be increased until $nt = n$ before testing can begin. In this latter process semaphore $b1$ plays a signalling role and semaphore $b2$ is used to admit processes to their Bi-test one at a time. With this informal sketch of meaning and function of the semaphores and variables I shall present Rem's solution without further annotation; thereafter I shall present a more formal treatment.

$P(m)$; $n := n + 1$;
do non $Bi \rightarrow$ **if** $nt = 0 \rightarrow V(m)$ ☐ $nt > 0 \rightarrow V(b2)$ **fi**;
                  $P(b1)$; $nt := nt + 1$;
                  if $nt < n \rightarrow V(b1)$ ☐ $nt = n \rightarrow V(b2)$ **fi**;
                  $P(b2)$; $nt := nt - 1$
od;
$n := n - 1$; Si;
if $n = 0 \rightarrow V(m)$
☐ $n > 0 \rightarrow$ **if** $nt < n \rightarrow V(b1)$ ☐ $nt = n \rightarrow V(b2)$ **fi**
fi

For our more formal treatment we introduce angle brackets in order to indicate that each action extending from an opening bracket until a next (closing) angle bracket denotes an atomic action. Atomic actions can be viewed as excluding each other in time. This is okay if each atomic action starts with a P-operation, ends with a V-operation, and has no such operations in between.

For each process we introduce two boolean ghost-variables ai ("in the antichambre") and wi ("in the waitingroom"). They are initially *false*; we shall use the notations $(\mathbf{N}\ j: aj)$ and $(\mathbf{N}\ j: wj)$ respectively to denote the number of processes for which ai and wi respectively are *true*. Furthermore we introduce a global ghost-boolean c —initially *false*— , the truth of which marks the states in which the implications $aj \Rightarrow$ **non** Bj need not hold. Labels have been inserted for later discussion. The annotated text of the program is as follows:

L0:$\langle P(m)\{$**non** c **and** $0 = nt \leqslant n\}$; $n := n + 1\{$**non** c **and** $0 \leqslant nt < n\}$;
    do non $Bi \rightarrow \{$**non** c **and** $0 \leqslant nt < n$ **and non** $Bi\}ai := true$;
            if $nt = 0 \rightarrow \{$**non** c **and** $0 = nt \leqslant n\}V(m)$
            ☐ $nt > 0 \rightarrow \{$**non** c **and** $0 < nt \leqslant n\}V(b2)$
            fi$\rangle$;
        L1: $\langle P(b1)\{c$ **and** $0 \leqslant nt < n\}$; $ai := false$; $wi := true$;
            $nt := nt + 1\{c$ **and** $0 < nt \leqslant n\}$;
            if $nt < n \rightarrow \{c$ **and** $0 \leqslant nt < n\}V(b1)$
            ☐ $nt = n \rightarrow c := false$; $\{$**non** c **and** $0 < nt \leqslant n\}V(b2)$
            fi$\rangle$;
        L2: $\langle P(b2)\{$**non** c **and** $0 < nt \leqslant n\}$; $wi := false$;
            $nt := nt - 1\{$**non** c **and** $0 \leqslant nt < n\}$
    od;
    $n := n - 1\{Bi$ **and** $0 \leqslant nt \leqslant n\}$;
    Si; $c := (nt < n)$;
    if $n = 0 \rightarrow \{$**non** c **and** $0 = nt \leqslant n\}V(m)$
    ☐ $n > 0 \rightarrow$ **if** $nt < n \rightarrow \{c$ **and** $0 \leqslant nt < n\}V(b1)$
              ☐ $nt = n \rightarrow \{$**non** c **and** $0 < nt \leqslant n\}V(b2)$
             fi
    fi$\rangle$
L3:

Indicating atomic actions by start- and end-label, we can denote the five atomic actions we have to consider as follows: L0-L1, L0-L3, L1-L2, L2-L1, and L2-L3. With the initialization $m = 1$, $b1 = b2 = 0$, we readily establish for all five the invariance of

$P0$: $m + b1 + b2 = 1$.

This establishes the property of the "split boolean semaphore" and tells us that, indeed, we are entitled to regard the five actions —each of which starts with a P-operation on one of the three semaphores and ends (dynamically) with a V-operation on one of the semaphores— as "atomic". In particular it guarantees that the Si are executed under mutual exclusion and under the initial truth of Bi.

Having established the atomicity, and taking the further initial values $nt = n = 0$ and $c = false$ into account, we next establish the invariant truth of

$P1$: $(m = 1 \Rightarrow ($**non** c **and** $0 = nt \leqslant n))$ **and**
       $(b1 = 1 \Rightarrow (c$ **and** $0 \leqslant nt < n))$ **and**
       $(b2 = 1 \Rightarrow ($**non** c **and** $0 < nt \leqslant n))$.

The invariance of $P1$ is easily established, as is indicated by the assertions that annotate the program text. (Note that it seems to be the function of the ghost-boolean c to make the three consequents mutually exclusive.)

With the further knowledge that initially all the wi are *false*, we easily establish the invariant truth of

$P2$: $(\mathbf{N} j: wj) = nt$.

Because $(\mathbf{N} j: wj) =$ the number of processes at L2, ready to perform $P(b2)$, we conclude now that on account of the third implication of $P1$, a deadlock cannot occur after execution of $V(b2)$.

With the further knowledge that initially all the ai are *false*, we easily establish the invariant truth of

$P3$: $(\mathbf{N} j: aj) = n - nt$.

Because $(\mathbf{N} j: aj) =$ the number of processes at L1, ready to perform $P(b1)$, we conclude now that on account of the second implication of $P1$, a deadlock cannot occur after execution of $V(b1)$.

(A "temporary" or "partial" deadlock can occur after execution of $V(m)$; then, however, the state $m = 1$ holds, and the assumption is that sooner or later another process will "join the game" via L0.)

Finally we establish the invariant truth of

$P4$: $(\mathbf{A} j: aj \Rightarrow (\textbf{non } Bj \textbf{ or } c))$,

which holds initially because then all antecedents are *false*. We shall check its invariance explicitly. L0-L3 and L2-L3 could make all Bj's *true* as a result of Si's modification of r; the assignment $c := (nt < n)$, however, makes all implications of $P4$ hold: if c is established by it, all consequents are *true*, if **non** c is established by it, we conclude $nt = n$, and $P3$ then tells us that all antecedents are *false*; in both cases all implications of $P4$ hold vacuously. L0-L1 and L2-L1 could only affect the ith implication, but they don't do so as $ai := true$ is executed under the truth of its consequent, viz. **non** Bi. In L1-L2, the assignment $ai := false$ strengthens an antecedent and is therefore safe; the assignment $c := false$ may strengthen any consequent, but —see $P3$— is executed under falsity of all antecedents and is therefore safe as well. This concludes our demonstration of the invariance of $P4$.

Combining (the first implication of) $P1$, $P3$, and $P4$ we conclude

$$m = 1 \Rightarrow ((\mathbf{N} j: aj) = n \textbf{ and } (\mathbf{A} j: aj \Rightarrow \textbf{non } Bj))   ,$$

thus expressing that no avoidable delay is introduced.

*   *   *

[1]   Hoare, C.A.R. "Monitors: an Operating System Structuring Concept", STAN-CS-73-401, November 1973

[2]   Hoare, C.A.R. "Towards a Theory of Parallel Programming", in *Operating Systems Techniques*, C.A.R. Hoare and R.H. Perrott (Eds.) London and New York, Academic Press, 1972

[3]   Brinch Hansen, Per, *Operating System Principles*, Englewood Cliffs, Prentice-Hall, 1973

[4] Dijkstra, Edsger W., "Hierarchical Ordering of Sequential Processes" in *Operating Systems Techniques*, C.A.R. Hoare and R.H. Perrott (Eds.) London and New York, Academic Press, 1972

NOTE. I have changed my mind and postpone the other solution's presentation to a later EWD report (End of note.)

Nuenen

PROF. DR. EDSGER W. DIJKSTRA
Burroughs Research Fellow

EWD635
Trip Report E.W. Dijkstra, Newcastle-upon-Tyne, 5–10 Sept. 1977

"Gawdamighty, wot a tongue! I wonder 'er own spit don't poison 'er. I wouldn't 'ang a dog on '*er* evidence."

Frank Crutchley on Mrs Ruddle [1]

At Schiphol Airport I met the colleagues van der Sluis, Blaauw, and van der Poel. I heard the absence of Verrijn Stuart explained (justified?) by an admiring reference to his mountaineering exploits in the Himalayas. I did not quote Miss Twitterton's comment when told that Frank Crutchley had taken good care of the cacti [1] because I wasn't *quite* sure of the quotation.

The strike of the British assistant air traffic controllers delayed my arrival in Newcastle by fifteen minutes, and my return in Nuenen by twelve hours. But flights with British Caledonian do have the advantage that the planes take off and land without music.

Upon arrival my Dutch colleagues and Goos from Germany wanted to go to Henderson Hall; for me there was someone from the University with a car to take me to the Computing Laboratory. His car —a 2CV— was much too small to take all five of us, and they had to take a taxi; it was an unintended case of one-upmanship, for which I hope I won't be blamed.

The purpose of the visit was attending the yearly "Joint International Seminar on the Teaching of Computing Science", sponsored by IBM and organized by the University of Newcastle. This year's topic was "Digital Systems Design", speakers were Professor D. Aspinall (UK), Professor I.M. Barron (UK), Professor Dr. G.A. Blaauw (The Netherlands), Dr. T.C. Chen (IBM, USA), Dr. E.L. Glazer (SDC, USA), Professor F.G. Heath (UK), Professor W.M. McKeeman (USA), Professor Z.G. Vranesic (Canada), Mr. J.G. Givens (Univ. of Newcastle) and Professor C.A.R. Hoare (UK) as a

319

stand-in for Professor Dr. Ing.R. Piloty (Germany) who was prevented from attending.

As usual the audience consisted mainly of professors of computing science; this time the speakers were mainly specialists in logic design. For many in the audience the exposure was a shock. At the level of component technology the change over the last fifteen years has been drastic: what used to be expressed in milliseconds is now expressed in microseconds, what used to be expressed in kilobucks is now expressed in dimes and quarters. This change has been so drastic that it is well-known. Much less known is that at the next levels, viz. of circuit design and logic design, the attention of the designers has been so fully usurped by the obligation to adapt to the ever changing technology, that at those levels design methodology has had no chance to mature from craft to scientific discipline. This is in sharp contrast to the developments in programming methodology, where during that period of fifteen years a fairly stable "base" could be enjoyed. Having witnessed that development in programming methodology at close quarters, I was overcome by the feeling of being exposed to the result of fifteen years of intellectual stagnation, and it was during Blaauw's lecture on the first afternoon that I asked my right-hand neighbour "Close your eyes, forget how you came here and guess in which year you are living."; without hesitation he came up with exactly the same year I had in mind: 1962.

In the corridors I later checked that that feeling of "they have failed to evolve" was much more general. It became even more justified when E.L. Glazer in his lectures and W.L. van der Poel in the discussion referred to logical design as an "art" or a "craft". In the last discussion session, on Friday afternoon, when the seminar was tied in with the general theme of teaching computing science, I raised the question whether the topic deserved the academic effort of trying to raise it from a craft to a scientific discipline. (With a few exceptions the talks had not been at an academic level, and under the assumption that the speakers had done justice to their subject, one could not avoid concluding that in its current state the topic is rather shallow; my question was essentially "Is more depth possible?".) The ensuing discussion —whom am I quoting?— "generated more heat than light". My clearest memory is that some violently objected to the idea, noteworthy I.M. Barron, who thought it appropriate to use the word "academic" in the pejorative sense in which it is so often used by the vulgar. (Later that evening, while waiting for the plane to depart, I read of the effort to prevent a further debasement of the word "academic" by defining it as "a term of opprobrium applied by those who do not know their business to those who do" [2].) I also concluded that H.A. Simon had been correct [3] when he observed that today's designers —he wrote this in 1968, but it could have been written now— are perfectly willing to use the results from other scientific disciplines, but are not ready to contemplate a "science of design" or to approach their *own* problems in a scientific manner.

Another overwhelming impression was the confusion between "economical" and "economic". Everybody agrees that considerations of economy play a predominant role in many aspects of computing science: it is to a large extent a science concerned with how not to waste resources. But several speakers could *only* deal with the (subtle) questions of economy after having translated them into the (crude) questions of economics, that is, after having equated "efficient" with "cheap". E.L. Glazer clearly demonstrated the confusion introduced by doing so. In *all* his lectures he mentioned the "cost equation" as his main guiding principle; at the same time he complained that its coefficients, even if known, were changing all the time. He concluded that, as a result, *design* was now very difficult; the only justified conclusion is that those changing values aggravate the already severe problems of *doing business*. The fact that in our field science and business often need each other seems in many minds to have blurred the distinction between the two, and the result is a confusing kind of unisex thinking. I.M. Barron went even further. He spoke entirely as an amateur economist, and argued that expected chip production capacity was so large, that research had to find new applications very quickly, lest the chip manufacturing firms collapse and their large investments be lost! (Thirty-six hours after my return I heard a proposal for automatically tuning radio sets, each equipped with a microprocessor for the decoding of the digital information to be supplied by the stations.)

T.C. Chen did in principle a good job, and his contributions were generally appreciated. With a number of very different and well-chosen examples he illustrated what novel problems may become relevant as the result of new technologies becoming available. But I found his method of presentation exasperating: he lectured as if addressing idiots. I attended his first lecture until the end, but the next day I could not envisage going through that torture again and I played truant. The third day, when he gave his last lecture, I decided to be a good boy again and to attend, but I am afraid that at the nth insipid visual I exploded. Also Aspinall showed how easily a lecture can suffer from prepared viewgraphs. (The things being prepared in advance, one can come away with cumbersome notations; furthermore the temptation to show irrelevancies seems hard to resist.)

The most informative talks were given by J.G. Givens, W.M. McKeeman, and C.A.R. Hoare. Givens described "The Work of the Digital Systems Laboratory at Newcastle-upon-Tyne" and did so very clearly. This I appreciated, independently of the fact that, if I had my way —which they are wise not to give me— I would presumably close the laboratory. When I heard the pride with which Givens told how at the end students were taught how to incorporate "more complex components", I was reminded of Donovan's article in the *Comm*.ACM [4] and shuddered. McKeeman's third talk "A Simple Computer" described an introductory course on computer architecture, given at Santa Cruz. His talk was informative and the course seemed indeed a broad and unbiased introduction to the problems; the associated laboratory work, however, made the course very time-consuming for the students. Hoare gave a very nice one-hour introduction to his "Communicating Sequential Processes"; he is still miles away from my ideal of defining semantics independently of any underlying computational model, but he has at least reached the stage that no one can make out whether he is talking about hardware or software. (Afterwards he wondered how many in the audience had noticed that in this respect he had not committed himself.) The reactions he evoked gave a surprising insight into some people's ignorance or small-mindedness.

During one discussion something very amazing surfaced. E.L. Glazer had described his problems in getting code for microprocessors right, and how they had been somewhat alleviated by additional hardware in which traditional debugging techniques —inspection and injection of individual register contents— could be used again. His problems had not been encountered by Fraser Duncan, who had found the good coding discipline of the late fifties again quite applicable, nor by Harry Whitfield who also had found these problems quite avoidable. So-called "cross-compilers" were mentioned as an obvious solution. Then Glazer told that he could get no one to write a cross-compiler because computing scientists who knew how to write a compiler did not want to have anything to do with microprocessors, for fear of status and for fear that, after having been contaminated with microprocessors, "they could never return to real computing again". Nowhere else had Glazer given us reason to doubt his words, so we believed him. But then there must be something very, very wrong. Here you have jobs, challenging enough for professors in computing science in Groningen and Bristol to spend a few days, a few weeks or a few months on in order to show that the job is perfectly doable, and in Silicon Valley the professionals, who should be able to do it, for some obscure (social?) reason look down on it, and the job isn't done decently. The story supported the definition of the problems of the real world as those that you are left with when you refuse to apply their effective solution. It left me very disturbed and I was reminded of a conversation with my wife, one evening a few months ago. We were talking about love of perfection, and I mentioned that R.M. Rilke always wrote flawless letters. When he made an error, he started the page afresh: as simple as that! I suggested that perhaps Rilke had carried a good principle too far. But my wife remarked immediately "I guess that Rilke learned very quickly how to avoid mistakes.". That conversation seemed so relevant that I told it to several people in Newcastle and I now include it in my trip report.

I did not join the excursion (boat tour this time) on Wednesday afternoon, but went with Fraser Duncan (now at the University of Bristol) to Brian Randell's house (where I was staying), where Fraser could say hello to Brian's wife. After a cup of coffee I left them because I wanted to do some writing. Later that afternoon Brian Randell, Gerhard Seegmüller, and Tony

Hoare returned (Fraser had gone to visit the Cathedral of Durham). At that moment I was trying to comment on a paper that a friend (not one of its authors) had mailed to me, and that for eighty percent is an ugly political pamphlet disguised as a scientific paper. An editor had sent it to Tony, asking him for a rebuttal, but having other things to do Tony had declined to do so. It was an amazing coincidence, and I welcomed the opportunity to discuss that paper.

That afternoon was the only moment of peace and quiet that week. On Monday evening the participants were the guests of the Randells. On Tuesday evening the University offered a sherry party, and afterwards I had dinner in Ewan Page's new house. On Wednesday evening the participants were offered a "Mediaeval Banquet" —to be eaten with knife and fingers: appropriately called "a digital dinner"— on Thursday evening we were offered the closing dinner in the new Town Hall (furnished with an unbelievable luxury) of Newcastle-upon-Tyne. The dinner was excellent; the only shortcoming was that the dining hall was very close to the kitchen where an oven produced a loud and high-pitched tone that became very painful.

*   *
*

Recalling the sarcasms from our survival kit I can only conclude that most talks have been pretty disappointing indeed. Of one speaker I remarked that his talk had been much better than I had feared, of another speaker it has been said that his talk had enhanced the quality of the others... "Reputations shredded while you wait." was Brian's apt comment. Brian always accuses me of a lack of tolerance and he is, of course, right that my naive idealism should not turn me into the complete misanthrope. But what is the alternative? Am I expected to cheer when Ewan Page defends their Digital Systems Laboratory by remarking that in other departments of the University much worse things happen? Am I expected to cheer when van der Poel explains to me that there is little point in trying to educate good designers because IBM has discovered that with poor designs more money is earned? Has the seminar made me a wiser man? I hope so. And also a sadder one? I sincerely hope not.

[1] Sayers, Dorothy L., *Busman's Honeymoon*, Gollancz 1937, Penguin Books 1962
[2] Gowers, Sir Ernest, *The Complete Plain Words*, Pelican Books 1977
[3] Simon, Herbert A., *The Sciences of the Artificial*, MIT Press, 1969
[4] Donovan, John J., Tools and Philosophy for Software Education, *Comm. ACM* 19, 8 (Aug. 1976), 430–436.

Nuenen   PROF. DR. EDSGER W. DIJKSTRA
                                                Burroughs Research Fellow

EWD636
Why Naive Program Transformation Systems Are Unlikely to Work

Look how carefully the title has been worded! No developer of a program transformation system need feel offended, for I have given him two escapes. Firstly, I am not arguing an impossibility, but only an unlikeliness — and we know that all startling advances have been made against seemingly overwhelming odds, don't we? Secondly, he has the option to declare that the program transformation system *he* is developing is not "naive" in the sense that I shall make more precise below.

*   *
*

I take the position that a serious programmer has at least two major concerns, viz. correctness and efficiency. And from existing software we can deduce that neither of these two concerns is a trivial one.

For years I have argued what I still believe, namely that, when faced with different concerns, we should try to separate them as completely as possible and deal with them in turn. For correctness and efficiency concerns this separation has been achieved up to a point. It is possible to treat the problem of program correctness in isolation from the problem of efficiency in the sense that we can deal with the correctness problem, temporarily even ignoring that our program text also admits the interpretation of executable code. It is also possible to investigate the various cost aspects of program execution independently of the question whether such execution of the program will produce a correct result.

Presented as in the previous paragraph, the separation sought seems to have been found. It is true that the separation is reachable as far as the program text itself is concerned; in the process of composing the text, however, the separation is less marked. There does exist a formal discipline that, when adhered to, cannot lead to an incorrect program. In its application, however, we have a great amount of freedom, and in the choice how to apply the discipline ensuring correctness, the designer always makes up his mind by considering his other concerns, such as efficiency. In other words, the more rigorous the concerns have been separated with respect to the program text itself, the more schizophrenic the act of program composition becomes: the programmer still remains a jack of many trades, switching all the time —and at a high frequency!— between various rôles, whose differences have only become more and more marked over the last decade.

*   *   *

Program transformations have been presented as a possible means to overcome the need for such a schizophrenic programmer behaviour. A number of so-called "semantics-preserving program transformations" have been discovered. Each such transformation, when applicable and applied to a program A generates a new program A' that, when executed, will produce the same result as the original program A, the difference being that the costs of execution of A and of A' may differ greatly. Program A' may also be derived by successive applications of a sequence of such transformations.

It was the discovery of (sequences of) such transformations that supported the idea of what I call "naive" program transformation systems. When using such a system for the development of a program, this development was envisaged to take place in two successive, clearly and rigorously separated, stages.

In the first stage the programmer would only be concerned with program correctness: unencumbered by efficiency considerations he would write a program, whose correctness could be established as easily as possible. In the ideal case, the program's correctness would be trivial to establish.

In the second stage —which in the dreams of some could or should be conducted by a different person, unfamiliar with the original problem— the correct but inefficient program would be subjected to semantics-preserving transformations from a library, until the program had become efficient as well. (At the moment this dream was dreamt, the available library of acknowledged transformations was admittedly still somewhat small, but it was constantly growing and hopes were high.)

*   *   *

When such systems were proposed to me I was very sceptical, but I was mainly so for a purely personal reason and accidental circumstance. Their advocates tried to convince me of the viability of their approach by composing according to their proposed method a program I had published myself. In their demonstrations, stage two required about ten pages of formal labour, while stage one had taken them between one day and one week.

It so happened that their demonstrations were not very convincing for me, because, heading schizophrenically towards a correct and efficient solution, I myself had solved the whole problem (without pencil and paper) in fifteen minutes. (It was the evident effectiveness of the *heuristics* applied that had prompted that publication: the problem itself was one of the kind I could not care less about.)

At the time I was not worried so much about the ten pages of stage two, since it was clear that most of it could be mechanized and would never need to see the light of day. I was much more worried about the discrepancy between one or several days for stage one on the one hand, and fifteen minutes for the whole job on the other, and I remember voicing this latter worry at a meeting of the IFIP Working Group 2.3 on "Programming Methodology".

One of the members —a pioneer in program transformations— suggested a possible explanation for the observed discrepancy: as programmers we had in the past been so terrorized by efficiency concerns that it was very difficult for us to come up with a trivially correct solution, no matter how grossly inefficient. He supported his explanation by stating a problem and presenting a solution for it that, indeed, was so ridiculously inefficient that it would never have entered my mind.

I was struck by his argument —otherwise I wouldn't have remembered it!— ; he made me doubt but could not convince me. The possible explanation for the discrepancy that I had considered was that, by ignoring efficiency considerations, the "admissible solution space" had become cumbersomely large: I felt that the efficiency considerations could provide a vital guiding principle. It seemed a draw, and for the next eight months I did not make up my mind any further about the chances of success for naive program transformation systems.

*   *
*

All the above was introduction. After the closing ceremony of IFIP77 in Toronto I had dinner with Jan Poirters and Martin Rem, and in a conversation about the rôle of mathematics in programming I ventured the conjecture that often an efficient program could be viewed as the successful exploitation of a mathematical theorem. I presented an efficient program as a piece of logical brinkmanship in which a cunning argument could show that the computational labour performed would be just enough for reaching the answer.

I came up with the example of the shortest subspanning tree between N points. There exists a simple one-to-one correspondence between the N^{N-2} different subspanning trees between N points and the N^{N-2} different numbers of $N - 2$ digits in base N. A naive computation A could therefore generate all N^{N-2} trees and select the shortest one encountered. But we know that there exists an efficient algorithm A' whose computation time is proportional to N^2. But the only way in which I can justify the latter algorithm is by using (a generalization of) the theorem that of the branches of the complete graph that meet in a single point, the shortest one is also a branch of the shortest subspanning tree.

In confirmation of our experience that everything of significance in computing science can be illustrated with Euclid's algorithm, Martin Rem came with that example. In order to compute the greatest common divisor of a positive X and Y, the correct algorithm A constructs a table of divisors of X, then a table of divisors of Y, then the intersection of the two tables, and from that (finite and nonempty) intersection the greatest value is selected. But good old Euclid already knew algorithm A' which I can only justify by appealing to (a generalization of) the theorem that $\gcd(x, y) = \gcd(x, y - x)$.

The next week David Gries told me about a speeding up of the Sieve of Eratosthenes —another classic!— for generating a table of prime numbers, a job for which many inefficient but correct algorithms can be created, e.g.

$$y, p := 1, 1;$$
$$\textbf{do } p < N \rightarrow p := p + 1; \ \textbf{do } \gcd(p, y) \neq 1 \rightarrow p := p + 1 \ \textbf{od};$$
$$\text{print}(p); \ y := y * p$$
$$\textbf{od} \quad .$$

David's program, however, relied on the theorem that there exists a prime number between n and $2n$.

In the meantime I have thought of a fourth example. The branches of a subspanning tree between N points provide a unique path between any two of the points and we can define the sum of the branches of such a path to be the "distance" between those two points. Which is the point pair with the maximum distance from each other? The simple algorithm A determines all $N(N - 1)/2$ distances and selects the longest encountered. The efficient algorithm A' uses the theorem that for an arbitrary point y the point x with the maximum distance from y is one of the end points of the longest path. We then determine the point z with the maximum distance from x, and the pair (x, z) is our answer.

The question now is: what are our chances of deriving an efficient program A' by applying (mechanizable) transformations from a finite library to the original program A? Because the transformations are semantics-preserving, program A' is correct if program A is. The correctness proof for A —which, ideally, is almost trivial— together with the derivation path from A to A' constitutes a correctness proof for A'. In none of the examples given does the theorem with which *we* proved the correctness of A' seem unnecessarily strong, i.e. in each case, from the *given* correctness of A' the corresponding theorem seems simply derivable. The supposed derivation path from A to A' therefore contains the major part not only of the justification of A', but also of the proof of the mathematical theorem that *we* used to justify program A' directly.

All our experience from mechanized mathematics tells us that therefore the derivation paths from A to A' —if, with a given library, they exist at all— can be expected to be long and difficult to find. Extending the library is only an improvement as long as the library is still very small; using a large library will be exactly as difficult as commanding a large body of mathematical knowledge. Furthermore, each intermediate product on the derivation path from A to A' must be a program that is semantically equivalent to A; for this constraint I can find no analogue in normal mathematical reasoning, and for many triples $\langle A, A', \text{library} \rangle$ it may make even the existence of such a derivation path questionable.

The stated hope that, once our system of mechanized program transformations is there, stage two can be left to a sort of "technical assistant" that need not know anything about the original problem and its underlying mathematics, but only needs to know how to operate the transformation system, now seems to me unwarranted. And if that hope is expressed as a claim, that claim now seems to me just as misleading as most advertising.

I do not exclude the possibility that useful program transformation systems of some sort will be developed —it may even be possible to derive some of the efficient algorithms I mentioned above— , but I don't expect them to be naive: the original goal of allocating the mathematical concern about correctness and the engineering concern about execution costs to two distinct, well-separated stages in the development process seems unattainable. It was good old Euclid who warned king Ptolemy I:

> "There is no 'royal road' to geometry."   ;

and those who think that that warning does not apply to *them* will be reminded of it the hard way. . . .

Acknowledgment

The argument displayed above contains enough loose expressions —such as "a major part of the proof"— to be regarded as fishy. I am not even myself perfectly sure of its convincing power. (How is *that* for a loose expression?) I therefore gratefully acknowledge the opportunity provided in Niagara-on-the-Lake, Aug. 1977, to confront members of IFIP WG2.3 with it and to solicit their comments. Although I found my feelings confirmed, it goes without saying that none of them can be held responsible for the views expressed in the above. I also thank Jan Poirters and Martin Rem for their contribution to a pleasant, yeah even memorable, dinner. (End of acknowledgment.)

Nuenen   PROF. DR. EDSGER W. DIJKSTRA
                                                   Burroughs Research Fellow

EWD637

The Three Golden Rules for Successful Scientific Research

This note is devoted to three rules that must be followed if you want to be successful in scientific research. (If you manage to follow them, they will prove almost sufficient, but that is another story.) They are recorded for the benefit of those who would like to be successful in their scientific research, but fail to be so because, being unaware of these rules, they violate them. In order to avoid any misunderstanding I would like to stress, right from the start, that this note is purely pragmatic. No moral judgements are implied, and it is completely up to you to decide whether you wish to regard trying to be successful in scientific research as a noble goal in life or not. I even leave you the option of not making that decision at all.

The first rule is an "internal" one; it has nothing to do with your relations with others, it concerns you yourself in isolation. It is as follows:

> Raise your quality standards as high as you can live with, avoid wasting your time on routine problems, and always try to work as closely as possible at the boundary of your abilities. Do this because it is the only way of discovering how that boundary should be moved forward.

This rule tells us that the obviously possible should be shunned as well as the obviously impossible: the first would not be instructive, the second would be hopeless, and both in their own way are barren.

The second rule is an "external" one; it deals with the relation between "the scientific world" and "the real world". It is as follows:

> We all like our work to be socially relevant and scientifically sound. If we can find a topic satisfying both desires, we are lucky; if the two targets are in conflict with each other, let the requirement of scientific soundness prevail.

The reason for this rule is obvious. If you do a piece of "perfect" work in which no one is interested, no harm is done. On the contrary, at least something "perfect", no matter how irrelevant, has been added to our culture. If, however, you offer a shaky, would-be solution to an urgent problem, you do harm to the world, which, in view of the urgency of the problem, will only be too willing to apply your ineffective remedy. It is no wonder that charlatanry always flourishes in connection with incurable diseases. (Our second rule is traditionally violated by the social sciences to such an extent that one can now question if they deserve the name "sciences" at all.)

The third rule is somewhere in the middle on the scale "internal/external". It deals with the relation between you and your scientific colleagues. It is as follows:

> Never tackle a problem of which you can be pretty sure that (now or in the near future) it will be tackled by others who are, in relation to that problem, at least as competent and well-equipped as you.

Again the reason is obvious. If others will come up with as good a solution as you could obtain, the world doesn't lose a thing if you leave the problem alone. A corollary of the third rule is that one should never compete with one's colleagues. If you are pretty sure that in a certain area you will do a better job than anyone else, please do it in complete devotion, but when in doubt, abstain. The third rule ensures that your contributions —if any!— will be unique.

*   *
*

I have checked the Three Golden Rules with a number of my colleagues from very different parts of the world, living and working under very different circumstances. They all agreed. And were not shocked either. The rules may strike you as a bit cruel.... If so, they should, for the sooner you have discovered that the scientific world is not a soft place but —like most other worlds, for that matter— a fairly ruthless one, the better. My blessings are with you

Nuenen   PROF. DR. EDSGER W. DIJKSTRA
                                             Burroughs Research Fellow

EWD639
The Introduction of MAES®

"Mathematics Inc. proudly announces MAES®, its knowledge-based Mathematical Articles Evaluation System. Developed and tested for internal usage by the World's Leading Manufacturer of first-class mathematical products, MAES® is an indispensable quality control tool for professional producers and consumers of Twentieth Century Mathematics. Being adopted by most of the International Mathematical Journals to replace their subjective, error-prone, labour-intensive and time-consuming refereeing process, MAES® will be welcomed by the Scientific Community as an enlightening new standard. In order to assist your mathematicians in the writing of the significant articles that give recognition to your Institute, Mathematics Inc. has acquiesced to give in all the leading Scientific Centers of the World our special three-day course "How to increase the MAES®-grade of your publications". Courses in London, Philadelphia, Moscow, Amsterdam, Grenoble, and Djakarta have already been planned, courses in Cambridge, Austin, Oxford, Brussels, Munich, Oslo, New York, Hong Kong, and Loempia are in a stage of active preparation. For the larger Scientific Institutes and Universities, the friendly specialists of Mathematics Inc. will be happy to give a personalized in-house Course, fully tuned and adapted to the special needs of your organization."

*   *
*

With the above text MAES® was announced to the World. Its announcement on the 1st of August 1976 gave exactly the stir and response we had anticipated. We could have done so earlier, but the date was carefully chosen in the wake of the Bicentennial 4th of July, Ulster's 12th of July and the Quatorze Juillet in France, during the summer when the papers have little politics to report on and during which we could take the Universities by surprise (in their Summer Sleep, so to speak). MAES® was the immediate success it deserved to be.

For the coming year institutional customers will be the main target of our promotion campaign; as soon as the Program Committees of the most important conferences and the Editorial Boards of the leading journals have adopted it, the individual, career-conscious mathematician is expected to provide for the next market extension. Mathematics Inc. is considering MAES®-grading service bureaus in the world's major scientific centers. It is still an open question whether they will be run by Mathematics Inc. itself or by one of our educational daughters, such as Instant Inspiration Company or Methodology Mechanics.

I must make a note to ask our PR-man for his advice; although it is not purely a PR-question, it has technical aspects as well. One of the distinctive features of MAES® is the knowledge-based determination of the metrics for the Exceptional Feature Attribute. KOD's ($=$ Key Occurrence Densities) are determined and compared to the statistical average, from which the Exceptional Feature Attribute favours deviations in various chosen directions. By being adopted MAES® will, therefore, not only influence the average style of mathematical publications but also —potentially at least— one of its own evaluation standards.

Within Mathematics Inc. there is a hot debate how to organize the ongoing MAES® adaptation. We have —like in every world-wide organization— the centralists who argue that only the Mathematics Inc. HQ in the Hosanna Building can coordinate and fully synchronize these successive releases; they furthermore argue that this synchronization is absolutely essential if MAES® is going to be accepted as an ISO Standard. On the other hand we have the decentralists who argue that, in view of the drastic differences in publication delays in the various parts of the world, some markets will be more successfully penetrated by a more slowly evaluating quality standard for mathematical publications, while other markets require a much more aggressively adapting grading system. Also they have, undoubtedly, a strong point. It is a hard battle; the issue is undecided yet and as Chairman of the Board I suppose that it will remain so until I have cut the Gordian knot.

Inside the Company we hope that in the meantime the MAES® concept of the Conceptual Paragraphs will somewhat ease the problem in that it makes the eventual MAES®-grade less sensitive to local changes in the preferred KOD deviations. Personally, I think that —more than its widely advertised Knowledge Base— the concept of the Conceptual Paragraphs will determine the MAES® success. After all, the introduction of Conceptual Paragraphing —which I suggested during its development— has in our internal usage already shown to be the most revolutionary enhancement of our grading techniques. It is so simple! And *we* have the patents, all over the world, so now I can divulge the secret! Not necessarily contiguous (!) sentences are grouped together in the same Conceptual Paragraph if, by doing so, we can increase the in*ter* and decrease the in*tra* cross reference correlation coefficients of the —of course: normalized— KOD's. It is as simple as that! By maximizing the one and minimizing the other, MAES®

Conceptual Paragraphing automatically arrives at the optimum retrieval modularization, which is the basis for *all* our Quality Attribute Metrics. Besides its intrinsic significance for the destructuralization of the flow of the SSR (= Symbol/Significance Ratio), MAES® Conceptual Paragraphing has the added advantage that the *place* of the optimal boundaries between the Conceptual Paragraphs is —as a result of the refined averaging procedures — statistically speaking less sensitive to fashions, as may be reflected in the Knowledge Base.

*   *   *

To give you some idea of the effectiveness of MAES®, let me report to you some of our in-house experience during the period 15th April 1976–14th of June 1976, during which nearly 4000 of our mathematical articles were subjected to MAES®-grading on an experimental basis. (Our market research people have guaranteed that those 4000 papers were a representative sample from our spring production.) The MAES®-grades given ranged from 0.632 to 0.944, with the exception of two articles with MAES®-grades under 0.3, one from our Loempia subsidiary, and one from the Grenoble one. (The latter exception is the more remarkable because on automatic evaluation systems particularly the French products tend to score very high.) The statistics collected by MAES® during that period are quite interesting. We detected significant metrics for quite a few new negative Quality Attributes.

Production of course material in Hebrew and in Japanese has been held up, pending the decision how it should be affected by the recent discovery of our Department of Mathematical Psychology, that the notion of deconceptualization should be represented by arrows that point backwards. In all other languages, I am happy to say, course material production is working full blast.

And it is high time too! Academic mathematicians are terribly slow in the uptake, and most of them have not yet understood that the era of soundly engineered mathematics is already here, today! They fool themselves —and worse: their students!— by closing their eyes to modern scientific techniques for the development and controlled growth of mathematics, they continue teaching their old, ad-hoc ways of doing research. But the wholesale introduction of MAES® will teach the reactionary bastards! At last their private, hobbyist norms will evaporate, for MAES® will *force* them to adopt the standards of the mathematical industry. Even the departments of pure math will now be forced to produce soundly engineered articles! This, no more and no less, is the Great Service that the introduction of MAES® will render to the World. Thanks to Mathematics Inc. Semper floreat at crescat!

Hosanna Building
Plataanstraat 5
5671 AL   Nuenen
The Netherlands

PROF. DR. EDSGER W. DIJKSTRA
Chairman of the Board of
Mathematics Inc.

EWD643
A Class of Simple Communication Patterns

WRITTEN IN CONJUNCTION WITH C.S. SCHOLTEN

We consider a finite, undirected graph each node of which contains a process. Processes contained in nodes directly connected by an edge of the graph are called each other's neighbours.

An act of communication is only possible between two neighbours. At any moment in time each process is ready to communicate with precisely one of its neighbours; the act of communication between two neighbours can only take place when each of them is ready to communicate with the other, and, as soon as they are both ready to communicate with the other, the communication is assumed to take place within a bounded period of time.

For each node there exists an (otherwise arbitrary) cyclic order of its neighbours, and the act of communication with one of its neighbours causes the node to become ready to communicate with its next neighbour, where "next" is to be understood in terms of that cyclic order. It is this rigid rule of the locally cyclic communication patterns that justifies the word "simple" in the title of this note. For such systems we shall determine the conditions characterizing the absence of the dangers of deadlock or starvation.

We represent the state of each process by the presence of one arrow from its node towards (the node of) the neighbour it is ready to communicate with: hence each node has always one outgoing arrow along one of the edges of the original undirected graph. In this representation, the act of communication between two neighbours takes place when they point to each other; the act of communication causes a "rotation" of both outgoing arrows. In this representation, the absence of deadlock is equivalent to the existence of at least one edge along which two arrows (in opposite directions) are present.

Let c be an arbitrary cycle of the undirected graph, in which neither a node nor an edge occurs more than once. (Such cycles contain at least 3

334

different nodes.) On this cycle we choose an arbitrary direction, which gives each node a "right-hand" neighbour and a "left-hand" neighbour in the cycle. Because such cycles contain at least 3 nodes, these two neighbours are different. For the outgoing arrow of a node x of that cycle we define a "signature with respect to c": if it points to a node that, in the cyclic order associated with x, lies in the range from (and excluding) the left-hand neighbour of x to (and including) the right-hand neighbour of x we call the arrow positive; otherwise we call the arrow negative.

Lemma 1. *No act of communication changes the truth-value of the predicate: the outgoing arrows of the nodes of the cycle c have the same signature with respect to c.*

PROOF. The value of the predicate can only change when the signature of the outgoing arrow of a node of c is changed. This can only happen at an act of communication with either its left-hand, or its right-hand neighbour in the cycle c. This is only possible when two communicating neighbours on the cycle had outgoing arrows of different signature. The act changes the signature of both arrows, so their signatures remain different from each other. In short: if the predicate is *false* it remains *false* in spite of the possibility of changing signatures, if it is *true*, it remains *true* because none of the signatures can change. (End of proof.)

Lemma 2. *The existence of a cycle c with outgoing arrows with the same signature causes local deadlock and, if the original graph is connected, total deadlock.*

PROOF. None of the outgoing arrows of the nodes of c can have its signature changed, hence for each node of c the number of acts of communication it can perform is bounded (by a bound lower than the number of its neighbours). By induction, the number of acts of communication of any node that is connected to c via a finite path, is bounded. (End of proof.)

Lemma 3. *In the case of total deadlock there is at least one cycle with all its outgoing arrows of the same signature.*

PROOF. Total deadlock means that no process has its outgoing arrow "matched" by an arrow in the opposite direction. Starting at any node, the step that consists of going from that node to the node its outgoing arrow points to can be repeated indefinitely. On a finite graph we must visit a node visited before, and hence a cyclic path (of at least 3 nodes) must exist: but that is a cycle with all its outgoing arrows of the same signature. (End of proof.)

Combining lemma's 2 and 3 we conclude our main

Theorem. *In the systems considered the absence/certainty of deadlock is equivalent to the absence/presence of at least one cycle of uniform signature.*

Lemma 4. *A deadlock-free system remains deadlock-free when, at a moment that there are no arrows along a certain edge, that edge is removed, provided at both its ends the cyclic order of the remaining neighbours remains the same.*

PROOF. The removal of an edge does not create new cycles. Because at both ends the cyclic order of the remaining neighbours remains the same, the definition of the signature of arrows with respect to the remaining cycles is not changed. Hence the assumed absence of cycles with outgoing arrows of uniform signature therefore remains. (End of proof.)

*   *
*

Our lemma's and theorem remain valid in a more general setting. We have assumed that each process would be ready to communicate with its neighbours "in some cyclic order". We have used that assumption only for two conclusions:

(1)   that contacts with left- and right-hand neighbours —i.e. the pair of neighbours on a cyclic path through the node in question— would alternate;

(2)   that each node will be ready to communicate with any of its neighbours within a bounded number of contacts.

When all local communication patterns satisfy properties 1) and 2), our conclusions remain valid provided we redefine the signature of an outgoing arrow of a node on a cycle c as follows: the arrow is positive if it points to the right-hand neighbour or will do so before pointing to the left-hand neighbour, the arrow is negative otherwise. These more general communication patterns are still "simple" in the sense that permanent nonactivity of a specific process will lead after a bounded number of communication acts to nonactivity of the whole network connected to it. Such networks are simple because the absence of the danger of deadlock implies then the absence of the danger of individual starvation.

For the sake of completeness we formulate

Lemma 5. *Consider a deadlock-free network with "a leaf", i.e. a node with only one neighbour. If the leaf, together with its outgoing arrow, is removed at a moment that its neighbour did not point to it, and the cyclic order of its neighbour's remaining neighbours remains the same, the resulting system is again deadlock-free.*

Lemma 5 is a variation on Lemma 4, and we leave its proof to the reader.

*   *
*

The theorem described and proved in this note is a theorem of the type the need of which I discussed last month at lunch with C.A.R. Hoare, when we met in Newcastle-upon-Tyne. At the end of that discussion we agreed that the discovery of a class of such theorems might be a proper thesis topic. Is the moral of this note that that topic might be unsuitable, because it is too small?

The theorem given in this note and its proof have been inspired in particular by the self-stabilizing systems designed earlier by L. Lamport and C.S. Scholten, in which processes at the nodes of a tree were considered. A discussion with C.S. Scholten on the topic of EWD642 (still in statu nascendi) was the incentive for its discovery.

Nuenen

PROF. DR. EDSGER W. DIJKSTRA
Burroughs Research Fellow

EWD648
"Why Is Software So Expensive?"
An Explanation to
the Hardware Designer

Recently I received an invitation from a sizeable (and growing) hardware company. For many years its traditional product line has been high-quality analog equipment; in the more recent past, however, digital components are beginning to play a more important rôle. The company's corporate management was aware of more or less unavoidably entering the (for the company unfamiliar) field of software, was aware of the existence of its many pitfalls without having a clear understanding of them, and I was invited to explain to the company's corporate management what the design of software is all about, why it is so expensive, etc.

Having many other obligations, I don't know yet whether I shall be able to accept the invitation, but, independently of that, the challenge absolutely delights me. Not only have I programmed for more than 25 years, but right from the beginning up till this very day I have done so in, over periods even close, cooperation with hardware designers, machine developers, prototype testers, etc. I think that I know the average digital hardware designer and his problems well enough to understand why he does not understand why designing software is so difficult. To explain the difficulty of software design to him is hard enough, almost as hard as explaining it to a pure mathematician. To explain it to a group of designers with their background and professional pride in high-quality *analog* equipment adds definitely a distinctive flavour to the challenge! Observing myself thinking about how to meet it and realizing that, even if I accept the invitation, my host will not have exclusive rights of my explanation, I decided to take pen and paper. Hence this text.

*   *   *

To the economic question "Why is software so expensive?" the equally economic answer could be "Because it is tried with cheap labour.". Why is it tried that way? Because its intrinsic difficulties are widely and grossly underestimated. So let us concentrate on "Why is software design so difficult?". One of the morals of my answer will be that with inadequately educated personnel it will be impossible; with adequately educated software designers it might be possible, but will certainly remain difficult. I would like to stress, right at the start, that current problems in software design can only partly be explained by identified lack of competence of the programmers involved. I would like to do so right at the start, because that explanation, although not uncommon, is too facile.

It is understandable: it must be very frustrating for a hardware manager to produce what he rightly considers as a reliable machine with a splendid cost/performance ratio and to observe thereafter that, by the time the customer receives the total system, the system is bug-ridden and its performance has dropped below the designer's worst dreams. And besides having to swallow that the software guys have ruined his product, he is expected to accept that while he works more and more efficiently every year, the software group is honoured for its incompetence by yearly increasing budgets. Without further explanations from our side, we programmers should forgive him his occasional bitterness, for by accusing us of incompetence he sins in ignorance.... And as long as *we* haven't been able to explain the nature of our problems clearly, *we* cannot blame him for that ignorance!

* *
*

A comparison between the hardware world and the software world seems a good introduction for the hardware designer to the problems of his software colleague.

The hardware designer has to simulate a discrete machine by essentially analog means. As a result the hardware designer has to think about delays, slopes of signals, fan-in and fan-out, skew clocks, heat dissipation, cooling, and power supply, and all the other problems of technology and manufacturing. Building essentially from analog components implies that "tolerances" are a very essential aspect of his component specifications; his quality control is essentially of a statistical nature and, when all is said and done, quality assurance is essentially a probabilistic statement. The fact that with current quality standards the probability of correct operation is very, very high should not seduce us to forget its probabilistic nature: very high probability should not be confused with certainty (in the mathematical sense) and it is therefore entirely appropriate that no piece of equipment is delivered without being exercised by test programs. As technology is pushed more and more to its limits —and it is so all the time— and tolerances become narrower and narrower, the control of these tolerances becomes a major concern for the hardware builders. Compared to the hardware designer who constantly struggles with an unruly nature, the software designer lives in heaven, for he builds his artefacts from zeros and ones alone. A zero is a zero and a one is a one: there is no fuzziness about his building blocks and the whole engineering notion of something being "within tolerance" is just not applicable. In this sense the programmer works indeed in a heavenly environment. The hypothetical one-hundred percent circuit designer who equates the problems of design and building with the problems of keeping the tolerances under control *must* be blind to the programming problems: once he has simulated the discrete machine correctly, all the really hard problems have been solved, haven't they?

To explain to the hardware world why programming still presents problems, we must draw attention to a few other differences. In very general terms we can view "design" as bridging a gap, as composing an artefact of given components; as long as "the target artefact" and "the source components" don't change, we can reuse the old design. The fact that we need to design continuously is because they do change. Here, however, hardware and software designers have been faced with very different, almost opposite types of variation, change, and diversity.

For the hardware designer the greatest variation has been in "the source components": as long as machines have been designed he has had to catch up with new technologies, he has never had time to become fully familiar with his source material because before he reached that stage, new components, new technologies appeared on the scene. Compared to the drastic variation in his "source components", his "target artefact" has almost remained constant: all the time he has redesigned and redesigned the same few machines.

For the programmer the variation and diversity is just at the other end: the hardware designer's target is the programmer's starting point. The programmer's "source components" have been remarkably stable —in the eyes of some, even depressingly so!— : FORTRAN and COBOL, still very much en vogue, are more than a quarter of a century old! The programmer finds the diversity at the other side of the gap to be bridged: he is faced with a collection of "target artefacts" of great diversity. Of very great diversity even; of an essentially very great diversity even, because here we find reflected that today's equipment, indeed, deserves the name "general purpose".

During the last decade, software designers have carried on an almost religious debate on "bottom-up" versus "top-down" design. It used to be "bottom-up", I think that now the "top-down" religion has the majority as its adherents. If we accept the sound principle that, when faced with a many-sided problem, we should explore the area of our greatest uncertainty first (because the solution of familiar problems can be postponed with less risk), we can interpret the conversion of the programming community from "bottom-up" to "top-down" as a slow recognition of the circumstance that the programmer's greatest diversity is at the *other* side of the gap.

Besides being at the other side of the gap to be bridged, the variation and diversity the programmer is faced with is more open-ended. For the understanding of his source components the hardware designer has always physics and electronics to fall back on as a last resort: for the understanding of his target problem and the design of algorithms solving it the software designer finds the appropriate theory more often lacking than not. How crippling the absence of an adequate theory can be has, however, only been discovered slowly.

With the first machine applications, which were scientific/technical, there were no such difficulties. The problem to be solved was scientifically perfectly understood and the numerical mathematics was available to provide the algorithms and their justification. The additional coding to be done, such as for the conversions between decimal and binary number system and for program loaders, was so trivial that common sense sufficed.

Since then we have seen again and again that, for lack of appropriate theory, problems were tackled with common sense, while common sense turned out to be insufficient. The first compilers were made in the fifties without any decent theory for language definition, for parsing, etc., and they were full of bugs. Parsing theory and the like came later. The first operating systems were made without proper understanding of synchronization, of deadlock, of danger of starvation, etc., and they too suffered from the defects that in hindsight were predictable. Again, the indispensable theory came later.

It is understandable that people have to discover by trying that common sense alone is not always a sufficient mental tool. The problem is that by the time the necessary theory has been developed, the pre-scientific, intuitive approach has already established itself and, in spite of its patent insufficiency, it is harder to eradicate than one would like to think. Here I must place a critical comment on a management practice that is not uncommon among computer manufacturers, viz. to choose as project manager someone with practical experience from an earlier, similar project: if the earlier project had been tackled by pre-scientific techniques, this is likely to happen to the new project as well, even if the relevant theory is in the meantime available.

A second consequence of this state of affairs is that one of the most vital abilities of a software designer faced with a new task is the ability to judge whether existing theory and common sense will suffice, or whether a new intellectual discipline of some sort needs to be developed first. In the latter case it is absolutely essential *not* to embark upon coding before that necessary piece of theory is there. Think first! I shall return to this topic later, in view of its management consequences.

*   *   *

Let me now try to give you, by analogy and example, some feeling for the kind of thinking required.

Since IBM stole the term "structured programming" I don't use it anymore myself, but I lectured on the subject in the late sixties at MIT. A key point of my message was that (large) programs were objects without any precedent in our cultural history, and that the most closely analogous object

I could think of was a mathematical theory. And I have illustrated this with the analogy between a lemma and a subroutine: the lemma is proved independently of how it is going to be used and is used independently of how it has been proved; similarly a subroutine is implemented independently of how it is going to be used and is used independently of how it has been implemented. Both were examples of "Divide and Rule": the mathematical argument is parcelled out in theorems and lemmata, and the program is similarly divided up into processes, subroutines, clusters, etc.

In the meantime I know that the analogy extends to the ways in which mathematical theories and programs are *developed*. By word of mouth I recently heard that Dana S. Scott described the design of a mathematical theory as an *experimental* science, experimental in the sense that adequacy and utility of new notations and concepts were determined experimentally, to wit: by trying to use them. This, now, is very similar to the way a design team tries to cope with the conceptual challenges it faces.

When the design is complete one must be able to talk meaningfully about it, but the final design may very well be something of a structure never talked about before. So the design team *must* invent its own language to talk about it, it *must* discover the illuminating concepts and invent good names for them. But it cannot wait to do so until the design is complete, for it needs the language in the act of designing! It is the old problem of the chicken and the egg. I know of only one way of escaping from that infinite regress: invent the language that you seem to need, somewhat loosely wherever you aren't quite sure, and test its adequacy by trying to use it, for from their usage the new words will get their meaning.

Let me give you one example. In the first half of the sixties I designed as part of a multiprogramming system a subsystem whose function it was to abstract from the difference between primary and secondary store: the unit in which information was to be shuffled between storage levels was called "a page". When we studied our first design, it turned out that we could regard that only as a first approximation, because efficiency considerations forced us to give a subset of the pages in primary store a special status. We called them "holy pages", the idea being that, the presence of a holy page in primary store being guaranteed, access to them could be speeded up. Was this a good idea? We had to define "holy pages" in such a way that we could prove that their number would be bounded. Eventually we came up with a very precise definition of "holy" that satisfied all our logic and efficiency requirements, but all during these discussions the notion "holy" only slowly developed into something precise and useful. Originally, for instance, I remember that "holiness" was a boolean attribute: a page was holy or not. Eventually pages turned out to have a "holiness counter", and the original boolean attribute became the question whether the holiness counter was positive.

If during those discussions a stranger would have entered our room and would have listened to us for fifteen minutes, he would have made the remark "I don't believe that you know what you are talking about.". Our answer would have been "Yes, you are right, and that is exactly why we are talking: we are trying to discover about precisely what we should be talking.".

I have described this scene at some length because I remember it so well and because I believe it to be quite typical. Eventually you come up with a very formal and well-defined product, but this eventual birth is preceded by a period of gestation during which new ideas are tried and discarded or developed. That is the *only* way I know of in which the mind can cope with such conceptual problems. From experience I have learned that in that gestation period, when a new jargon has to be created, an excellent mastery of their native tongue is an absolute requirement for all participants. A programmer that talks sloppily is just a disaster. Excellent mastery of his native tongue is my first selection criterion for a prospective programmer; good taste in mathematics is the second important criterion. (As luck will have it, they often go hand in hand.)

I had a third reason for describing the birth of the notion "holy" at some length. A few years ago I learned that it is not just a romantization, not just a sweet memory from a project we all liked: our experience was at the heart of the matter. I learned so when I wished to give, by way of exercise for myself, the complete formal development of a recursive parser for a simple programming language, defined in terms of some five or six syntactic categories. The *only* way in which I could get the formal treatment right was by the introduction of *new syntactic categories*! Those new syntactic categories characterized character sequences that were *meaningless* in the original programming language to be parsed, but *indispensable* for the understanding and justification of the parsing algorithm under design. My formal exercise was very illuminating, not because it had resulted in a nice parser, but because in a nice, formal nutshell it illustrated the need for the kind of invention software development requires: the new syntactic categories were exemplary of the concepts that have to be invented along the way, concepts that are meaningless with respect to the original problem statement but indispensable for understanding the solution.

*   *
*

I hope that the above gives you some feeling for the programmer's task. When dealing with the problems of software design, I must also devote a word or two to the phenomenon of the bad software manager. It is regrettable, but bad software managers do exist and, although bad, they have enough power to ruin a project. I have lectured all over the world to programmers working in all sorts of organizations, and the overwhelming impression I got from the discussions is that the bad software manager is an almost ubiquitous phenomenon: one of the most common reactions from the audience in the discussion after a lecture is "What a pity that our manager isn't here! We cannot explain it to him, but from you he would perhaps have accepted it. We would love to work in the way you have described, but our manager, who doesn't understand, won't let us.". I have encountered this reaction so often that I can only conclude that, on the average, the situation is really bad. (I had my worst experience in a bank, with some government organizations as good seconds.)

In connection with bad managers I have often described my experience as a lecturer at IBM, Hursley, because it was so illuminating. Just before I came, the interior decorator had redone the auditorium, and in doing so he had replaced the old-fashioned blackboard by screen and overhead projector. As a result I had to perform in a dimly lighted room with my sunglasses on in order not to get completely blinded. I could just see the people in the front rows.

That lecture was one of the most terrible experiences in my life. With a few well-chosen examples I illustrated the problem solving techniques I could formulate at that time, showed the designer's freedom on the one hand, and the formal discipline needed to control it on the other. But the visible audience was absolutely unresponsive: I felt as if I were addressing an audience of puppets made from chewing gum. It was sheer torture, but I *knew* that it was a good lecture and with a dogged determination I carried my performance through until the bitter end.

When I had finished and the lights were turned up I was surprised by a shattering applause... from the back rows that had been invisible! It then turned out that I had had a very mixed audience, delighted programmers in the back rows and in the front rows their managers who were extremely annoyed at my performance: by openly displaying the amount of "invention" involved, I had presented the programming task as even more "unmanageable" than they already feared. From their point of view I had done a very poor job. It was at that occasion that I formulated for myself the conclusion that poor software managers see programming primarily as a management problem because they don't know how to manage it.

These problems are less prevalent in those organizations —I know a few software houses— where the management consists of competent, experienced programmers (rather than a banker with colonial experience, but still too young to retire). One of the problems caused by the non-understanding software manager is that he thinks that his subordinates have to produce code: they have to solve problems, and in order to do so, they have to *use* code. To this very day we have organizations that measure "programmer productivity" by the "number of lines of code produced per month". This number can, indeed, be counted, but they are booking it on the wrong side of the ledger, for we should talk about "the number of lines of code spent".

Coding requires great care and a non-failing talent for accuracy; it is labour-intensive and should therefore be postponed until you are as sure as sure can be that the program you are about to code is, indeed, the program you are aiming for. I know of one very successful software firm in which it is a rule of the house that for a one-year project coding is not allowed to start before the ninth month! In this organization they know that the eventual code is no more than the deposit of your understanding. When I told its director that my main concern in teaching students computing science was to train them to think first and not to rush into coding, he just said "If you succeed in doing so, you are worth your weight in gold." (I am not very heavy).

But apparently, many managers create havoc by discouraging thinking and urging their subordinates to "produce" code. Later they complain that 80 percent of their labour force is tied up with "program maintenance" and blame software technology for that sorry state of affairs, instead of themselves. So much for the poor software manager. (All this is well-known, but occasionally needs to be said again.)

*   *   *

Another profound difference between the hardware and the software worlds is presented by the different roles of testing.

When, 25 years ago, a logic designer had cooked up a circuit, his next acts were to build and to try it, and if it did not work he would probe a few signals with his scope and adjust a capacitor. And when it worked he would subject the voltages from the power supply to 10 percent variations, adjust, etc., until he had a circuit that worked correctly over the whole range of conditions he was aiming at. He made a product of which he could "see that it worked over the whole range". Of course he did not try it for "all" points of the range, but that wasn't necessary, for very general continuity considerations made it evident that it was sufficient to test the circuit under a very limited number of conditions, together "covering" the whole range.

This iterative design process of trial and error has been taken so much for granted that it has also been adopted under circumstances in which the continuity assumption that justifies the whole procedure is not valid. In the case of an artefact with a discrete "performance space" such as a program, the assumption of continuity is *not* valid, and as a result the iterative design process of trial and error is therefore fundamentally inadequate. The good software designer knows this; he knows that from the observation that in the cases tried his program produced the correct result he is *not* allowed to extrapolate that his program is okay; therefore he tries to prove mathematically that his program meets the requirements.

The mere suggestion of the existence of an environment in which the traditional design process of trial and error is inadequate and where, therefore, mathematical proof is required, is unpalatable for those for whom mathematical proofs are beyond their mental grasp. As a result, the suggestion has encountered a considerable resistance, even among programmers who should know better. It is not to be wondered that in the hardware world the recognition of the potential inadequacy of the testing procedure is still very rare.

Some hardware designers are beginning to worry, but usually not because they consider the fundamental inadequacy of the testing approach, but only because the "adjustment" has become so expensive since the advent of LSI-technology. But even without that financial aspect they should already worry, because in the meantime a sizeable fraction of their design activity does take place in a discrete environment.

Recently I heard a story about a machine —not a machine design by Burroughs, I am happy to add— . It was a microprogrammed multi-processor installation that had been speeded up by the addition of a slave store, but its designers had done the addition badly; when the two processors operated simultaneously on the two halves of the same word, the machine with the slave store reacted differently from the version without it. After a few months of operation a system breakdown was traced back to this very design error. By testing you just cannot hope to catch such an error that becomes apparent by coincidence. Clearly the machine had been designed by people that hadn't the foggiest notion about programming. A single competent programmer on the design crew would have prevented that blunder: as soon as you complicate the design of a multiprocessor installation by introducing a slave store, the obligation to *prove* —instead of just believing without convincing evidence— that after the introduction of the slave store the machine still meets its original functional specifications is obvious to a competent programmer. (Such a proof doesn't seem to present any fundamental or practical difficulties either.) To convince hardware designers of the fact that they have moved into an environment in which their conventional experimental techniques for design and quality control are no longer adequate is one of the major educational challenges in the field.

I called it "major" because, as long as it isn't met, hardware designers won't understand what a software designer is responsible for. In the traditional engineering tradition, the completed design is the designer's complete product: you build an artefact and, lo and behold, it works! If you don't believe it, just try it and you will see that "it works". In the case of an artefact with a discrete performance space, the only appropriate reaction to the observation that it has "worked" in the cases tried is: "So what?". The only convincing evidence that such a device with a discrete performance space meets its requirements includes a mathematical proof. It is a severe mistake to think that the programmer's products are the programs he writes; the programmer has to produce trustworthy solutions, and he has to produce and present them in the form of convincing arguments. Those arguments constitute the hard core of his product and the written program text is only the accompanying material to which his arguments are applicable.

*   *
*

Many software projects carried out in the past have been overly complex and, consequently, full of bugs and patches. Mainly the following two circumstances have been responsible for this:

(1) dramatic increases of processor speeds and memory sizes, which made it seem as if the sky were the limit; only after the creation of a number of disastrously complicated systems it dawned upon us, that our limited thinking ability was the bottleneck

(2) a world that became over-ambitious in its desire to apply those wonderful new machines; many programmers have yielded to the pressure to stretch their available programming technology beyond its limits; this was not a very scientific behaviour, but perhaps stepping beyond the limit was necessary for discovering that limit's position.

In retrospect we can add two other reasons: for lack of experience programmers did not know how harmful complexity is, and secondly they did not know how complexity can usually be avoided if you put your mind to it. Perhaps it would have helped if the analogy between a software design and a mathematical theory had been widely recognized earlier, because everyone knows that even for a single theorem the first proof discovered is seldom the best one: later proofs are often orders of magnitude simpler.

When C.A.R. Hoare writes —as he did early this year— "...the threshold for my tolerance of complexity is *much* lower than it used to be" he reflects a dual development: a greater awareness of the dangers of complexity, but also a raised standard of elegance. The awareness of the dangers of complexity made greater simplicity a laudable goal, but at first it was entirely an open question whether that goal could be reached. Some problems may defy elegant solutions, but there seems overwhelming evidence that much of what has been done in programming (and in computing science in general) can be simplified drastically. Numerous are the stories of the 30-line solutions concocted by a so-called professional programmer —or even a teacher of programming!— that could be reduced to a program of 4 or 5 lines.

To educate a generation of programmers with a much lower threshold for their tolerance of complexity and to teach them how to search for the truly simple solution is the second major intellectual challenge in our field. This is technically hard, for you have to instil some of the manipulative ability and a lot of the good taste of the mathematician. It is psychologically hard in an environment that confuses between love of perfection and claim of perfection and, by blaming you for the first, accuses you of the latter.

How do we convince people that in programming simplicity and clarity —in short: what mathematicians call "elegance"— are not a dispensable luxury, but a crucial matter that decides between success and failure? I expect help from economic considerations. Contrary to the situation with hardware, where an increase in reliability usually has to be paid for by a higher price, in the case of software unreliability is the greatest cost factor. It may sound paradoxical, but a reliable (and therefore simple) program is much cheaper to develop and use than a (complicated and therefore) unreliable one. This "paradox" should make us very hesitant to attach too much weight to a possible analogy between software design and more traditional engineering disciplines.

Nuenen

PROF. DR. EDSGER W. DIJKSTRA
Burroughs Research Fellow

EWD650
A Theorem About Odd Powers of Odd Integers

Theorem. *For any odd $p \geq 1$, integer $K \geq 1$, and odd r such that $1 \leq r < 2^K$, a value x exists such that*

R: $1 \leq x < 2^K$ **and** $2^K | (x^p - r)$ **and** $\mathrm{odd}(x)$.

NOTE. For "$a | b$" read: "a divides b". (End of note.)

PROOF. The existence of x is proved by designing a program computing x satisfying R.

Trying to establish R by means of a repetitive construct, we must choose an invariant relation. This time we apply the well-known technique of replacing a constant by a variable, and replace the constant K by the variable k. Introducing $d = 2^k$ for the sake of brevity, we then get

P: $d = 2^k$ **and** $1 \leq x < d$ **and** $d | (x^p - r)$ **and** $\mathrm{odd}(x)$.

This choice of invariant relation P is suggested by the observation that R is trivial to satisfy for $K = 1$; hence P is trivial to establish initially. The simplest structure to try for our program is therefore:

$x, k, d := 1, 1, 2\{P\}$;
do $k \neq K \rightarrow$ "increase k by 1 under invariance of P" **od** $\{R\}$.

Increasing k by 1 (together with doubling d) can only violate the term $d | (x^p - r)$. The weakest precondition that $d := 2 * d$ does *not* do so is —according to the axiom of assignment— $(2 * d) | (x^p - r)$. Hence an acceptable component for "increase k by 1 under invariance of P" is

$$(2 * d) | (x^p - r) \rightarrow k, d := k + 1, 2 * d   .$$

In the case **non** $(2*d) \mid (x^p - r)$ we conclude from $d \mid (x^p - r)$ that $x^p - r$ is an odd multiple of d. Because d is even, and p and x are odd, the binomial expansion tells us that $(x + d)^p - x^p$ is an odd multiple of d, and that hence $(x + d)^p - r$ is a multiple of $2*d$. Because also d is doubled, $x < d$ remains true under $x := x + d$, because d is even odd(x) obviously remains true, and our program becomes:

$x, k, d := 1, 1, 2 \{P\}$;
do $k \neq K \to$ **if** $(2*d) \mid (x^p - r) \to k, d := k + 1, 2*d \{P\}$
           $[\!]$ **non** $(2*d) \mid (x^p - r) \to x, k, d := x + d, k + 1, 2*d\{P\}$
          fi $\{P\}$
od $\{R\}$.

Because this program obviously terminates, its existence proves the theorem. (End of proof.)

*   *
*

With the argument as given, the above program was found in five minutes. I only mention this in reply to Zohar Manna and Richard Waldinger, who wrote in "Synthesis: Dreams $\Rightarrow$ Programs" (SRI Technical Note 156, November 1977)

> Our instructors at the Structured Programming School have urged us to find the appropriate invariant assertion before introducing a loop. But how are we to select the successful invariant when there are so many promising candidates around? [...] Recursion seems to be the ideal vehicle for systematic program construction [...]. In choosing to emphasize iteration instead, the proponents of structured programming have had to resort to more dubious (sic!) means."

Although I haven't used the term Structured Programming any more for at least five years, and although I have a vested interest in recursion, yet I felt addressed by the two gentlemen. So it seemed only appropriate to record that the "more dubious means" have —again!— been pretty effective. (I have evidence that, despite the existence of this very simple solution, the problem is not trivial: many computing scientists could not solve the programming problem within an hour. Try it on your colleagues, if you don't believe me.)

Nuenen

PROF. DR. EDSGER W. DIJKSTRA
Burroughs Research Fellow

EWD671
Program Inversion

Let the integer array $p(0..M-1)$ be such that the sequence $p(0), p(1),...,p(M-1)$ represents a permutation of the numbers from 0 through $M-1$ and let the integer array $y(0..M-1)$ be such that $(\mathbf{A}\ i: 0 \leqslant i < M: 0 \leqslant y(i) \leqslant i)$. Under those constraints we are interested in the relation

$$(\mathbf{A}\ i: 0 \leqslant i < M: y(i) = (\mathbf{N}\ j: 0 \leqslant j < i: p(j) < p(i))) \quad . \quad (1)$$

(*Legenda*: "$(\mathbf{N}\ j: 0 \leqslant j < i: p(j) < p(i))$" should be read as "the number of mutually different values j in the range $0 \leqslant j < i$, such that $p(j) < p(i)$".)

We can now consider the two solvable problems

(*A*) Given p, assign to y a value such that (1) is satisfied.
(*B*) Given y, assign to p a value such that (1) is satisfied.

Because we want to consider programs whose execution may modify the given array, we rephrase:

(*A*) Given p, assign to y a value such that (1) holds between the initial value of p and the final value of y.
(*B*) Given y, assign to p a value such that (1) holds between the initial value of y and the final value of p.

If A transforms p into a (standard) value which is its initial value in B, and if B transforms y into a (standard) value which is its initial value in A, then transformations A and B are *inverse* transformations on the pair (p, y). We are interested in these inverse transformations because in general problem A is regarded as easier than B: we have solved problem B as soon as we have for A a reversible solution!

Our First Effort

Let the standard value for p be such that $(\mathbf{A}\ i: 0 \leqslant i < M: p(i) = i)$. From (1) we immediately deduce that a permutation of the values $p(0),\ldots,$ $p(k - 1)$ does not affect the values of $y(i)$ for $i \geqslant k$. This suggests the computation of the values $y(k)$ in the order of increasing k, each time combining the computation of $y(k)$ with a permutation of $p(0),\ldots,p(k)$. Because the final value of p should be sorted, we are led most naturally to a bubble sort:

```
k := 0; {p(0),...,p(k − 1) is ordered}
do k ≠ M → "make p(0),...,p(k) ordered";
            k := k + 1 {p(0),...,p(k − 1) is ordered}
od     .
```

The standard program for the bubble sort is

```
k := 0;
do k ≠ M → j := k;
            do j > 0 cand p(j − 1) > p(j) → p:swap(j − 1, j);
                                             j := j − 1
            od {here j = the value y(k) should get};
            k := k + 1
od {A i: 0 ≤ i < M: p(i) = i}     .
```

We initialize with $y := (0)$ the array variable y as the empty array with $y.lob = 0$, each time extending it with a new value as soon as that has been computed. Because $k = y.dom$ would be an invariant, variable k can be eliminated.

Program A1:
```
y := (0); {y.dom = 0}
do y.dom ≠ M → j := y.dom {this is an initialization}; {j = y.dom}
                do j > 0 cand p(j − 1) > p(j) → p:swap(j − 1, j);
                                                 j := j − 1
                                                 {j < y.dom}
                od; y:hiext(j) {j's value is no longer relevant}
                {y.dom > 0}
od {A i: 0 ≤ i < M: p(i) = i}     .
```

Inverting it we construct

Program B1:
```
p := (0); do p.dom ≠ M → p:hiext(p.dom) od;
{A i: 0 ≤ i < M: p(i) = i}
do y.dom ≠ 0 → j, y:hipop {this is an initialization of j};
                do j ≠ y.dom → j := j + 1; p:swap(j − 1, j) od
                {j's value is no longer relevant}
od     .
```

This inversion was easy because the postcondition of each repeatable statement implies the negation of the stated precondition of the repetitive construct as a whole; furthermore we have used the fact that $y: hiext(j)$ and j, $y: hipop$ are each other's inverse, that $j := j + 1$ and $j := j - 1$ are each other's inverse, and that $p: swap(j - 1, j)$ is its own inverse.

We leave to the reader the insertion of provable assertions in program B1 that would justify the derivation of A1 from B1 by inversion.

Our Second Effort

We can also compute the values $y(k)$ in the order of decreasing k. (Here it is as if our standard value of p is the empty array with $p.lob = 0$ and the standard value of y is the empty array with $y.hib = M - 1$.) We make three observations:

(1) As soon as the $y(i)$ for $i \geq k$ have been computed, the $p(i)$ for $i \geq k$ no longer matter, i.e. we can work with a single array, $v(0..M-1)$ say, where in A/B, in relation (1) p refers to the initial/final value of v, and y refers to the final/initial value of v.
(2) Denoting with $Q(k)$: "the sequence $p(0)$, $p(1),\ldots,p(k)$ represents a permutation of the numbers $0,\ldots,k$", we can write $Q(k) \Rightarrow y(k) = p(k)$.
(3) Decreasing in the range $0 \leq i < k$ all $p(i)$ such that $p(i) > p(k)$ by 1 leaves all $y(i)$ with $0 \leq i < k$ unaffected.

These observations lead to the following program (in which we can view the elements $v(i)$ with $i < k$ as the corresponding elements of (a changing) p and the $v(i)$ with $i \geq k$ as the corresponding elements of a growing y).

```
k := M; {k = M and Q(k − 1) and v = p}
do k ≠ 0 → k := k − 1; {Q(k)}
              i := 0; do i ≠ k → if v(i) > v(k) → v:(i) = v(i) − 1
                                                  {v(i) ⩾ v(k)}
                             ▯ v(i) < v(k) → skip{v(i) < v(k)}
                       fi; i := i + 1
                  od {i = k and Q(k − 1)}
od {k = 0 and v = y}
```

In the alternative construct the postconditions have been added in order to ease the inversion:

Program B2:
$k := 0\{v = y\}$;
do $k \neq M \rightarrow i := k$;
        do $i \neq 0 \rightarrow i := i - 1$;
               if $v(i) \geqslant v(k) \rightarrow v{:}(i) = v(i) + 1$
               [] $v(i) < v(k) \rightarrow skip$
               fi
        od $\{i = 0\}$;
        $k := k + 1$
od $\{k = M$ **and** $v = p\}$.

*   *   *

I had invented problems A and B for examination purposes. After the students had handed in their work, it was W.H.J. Feijen who suggested that it would be nice to derive the one program from the other using inversion. Because in this case we have a deterministic program in which no information is destroyed, the inversion is a straightforward process. What remains of these techniques in the general situation remains to be seen. Is it possible to show that a program with nondeterministic elements leads to a unique answer because in its inverse no information is destroyed? Who knows.... In the meantime I have derived a program —B2 to be precise— that was new for me.

Nuenen

PROF. DR. EDSGER W. DIJKSTRA
Burroughs Research Fellow

EWD673

On Weak and Strong Termination

In the literature we find two concepts of "termination". We shall call them "weak" and "strong" termination respectively. They are equivalent within the realm of continuous functions, but different in the presence of unbounded nondeterminacy. It will be shown that in the realm of continuous functions the generality of (infinite) well-founded sets is of no essential use for proofs of termination, as partially ordered finite sets will do just as nicely.

*   *   *

In a proof of weak termination we demonstrate the impossibility that a computation will continue "forever", although an upper bound on the "time" it will take need not exist; in a proof of strong termination we demonstrate that the computation will have terminated within a certain amount of "time".

For proofs of strong termination the conceptually simplest tool is the so-called "variant function", an integer-valued function of the state which is bounded from below (≥ 0, say), and decreased by at least 1 at each "step" of the computation.

For proofs of weak termination Floyd [1967] has suggested to replace, as range of the variant function, the natural numbers by the elements of a so-called "well-founded set". A well-founded set is a set on which a (partial) ordering has been defined such that no element is the first of an infinite decreasing sequence of elements from the set. A well-known example of a well-founded set is the one consisting of the pairs (x, y) of natural numbers with the ordering defined as

$$(x', y') < (x, y) \underset{def}{=} x' < x \textbf{ or } (x' = x \textbf{ and } y' < y) \quad .$$

355

This well-founded set would be the proper vehicle for proving the weak termination of —X and Y being natural constants—

S: $x, y := X, Y$;
  do $x > 0 \rightarrow x, y := x - 1$, any natural number
  $\rrbracket\ y > 0 \rightarrow y := y - 1$
  od

where "any natural number" denotes a function of unbounded nondeterminacy, i.e. such that

$$wp(\text{"}y := \text{any natural number"}, y \geqslant 0) = T \qquad \text{and}$$
$$wp(\text{"}y := \text{any natural number"}, y \leqslant k) = F \qquad \text{for all } k \qquad .$$

Note that in general program S does not enjoy the property of strong termination, because for $X > 0$ no upper bound for y can be given.

The well-founded set of the pairs (x, y) used above illustrates nicely the way in which well-founded sets are a true generalization of the natural numbers. Each natural number n is the first element of only finite decreasing sequences, but only of a finite number of them —2^n, to be precise— that, therefore, have a maximum length —$n + 1$, to be precise— . In the more general well-founded set we considered, each element (x, y) with $x \geqslant 1$ is the first element of only finite decreasing sequences, but of infinitely many of them, whose lengths have no maximum. Our example also suggests that the generality the well-founded sets offer over and above the natural numbers is the last thing we need.

With program S we showed how, under assumption of the availability of the function "any natural number" of unbounded nondeterminacy, we could implement a weakly terminating program that was not strongly terminating. On the other hand it is quite easy to derive from *any* weakly terminating program that does not terminate strongly a computation of "any natural number": just add to it a count of the number of "steps" executed. Therefore the availability of the function "any natural number" of unbounded nondeterminacy is equivalent to the existence of programs that terminate weakly, but not strongly. Furthermore it is known —see, for instance, Dijkstra [1976], Chapter 9— that unbounded nondeterminacy is incompatible with the constraint of continuity.

Several conclusions present themselves:

(1) Within the realm of continuous functions, where nondeterminacy is bounded, weak termination and strong termination are equivalent.
(2) We only need the greater generality of the well-founded sets over and above the natural numbers, when we decide to leave the realm of the continuous functions. As long as there is very little incentive to do so, the greater generality of (infinite) well-founded sets is of no essential use, and (partially) ordered finite sets will do just as nicely. (Since a partial order on a finite set can always be embedded in a total order, the prevalence of the use of the range of natural numbers —the first K,

for some sufficiently large K, to be precise— now becomes fully understandable.)

Dijkstra, Edsger W. [1976] *A Discipline of Programming*, Prentice-Hall, Englewood Cliffs, NJ, U.S.A.
Floyd, R.W. [1967] "Assigning Meanings to Programs". *Proc. Symp. in Applied Mathematics*, vol. 19 (J.T. Schwartz, ed.), American Mathematical Society, Providence, RI, U.S.A.

Nuenen

PROF. DR. EDSGER W. DIJKSTRA
Burroughs Research Fellow

EWD675

The Equivalence of Bounded Nondeterminacy and Continuity

Unbounded nondeterminacy is presented by the function "any natural number" such that

$$wp(\text{"}x := \text{any natural number"}, 0 \leqslant x) = T$$
$$wp(\text{"}x := \text{any natural number"}, x \leqslant k) = F \qquad \text{for all } k \qquad .$$

Program S is *continuous* —see Chapter 9 of "A Discipline of Programming", where this property is called Property 5— means that for any infinite sequence of predicates $C_0, C_1, C_2, \ldots$ such that

$$\text{for } r \geqslant 0 \qquad C_r \Rightarrow C_{r+1} \qquad \text{for all states}$$

we have for all states

$$wp(S, (\mathbf{E}\, r\colon r \geqslant 0\colon C_r)) = (\mathbf{E}\, s\colon s \geqslant 0\colon wp(S, C_s)) \qquad (1)$$

and in the same chapter I have shown that all programs that could be written in my programming language fragment —with finite (!) guarded command sets— are continuous.

It is further shown that the program "$x := $ any natural number" is not continuous, and therefore cannot be written in that programming language fragment. For the sake of completeness, we repeat the proof. Assume the program S: "$x := $ any natural number" to be continuous. We then have:

$$T = wp(S, 0 \leqslant x)$$
$$= wp(S, (\mathbf{E}\, r\colon r \geqslant 0\colon 0 \leqslant x \leqslant r))$$
$$= (\mathbf{E}\, s\colon s \geqslant 0\colon wp(S, 0 \leqslant x \leqslant s))$$
$$= (\mathbf{E}\, s\colon s \geqslant 0\colon F) = F$$

a contradiction that leads to the conclusion that "$x := $ any natural number" cannot be continuous, i.e. that continuity implies bounded nondeterminacy.

In the sequel of this note we shall show that the inverse holds as well, viz. that the existence of a noncontinuous program implies the inclusion of unbounded nondeterminacy. (The following argument was suggested to me by C.S. Scholten almost instantaneously when I had posed the problem.)

Assume the existence of a program S and an infinite sequence of predicates C_r satisfying $C_r \Rightarrow C_{r+1}$, such that (1) does not hold. Because in (1) the right-hand side trivially implies the left-hand side, this means that we assume

$$wp(S, (\mathbf{E}\ r: r \geq 0: C_r))\ \text{and non}\ (\mathbf{E}\ s: s \geq 0: wp(S, C_s)) =$$
$$wp(S, (\mathbf{E}\ r: r \geq 0: C_r))\ \text{and}\ (\mathbf{A}\ s: s \geq 0: \text{non}\ wp(S, C_s)) \qquad (2)$$

to be different from F.

Consider now the program

$$S; x := (\mathbf{MIN}:\ k:\ C_k)$$

started in an initial state satisfying (2). Because the initial state satisfies $wp(S, (\mathbf{E}\ r:\ r \geq 0:\ C_r))$, this program terminates and is guaranteed to establish $0 \leq x$. On the other hand, the assumption that for some K it is certain to establish $x \leq K$ means that S is certain to establish C_K, a conclusion that is incompatible with the second term of (2). Hence its nondeterminacy is unbounded. (The fact that our program of unbounded nondeterminacy is not a total program, but only defined for initial states satisfying (2), is not relevant here: the essential thing is that (2) differs from F, i.e. that the set of states satisfying (2) is not empty.)

We have established the *equivalence* of continuity and the boundedness of nondeterminacy. In EWD673 we established the equivalence of the boundedness of nondeterminacy and the equality of weak and strong termination. Hence the three criteria

(1) continuity or not
(2) nondeterminacy bounded or not
(3) weak and strong termination equivalent or not

are three different aspects of the *same* dichotomy. All this is very satisfying. (The arguments are so simple that, presumably, this is already known. But it was new for me, and I like the arguments.)

Plataanstraat 5
5671 AL   Nuenen
The Netherlands

PROF. DR. EDSGER W. DIJKSTRA
Burroughs Research Fellow

EWD678
A Story that Starts with a Very Good Computer

Once upon a time, a long time ago, an organization decided to get a computation centre. The organization hired a manager to manage the computation centre, and he was a very competent manager, for he hired a very good computer to do the computing and a very good programmer to do the programming. The manager's high quality was shown by his choice of computer: knowing that in the work of his organization, sorting would play a very big role, he selected the one and only computer on the market that had a very fast, built-in sort instruction, called "SORT", in its instruction code. The manager's high quality also manifested itself by the choice of the programmer, as will become clear in the sequel.

The machine was installed, and the main application program, in which the instruction SORT occurred 77 times, was written and proved to be correct. The programmer could do so because for each of the instructions of the order code, SORT included, the reference manual gave him the functional specifications on which to base his correctness proof. The main application program was put in operation and everybody in the whole organization was instantaneously happy... until, after the first month of operation, the electricity bill arrived! The bill was very high....

Suspicion, quite naturally, fell on the new computer and the manager inspected its power consumption more closely. He discovered that the SORT-instruction was the culprit, and asked his programmer, whether he could reduce the power consumption of his program. The programmer made a more detailed study of the power consumption of the SORT-instruction and discovered that it rose steeply —more than quadratically, as a matter of fact— with the length of the array to be sorted. And since almost all his 77 calls of the SORT-instruction were on rather long arrays, he understood the height of the bill immediately, and also realized his only hope for reducing the power consumption: shortening the length of the arrays supplied to the SORT-instruction.

He decided to replace all 77 occurrences of the SORT-instruction in his main application program by calls on a subroutine (still to be written) that he modestly called "*save*0", and in order that the correctness proof of the main program would remain valid, he decided that the functional specifications of *save*0 would be identical to those of SORT.

He thought for a long time how to construct the body of *save*0. He then came up with the following idea. If the array consists of less than two elements, it is sorted by definition, and control can return immediately. Otherwise, by (if necessary, repeatedly) swapping two values when the larger was to the left of the smaller, he managed to rearrange and divide the array in such a way, that the largest element in the left-hand section did not exceed the smallest element in the right-hand section; thereafter he gave two SORT-instructions, one for each section.

The programmer was very pleased by what he had done: the correctness proof for the main application program remained automatically valid, his only additional proof obligation had been to prove the correctness of the body of *save*0 —but he had already some experience in proving the correctness of programs using the SORT-instruction and that helped— .

Also the manager was very pleased, for this minor program change —it was hardly a "change": it was almost only an addition— indeed had cut the electricity bill by more than a factor of two! But improvement, like all novelty, wears out, and after a few months the manager asked the programmer whether he could reduce the still high power consumption yet further. This time the programmer said instantaneously "Oh yes.", for now he knew the trick: he introduced a subroutine *save*1, the body of which was a copy of the body of *save*0, and thereafter replaced in the body of *save*0 the two occurrences of the SORT-instruction by calls on *save*1. The programmer was extremely pleased with himself, for this time he had reduced the power consumption by a further factor of two, but had done so without any further proof obligations!

The manager was also pleased, but only for a month or two. When he asked his programmer again, whether he could reduce the power consumption still further, the programmer, again, said immediately "Oh yes." but went to his desk to do some sensible coding. He could have repeated the trick by introducing a new subroutine *save*2, etc., but by now he knew that, a few months later, the manager would come again. Besides that, he did not like the prospect of filling more and more of the store with almost equal copies of the same subroutine. He decided to map the texts of *save*0, *save*1, *save*2, etc. on the same general text —which he called *saven*— at the expense of a global variable n —initialized in the main program at zero— the value of which should indicate whether a call on *saven* should act as *save*0, *save*1, *save*2, etc. The body of *saven* was derived from the ones of *save*0, *save*1, etc.: upon entry, n was increased by 1, just before return, n was decreased by 1, and the internal calls on the next *save* or on SORT were replaced by

if $n < N \rightarrow$ *saven* [] $n = N \rightarrow$ SORT **fi**   (1)

and he satisfied his manager by setting the constant $N = 3$. As he had foreseen, a month later he was asked to reduce the power consumption still further: he just increased N by 1.

Having thus mechanized the optimization process that reduced the power consumption, the programmer gladly increased N by 1, every time he was asked to reduce the power consumption, and that was about once a month.

After a year or so, the manager discovered that, lately, his programmer's optimizations had become less and less effective. Since he was a very competent manager, he investigated the matter; in the course of his investigations he discovered that the SORT-instruction was hardly invoked at all! This discovery worried him, because for that SORT-instruction his organization paid a lot of money: for a much lower rental price the manufacturer offered a model without SORT-instruction, but otherwise identical. The manager went to the programmer, telling him his observation that the SORT-instruction was hardly exercised: could the programmer avoid its use completely? For then they could replace their expensive machine by the cheaper model!

This time, the programmer had to think again. Looking at (1) —the only place left where the SORT-instruction still occurred— he realized that if n remained under an upper bound, he could choose N larger than that upper bound, with the result that the second alternative of (1) would never be selected! By inspecting his main application he could prove that $N = 25$ would be large enough, and he replaced (1) by

if $n < 25 \rightarrow$ *saven* **fi**   .   (2)

Later he realized that, having proved that the guard would always be true, he could simplify the program still further by replacing (2) just by

saven   .   (3)

Now he was completely happy: with the last simplification the correctness of his program was no longer dependent on the exact value of the upper bound, but only on its existence. The machine was replaced by the simpler model and the manager, too, was happy ever after.

*   *   *

The above fairy tale —like all fairy tales, for that matter— has been written for educational purposes. It deserves to be remembered because it is a sobering thought that, upon instigation of his manager, a programmer engaged on optimization could have discovered all this —with the exact nature of the proof obligation included!— long before mathematicians called it Recursion.

Nuenen

PROF. DR. EDSGER W. DIJKSTRA
Burroughs Research Fellow